Divided We Stand

POLITICS AND SOCIETY IN TWENTIETH-CENTURY AMERICA

SERIES EDITORS
William Chafe, Gary Gerstle, and Linda Gordon

A list of titles in this series appears at the back of the book

Divided We Stand

AMERICAN WORKERS AND THE
STRUGGLE FOR BLACK EQUALITY

Bruce Nelson

PRINCETON UNIVERSITY PRESS

PRINCETON AND OXFORD

Copyright © 2001 by Princeton University Press
Published by Princeton University Press, 41 William Street,
Princeton, New Jersey 08540
In the United Kingdom: Princeton University Press,
3 Market Place, Woodstock, Oxfordshire OX20 1SY
All Rights Reserved

Library of Congress Cataloging-in-Publication Data

Nelson, Bruce, 1940-
Divided we stand : American workers and the struggle for
Black equality / Bruce Nelson.
p. cm. — (Politics and society in twentieth-century America)
Includes bibliographical references and index.
ISBN 0-691-01732-8 (alk. paper)
1. Afro-Americans—Employment—History. 2. Minorities—Employment—
United States—History. 3. Alien labor—United States—History. 4. Discrimination in
employment—United States—History. 5. Race discrimination—United States—History.
6. Afro-american iron steel workers—United States—History. 7. Afro-American
stevedores—United States—History. I. Title. II. Series.
HD8081.A65 N45 2000
331.6′396073—dc21   00-040094

This book has been composed in Goudy

The paper used in this publication
meets the minimum requirements of
ANSI/NISO Z39.48-1992 (R1997)
(*Permanence of Paper*)

www.pup.princeton.edu

Printed in the United States of America

1   2   3   4   5   6   7   8   9   10

IN MEMORY OF

ED MANN

ARCHIE NELSON

MARVIN WEINSTOCK

WALTER WILLIAMS

Contents

CONTENTS

Illustrations

Acknowledgments

It is a pleasure to acknowledge the generous assistance I have received from many people in the course of researching and writing this book.

For several years I contemplated writing entirely about Youngstown, and for a decade—even when it had become a single chapter in a much larger project—I visited the area many times. My greatest debt is to Alice and Staughton Lynd, who first encouraged me to come to Youngstown, welcomed me into their home, and introduced me to members of the remarkable community they have helped to build in the Mahoning Valley over a period of nearly thirty years. Alice transcribed the first, and longest, of my oral history interviews. Staughton helped arrange many of those interviews and made research materials available to me from his own substantial archives. Although Staughton and I have found much to disagree about as the book's line of argument has developed, he and Alice have remained generous hosts, allies, and friends throughout the process.

Thanks to the generosity of Theresa and Jim Strock, I was fortunate enough to have a second home away from home in the Youngstown area. I met Theresa at a demonstration protesting the widespread use of toxic chemicals in the workplace. In spite of the debilitating effect of those chemicals on her health, she always found the energy to welcome me to her home, overwhelm me with good food, and regale me with stories about her battles with foremen and doctors and her adventures in the classroom as she went back to school and became an honors student.

And then there are the "men of steel" who are at the heart of my story. Ed Mann, Archie Nelson, and Marvin Weinstock spent many hours reminiscing with me about their experience in the United Steelworkers' union and teaching me about the dynamics of day-to-day working life in the mills. In a very real sense, Ed got me started. He was my first interviewee; after that there was no turning back. Marv shared many documents with me and, on his own initiative, went to the public library and photocopied numerous articles about the campaign to desegregate Youngstown's public swimming pools. Archie showed extraordinary trust and generosity in making personal mementos available to me.

Sadly, Ed, Archie, and Marv have all "crossed the bar" and will not be able to pass judgment on the fruits of my work or know how much I appreciate their help and their friendship. I dedicate this book to them and to longshoreman Walter Williams.

I am also grateful to the many other steelworkers and steel-related people I interviewed in the Mahoning Valley, including Willie Aikens, Miyo Barbero, Sam Camens, Jim Davis, Gerald Dickey, Ken Doran, Agnes Griffin, Frank Leseganich, Merlin Luce, Betty Mann, Heybert Moyer, Betsy Murphy, Daniel P. Thomas, and James Trevathan.

Oliver Montgomery lives in Pittsburgh now, but he is a Youngstown man. I interviewed Oliver twice, the second time in his office overlooking the famous three rivers that converge in downtown Pittsburgh. He has been extraordinarily generous from the beginning, and he and his close friend Jim Davis have taught me much.

At the *Youngstown Vindicator*, Martha Clonis guided me through the archives many times over the years. Bob Yosay, also of the *Vindicator*, was enormously helpful with photographs. Bill Mullen arranged for me to discuss my work at Youngstown State University, where I spoke to one of the most diverse and knowledgeable audiences I have encountered in my twenty-plus years in academia. Gerald Dickey, who still works in steel, located many more prospective interviewees than I was able to follow up on. Agnes Griffin shared valuable photos and historical documents relating to her husband's (James Griffin) career in the United Steelworkers. Merlin Luce provided numerous documents, along with vivid recollections of the Socialist Workers party's heyday in Youngstown. Betty Mann welcomed me to her home whenever I visited the area and, along with her daughter, Beth Hepfner, shared many memories of Ed Mann with me.

In my research on longshoremen in Pacific Coast ports, above all in the port of Los Angeles, Bob Cherny, Nancy and Jeff Quam-Wickham, Tony Salcido, Harvey Schwartz, and Gene Vrana have all been generous beyond belief. Nancy steered me back to the waterfront, first by writing a valuable essay that commanded my attention, and then by sharing numerous research materials and encouraging me to go beyond the parameters of her own essay. Bob, who is writing what will surely be the definitive biography of Harry Bridges, shared many documents with me and gave several of my chapters a careful reading. Tony, a longshoreman and oral historian, sent me more documents than I could digest, made numerous audiotapes of his oral history interviews with San Pedro longshoremen available to me, and contributed in countless ways. When Tony and his wife, Bea, came east to have a look at the fall colors in New England, my wife, Donna, and I spent a memorable evening with them. By picking up the tab for dinner, I was able to repay Tony a tiny fraction of what I owe him. Fortunately, he is not keeping score.

Harvey Schwartz has also been extraordinarily generous over the years. Recently he has gone to great lengths to help me find photographs for the book. If the chapters on longshoremen *look* good, most of the credit is due to Harvey. Finally, Gene Vrana, the archivist and librarian at the International Longshore and Warehouse Union, has been enormously helpful as a professional and warm and welcoming as a friend, even after it became clear that some of what I had to say was critical of the union with which he has long been associated. Gene's honesty and willingness to come to terms with a complex record exemplify the very best traditions of the labor movement.

Ireland—and analyzing the historical process of becoming Irish in Ireland's far-flung diaspora—was barely on my horizon when I started researching this book, but its importance has grown apace over the years, sometimes "like Topsy," it would seem. I am especially grateful to Perry Curtis, Dermot Keogh, and Kevin Whelan for tutoring me in the basics, and the complexities, of Irish history. Perry has been generous with his knowledge and with his extraordinary collection of "apes and angels." Kevin read several chapters of my book, helped me locate valuable photographs in the National Library of Ireland, and, generally, turned our encounters—in Hanover, in Dublin, even on the Burren—into freewheeling seminars. Thanks also to the Feeneys in Inverin, County Galway, to the Keoghs in Cork City, to Anne Kearney in Dublin, and to my cousins Mary and Pat Rodgers in Ballynahinch, County Down, for their warmth and hospitality.

It is also a pleasure to express my gratitude to archivists, librarians, and friends in the many other locations where I did my research. Penn State University, the home of the United Steelworkers' archives, has been a vitally important place for me. I am grateful to the staff of the Historical Collections and Labor Archives at Penn State, first and foremost to Denise Conklin, who has provided indispensable assistance for nearly a decade; and to my fellow historian Dan Letwin, whose friendship and hospitality made my sojourns at Penn State as enjoyable as they were useful. Thanks also to Cliff Kuhn in Atlanta and to Bob

Dinwiddie and the staff of the Southern Labor Archives at Georgia State University; to Tim Meagher and Mary Beth Fraser at the Catholic University of America Archives; to Mireya, Jose, and Maria Garcia and Steve Rosswurm in Chicago and to Archie Motley and the staff of the Chicago Historical Society; to Joe Doyle in New York City and to Debra Bernhardt, another indispensable helpmate and friend, at the Tamiment Institute Library at New York University; to Robert Marshall at California State University Northridge; and to the staffs of the Youngstown Public Library, the Youngstown Historical Center of Industry and Labor, the State Historical Society of Wisconsin, the Amistad Research Center at Tulane University, the Moorland-Spingarn Research Center at Howard University, the Manuscript Division of the Library of Congress, and the National Library of Ireland.

Several fellowships made it possible for me to engage in sustained periods of research, reflection, and writing. In 1991, long before I knew what I was doing, a fellowship at the Carter G. Woodson Institute and the University of Virginia made it possible for me to explore the subject of race and labor and to begin writing about Youngstown. Darryl Scott, Marshall Stevenson, Patricia Sullivan, Ed Ayers, Paul Gaston, Mel Leffler, and—above all—Eileen Boris and Nelson Lichtenstein helped make my sojourn in Charlottesville a productive and enjoyable one. In 1995, thanks to the generosity of Tony Badger, I spent the autumn term at Cambridge University, where—notwithstanding my distance from the world of steel—I managed to complete several chapters. Thanks also to Gordon Johnson, the president of Wolfson College, Cambridge; and to Brendan Bradshaw and Peter Gray, who responded with patience and good humor to my budding interest in Irish history.

I am also deeply grateful to the National Endowment for the Humanities, which awarded me a Fellowship for College Teachers and Independent Scholars in 1996, and to the Woodrow Wilson International Center for Scholars, in Washington, D.C., where I spent six months in 1997. At the Wilson Center, Ann Sheffield was unfailingly generous; Lindsay Collins's warmth and humanity provided a lift every day; Mike Lacey turned the lunch hour into a seminar that sometimes went on well into the afternoon; and fellow scholars Tom Edsall, Temma Kaplan, Henry Munson, Steve Pincus, and Dorothy Ross provided intellectual stimulation and many enjoyable moments. Thanks, especially, to Mary and Tom Edsall for their warm hospitality and to my daughter, Ellen, who in spite of her busy schedule made sure her dad was well taken care of during his six months away from home.

Dartmouth College has generously facilitated my research and time away from teaching. I am grateful to the History Department and the Dean of the Faculty Office; to Patsy Carter and Marianne Hraibi at Interlibrary Loan; to Susan Bibeau and Otmar Foelsche at Humanities Computing; and to the many students who have provided invaluable research assistance, including Meeta Agrawal, Iris Chiu, Kirsten Doolittle, David Engstrom, Debbie Greenberger, Martin Kessler, David McCarthy, John Pellettieri, Karen Rose, Andy Schopler, Kate Stone, and Jordy Urstadt.

I have also been blessed by the friendship, instruction, and inspiration that many of my fellow scholars have provided. Alex Bontemps, Michelle Brattain, David Brody, Bob Cherny, Lizabeth Cohen, Joe Doyle, Tom and Mary Edsall, Ron Edsforth, Josh Freeman, Mike Honey, Temma Kaplan, Mike Lacey, Staughton Lynd, Tim Meagher, Bill Mello, Darryl Pinckney, Steve Rosswurm, Tom Sugrue, Kevin Whelan, Jim Whitters, and Bob Zieger all read various sections of my manuscript as it progressed and provided vitally important criticism, encouragement, and affirmation. Eric Arnesen, David Brundage, Rick Halpern, John Hoerr, Bill Mello, and Steve Rosswurm shared valuable research materials with me; and Ken Durr, John Hinshaw, Ruth Needleman, and Jim Rose shared their impressive work in progress on steel. Nelson Lichtenstein has read most if not all of my manuscript and has taught me much, even when we have agreed to disagree. Robin Kelley and David Roediger have inspired me with their scholarship and personal generosity. Their encouragement and support at critical stages of my work have been like the proverbial balm in Gilead. Kevin Boyle read the entire manuscript and provided a number of astute criticisms that I probably should have taken to heart more than I did. Herbert Hill not only read every word of the manuscript but provided me with rich research materials from his personal papers and offered indispensable friendship, support, and criticism along the way. Herb's wife, Mary Lydon, from County Donegal in Ireland's beautiful northwest, has also been a generous friend and an inspiration. Gary Gerstle, who has served as my editor for the last four years, has read and reread every chapter several times. His criticisms have been indispensable; his encouragement and belief in the importance of my work have gone far beyond the call of duty.

At Princeton University Press, Brigitta van Rheinberg has enthusiastically supported the publication of this book from day one, which seems a long time ago. I very much appreciate her assistance and encouragement.

And finally, there is my wife, Donna. She has wisely refrained from reading the manuscript, but she has been deeply affected by it, in ways that have not always been positive. Through it all, she has demonstrated unbelievable patience and support. Best of all, she has persuaded me to step back from the precipice again and again in order to "smell the flowers." Through much of the decade that it has taken me to finish this book, she has joined me for bike rides on the back roads of Vermont; for hikes in Ireland, on a great arc stretching from Mizen Head in West Cork to Malin Head in Donegal; and most recently, for rambles on Scotland's Isle of Skye and in search of the remains of Gavin Maxwell and his beloved Edal on a wild sea loch in the Western Highlands. These "distractions" have perhaps delayed the completion of the book, but they have provided necessary time to reflect and renew. For that, and so much more, I am indebted to Donna, as I am to my children, Ellen and Chris, who as young adults continue to enrich my life.

Permissions

PORTIONS OF CHAPTER 3 appeared, in somewhat different form, in two essays previously published by the author: "Class and Race in the Crescent City: The ILWU, from San Francisco to New Orleans," in *The CIO's Left-Led Unions*, ed. Steve Rosswurm (New Brunswick, N.J.: Rutgers University Press, 1992), 19–45, 210–16; and "The 'Lords of the Docks' Reconsidered: Race Relations among West Coast Longshoremen, 1933–61," in *Waterfront Workers: New Perspectives on Race and Class*, ed. Calvin Winslow (Urbana: University of Illinois Press, 1998), 155–92.

Portions of chapter 6 appeared, in somewhat different form, in an essay previously published by the author: " 'CIO Meant One Thing for the Whites and Another Thing for Us': Steelworkers and Civil Rights, 1936–1974," in *Southern Labor in Transition, 1940–1995*, ed. Robert H. Zieger (Knoxville: University of Tennessee Press, 1997), 113–45.

I am grateful to Rutgers University Press, the University of Illinois Press, and the University of Tennessee Press for permission to reprint this material.

Introduction

THE ELEVEN-YEAR journey that has led to the completion of this book began, more or less by happenstance, at the home of Ed and Betty Mann in December 1988. Ed Mann, who died in 1992, was a steelworker, cantankerously independent socialist, and legendary activist in the Youngstown/Mahoning Valley area of northeast Ohio. I met him through my friend and fellow historian Staughton Lynd, who had encouraged me to study Youngstown's rich labor history and who regarded Ed as the best person to begin telling that largely untold story.[1]

Although I had few clear ideas about where my research would take me, I was already committed to exploring the record of the unions affiliated with the Congress of Industrial Organizations (CIO) on issues of race, and I decided that questions about how white workers in the mills had responded to the struggle for black equality should be a major focus of my discussions with Ed. With characteristic candor and generosity, he shared his recollections with me for the better part of two days. This led to an extended series of interviews with workers, black and white, who had played a leading role in building the steelworkers' union in the Mahoning Valley. I remember, in particular, my first meeting with Archie Nelson. By the time I met Archie, his health was failing, and as he lay on his living room couch or sat at his kitchen table, the pain he was suffering was evident—in his face, his voice, his body language. Nonetheless, he spoke of his experience in the mills with passion and eloquence, in a richly colloquial dialect that was rooted in his formative years in Alabama. To this day I can hear him recalling his arrival in "God's country" during World War II. "As I looked around there," he said of his first encounter with Youngstown's steel mills, "every job I saw that was a decent job, it was held by whites. And all the greasy, nasty, cheap jobs was held by blacks." In the coke plant, in the blast furnace, in the plate mill, wherever there was "nasty work, it was *loaded* with blacks."[2]

What struck me most forcefully about my interviews with black steelworkers was that in describing the racial discrimination they encountered in the workplace, they rarely distinguished between steel

Fig. intro. 1. Ed Mann, Youngstown, 1989: "retired" but still walking the picket line. Credit: *Youngstown Vindicator*

management and white workers. When pressed, to be sure, they remembered whites who had been decent and honorable in their relations with blacks, and they readily acknowledged management's overall responsibility for the structure of racial inequality in the mills. But to them management and white workers acted in tandem. The foremen they knew were often the brothers or cousins of white workers in the same departments; and, together, they actively defended the "wages of whiteness" on the shop floor. When black workers organized to challenge this regime, whites responded with wildcat strikes or with less overt but more tenacious forms of resistance that sometimes placed black workers' lives in jeopardy. In other words, the "agency" of white workers was clear and direct, and there was no hint of "false consciousness" in their activity. Whites acted to defend an employment structure that benefited them, materially and psychologically. And although local unions sometimes took a stand in support of racial equality, all too often the United Steelworkers—at the local, district, and national levels—served as the guardian of "white job expectations."[3]

Listening to Archie Nelson—and to Willie Aikens, Jim Davis, Oliver Montgomery, James Trevathan, and other African American steelworkers—marked the beginning of my reeducation about the dynamics of class and race in American society and the first major step in an odyssey that has culminated in *Divided We Stand*. Of course, everyone this side of comatose knows something about race and racism in the United States. The "new" labor history with which I have been associated for twenty years emerged in the 1960s, at a time when race and the struggle for black equality were major motifs of the experience of an entire generation. For me, a product of suburbia, elite schooling, and conservative parents, the sixties represented a bracing challenge to the assumptions and mores that had shaped my parochial world, and the Civil Rights movement was the crucible in which I came of age politically. Unlike Bob Moses, Charles Sherrod, Jane Stembridge, and other heroes of mine from the Student Nonviolent Coordinating Committee, I was not a full-time activist in the South. But like many young people of my generation, I marched and picketed for civil rights, and in March 1965 I even had a brief but unforgettable moment on the front lines of battle in Selma. What was true for me must have been true in equal or greater measure for many cadres of the new labor history who were students and political activists in the 1960s. Martin Luther King, Jr., and Malcolm X, Fannie Lou Hamer and Bob Moses, Stokely Carmichael and the Black Panthers, were our generational icons; they played a pivotal role in defining our values and shaping our politics. Surely *we* could not have lost sight of the centrality of race in American history.

Yet we have often been accused of doing just that. "The new labor history has a race problem," Nell Irvin Painter charged in 1989 in a brief essay in which she concluded that some of its leading practitioners were guilty of "the deletion of black workers and white racism" from the historical record. Painter was adding her voice to that of Herbert Hill, a scholar at the University of Wisconsin and former labor secretary of the National Association for the Advancement of Colored People (NAACP), who has long engaged in a crusade not only against racism in American society but also against what he regards as the willful blindness of labor historians. "The tendency to deny race as a crucial factor, to permit questions of class to subsume racial issues," Hill declared in 1988, "is based on a perspective that ignores racism as a system of domination, as it ignores the role of racist ideology in working class history." As late as 1996 he charged that "with some noteworthy exceptions, . . . contemporary labor historians have failed to confront the fundamental issue: the historical development of working-class identity as racial identity."[4]

Hill's unrelenting critique of the new labor history has ruffled many feathers and engendered a vigorous counterattack.[5] My own sense is that, for at least a generation, there *was* a widespread, and largely un-conscious, tendency to portray the working class as white (and usually male)—either to minimize the importance of race in writing the his-tory of American workers or to assign it a distinctly secondary role as an explanatory factor. As late as 1990, this tendency was all too evident in *Perspectives on American Labor History*, a volume of essays in which seven leading historians of the American working class attempted to sum up the state of the field. Although the essays by Mari Jo Buhle and Alice Kessler-Harris sought to provide a gendered perspective on working-class history, none of the authors made race central to their analysis, and several barely mentioned it. Indeed, Alan Dawley was so certain of the analytical primacy of class, and so sure capitalists were the prime movers in the generation of racism, that he asked with a rhetorical flourish: "Does anyone believe that if by some sudden magic 70 percent of the richest Progressive Era tycoons became Afro-Ameri-can instead of Anglo-American, white supremacy would have lived another day?"[6]

No less than the distinguished authors of *Perspectives on American Labor History*, I was inclined to assume that although racism was an unfortunate obstacle to labor solidarity, the explanation for this prob-lem was "rooted in the economic interests of dominant classes."[7] In fact, this premise was one of the foundation stones of *Workers on the Waterfront*, my book on the occupational culture and insurgent activ-ism of longshoremen and seamen in the 1930s. After nearly a decade on the shop floor, I had returned to graduate school to study labor history, and there I belatedly encountered E. P. Thompson's *Making of the English Working Class*. Like most labor historians of my generation, I was deeply impressed by the sweep and grandeur of Thompson's work and by what William Sewell has called his "revolutionary enlargement of the scope of working-class history." I, too, devoured his articles and essays and got lost—sometimes literally—in the 832 pages of the magisterial *Making*. "We can see a *logic* in the responses of similar occupational groups undergoing similar experiences," Thompson declared in his book's famous preface, "but we cannot predicate any *law*. Consciousness of class arises in the same way in different times and places, but never in *just* the same way." In the San Francisco general strike of 1934, in the formation of the Maritime Federation of the Pacific Coast, in marine workers' political strikes and demonstrations in solidarity with Republican Spain, I found "consciousness of class." I also encountered many fault lines—most notably, of craft, ethnicity, and race—that divided maritime workers. But in the Communist-led International Longshoremen's and Warehousemen's Union (ILWU), there were inspiring examples of interracial solidarity and thus an apparent validation of my long-standing conviction that where conditions were favorable, and the right leadership was in place, "class" would triumph over "race."[8]

Workers on the Waterfront focused mainly on the 1930s, a time when issues of black-white relations remained relatively quiescent on the West Coast because a stagnant economy slowed the pace of the Great Migration and offered African Americans few opportunities to challenge the region's racially segmented employment structure. But these conditions changed dramatically in the 1940s, and Nancy Quam-Wickham's essay "Who Controls the Hiring Hall? The Struggle for Job Control in the ILWU during World War II" threatened to turn some of my most cherished assumptions upside down. During the war the Pacific Coast's major port cities became vital hubs of the "arsenal of democracy," and African Americans were drawn in unprecedented numbers to job opportunities that appeared to exist in shipyards, in aircraft manufacturing plants, and—more than ever before—on the docks. In examining this volatile environment, Quam-Wickham not only concentrated on the union leadership's stated policies but also drew on extensive oral history interviews with veteran longshoremen in the port of Los Angeles that revealed a pattern of intense rank-and-file resistance to the influx of these black "strangers"; so much so, she argued, that the ILWU's vaunted "rank-and-filism" became "racism." Faced with stubborn opposition at the grassroots, ILWU leaders responded cautiously, and sometimes with little more than rhetoric; for as Quam-Wickham observed, aggressively attacking racism would have required a head-on collision with the union's rank-and-file members and the control they had established at the point of production.[9]

For me, the key issue in Quam-Wickham's essay was not the failure or success of the ILWU leadership but the actions and beliefs of rank-and-file longshoremen. They were, after all, members of a Left-led union that was famous for its traditions of democracy and rank-and-file activism. Throughout the 1930s, often on their own initiative, dockworkers had aggressively expanded their control of the workplace. Their physical prowess and fearless assault on managerial authority transformed them into proud symbols of working-class manhood up and down the coast. Moreover, ILWU members demonstrated against fascism; they marched in May Day parades; in their "self-activity," they merged the themes of "porkchops" and politics. How could *they* have been a party to the exclusion of black workers?

Fortunately, at just the moment I began to address this question, a number of historians were developing new approaches and insights that have transformed our understanding of the ways in which class and race have intersected in the United States. African American scholars such as Joe Trotter, Earl Lewis, Robin Kelley, and Tera Hunter have taken the lead in creating richly textured portraits of black workers, thus restoring their agency in the larger black community and in the making of the American working class. These scholars emphasize the degree to which blacks and whites lived and socialized in separate worlds and argue that both groups' sense of themselves as racial subjects was closely intertwined with their identities as working people. Perhaps no one has explored these themes with more insight and imagination than Robin Kelley, especially in his rethinking of "black working-class opposition in the Jim Crow South." As the author of a book on Alabama Communists during the Great Depression, Kelley is keenly aware of the moments of interracial solidarity, large and small, that have enriched the history of the American working class. But far more typical of that historical experience, he argues, was the day-to-day interaction in the workplaces of the South that served to accentuate difference and hierarchy much more than it created a sense of common ground. He points out that "black workers endured some of the most obnoxious verbal and physical insults from white workers, their supposed 'natural allies,'" and concludes that "racist attacks by white workers did not need instigation from wily employers. Because they ultimately defined their own class interests in racial terms, white workers employed racist terror and intimidation to help secure a comparatively privileged position within the prevailing system of wage dependency."[10]

The most provocative and important book on how race has affected the development of white working-class identity is David Roediger's *Wages of Whiteness*.[11] Roediger has sought to understand "the whiteness of the white worker in the broad context of class formation" and against the backdrop of chattel slavery. He has argued that relatively few white workers faced significant job competition from blacks in the nineteenth century, but the great majority measured their well-being against the cultural symbolism of "slaving like a nigger." By daring to "explore working-class 'whiteness' and white supremacy as creations, in part, of the white working class itself," he has issued a sharp challenge not only to classical Marxism but to many practitioners of the new labor history. But like Kelley, Roediger has resisted the temptation to pit race against class and to elevate the former above the latter in constructing the building blocks of consciousness. Debates about priority necessarily become a "zero-sum game," he argues, and "an increasing emphasis on one 'variable' leads inexorably to a diminished emphasis on the other." The key is to see how class, gender, and racial identities are intertwined, and to understand identity as a process of *becoming* that crystallizes at particular historical moments but also continues to change over time.[12]

• • • • •

Although charting its own course, *Divided We Stand* attempts to build on the foundation that scholars such as Kelley and Roediger have constructed and to learn from, and engage in, the increasingly vibrant debates that reshaped the no-longer new labor history in the 1990s. The book focuses mainly on longshoremen and steelworkers, mostly in the twentieth century, and illuminates three central—and overlapping—areas of inquiry: first, the relative importance of employers and workers in shaping racially segmented hierarchies in the workplace; second, the relationship between organized labor and the struggle for black equality and the role of trade unions in diminishing or—in some cases—deepening racial inequality; and third, the question of working-class agency. What did workers want? What forces shaped what they could "do and dream"? What role did they play in forging the predominant patterns of race relations and racial subordination in American society?[13]

It is necessary to acknowledge at the outset that in the late nineteenth and early twentieth centuries capitalists were the decisive force in creating innovative occupational structures in auto, steel, meatpacking, and other mainstays of the new industrial regime. In large-scale, capital-intensive industries, it was the power of employers that mattered. They shaped and controlled their enterprises in accordance with their own profit-maximizing objectives, and when workers resisted they were usually crushed. But to conclude, therefore, that "racial prejudice" developed first and foremost in the workplace, as a result of the "deliberate policies" of capital, ignores the long-term process of class and racial formation and obscures vitally important questions of working-class agency.[14] Long before the consolidation of corporate capitalism and the triumph of the robber barons, white workers were driving free blacks from their jobs, burning them out of their homes, and developing plebeian cultural forms that idealized the plantation South as a rural Arcadia. Thus it is necesary to understand how the larger society shaped workers' perceptions of race and to be cognizant of the cultural baggage they brought with them *to* the workplace.

Although few workingmen were organized into trade unions in the first half of the nineteenth century, many could rely on their skill, and on ethnic, familial, and religious networks, to exert some power on the job. Indeed, the greater their skill and sense of group cohesion, the greater their power to determine who worked and who did not. Although unskilled laborers generally exercised much less control in the workplace than their skilled counterparts, they, too, were sometimes able to influence the complexion of the labor force. Nowhere was this more evident than on the New York and Philadelphia waterfronts, where Irish immigrants not only drove blacks from the docks but made their attempted return as strikebreakers appear to be an "invasion" of the "property rights" of others.[15]

Not that the Irish and other Europeans arrived in the United States with fully formed ideas about the meaning of whiteness and blackness. On the contrary, many immigrants were racially "in between" themselves, and only gradually did they internalize the prevailing racial mores and come to regard the wages of whiteness as an entitlement. For native and newcomer alike, moreover, the workplace was not the only, or even the most important, arena for learning these lessons. The minstrel show and vaudeville stage, the maelstrom of partisan politics, and the burgeoning culture of consumption played vital roles in rooting the racial self and its racialized antithesis in the fabric of everyday life, making race omnipresent even when flesh-and-blood African Americans were not. Minstrelsy emerged in the antebellum era as a distinctively urban and working-class form of entertainment. It celebrated the lost rhythms and presumed innocence of rural life; it counterposed unrestrained male sexuality to the puritanical sexual mores of evangelical religion; above all, it affirmed the racial superiority of white men. Minstrel entertainers appropriated the music and dance of African Americans in order to portray the South and slavery in a benign light and to convey the slaveowners' view of race to a northern plebeian audience.[16]

As a medium of education and entertainment, the Democratic party played a strikingly similar role. "The Democracy" won the allegiance of many urban workingmen and became a vitally important instrument for socializing the Irish and other European immigrants into the culture of white supremacy. Democratic politicians like Stephen A. Douglas of Illinois combined intense Negrophobia and an apologia for chattel slavery with an enthusiastic embrace of immigrants "from every branch of the Caucasian race." Walt Whitman, a product of the artisanal culture of New York City and the Democratic party's poet laureate, propagated the same themes in the pages of the staunchly partisan *Brooklyn Eagle*. "Who believes that Whites and Blacks can ever amalgamate in America?" Whitman declared in an 1858 editorial. "Or who wishes it to happen? . . . Is not America for the Whites? And is it not better so?"[17]

The emerging, and soon to be omnipresent, culture of consumption reinforced the same lessons and transferred them from the masculine arena of electoral politics to the household and other feminine spheres. At a time when black women—and in the North, black men as well—were largely confined to domestic service or some other niche in the broader service sector, the marketing of consumer products served to reify this pattern of subservience and reinforce the association of "blackness" with inferiority. Perhaps the most popular symbols linking African Americans with servitude were the packaged-food icons Aunt Jemima, Uncle Ben, and Rastus the Cream of Wheat man. Aunt Jemima, who was adapted from a minstrel performance in Saint Joseph, Missouri, became a national mammy. As she served up "the romance of the old plantation" with her pancakes, she no doubt helped immigrant, working-class consumers recognize themselves as white.[18]

When emphasizing the power and apparent ubiquity of race, however, we cannot afford to portray whiteness and working-class racism as absolute, monolithic, and unchanging. The fact that race is historically constructed compels us to analyze a long-term process of development *and* to pay close attention to the particularity of time and place. In the making and remaking of the American working class, newcomers learned the lessons of race unevenly and only gradually, and the meaning of race was contested terrain. Always there were voices—among abolitionists and Radical Republicans, working-class socialists and middle-class feminists, mainstream Protestants and marginalized Pentecostals—challenging the prevailing racial mores and daring to envision a "more perfect union." Above all, African Americans themselves refused to be mere clay in the hands of their oppressors. They fought, in diverse ways, to affirm their humanity and to achieve at least a modicum of justice—by building schools and churches, by starting their own businesses and organizing unions, and even by purchasing articles of mass consumption and thereby confronting whites with the "shock of sameness."[19]

The unevenness and complexity of the process of class and racial formation is vividly evident in Chicago's packinghouses and in the defeat of union-organizing campaigns there in the early twentieth century. Throughout this period the workforce in meatpacking was changing, as Poles and other eastern Europeans moved up to semiskilled jobs on the "killing floor" and thousands of southern black migrants took their place at the bottom of the industry's occupational hierarchy. Any hope of unionization depended on forging unity among these disparate elements—above all, solidarity between blacks and recent immigrants from southern and eastern Europe. As the largest single group in packing town, not only were Polish workers enthusiastically prounion, but their attitude toward the African Americans with whom they shared the workplace was unusually (but by no means uniformly) benign. For Poles were still relative newcomers to America. Many of them regarded blacks as fellow sojourners—and fellow workers—in a larger environment that remained unfamiliar and often hostile. Blacks, however, were divided in their attitude toward the organizing campaign. On the basis of years of experience on the killing floor, "northern Negroes" were actively prounion and aware of the necessity of building interracial alliances in the workplace. But migrants from the South, who far outnumbered their northern counterparts, were inclined to credit the employers with providing jobs that offered a dramatic improvement in their standard of living. The vast majority of southern migrants refused to join the Stockyards Labor Council, which they viewed, with fear or disdain, as the "white man's union." Thus the packinghouse labor force was bifurcated, but as much by the unevenness of workers' experience of the factory regime as by race. In 1919 the balance was finally tipped toward racial polarization by conflicts that owed their destructive force mainly to the virulent antagonism of important segments of the Irish community toward African Americans. Acting as "the military arm of the Irish political machine," a number of Irish "athletic clubs" were looking for an excuse to make war on Chicago's black community. One of these clubs, in particular, acted as the catalyst. Based in the "shanty" Irish neighborhhood of Canaryville and named for its sponsor, Democratic alderman Frank Ragen, Ragen's Colts instigated the street battles that left twenty-three blacks and fifteen whites dead and in the process derailed the packinghouse organizing campaign.[20]

Chicago in the "red" summer of 1919 highlights the essential fact that racial identity developed slowly and unevenly and that racism was, in historian James Barrett's words, a "learned value."[21] In 1919 Poles had not yet inhaled the atmosphere of America and internalized its racial folkways; they were still racially in between. But the Irish were at a very different stage of their development as an ethnic group. They had come to the United States by the millions in the nineteenth century, and their Gaelic "backwardness," Catholic faith, and formidable—sometimes overwhelming—numbers had provoked an intense nativist reaction. Indeed, their own status as white had been precarious for many years, and it was the coming of the next great wave of immigration, beginning in the 1880s, that had helped incorporate them into the White Republic. By then Irish Americans had pulled themselves up several rungs on the social ladder. Many had settled into jobs—as skilled craftsmen, foremen, union officials, and the proverbial cop on the beat—that put them in direct contact with the new immigrants.[22] This positioned the Irish to play a dual role—as guides to the ways of America and as gatekeepers who were afforded the opportunity to harass and humiliate and to sharpen the lines between the hyphenated American and the "greenhorn." Thus, in New York's East Harlem, Robert Orsi noted in 1985, friction between Italian laborers and their Irish foremen "left wounds so deep that [they are] remembered to the present." Similarly, in the steel valleys of western Pennsylvania, Slovak American Thomas Bell recalled in 1941 that his forebears had had "intimate contact" with the Irish, "in town as neighbors and in the mill as pushers and gang foremen, and to this must be ascribed much of the subsequent bitterness between them." In the opinion of Slovak steelworkers, said Bell, "the outstanding Irish characteristic was a dirty mouth." The novelist James T. Farrell also revealed the chasm that separated the old immigrants from the new in the Chicago of his youth in his unforgettable portrait of Studs Lonigan. The Lonigan family, which Farrell placed in the ranks of the arriviste middle class, was several steps removed from Canaryville and the world of Ragen's Colts, but the adolescent Studs was nonetheless drawn to the streets, parks, and taverns where many young Irish American males prepared themselves for manhood by terrorizing Jews and equating "Polacks" and "Dagoes" with "niggers." Although they regarded a "white Jew" as an impossibility, and Studs contemplated telling the maddeningly articulate socialist waiter at the local Greek restaurant to "get the hell out of a white man's country," the main focus of their fear and antagonism was the blacks who were trespassing on their turf. "One of these days," they warned in a fantasy of the conflagration that exploded in 1919, "all the Irish from the back of the yards will go into the black belt, and there'll be a lot of niggers strung up on lampposts with their gizzards cut out."[23]

There was, of course, a far more generous side to the Irish. In spite of Bell's harsh assessment of his Hibernian neighbors, men named Maloy, McDonald, Mullen, and Murray would lead "Hunky" steelworkers into the promised land of industrial citizenship in the 1930s. And long before the thirties, Irish Catholics headed more than fifty of the affiliated national unions of the American Federation of Labor and were a major segment of the unions' second-level and shop-floor leadership. In this capacity, Barrett writes, they often played the role of "Americanizers" for the foreign-born. At the same time, Irish American politicos made the new immigrants junior partners in New York's Tammany Hall and other urban political machines and initiated significant legislative reforms that dramatically improved the quality of the immigrants' lives.[24] There were even elements in the Irish community that actively supported the cause of racial equality. Patrick Ford, a native of Ireland's County Galway who immigrated to Boston in 1845, was a leader of the Irish Land League in the United States and the founder and editor of the *Irish World and Industrial Liberator*. Calling the "colored brother" a "defrauded workingman," Ford fought against racism in the Land League and the labor movement and sought to build solidarity between the Irish and other colonized peoples around the world.[25] Terence V. Powderly, whose parents emigrated from Ireland to Carbondale, Pennsylvania, in the 1820s, became the grand master workman of the Knights of Labor and by the mid-1880s the nation's best-known labor leader. (He was also a national officer in both the Land League and the Clan na Gael, a secret society dedicated to the violent overthrow of British rule in Ireland.) Powderly forthrightly championed biracial trade unionism in the South and insisted that "in the field of labor and American citizenship" the Knights recognized "no line of race, creed, politics, or color." A generation later, William Z. Foster, whose father was a native of County Carlow and a Fenian political refugee in the United States, directed the packinghouse-organizing campaign in Chicago and encouraged the organization of black workers as a matter of principle and practical necessity. His patron in the Windy City was John Fitzpatrick, a native of County Westmeath who arrived in Chicago at the age of eleven, went to work in the stockyards' killing pens at thirteen, and eventually became president of the Chicago Federation of Labor (CFL). In the heady days of the postwar era, when all things seemed possible, Fitzpatrick and other CFL progressives combined aggressive advocacy of Irish independence and support for the recognition of the Soviet Union with a genuine commitment to interracial unionism in packing town.[26]

More commonly, however, the Irish taught newcomers different lessons: that to become American one must become white, that American citizenship required the drawing of a racial line between "us" and "them," and that whiteness was not only about skin color but also about ascribed characteristics separating the saved from the damned and from the purgatory of racial in betweenness. This, after all, had been their own experience in the nineteenth century. Through the agency of the Democratic party and blackface minstrelsy, and over against the social mirror of slavery, the Irish had learned who they were by learning who they were not. In part they had done so on their own terms, as their aggressive embrace of Catholicism in a Protestant nation signified. But when it came to race, they had seen no middle ground that offered any hope of redemption. They became so intent on laying claim to the wages of whiteness that for African Americans *Paddy* gradually emerged as a derogatory synonym for *white*.[27]

· · · · ·

It is in this larger context of class and racial formation that we must evaluate the development of trade unionism and organized labor's relationship to the struggle for black equality. Some unions, like the International Association of Machinists, explicitly limited their membership to "white, free born male citizens of some civilized country." But even when they did not insert whites-only clauses in their constitutions, many labor organizations functioned as ethnic and familial job trusts whose benefits were passed down to the same narrow constituency from generation to generation. To be sure, the leadership of the American Federation of Labor (AFL) routinely voiced its opposition to racial discrimination but then argued, in 1901, that "the antipathy . . . some union workers have against the colored man is not because of his color, but because of the fact that generally he is a 'cheap man.' " Already the onus was clear. Insofar as AFL unions excluded African Americans, it was because blacks allowed themselves to be used by unscrupulous employers as "an impediment to the attainment of the worker's just rights." And soon their activity became indicative of an ascribed racial essence and of the alleged lack of those attributes of "temperament such as patriotism, sympathy, sacrifice, etc., which are peculiar to most of the Caucasian race." By 1905 AFL president Samuel Gompers was portraying trade unions as agents of "Caucasian civilization" and warning that "if the colored man continues to lend himself to the work of tearing down what the white man has built up, a race hatred far worse than any ever known will result."[28]

For the next half century, most AFL unions that organized black workers did so reluctantly, as a matter of practical necessity, and then consigned them to separate—and subordinate—locals. But in the mid- and late 1930s, the Congress of Industrial Organizations emerged as a formidable challenger to the AFL's hidebound record and leadership. Given the inclusive character of industrial labor markets, CIO leaders knew instinctively that they had to organize blacks as well as whites if their unions were to survive. Moreover, the leavening presence of a substantial left-wing cadre meant that some sections of the CIO developed a deep ideological commitment to the goal of racial equality. Representatives of civil rights organizations were quick to hail the new federation as a "lamp of democracy." Walter White, the executive secretary of the NAACP, declared during World War II that "the CIO has proved . . . it stands for Negro advancement. It has fought for our people within the unions and outside the unions." This view has been reaffirmed recently by several leading historians of American labor. Robert Zieger, the author of a comprehensive overview of the CIO's twenty-year history, argues that its willingness to address the concerns of African Americans was "unprecedented in the American labor movement." In her widely praised study of industrial workers in Chicago, Lizabeth Cohen concludes that "the CIO . . . went further in promoting racial harmony than any other institution in existence at the time." At a deeper level, Nelson Lichtenstein argues, the overlapping CIO and Civil Rights eras were a time "when the fortunes of the movement for workers' rights and civil rights were linked in progressive and fruitful synthesis."[29]

There was indeed a logic of solidarity that compelled the CIO to reach out to black workers and a leadership that combined a principled sense of obligation with an awareness of practical necessity. This led to remarkable breakthroughs, in the unionization of mass-production industries such as auto and steel and—at times—in addressing the concerns of African Americans. The hundreds of thousands of black workers who joined the CIO were at the forefront of efforts to transform race relations.[30] Radical activists from the Communist and Socialist parties offered vital support to this struggle, enhancing its interracial character and strengthening its trade union base. But white workers continued to make up the overwhelming majority of the CIO's membership, and many of them demonstrated little or no interest in relinquishing the privileges that positioned them a notch or two above African Americans in the social order.

Here the CIO's logic of solidarity came up against a different logic—of majoritarian democracy, which in the United States has always been deeply intertwined with racialized perceptions of self and society. Originally the CIO leadership had hoped to supplant the AFL as the representative voice of the American working class. Although that hope was quickly dashed by the AFL's resurgence in the late 1930s, the intense rivalry between the two labor federations compelled the CIO to expand or die. The more the new federation succeeded in expanding its base, however, the more it was constrained by a membership majority that had little or no commitment to a broad-gauged social-democratic agenda.[31] Institutionally, to be sure, the CIO remained a consistently liberal force. When bread-and-butter concerns were on the table, its mass base was often reliably liberal as well. But especially when racial issues came to the forefront, Lichtenstein's "progressive and fruitful synthesis" often unraveled. Thus in Detroit, where the CIO claimed as many as three hundred fifty thousand members in 1945, attempts to forge a progressive labor politics continually foundered—on the rock of competition between the rival labor federations but also because of white workers' growing opposition to black "invasion" of their neighborhoods. This issue hit so close to home that in the 1950s, when sociologist Arthur Kornhauser conducted a survey entitled "Detroit as the People See It," he found that 85 percent of poor and working-class whites supported racial segregation; and CIO members were "even more likely than other white Detroiters to express negative views of African Americans."[32]

The CIO's new immigrant constituency is especially important in this regard. Along with their American-born sons and daughters, immigrants from southern and eastern Europe constituted the vital core of the industrial working class and the largest single component of the CIO's membership. In the context of the 1930s and 1940s, they finally solidified their claim to first-class citizenship. But as they became fully American, they also became unambiguously white. Just as the Irish had learned America's racial folkways through the medium of blackface minstrelsy, so the new immigrants were Americanized through Hollywood movies, which adapted blackface to the silver screen and celebrated the glories of the melting pot while graphically excluding African Americans from the mix. Those who joined the armed forces during World War II, and even during the Korean War, learned the same lesson in a deeper way. Uncle Sam integrated Jews from Brooklyn, Poles from Chicago, and "rednecks" from Appalachia into the same units, but blacks remained segregated, and suspect as fighting men. Ironically, the Civil Rights movement, which drew on deep wellsprings of American and Christian idealism, helped to crystallize a countermyth of immigrant struggle and self-reliance and to give rise to a new phenomenon, the "white ethnic." Increasingly, for white ethnics, the mythology of a shared historical experience across the once formidable lines of European nationality led to a common sense of entitlement for "us" in the face of a widening array of demands from "them."[33]

．　．　．　．　．

Debates about the role of white workers in the creation of white supremacy and the consolidation of racial inequality in the workplace and the larger society have become especially contentious in recent years.[34] As that argument has unfolded, the experience of Irish immigrants in the nineteenth century has served as an important laboratory for analyzing the relationship between structure and agency, freedom and constraint, in the making of working-class whiteness. Few would disagree with the assertion that the Irish in the United States enthusiastically embraced white supremacy and quickly developed an almost maniacal antagonism toward African Americans.[35] But the question of how this happened and whether the Irish were free to choose another course remains contested terrain. In a pioneering article on the failure of William Lloyd Garrison and his coworkers to win Irish immigrants to the cause of abolitionism, Gilbert Osofsky declared that "the working-class, Roman Catholic, poverty-stricken, and much-abused Irish immigrant could not afford the luxury of political radicalism." According to Osofsky, the Irish were "too busy scraping together a simple sustenance" to pay attention to "extraneous issues." More recently, Peter Way has characterized Irish emigration as "an ultimatum more than a free choice," and he has argued that "by rescuing those at the bottom of society from historical limbo and conferring agency upon them, [labor] historians have abstracted the masses from their essentially powerless position." Even Roediger maintains that "the ways in which the Irish competed for work and adjusted to industrial morality in America made it *all but certain* that they would adopt and extend the politics of white unity offered by the Democratic party."[36]

Hundreds of thousands of Irish men and women emigrated to the United States and developed a significant presence in the labor markets of industrializing America, long before the Great Famine. Inevitably, they encountered African Americans and competed with them for jobs in cities such as Boston, New York, and Philadelphia, because black men were often employed as waiters, boot cleaners, barbers, and common laborers, and black women worked in domestic service and several closely related occupations. Over time, however, Negroes became increasingly marginal economic competitors—not because they lacked skill or experience, but because the numerical preponderance of the immigrants and the growing virulence of color prejudice combined to overwhelm them. Thus by the 1840s native-born white Americans, Germans, and even other Irish men and women were much more likely to offer effective competition for employment. But no matter who provided the competition, Irish success in establishing one labor market niche after another is striking. Thomas Mooney, an itinerant Irishman from Cork and author of the guidebook *Nine Years in America*, observed in 1850 that his countrymen did "almost all the rude and heavy work" in New York City; and according to historian David Doyle's calculations, by 1855 a majority of Irish males in New York had moved from "rude and heavy work" into skilled and semiskilled jobs.[37]

One can hardly argue, then, that economic competition as such was decisive in creating and hardening Irish American antagonism toward African Americans. The Democratic party in its various guises, from the pragmatic politicos of Tammany Hall to roughneck Bowery radicals such as Irish-born Mike Walsh, offers a more compelling motive force, as does the Roman Catholic Church. The question of slavery divided

Catholics, as it did Protestants. Leading Catholic spokesmen in Ireland—notably, Father Theobald Mathew, the great temperance crusader, and the even more famous layman Daniel O'Connell—were outspoken opponents of slavery. Father Mathew, whose main following was among the rural Catholic poor, apparently was "endowed in the popular mind with miraculous powers"; and O'Connell, the leader of the Catholic emancipation movement and, by reputation, Ireland's liberator, "assumed the stature of a messiah who would deliver the Irish from bondage and usher in the promised millennium." "Irishmen and Irishwomen!" these two icons of Irish society declared in a famous antislavery appeal to their compatriots in the United States, "treat the colored people as your equals, as brethren. By all your memories of Ireland, continue to love liberty—hate slavery—CLING BY THE ABOLITIONISTS—and in America you will do honor to the name of Ireland."[38]

But could the Irish in America "cling by the abolitionists" when, as even O'Connell acknowledged, some of them were "wicked and calumniating enemies of catholicity and of the Irish"? As Protestantism, nativism, and antislavery sentiment became more closely intertwined in the United States, O'Connell's association with Protestant reformers sullied his image among many of his exiled compatriots. The problem was compounded by his criticism of America's Manifest Destiny and the westward expansion of slavery in the 1840s. Many Irish men and women wondered how O'Connell could denounce the United States and appear to align himself with British opposition to American policy when it was clear that "notwithstanding the slavery of the negro, [America] is liberty's bulwark and Ireland's dearest ally." Moreover, as the crisis of subsistence in the Irish countryside reached catastrophic proportions during the Great Famine, there was a widespread tendency to argue that the Irish people were treated as badly as American slaves. In 1845 even the black abolitionist Frederick Douglass could write from Ireland: "I see much here to remind me of my former condition and I confess I should be ashamed to lift my voice against American slavery, but that I know the cause of humanity is one the world over." O'Connell also believed that the cause of humanity was one the world over, and for that very reason (although he wavered on occasion) he would not heed the growing number of critics who maintained that his opposition to slavery was interfering with Ireland's vital interests. Increasingly, however, his voice was superseded by others, especially by the uncompromising nationalists in the Young Ireland movement of the 1840s, who argued that the Irish people could not allow themselves to be diverted from the essential and immediate task of liberating their beloved homeland from hunger and oppression.[39]

In the United States, the growing power of a nativism that was at once anti-Irish and proudly Protestant persuaded the Catholic Church to declare its loyalty to "American institutions," and thus to embrace a Constitution that clearly countenanced slavery. When informed of the famous antislavery appeal that bore the signatures of sixty thousand Irish men and women, Irish-born Bishop John Hughes of New York at first declared it a forgery, then added that if it were genuine, every Irish American should nonetheless reject it as unwarranted interference in the internal affairs of the United States. Far more than they opposed slavery, Hughes and other Catholic leaders abhorred the Garrisonians—the "fanatics" and "nigger-worshippers"—who denounced the Constitution as "an agreement with hell." Indeed, some Catholic bishops actually owned slaves, and many who did not became apologists for the "peculiar institution" and the political interests of southern slaveholders. Hughes himself defended the slave trade, asked only that slave owners treat their chattel humanely, and allowed the *Freeman's Journal*, which served as the semiofficial voice of the New York diocese, to print crudely racist articles that routinely depicted African Americans as "ugly black niggers."[40]

But beyond the Catholic Church and the Democratic party, there was—as O'Connell discovered to his great sorrow—"something in the 'atmosphere' of America" that poisoned the well of human sympathy where white attitudes toward blacks were concerned. It derived in large measure from the centrality of chattel slavery in the American experience and from the close association between race and slavery in the popular mind. Even many who opposed the "peculiar institution" assumed that the enslavement of blacks was the result of their own predisposition toward "slavishness." Blacks—whether slave or free—were widely viewed as degraded and dependent by nature, and "whiteness" emerged as a set of cultural attributes defined in opposition to "blackness."[41]

Far more than British or even German immigrants, the Irish were at a disadvantage in adapting to this highly charged racial symbolism, for in the eyes of Anglo-Protestant America, their whiteness was very much in question. As early as 1818 an angry nativist lamented the presence of "Irish negroes" in New York City and expressed the fervent hope that the ships that imported them would "go to the bottom and be damn[ed]." By the 1840s the tendency to portray the Irish in "distinctly racial" terms—as apelike creatures who were laughably crude and lamentably violent—had become widespread if not universal, in Britain as well as in the United States. Thus a meditation on the "Celtic physiognomy" in *Harper's Weekly* commented on "the small and somewhat upturned nose [and] the black tint of the skin." The English journal *Punch* characterized the "Irish Yahoo" who populated "the lowest districts of London and Liverpool" as "a creature manifestly between the Gorilla and the Negro," "a climbing animal [who] may sometimes be seen ascending a ladder with a hod of bricks." As late as 1882, in the American journal *Puck*, Frederick Opper rendered the Irish peasant as the "King of A-Shantee," a subhuman and distinctly simian creature. In his play on the word *Ashanti*, Opper linked Irish Celts to black Africans.[42]

Thus, for the Irish, to "merge socially and politically with the American people," as Bishop Hughes recommended, came to mean seizing the mantle of whiteness as their own and defining themselves over against the blackness of the free Negro as well as of the slave. In so defining themselves, they turned their backs on O'Connell's appeal to the generous and humane dimensions of Irishness and chose the low road of white racial identity. Perhaps, as David Brundage has argued, their destiny was one of "closed avenues and limited options, fears and necessities." But the choice they made had enormous consequences for the long-term development of the American working class, for the Irish were strategically positioned to point the way for the immigrant nationalities that followed. In so choosing, moreover, Irish workers were hardly the mere tools of capital. They acted in their own interests, as they understood them; and relative to their employers, they often represented the "hard" side of American racism. We can argue about the extent of their freedom but not about their agency or its effects.[43]

In the final analysis, to play structure and agency off against each other is to create a false dichotomy. Workers were indeed "made"—by economic and technological forces, by urbanization and immigration, by religious institutions, political parties, and the state, and by the cultures of minstrelsy and mass consumption. But they also made themselves. To emphasize their agency is to suggest not that they were free to shape the world as they wished but rather that they were not merely acted upon. They acted on their own behalf, and like all historical actors they bear some moral responsibility for the choices they made. As historian Laura Lee Downs has argued in the British context, "The relative powerlessness of white workers is too easily taken to signify a

Fig. intro. 2. "The King of A-Shantee": Frederick B. Opper's cartoon drawing not only reinforced the image of the Irish as "white chimpanzees" but in its play on the word *Ashanti* linked them to black Africans (*Puck*, Feb. 15, 1882). Credit: L. Perry Curtis, Jr.

complete lack of agency, so that working-class racism becomes mere weak-kneed collusion with the powers that be. But . . . the white working class was present at and active in its making as a *white* working class. As such, it bears its own portion of responsibility for racism's enduring grip in modern Britain." Can we say any less with regard to racism's enduring grip in the United States?[44]

Unlike many of my fellow labor historians, I find this perspective most compelling—not in human or political terms but in terms of the weight of the historical evidence. I readily acknowledge, however, that this is a story of enormous complexity, and I readily concede the dangers inherent in referring, without qualification, to the white working class. Having spent many hours with Ed Mann and Marvin Weinstock in Youngstown over a period of years, having learned—from Mann and Staughton Lynd and others—the legend of John Barbero, who died in a tragic accident long before my arrival in the Mahoning Valley, I know something of the deep wellsprings of humanity that these and other men of steel embodied. I learned these lessons, in a more personal and sustained way, during my nine years of working as a truck assembler, machine operator, warehouseman, and even, on occasion, longshore-man during the 1970s. The generosity, humor, intelligence, and warmth I encountered in and around the workplace on a daily basis are forever etched in my memory.

For me, much about the long-term history of the American working class remains heroic and inspiring. Anyone who has studied the CIO era cannot help but marvel at the courage and solidarity that built the new unions in the steel, meatpacking, maritime, and auto industries. It was a time when "ordinary" people did extraordinary things and changed the course of American history for the better. It was also a time, lest we forget, when "white workers . . . not only struggle[d] side by side with Negroes, but . . . follow[ed] them as leaders and honor[ed] them as martyrs."[45] Quite apart from these spectacular moments of solidarity, there were no doubt many small acts of kindness and humanity across the lines of race during this era. Horace Cayton and St. Clair Drake recorded some of them in *Black Metropolis* (published in 1945); others remain hidden from history.

But when looking at the larger picture it appears undeniable that too often the center of gravity was not the small acts of kindness and spectacular moments of solidarity. Until recent decades at least, the history of the white working class, *in its majority*, was one of self-defini-tion in opposition to an often-demonized racial Other and intense re-sistance to the quest of African Americans for full citizenship. In this sense white workers hardly constituted a class apart. Rather, many of them shared in the white supremacist cultural reflexes of the larger society and eagerly laid claim to the "public and psychological wage" that they hoped membership in the "ruling nation" would afford.[46]

• • • • •

Divided We Stand is itself divided, into two parts—the first is on long-shoremen; the second, on steelworkers. When I chose to focus on these particular occupations, it was, initially at least, for reasons that were largely subjective and even—to some degree—accidental. But over time it has become apparent to me that my decision to journey to Youngstown in 1988, with tape recorder in hand, has been especially fortuitous, for the steel industry and the waterfront both illuminate the historical process of class formation in the United States in clear and compelling ways. That process has been driven by economic imperatives, but it has also been shaped by a series of Great Migrations that began in the 1840s and have continued into our own time. In recent years the streams of this migration have flowed from all over the world. But for nearly a century they came overwhelmingly from Europe—cresting first, in the 1840s and 1850s, with millions of immigrants from Ireland and Germany; and then, from the late nineteenth to the early twentieth century, with a far larger wave from Italy, Poland, and other regions of southern and eastern Europe. From the beginning of the Great Famine in 1845 to the establishment of the Irish Free State in 1922, nearly five million Irish men and women emigrated to the United States.[47] In spite of the Catholicism that initially marked them as ominously different from the ethnoculture of Anglo-Protestant America, the Irish became the quintessential representatives of the old immigration. In New York, Boston, New Orleans, San Francisco, and Buffalo and other Great Lakes ports, the waterfront quickly became a distinctively Irish space. Indeed, the experience of Irish immigrants and their descendants on the docks illuminates several important motifs of the making of the American working class, above all, perhaps, the way a "race" of "strangers" emerged from the crucible of class formation as American and white.

There were plenty of Irish immigrants in steel, too. But the steel industry's greatest growth coincided with the era of the new immigration, when "birds of passage" from southern and eastern Europe were coming to the United States by the millions. As Thomas Bell's *Out of This Furnace* evocatively reveals, the human history of the steel industry is much less about Andrew Carnegie's meteoric rise from his immigrant roots than it is about the gradual and uneven transformation of another, and more heterogeneous, "race" of "strangers" into Americans and white ethnics.

Vital to this process was yet another group of migrants—this time from within the United States for the most part, but with no prospect of becoming white. As freemen and slaves, African Americans worked on the docks of New York and Baltimore, Charleston and New Orleans, and in the iron mills of the Old South. After the Civil War, they headed North when they could get away. They came to Pittsburgh and Youngstown not as birds of passage but as permanent settlers and withstood the harsh taunts (and worse) of the Irish- and Welshmen who dominated the shape-up outside the mill gates. Thus black migrants were also a part of the making of the American working class. Although often pushed to the margins of the labor market, they nonetheless served as a vitally important presence—teaching European immigrants, old and new, what they must not be and what they must become. Together, these three migrations reveal that class has meant the long-term negotiation of identities and allegiances that have always been conditioned by race, gender, and emergent ethnicity. Are there better sites than the steel industry and the waterfront from which to witness the unfolding of this distinctly American process of becoming? No doubt—especially from the standpoint of gender—there are more representative industries and occupations, but few that would have changed the central components of the story.

Chapter 1 offers a portrait of dock labor and an overview of the nation's waterfronts, concentrating mainly on New York between the 1850s and the 1920s. Chapter 2 is almost entirely about the New York waterfront from the 1920s through the 1960s and relates the saga of the International Longshoremen's Association (ILA). The port of New York was by far the largest in the United States. As late as 1936, it "handled approximately 54 percent by value and 21 percent by volume of the nation's grand total of foreign maritime commerce." Moreover, it provided employment for nearly fifty thousand longshoremen at a time when the West Coast's twenty ports employed a total of twelve thousand.[48] Because of the predominance of the Irish, and later the Italians, in the port's labor force, this is a story of ethnicity as much as of race. Indeed, the New York waterfront brings us face to face with ethnicity and—especially among the Irish—religion not as a problem to be lamented but as a pillar around which working-class life often revolved. It also casts a bright light on the uneven rhythms of working-class mobilization and protest, the coalescence of ethnic identities into a wider sense of white ethnicity, and the enormous disparity in the historical experience of African Americans and European immigrants.

Chapter 3 focuses mainly on the West Coast, where race relations ranged from San Francisco's aggressive egalitarianism to Portland's obstinately "lily-white" stance. It assesses how a Communist-led union responded to the struggle for black equality in several key locals. Above all, it analyzes how veteran white longshoremen in the port of Los Angeles effected and rationalized the marginalization of their African

American counterparts. For comparative purposes, the chapter also examines the port of New Orleans and the racial practices of the ILA in the Crescent City. From the vantage point of the Pacific Coast, General Longshoremen's Local 1419 appeared to be an unfortunate survival of Jim Crow in the Civil Rights era. To its defenders, however, it was the nation's "largest and most powerful all Negro union," and it signified a rational determination on the part of black workers that their interests could best be protected by following the path of racial separation.[49]

Chapter 4 examines the long nonunion era that preceded the successful organization of the steel industry in the late 1930s. It focuses on steel's extraordinarily complex occupational hierarchy and on the ethnic and racial segmentation of the industry's internal labor market. It compares the histories of black and new immigrant workers in steel and once again charts the remarkable differences in their experience. Chapters 5 and 6 examine the successful unionization of the steel industry during the CIO era—first through the agency of the Steel Workers Organizing Committee (SWOC), and then under the aegis of the United Steelworkers of America (USWA). The USWA was one of the CIO's most centralized unions and, by reputation, one of its least democratic. Given the power of the steel masters and the authoritarian control union leadership exercised, it follows logically that rank-and-file workers would have played a very small role in shaping the racial practices of the industry and even of their union. Or does it? These two chapters look at the shop floor in steel mills across the nation to demonstrate how workers and managers colluded to maintain a complex pattern of ethnic diversity and racial subordination. They demonstrate, too, how black workers were compelled to organize autonomously and to link up with civil rights organizations such as the NAACP in the struggle against discrimination in the mills.

Chapter 7 brings us full circle—back to Youngstown, where the journey began for me. It is a case study of steel unionism and race relations in two of the most important United Steelworkers' locals in the Mahoning Valley of northeast Ohio. More than any other chapter, this one tries to identify and flesh out larger patterns of development by focusing on individuals whose lives have remained hidden from history because—until the shutdown of the mills in the 1970s and 1980s made them visible, as victims and as scapegoats—they disappeared into an "iron house" every day and labored there in relative obscurity. Concluding with the shutdown of the mills compels me to end on a note of tragedy, and yet any history of race in America necessarily involves the tragedy of lives stunted by dehumanization and discrimination, of hopes for justice undermined by the power of the "aristocracy of the human skin,"[50] of visions truncated by the weight of racialized identities. But the story of race, class, and unionism in Youngstown is also filled with small triumphs, and, above all, with examples of humanity that nourish the spirit and compel admiration for the extraordinary courage and resilience of ordinary people.

PART ONE

LONGSHOREMEN

The Logic and Limits of Solidarity, 1850s–1920s

FEW OCCUPATIONAL GROUPS better illustrate the unevenness of work-ing-class consciousness and the complexities of ethnic and racial con-flict and accommodation in the United States than the men who la-bored "along shore," loading and unloading ships. The longshoremen were classically proletarian. They worked with their hands, developed a muscular workplace culture, and were rooted in dense communal networks that merged class, ethnic, and racial identities. They orga-nized unions as early as the 1840s and engaged in strikes that paralyzed the economic life of major metropolitan areas. They were at once insu-lar and cosmopolitan—reflecting the relatively self-contained mores of their neighborhoods and yet linked by their work to a wider world of commerce and culture, intensely local in their allegiances but willing to turn for leadership to Communists, syndicalists, and other critics of capitalism.

In the nineteenth century, immigrants from Ireland and Germany competed for employment on the docks with northern free blacks and southern slaves. In the early twentieth century, new immigrants from southern and eastern Europe entered the labor market in large numbers and changed the face of the waterfront. The embattled Irish succeeded in maintaining several major enclaves. Blacks were driven from the docks in some cities but predominated in others. Mexicans gradually created a niche for themselves on the Texas Gulf Coast and in the booming port of Los Angeles. Along with "swarthy" Italians, they com-plicated the question of race by creating a sizable intermediate stratum of people who were not "black" but not yet "white" either.

In organizing unions and exercising some control of their work envi-ronment, longshoremen continually came up against questions of race and ethnicity. Who qualified as one's fellow worker? Was it only kin, neighbor, and countryman? Or was it any able-bodied candidate who joined the ranks of job seekers at the "slave markets" where dockwork-ers vied for employment each day? There was no single answer to these questions. For many years longshoremen in each port worked out their own solutions. In the twentieth century, however, when trade unions finally developed a stable presence, they sought to impose more uniform patterns not only of wages and conditions but also of racial accommodation and exclusion.

Of course, employers, the state, and other forces in the larger society played an important role in determining the complexion of the longshore labor force. Successive waves of new immigrants pressed against the ramparts of protected ethnic niches. Employers sought to increase the supply of labor and to exploit ethnic and racial differences for their profit-maximizing purposes. The state endeavored to bring a modicum of order to a notoriously disorderly environment and sometimes intervened in the chaotic rhythms of maritime commerce. Nonetheless, a long-term perspective suggests that the self-activity of the longshoremen themselves was vital, and sometimes decisive, in shaping patterns of ethnic and racial inequality on the waterfront.

· · · · ·

Today technology has rendered the longshoreman almost obsolete; the giant cargo container, which has dramatically reduced the need for labor in the loading and unloading of ships, is rightly called the longshoreman's coffin. But for centuries, wherever there was a harbor and waterfront commerce, an abundant supply of men labored along the shore. Their work routine was erratic, for ships sailing from distant ports and facing the vagaries of weather along the way could hardly be expected to keep a predictable schedule. And so the longshoreman waited, and then, if lucky enough to be chosen to work the ship's cargo, he might face twenty (or thirty, or even more) consecutive hours of frantic effort, stowing lumber or cotton, throwing sacks of coffee or sugar—in short, handling anything from steel beams to a passenger's luggage—driven always by the stern injunction that "the ship must sail on time." The transition from sail to steam reduced the unpredictability somewhat, but with its alternating rhythms of enforced idleness and hard, often dangerous, work, the waterfront remained a quintessential site of "casualism."[1]

Longshoremen lived out these rhythms in an environment characterized by extraordinary occupational diversity and geographic range. Waterfront communities, varying in size from the massive port of New York to the smallest lumber port in the Pacific Northwest, dotted a vast coastline stretching from Down East Maine all the way to Brownsville,

Texas, and from San Diego to the Canadian border. In addition, there was a complex network of inland waterways, centered on the Great Lakes and the Mississippi and Ohio Rivers. The centerpiece of this far-flung system was the port of New York, by far the largest in the nation. With more than 770 miles of shoreline and 350 miles of developed water frontage, the port encompassed seven major bays, the mouths of four large rivers, and four estuaries, stretching from Manhattan to Brooklyn to Staten Island and along the New Jersey coastline to Bayonne, Hoboken, Jersey City, and Port Newark. Perhaps 300,000 workers were employed in the handling of waterborne commerce in the port of New York—as seamen, longshoremen, checkers and weighers, tugboat and lighter men, truck drivers and freight handlers, railroad and shipyard workers, ship chandlers, and customs brokers. Among these occupations, the longshoremen were by far the most numerous. In 1914 well-informed observers estimated that between 40,000 and 60,000 dockworkers worked in the port. As late as 1938, a careful student of "the waterfront labor problem" concluded that New York accounted for about a third of the 150,000 longshoremen employed in the United States.[2]

Some dockworkers were specialists who handled only one type of cargo—coal heavers, grain shovelers, cotton screwmen, lumber handlers, and banana "fiends." They worked in gangs that ranged from four men in lumber and cotton to more than thirty in the case of banana handlers. General longshoremen, who dealt with the wide array of goods that most ships transported, were divided into three groups that constituted a clear but permeable occupational hierarchy. The most skilled men worked on deck, operating winches, rigging gear, and guiding the cargo from one place of rest to another. Then came the hold men, whose ability to stow cargo evenly was vital to a ship's safety. Finally, the dock men loaded and unloaded goods on the pier. Although the dock men began as the lowest stratum of the longshore hierarchy, the intoduction of motorized vehicles and other mechanized equipment on the piers gradually propelled them ahead of their counterparts in the hold. "I worked in the [hold] for ten years before I got outta there," New York longshoreman Roy Saunders recalled in 1989. "That was the dogs. That was the worst. Cold in the wintertime, hot in the summer. They thought the men in the hold was the lowest."[3]

In the popular idiom, the longshoreman—wherever he worked—was a stereotypical creature, large of back but small of mind, at once a free spirit and the passive victim of oppressive circumstance. The long bouts of enforced waiting led to the portrayal of "men with a small capacity for mental analysis who are taking things exactly as they find them." In the novelist Theodore Dreiser's words, "They stand or sit like sheep in droves awaiting the call of opportunity. You see them in sun or rain, on hot days or cold ones, waiting." But another novelist captured a quite different dimension of the longshoreman: the happy-go-lucky fellow who, according to Ernest Poole, was "huge of limb, and tough of muscle, hard-swearing, quick-fisted, big of heart." Living in a waterfront world that was "enlivened with the most picturesque aspects of human nature," he cursed, he drank, he fought, and he lived for the moment and gave little thought to the morrow. The journalist J. Anthony Lukas provided a memorable portrait of such a man in his depiction of a Boston longshoreman who fought a barroom battle with cargo hooks; and then, after his opponent had driven a hook through his lip and out the middle of his chin, the bloody but unbowed victim "staggered to the bar and knocked back a shot of whiskey, which dribbled out through the hole in his chin."[4]

Beyond the stereotypes were the realities that the world "uptown" showed little interest in acknowledging. The hard-drinking, hard-swearing longshoreman of legend was often a family man who struggled against great odds to provide for his wife and children, engaging in a race with time against injury and the physical debilitation that years of dock labor inevitably wrought. In Liverpool it was said that a man could not work as a coal heaver for more than five years; in New York a veteran longshoreman told the federally appointed Commission on Industrial Relations that work on the docks used men up in ten years. And yet somehow they persevered. According to an estimate in an official report on dock employment in the port of New York, the majority of the longshoremen were between thirty and forty. Charles Barnes, the most careful observer of waterfront labor in the early twentieth century, implied that the average age was closer to fifty. Barnes and others were struck by the absence of young men on the docks. No doubt many younger men came and went. For those who stayed, the waterfront became a way of life. "After a man works at [the trade for] ten or fifteen years," said the superintendent of New York's largest stevedoring firm, "he gets into a groove and is not good for anything [else]."[5]

But he was, of necessity, good at what he did. Technically, longshoring was not skilled work; it was not acknowledged as a craft and did not require a formal apprenticeship. But in a workaday environment

6

where human error and the ravages of weather could—and frequently did—bring injury and death, doing the job right required a touch that only "intelligence, experience, and superior judgment" could provide. A Liverpool union official declared that the "all-round" dockworker required "the intelligence of a Cabinet Minister . . . [,] the mechanical knowledge and resource of a skilled engineer, and, in addition, the agility and quick-wittedness of a ring-tailed monkey." More prosaically, the author of a comprehensive government survey entitled "Longshore Labor Conditions in the United States" concluded that "when it comes to handling the ship's winches or to stowing the cargo in the ship's hold, . . . such work can be learned only after several years of constant and persevering application."[6]

On the job, moreover, the longshoreman was not a free-spirited individual but a participant in a collective endeavor that required constant cooperation in order to equalize the expenditure of energy and to prevent accident or death. "They work in gangs so much," said one close observer of the waterfront, that "they learn the value of fellowship in . . . way[s] that other men largely have not." One form this fellowship took was the tradition of monetary support for workers who had been hurt on the docks. Although they labored in one of the most dangerous occupations in the United States, longshoremen were seldom compensated for their injuries by the employers or the state. Thus they developed an informal system for taking care of their own. In 1907 Ernest Poole noted that on payday, at almost every pay window, "stood a man with an empty cigar box, into which each docker dropped fifty cents or one quarter out of his pay." John Dwyer, a longshoreman born in 1915, affirmed the remarkable longevity of this tradition. "If somebody got hurt," he recalled in 1989, "they had a box every payday. The guys were good about throwing [in] a buck or two. . . . If you got hurt, you got whatever was in the box."[7]

Another mode of fellowship was more combative. Barnes observed that although dockworkers rarely obtained formal recognition from the shipowners and were almost invariably defeated when they went on strike, they nonetheless developed a tradition of solidarity that allowed them to exert considerable influence on the job, often informally, in a single gang or on a single pier. Generally, unions played no direct role in this activity, but longshoremen acting in concert were still able to compel wage increases, affect the pace of their labor, and have some say over the size and composition of their work gangs. "Whenever an advance in wages has been secured," Barnes wrote, "it has been the

7

Fig. 1.1. "The Ship Must Sail on Time": longshoremen at work. Credit: *Dispatcher*, International Longshore and Warehouse Union

result of a demand pressed with calm determination." In many instances the companies were "forced to yield by the united resolution of the men to hinder the work in all possible ways until they won their point." Barnes found, moreover, that unions were gradually able to compel informal recognition on some of the most important piers in New York, until the companies instructed their hiring foremen not to reject union members. If a foreman were to do so, the men "would all quietly quit work."[8]

In sharp contrast to this quiet but proud tradition of solidarity, there was another reality on the docks: of raw exploitation, routine humiliation, and the common perception of the longshoreman as a hapless victim of a harsh environment. "When an accident takes place," said one observer, "often a man will lie there on the pier . . . and in winter will be swept by the wind and snow for . . . hours before anyone gets around to him." The city hospitals had a "thoroughly bad reputation" in this regard, for "a longshoreman[,] when he comes up from the hold[,] is generally so dirty and dusty . . . that he is the last sort of person they want in the hospital; and if they can let him lie there they let him lie there." Far more common, but no less humiliating, was the daily reality of "bull driving" by foremen who were determined to get as much work out of their charges as possible. Often men were compelled to carry heavy sacks, weighing hundreds of pounds, "on the run," up and down gangways made slippery by rain, sleet, or snow. "There is too much bullying," said longshoreman Timothy Carroll. "The foremen are after you all the time, and they don't treat you like men. . . . If you want to go to the toilet or anywhere, they go down and pull you out." When asked to compare the pace of work in New York with that in his native Liverpool, Carroll replied, "I think this is Chinese labor [compared] to . . . Liverpool." Carroll was a recent immigrant, but already he had intuited that "Chinese labor" symbolized the antithesis of "American manhood."[9]

Here was another contradiction. Hard physical labor on the docks and at construction sites engendered its own mystique of manhood. Although the work was exhausting and irregular, it implied physical prowess and independence in ways that white-collar employment, and even the confining regimen of the factory, did not. But the "bull-driving" foremen and the imperative that "the ship must sail on time" threatened this mystique.[10] One response was overcompensation and a cult of hypermasculinity. Many longshoremen took a perverse pride in the danger of their work environment and in their ability to withstand the bull driving. To outsiders, they often appeared "swaggering and overbearing," and their quickness to settle disputes with their fists was "alarming." Drink provided another form of release. Alcoholism allegedly reached epidemic proportions in waterfront neighborhoods. And men who were robbed of their self-respect on the job were sometimes inclined to take out their frustrations on wives and children. Harold Gates, a teamster who grew up among longshoremen in working-class Greenwich Village, remembered it as "a terrible life."[11]

But there were compensations—in familial and ethnic networks, in the church, and even on the job. Dockworkers Sam Madell and Roy Saunders recalled one legendary aspect of longshoring. "There was a lot of stealing going on around the docks," said Madell. "It became particularly prevalent when a whiskey ship came in[. Then] it seemed like everyone on the waterfront would descend on the ship." Saunders agreed.

The whiskey business was bad, guys takin' cases and stashin' it. . . . And rum. When that rum was comin' in there in sixty-gallon barrels, 161 proof, the guys used to go down there and drill a hole in the barrel, make a peg first, so that when he fill up his pail, he sticks that peg in there to stop it from runnin'.

Well, he'd go out and buy a nickel's worth of ice from the hot-dog man, and he'd put four or five Pepsi-Colas in it, and come around like a water boy. He'd walk right by the boss with that thing. One half a pail would make twenty-one men drunk. That was the whole gang.[12]

At the heart of the longshoreman's world, his curse as well as the key to his survival, was the shape-up, the daily routine at the pier head where the hiring foreman—the waterfront's true autocrat—selected the men needed to work a ship. As early as 1861, Henry Mayhew, the great English chronicler, gave an unforgettable portrayal of the "shape" in the port of London, where the livelihoods of twelve thousand workers depended on the docks but there was sufficient work for only four thousand. It was, Mayhew wrote, "a sight to sadden the most callous, to see thousands of men struggling for only one day's hire; the scuffle being made the fiercer by the knowledge that hundreds out of the number there assembled must be left to idle the day out in want." In New York there was perhaps less scuffling, but as late as the 1950s a journalist saw the same "anxiety, eagerness, and fear" among the men in the shape, the same "relief and joy" among those chosen, and "bleak disappointment," even "despair," among those who were rejected.[13]

The shape-up was the means by which the employer guaranteed himself a surplus of labor and ensured a high rate of productivity from workers driven by the fear of the men "waiting at the gate" to replace them. The International Longshoremen's Association (ILA), the predominant labor organization in the industry, also favored the shape-up because it swelled the number of union members, kept their dues flowing into the ILA treasury, and offered ILA officials numerous ways to pad their pockets via kickbacks and other forms of graft. For all of these reasons, trade union and social reformers issued persistent calls for the abolition of the shape. In 1943 a U.S. Senate subcommittee declared with exasperation that it "is wasteful and inefficient; it has been condemned for over thirty years; it should be tolerated no longer." But many longshoremen appear to have accepted the shape—for some, even among the regularly employed, because it reflected their "casual frame of mind"; for others, because it offered at least the hope of a

10

day's work at relatively high hourly wages, an opportunity that the implementation of any decasualization plan might have foreclosed. "It was one thing to stop new men entering the trade," wrote historian Eric Hobsbawm of the British experience; "quite another to throw Bill and Jack (and perhaps oneself) out on the streets."[14]

Critics of the shape-up were correct to point out that it encouraged a vast oversupply of labor and hence favoritism in the assignment of jobs. But even in New York the employers' need for a skilled and stable labor force and the longshoremen's need for a modicum of security and a living wage led to the development of regular gangs of twenty or more men who asserted their right to priority on a given pier and established local patterns of "custom and practice." Foreign-owned steamship companies such as Hamburg-American and North German Lloyd in Hoboken and the Cunard and White Star Lines in Manhattan hired workers "on a more or less permanent basis," beginning in the early years of the twentieth century (perhaps earlier). In 1938 a survey of dockworkers living in Greenwich Village noted the prevalence of regular gangs on Manhattan's West Side and pointed out that extra men were hired only after the regulars had been assigned. "A steady gang sticks to one pier," the survey team concluded, "and has an agreement with the stevedore that they will get work whenever there is any on that pier."[15]

The men who worked in steady gangs made up the core of the port's dock labor force, but they may have accounted for no more than half of the total. The regulars predominated in the foreign trade; the "extras," or "casuals," were more common in the coastwise trade. But virtually every dock attracted about twice the number of men it needed on a day-to-day basis. Moreover, the persistence of an unregulated and overabundant supply of labor inevitably meant that even the regulars faced economic insecurity and, sometimes, a condition close to poverty. This becomes strikingly evident from the data collected by the Greenwich Village survey team among longshoremen in one of the port's better and more secure working environments. Of course, 1938 was a Depression year, and that fact had a significant bearing on the data collected by the survey team. But in talking to 278 longshoremen, 217 of whom were heads of households, the Greenwich Village researchers found a level of deprivation that owed nearly as much to the character of the waterfront labor market as it did to the temporary weight of the Great Depression. The average annual family income of these men was nine hundred dollars, which at the prevailing rate of pay on the docks indicated that many of them had worked no more than half of the normal working days in the previous year. Many families depended on more than one breadwinner, although "usually it was the son or daughter who went to work, seldom the wife." Remarkably, after nearly a full decade of the Great Depression, only 29 percent of the families had ever been on relief, but this reflected their dogged aversion to the dole more than their economic circumstances. The survey team found that many of the families had lived in the same neighborhood, even the same house, for more than ten years, and in some cases more than twenty. And yet 91 percent of them still resided in old, walk-up tenements, and nearly half (47 percent) were compelled to use shared toilets in the hallways of their tenements. "From two to four families shared this kind of toilet," the survey team reported, "no matter how many people there were in the families. In many houses the toilets were so neglected by the janitor that foul odors permeated all the poorly ventilated halls."[16]

· · · · ·

Whether they labored on Manhattan's West Side or along the East River, or for that matter in Boston or Baltimore, longshoremen were likely to be members of kinship, neighborhood, and ethnic networks that revolved around the waterfront's peculiar rhythms but also provided sustenance and solace against its harsh realities. In a trade where men labored collectively, under conditions that were often life-threatening, easy communication and mutual trust were vital to their well-being; and this trust developed most readily among family members, neighbors, and men of the same ethnic group. In the cities along the Mid- and North Atlantic coast, ethnicity was deeply ingrained in the dynamics of urban geography and politics. For those seeking work on the waterfront, the labor contractor and hiring foreman held the key, and winning their favor was often facilitated by ties of race and nationality. Thus ethnic camaraderie was a natural, even necessary, feature of waterfront life, and a distinct and resilient tradition of ethnic particularism continued to characterize the longshore labor market well into the twentieth century.[17]

The Irish became the dominant force on the New York waterfront in the 1850s, and as late as 1880 95 percent of the city's longshoremen were Irish and Irish American. (The remaining 5 percent, Barnes estimated, was made up of "Germans, Scotch, English, and Scandinavians.") But the question of how the Irish established their ethnic niche and which groups they displaced requires closer scrutiny. Is it possible that many of their predecessors were not native-born whites or other European immigrants but African Americans? And did the Irish feel compelled not only to displace blacks from dock labor but to erase any memory of their presence and to reconstruct the waterfront as "white" space?[18]

Recent historical investigation has confirmed that slaves and free blacks worked as seamen and dock laborers during the colonial period, and they continued in these roles during the early years of the new republic.[19] In the 1790s a British visitor to the United States recorded his impression that most of the "inferior" labor in New York City was performed by blacks; and census data and city directories reveal that in the early years of the nineteenth century 40 percent of the free black male heads of household were "laborers or mariners." Since more than a third of the nation's trade passed through the port of New York, it is likely that many of those who showed up in the city directories as laborers worked as longshoremen, and that blacks were prominently represented among them. As late as the 1830s, blacks still worked as sail makers, shoemakers, tailors, carpenters, and blacksmiths in New York; another British visitor observed that the men who worked as scavengers, porters, dock laborers, barbers, and waiters in hotels were "all, or nearly all, black," and that "nearly all of the maid servants were . . . black women." Increasingly, however, white aggression was pushing African Americans to the margins of the job market. According to historian Paul Gilje, the rioters who terrorized New York's black community during the infamous July Days of 1834 were mainly "journeymen and mechanics sliding down the economic scale or young workers whose hold on an occupation was tenuous." The riots began with attacks on the homes and churches of white abolitionists whose alleged crime was the advocacy of "immediate emancipation" and the "amalgamation" of the races. From there the reign of terror spread to the black community. Not only did the rioters attack individual workers and work sites, but they also demolished black schools and churches and ransacked black homes. Their targets imply a rage whose roots were deeper than the competition for bread. For many whites, especially those who found little stability and sense of community in their own daily existence, black schools and churches represented a mature and stable associational life that seemed to signify an inversion of the "natural order."[20]

Although job competition between blacks and whites was real enough in the early years of the republic, African Americans were soon inundated by the great surge of immigration from Britain, Ireland, and Germany that began in the 1820s. New York City's population quadrupled between 1830 and 1860. In the late 1840s and early 1850s, between 200,000 and 400,000 immigrants landed in the city every year; and by 1855, when the census recorded only 11,840 African Americans in New York, 51 percent of the city's population of 630,000 was foreign-born. No wonder Frederick Douglass lamented the fact that "every hour sees the black man elbowed out of employment by some newly arrived emigrant whose hunger and whose color are thought to give him a better title to the place."[21]

The Irish were prominent among those doing the elbowing. During the thirty years preceding the onset of the Great Famine in 1845, between 800,000 and 1 million Irish men, women, and children emigrated to North America. For more than a century the overwhelming majority of those sailing westward had been skilled and Protestant and from the northern counties of Ulster, but by the end of the 1830s it was the unskilled and the Catholic, from the Gaelic South and West, who predominated in the emigrant stream. The famine not only added to the flow (between 1847 and 1851 nearly 850,000 Irish entered the United States through the port of New York) but accentuated its poor and "papist" character. By 1860 New York had become the world's most Irish city; its Irish-born population of 203,000 surpassed that of any city in Ireland.[22]

"The poor Irishman," said Ralph Waldo Emerson, "the wheelbarrow is his country." Indeed, Irish immigrants built canals and railroads in the United States; they worked in the "sweated" trades; and they quickly came to dominate the fields of domestic service and common labor. Their destiny, it seemed, was to "dig and delve, and drudge, and do domestic work." But only gradually did they build an inclusive Irish identity. In the United States as well as in Britain, immigrants from Ireland were notorious for the intensity of their local and regional loyalties. "I am unable to hire a Connaught man," one Liverpool employer reported; "he is always spoken of in terms of contempt" by his fellow workers, who in this case were likely to be from the eastern province of Leinster or the northeast of Ulster. A Connaught man "is discovered immediately," lamented the employer, "and they will persecute him till he quits." Among canal diggers in the United States, there were murderous feuds between Connaught men and "Corconians." "So deadly was the character of their enmity towards each other," an Irish immigrant observed, "that one of a different party even passing by the other party would be run down like a rabbit by a pack of bloodhounds, & murdered on the spot." Often these faction fights reflected the precarious position of immigrants and native-born workers in an intensely competitive labor market. But increasingly, Anglo-Protestant Americans were loath to distinguish between different groups of Irishmen, all of whom were stereotyped as "drunken, dirty, indolent, and riotous," as a threat not only to law and order but—insofar as they were Catholic—to the very principles of liberty upon which the American nation was founded. Nativist hostility endowed the Irish with a dramatically enhanced sense of how much they had in common. The tragedy of the famine, the surge of nationalism that developed in its wake, and the remarkable institutional development of the Catholic Church all served to deepen and consolidate a shared sense of Irishness, until it became an indelible part of the American landscape.[23]

In seaboard cities such as Boston, New York, and Philadelphia, the Irish overwhelmed their competitors in the lower echelons of the labor market. By 1855 there were 21,749 Irish-born laborers and porters in New York, compared with 702 blacks. Thomas Mooney, a temperance advocate and unabashed moralist, lamented the predominance of the Irish in longshore work, because its inherent casualism resulted in "an idle, lazy kind of life" that "seldom yields to those who stick to it any other result than hardship." But in turning to the waterfront for employment, Irish immigrants were only following the well-worn path trod by their countrymen in British ports such as Liverpool, Glasgow, and London. By 1848 an Irishman in Liverpool could observe that the Irish "perform nearly all the labour requiring great physical powers and endurance. Nine-tenths of the ships that arrive in this great port are discharged and loaded by them." In Glasgow two-thirds of the dock-workers were estimated to be Irish-born by the 1850s, and that percentage remained remarkably constant for the rest of the nineteenth century. In London it was said that "the loading and unloading of ships, and the principal hard work all down the [Thames], was done by Irishmen." Irish domination of some docks became so pronounced that "the story was told of a foreman named Donovan, who was said to have taken on 57 Donovans for work in one day, and was only stopped by the men threatening him with violence if he took on any more relations!" The secretary of the dockworkers' union, himself a London Irishman, admitted that by the 1880s his organization had become a "close hereditary corporation."[24]

In New York, on any given day, five thousand to six thousand men were likely to be employed in the loading and unloading of ships. They were hired, even then, via the shape-up, and they faced the same irregularity of work and oversupply of labor that were endemic to the trade. Thus it became important to limit their numbers, if possible to kin, neighbors, and countrymen. Three instruments—the labor contractor, the ethnic neighborhood, and the trade union—played a vital role in the attainment of this objective. The labor contractors, or stevedores, were often former dockworkers. As the longshore workforce became increasingly Irish, so too did the ranks of the stevedores, who then helped to hasten and consolidate the process of niche formation by giving priority to their countrymen in the assignment of jobs. Then, in the Irish neighborhoods that adjoined the West Side waterfront, especially Greenwich Village, Chelsea, and Hell's Kitchen, Irish-born and Irish American residents developed a sense of entitlement and fought—sometimes literally—to defend the jobs they regarded as theirs by right against incursions by "strangers." Finally, in an industry characterized by multiple actors and interests and a high degree of decentralization, trade union organization tended to be highly decentralized as well. Often informal boycotts, slowdowns, and other acts of solidarity on an individual pier proved more effective than strikes, and the bonds that derived from kinship, ethnicity, and community provided the fertile soil in which this sense of affinity could take root and grow.[25]

Dock unionism was "resilient rather than continuous," historian David Montgomery reminds us; "unions in all the major ports were incessantly formed, broken, and reformed." The first union that survived for any length of time on the New York waterfront was the Longshoremen's United Benevolent Society. In October 1852 the city's dockworkers met and resolved that because the "necessaries of life . . . have been for a long time beyond our reach," they would refuse to work for any stevedore or merchant who would not consent to accept the rate of thirteen shillings a day for laborers and fifteen shillings for foremen. They also warned that should anyone in their ranks attempt to work for less, "we will denounce him as a recreant and an enemy to his class and consider it a degradation to be seen in his society." The following evening the dockworkers met again and formed the Longshoremen's United Benevolent Society. One hundred forty-two men came forward to pay a one-dollar initiation fee and thereby signify their membership in the new organization, which soon claimed fourteen hundred members.[26]

The character of the society was vividly evident in the banner its members carried in New York City's Fourth of July procession in 1854. One side of the banner featured the flags of eight European nations and above them, the stars and stripes of the United States and the word "Unity." At the top of the banner the words "We know no distinction but that of merit" were inscribed. The other side featured the figure of Charity, holding two orphan children by the hand and presenting them to members of the society for protection. Although it was not evident on the banner, the society also existed to represent its members' economic interests and to negotiate with the shipowners on their behalf. The society's leaders affirmed their commitment to establishing and sustaining "that spirit of cordial feeling which should always exist between workingmen and their employers." But when the latter refused to listen to reason, the organization simply stated the wages for which its members would work and then prepared to "stand out" if the shipowners were unwilling to accommodate them. Any member who was "unmanly" enough to work for less than the wages the society established faced the prospect of expulsion. Always, however, the leadership's emphasis was on compromise and forbearance in relations with the employers and virtuous conduct on the part of the society's members. The society's vice-president recommended "abstinence from all intoxicating drinks . . . and an orderly and obliging demeanor"; its president declared that "we are peaceable and law-abiding citizens, who seek to earn our bread in the sweat of our brow, and disclaim all connection with riotous and disorderly proceedings."[27]

But "riotous and disorderly proceedings" were a recurring fact of life on the waterfront, especially when the shipowners tried to drive down the price of labor. Strikes by longshoremen and seamen ranged from nonviolent mass mobilizations marked by "great coolness and order" to angry bursts of activity that one historian has called "collective bargaining by riot." In 1825 there were reports of "wharves thronged with crowds of labourers standing out for higher wages" and effectively disrupting "nearly all the ships in port." On this occasion, "two very active and noisy individuals who employed themselves in . . . preventing those disposed to work from doing so" were arrested and thrown in jail. Three years later the *New York Evening Post* reported that "between two and three hundred riggers, stevedores and laborers" struck to protest a wage cut and were "guilty of . . . irregularities" that included throwing paving stones at those who resisted their demand to quit work. Order was restored only when scores of policemen and a troop of cavalry arrived on the scene and arrested some of the rioters. In 1836 parades of striking dockworkers pulled "more than eight hundred men" off their jobs and effectively shut down the port. Although they had no trade union organization, the workers published a lengthy statement of their grievances and carried their own trade banner as they marched along the waterfront. But the authorities were unimpressed. When attempts to disperse the protesters landed a policeman in the hospital with a fractured skull, the mayor called out a militia regiment and compelled the strikers to return to work. A decade later about five hundred Irish longshoremen on the Atlantic Dock in Brooklyn demanded higher pay and reduced hours of work, and they went on strike to enforce their demands. When the employers turned to recently arrived German immigrants to break the strike, the result was bitter ethnic conflict and a level of violence that again led to the use of militiamen against the strikers.[28]

In some of the earliest strikes, newspaper reports and court records highlighted the participation of blacks as well as whites but did not otherwise identify workers by nationality. Thus a seamen's protest in 1802 involved separate black and white contingents, with the blacks acting "in a subordinate capacity"; and the longshoremen's strikes of 1825 and 1828 included "both white and colored persons." Thereafter, however, there were no references to race, until blacks appeared as strikebreakers in the 1850s. In the meantime, the massive influx of European immigrants had driven African Americans to the margins of the labor market and triggered a sustained period of interethnic rivalry and accommodation.[29]

The fact that the flags of eight European nations adorned the Long-shoremen's United Benevolent Society's banner in 1854 suggests that at the outset the organization was committed to incorporating the multinational immigrant constituency that had transformed the waterfront workforce in the 1830s and 1840s. From the beginning, however, men named Kelly, Donohue, McManus, and McGrath were prominent in the society's leadership, and the dynamics of immigration and occupational networking were turning the dock labor force "green." By the end of the 1850s, the society's members were "overwhelmingly Irish." They turned out, "six hundred strong," in New York's Saint Patrick's Day parades, "dressed in handsome green and gold regalia and carrying Irish and American flags and the Society's imposing banners." This became an enduring—almost sacrosanct—tradition. In "The Day We Celebrate," Irish American playwright and songwriter Edward Harrigan paid homage to the groups that headed the massive Saint Patrick's Day parades of the 1870s:

> The Ancient Order of Hibernians, Father Mathew's Temperance men,
> The Sprig of Shamrock and Fenians too, on the 17th of March fall in.
> The longshoremen are next in line, all hearty, stout and tough.
> Their hearts are made of Irish Oak, although their hands are rough.[30]

Harrigan took it for granted not only that New York's longshoremen were an integral part of the larger Irish American community, but that in this case occupation and ethnicity had grown together as naturally as the oak tree sank its roots into Irish soil. What remained unspoken was the means by which other European immigrants, and above all African Americans, had been displaced from the docks.[31]

The extensive use of African Americans as strikebreakers began in the mid-1850s. Apparently, by that time blacks had come to see strike-breaking as the only means to regain access to a field of labor where they had once been prominently represented. They were offered employment during a strike in 1855 and, predictably, "anti-Negro violence resulted." When the strike ended, almost all of the strikebreakers were discharged, and the issue of race apparently did not flare up again until 1862 and, even more so, 1863, when the waterfront became the site of a "labor war" that reached a gruesome crescendo with the infamous draft riots in July. The claim that "hordes of darkeys" would soon over-run the northern states and work for "half wages" was for the most part a demagogic scare tactic, but on the waterfront job competition between blacks and whites had become a stark and dangerous reality, not only in New York City but also in Albany, Boston, Buffalo, Chicago, Cleveland, and Detroit. In each of these cities, employers used black labor to break strikes by white longshoremen in 1863. In April, on the Manhattan waterfront, hundreds of Irish longshoremen, who were allegedly "inflamed by drink," shouted "Kill the niggers" as they assaulted black strikebreakers. In June New York dockworkers went on strike "*en masse*" and formed the Longshoremen's Association, which enrolled three hundred members within a week. In Buffalo a confrontation between Irish strikers and black strikebreakers in early July left three Negroes dead and twelve others badly beaten.[32]

A week later the draft riots erupted in New York City, with the goal of preventing the implementation of the new federal Conscription Act and its lottery system of recruiting fresh troops for the Union Army. Although the riots involved a wide swath of the city's population, the role of the Irish caused much comment. Influential Irish Catholic voices—above all, the *Freeman's Journal and Catholic Register*—had damned the Emancipation Proclamation as a "crime . . . against . . . the holy precepts of Christianity," denied that slavery was a sin, and denounced African Americans as a "semi-savage race" (a term that many Anglo-Protestants were wont to use in describing the Irish). The longshoremen and their communal allies used the riots as a pretext to drive blacks from the docks. But far more than job competition was at stake in their murderous pogrom. Themes of amalgamation, sexual conquest, even annihilation, were dramatically evident in the behavior of the mobs. On the first day of the riots, a waterfront lynching party hanged William Jones and burned his body. The next morning,

> black sailor William Williams was assaulted by longshoreman Edward Can-field and two other laborers . . . when he walked ashore at an Upper West Side pier to ask directions. Like many racial murders, this attack developed into an impromptu neighborhood theater with its own horrific routines. Each member of the white gang came up to the prostrate sailor to perform an atrocity—to jump on him, smash his body with a cobblestone, plant a knife in his chest—while the white audience of local proprietors, workmen, women, and boys watched with a mixture of shock, fascination, and, in most instances, a measure of approval.

After purging the harbor district of African Americans, the longshore-men announced that henceforth "work upon the docks . . . shall be attended to solely and absolutely by members of the 'Longshoremen's Association' and such white laborers as they see fit to permit upon the premises."[33]

In the midst of a rebellion against duly constituted authority, Irish longshoremen were aggressively claiming full citizenship in the White Republic. It was a claim that would be greeted with widespread skepti-cism for another generation. To the guardians of American manners and morals, the Irish could become "white" only when they became "civilized" and abandoned the alleged traits of character that bound them to the Negro. But to the Irish becoming "white" meant creating social and psychological distance between themselves and African Americans and, as a first priority, severing the occupational and resi-dential ties that linked the two groups in the popular imagination. Frederick Douglass warned that in taking jobs away from blacks the Irish would "assume our degradation." But Irish longshoremen devel-oped a compelling answer. To avoid the "taint of blackness," and the heavy psychological burden of "slaving like a nigger," they would drive blacks from the labor market altogether and, in the process, redefine the jobs they appropriated as "white."[34]

Remarkably, however, the day after the draft riots ended, some blacks dared to reclaim their jobs, and the fact that they survived unmolested encouraged others to do the same. Some black longshoremen even returned to the Erie Railroad Company piers, which suggests that the crusade for an "all-white" waterfront may not have been entirely successful after all. Although few outsiders—least of all blacks—were able to circumvent the Irish near monopoly on the docks, there are indications that African Americans retained a marginal presence there between the draft riots and the next great upheaval, in 1887. In 1879 Charles H. Farnham recorded his impressions of a day spent on the New York waterfront for *Scribner's Monthly*. Characteristically, he found much that alternately fascinated and repelled him in an environment that featured "toilers and idlers, drift and treasure, blooming youth and cold cadavers." But in the case of the black laborers he encountered, the tone was entirely one of fascination. Although bales of cotton weighed five hundred pounds, he reported seeing "two negroes put fourteen of them, or 7,000 pounds, from the ground upon a wagon in nine minutes. It was a treat to watch their sinewy arms and strong backs as they tossed the bales about with apparent ease."[35]

Gradually, mass emigration from southern and eastern Europe built up a reserve army of labor that the shipowners were bound to use to their advantage. In January 1887 a lockout of about 150 coastwise longshoremen employed by a single steamship line triggered a general strike that spread across the entire waterfront and became—in Barnes's words—the "greatest sympathetic strike which . . . had ever taken place in New York City." Although the dispute continued for months at some piers, the general strike ended in defeat for the longshoremen on whose behalf it had been fought, and many employers took advantage of the situation to impose another wage cut. Even more important, the strike marked the beginning of what Barnes called the "Italian invasion in waterfront work." Barnes estimated that as of 1912, "while the Irish (including Irish-Americans) were still in excess of any other nationality, the Italians ranked a close second, making up about one-third of the total." Two years later, when the Commission on Industrial Relations investigated conditions on the New York waterfront, several informed observers expressed the belief that the Italians constituted as much as half of the estimated longshore labor force of about forty-five thousand men.[36]

Ironically, it was the "invaders" from Italy, along with Slavs and Jews from eastern Europe and Greeks and Syrians from the eastern Mediterranean, who made the Irish appear more American, and "white," to their WASP counterparts. By the 1880s, when the new immigration accelerated, a substantial Irish middle class had developed, many an Irish worker had made the transition from unskilled to skilled labor, and the Catholic Church had demonstrated its mettle as an instrument of Americanization and social control. In the popular imagination, riotous Paddy was giving way to genial Pat. To be sure, Pat was still a clumsy figure, prone to drink and disorder. But traits that had once seemed ominous now became hilarious, especially on the vaudeville stage. And in any case, the key comparison was no longer with the "wild Irish" of old but with the seemingly unassimilable Italians, Jews, and Hunkies, who—according to an eminent Protestant clergyman— were "races of far greater peril to us than the Irish." Relative to the new immigrants, a New England Yankee declared, the Irish "do not bring habits or institutions differing greatly from those of the Americans themselves."[37]

On the waterfront, however, the Irish found that their newly minted whiteness was not necessarily something they could take to the bank. Indeed, for the most part they were helpless to stop the flow of "strangers" to the docks, and the steamship companies were willing to exploit their resentment to hasten the process of displacement. Barnes reported that "if a gang of 'Ginnies,' or 'Dagoes' . . . was put in the hold with the Irish, the latter would quit. Accordingly, sharp foremen . . . took advantage of the irascibility of the Irish to force them out and so gain the advantage of employing the Italians." Brooklyn, especially, became an Italian stronghold. "When you come down to the Bush [Terminal]," Barnes wrote of the port's largest concentration of shipping, "probably two-thirds of the men . . . are Italians, and, of course, conditions are a little worse."[38]

In Barnes's interviews with veteran longshoremen, and in the hearings of the Commission on Industrial Relations, the theme of declension was nearly pervasive. "Years ago we had the Irishm[e]n," said the superintendent of the port's largest stevedoring firm. They were "all good men—good, able men; the best men physically for hard labor." Lamentably, "them people have all died out," and an imagined but nonetheless resonant golden age died with them. But the Irish managed to defend several key enclaves, especially along the Hudson (or

North) River in Manhattan, where the Cunard, White Star, and other European steamship lines docked their great passenger liners. Here, two thousand or more men worked in regular gangs and earned wages well above the average. The White Star Line's Pier 60 was unique in this regard. By reputation, it was a place where "the gangs work . . . steadily all the time" and thus a "place to make a big week."[39]

When the Irish monopoly of these jobs was threatened, the longshoremen—and members of the West Village and Chelsea communities—fought desperately to defend their turf. This became vividly evident during a portwide strike in 1907, when the shipowners employed Italian strikebreakers on the North River piers, including Pier 60. At the conclusion of the strike, the White Star Line paid off these men, and three hundred of them ran "like frightened deer" to the nearest elevated railway stations. According to the *New York Times*, strikers "armed with cotton hooks, clubs, and paving stones" attacked them; the strikebreakers "drew stilettos and turned upon their pursuers, but before they had a chance to use the knives they were knocked down, kicked, and trampled upon." Several blocks away, a crowd of women cornered a group of fourteen strikebreakers and assaulted them with "all kinds of missiles." One woman, "armed with an iron poker," knocked down three Italians and pounded them on the head with it. Another woman, the *New York Times* reported, "was seated upon an Italian and was pounding him with a baseball bat." At a third site, police reserves attacked strikers with fists and clubs, and women in nearby tenement windows retaliated by hurling flower pots, iron cookware, and bottles at the police below them. When the officers charged up the stairs of the buildings, most of their targets managed to flee across the rooftops and climb down fire escapes to safe havens below. Only one woman, the wife of a striking longshoreman, who was "caught in the act of throwing an iron pot at a policeman," was arrested and jailed.[40]

Over time, the Italians earned at least a marginal place even on these bitterly contested piers, first as coal heavers, then as regular longshoremen. But the Irish remained unreconciled to their presence. Caroline Ware, the author of a pioneering ethnographic study of working-class life in Greenwich Village, found in the early thirties that Italian dockworkers could not "use the 'longshoremen's rest' maintained by the union because the place was full of Irish ready to run them out." As late as 1938 members of the Greenwich House survey team were struck by "the strong feeling of superiority of the Irish-Americans." Above all, Irish Americans resented "the intrusion of the Italians," whom they blamed for "bad conditions" on the waterfront.[41]

The Italians were allegedly "tractable" and helpless in the face of the "foremen of their race" who controlled their access to employment and regularly skimmed off a part of their wages. Above all, they were not yet white. Testimony before the Commission on Industrial Relations drove this point home again and again. A management representative from Pier 60 informed the commission that neither Italians nor "Polaks" qualified as white men. "In other words," a commission investigator asked, "you may employ seven gangs of white men and one gang of Italians on a ship?" "Yes, sir," was the reply. Another management spokesman, from the American Hawaiian pier in Brooklyn, affirmed that "in discharging [the ship] we employ all Italians, and in loading all white men." The Italians were almost universally regarded as a lower class of labor, and on some piers it was said that "one 'white man' is as good as two or three Italians." This frame of reference was particular— but by no means unique—to the waterfront. According to historian John Higham, in all sections of the United States, "native-born and northern European laborers called themselves 'white men' to distinguish themselves from the southern Europeans whom they worked beside. . . . In every section, the Negro, the Oriental, and the southern European appeared more and more in a common light." For Irish longshoremen, their status as white men conferred real but limited rewards—readier access to skilled and supervisory employment throughout the port, a continuing (albeit precarious) hold on the best piers, and a sense of superiority that could offer psychic gratification one moment but a sense of vulnerability, even betrayal, the next.[42]

At first the Italians were not especially concerned about differentiating themselves from blacks. Perhaps, as newcomers eager for virtually any employment, they were willing to take this new and unfamiliar world pretty much as they found it. But America had many lessons to teach, and the Irish, if only by example, were among the best teachers. Sociologist E. Franklin Frazier found that by the early 1920s, "in order to insure their own standing," Italian longshoremen were assimilating "the prejudices of the white men" toward blacks. In the classic immigrant tradition, they were learning the "values" of their predecessors and, in the process, becoming white.[43]

Like the Italians, African Americans served as strikebreakers in 1887, and they were able establish a more secure foothold in 1895, when the Ward Line employed a contingent of blacks to break a local strike in Brooklyn and thereafter relied on Negro labor "to the exclusion of all other races."[44] By 1902 there were ten regular gangs of Negro longshoremen in the port, and the number increased to thirty-five in 1904. Census data indicated a total of 1,119 Negro dockworkers in 1910. "At dusk," Mary White Ovington wrote in her book on the Negro in New York, "Brooklynites see these black, huge-muscled men, many of them West Indians, walking up the hill at Montague Street. In [Manhattan] they live among the Irish in Hell's Kitchen and on San Juan Hill." It appears that many—perhaps most—blacks gained access to longshore work through strikebreaking. In *Home to Harlem*, the Afro-Caribbean novelist Claude McKay offered a frank, often lurid, portrait of the black migrants from the rural South and the West Indies who carved out a place for themselves on the margins of the tight wartime labor market. One of them, a longshoreman named Zeddy, bragged unashamedly that "I'll scab through hell to make mah living. Scab job or open shop or union am all the same jobs to me." On a more sober note, Frazier observed that these men "pa[id] with their blood" for whatever inroads they made. A hiring foreman told him that "he could recall the time when a Negro could not walk on Atlantic Avenue," one of the main thoroughfares intersecting the Brooklyn waterfront.[45]

Although it was common to employ blacks, Italians, and, for that matter, even "white men" as strikebreakers, blacks and Italians were strikers and union members too. There were two major portwide work stoppages in the early twentieth century—the first in 1907, the second in 1919. Both mobilized large numbers of workers—thirty thousand in 1907, forty thousand or more in 1919. Both succeeded in disrupting the normal life of the port; in fact, the 1919 strike idled nearly six hundred vessels and tied up shipping for almost a month. The 1907 strike was triggered by black longshoremen who worked on the Ward and Mallory Line docks. They struck, on their own, for a wage increase to bring their pay up to the standard rate in the port; and although—like the great majority of strikers—they were not members of any recognized union, the chairman of their negotiating committee informed the press that they had their own organization and that they planned to apply for an AFL charter. There were moments of broad and militant solidarity—most notably, on May First, when columns of strikers (most of them Italians who, clearly, were no longer "tractable") marched along the waterfront behind red banners and the flags of Germany,

Ireland, Italy, and the United States. But for the most part demands were formulated, and the battle was fought, pier by pier, with black strikers pitted against Italian strikebreakers in one section of the port, Italian strikers facing black strikebreakers in another, and the Irish fighting to protect their North River enclave from Italian and black scabs.[46]

By 1919 unionism had finally come to stay; the International Long-shoremen's Association had defeated its rivals and claimed fifty-four locals throughout the port. But the strike developed in defiance of the ILA leadership, which opposed it from the beginning. According to the *New York Times*, the strike was a "wild repudiation of all union leadership," and for good measure the strikers defied Secretary of Labor William B. Wilson and the navy and war departments. As in 1907, there were impressive moments of solidarity. The Italians marched over the Brooklyn Bridge to Manhattan again, in what the leadership of the ILA—men named O'Connor, Riley, and Ryan—clearly regarded as an invasion of Irish territory. And at a packed union meeting, a black longshoreman declared, to thunderous applause, that although "the Negro in New York is suffering more than any other [group] in the city, . . . the Negro will stick with the men and do as they do." But there was also extensive strikebreaking, by blacks as well as Italians. And even when men from many nations stood shoulder to shoulder in turbulent strike meetings, the ultimate frame of reference remained the grievances on one's own pier, and the most trusted ally was the worker, neighbor, and countryman with whom one had labored side by side for years.[47]

· · · · ·

This persistent localism was reflected in—but also challenged—the "Irish Patriotic Strike" that occurred in the port of New York in August and September 1920. The strike—actually a boycott of British shipping waged by rank-and-file longshoremen and their allies with no support from the ILA—began on August 27 and spread from Manhattan to Brooklyn and then to Boston.[48] This was a pivotal moment in the Irish independence struggle, as guerrilla warfare raged between the Irish Republican Army and British forces in Ireland, and street speakers rallied the faithful in New York's Irish neighborhoods to the fight for Irish freedom. The immediate cause of the strike was the fate of two Irish patriots who were very much in the headlines at that time. The first was Daniel Mannix, the Roman Catholic archbishop of Melbourne,

Australia; the second was Terence MacSwiney, the republican lord mayor of Cork, who two weeks earlier had begun a hunger strike to protest his arrest by British authorities. Even before his death, after seventy-four days of fasting, MacSwiney's sacrificial act electrified partisans of Irish independence throughout the diaspora. Comparing him to Christ, his supporters declared that "One Man Can Save a Nation as One Man Saved the World."[49]

Mannix played an even more direct role in triggering the Irish Patriotic Strike. A former president of Ireland's National Seminary at Maynooth, he had emigrated to Australia in 1913 and almost immediately had become a towering, and fiercely controversial, figure. He supported the Australian Labour party and helped to make Irish Catholic workers its chief constituency. He denounced World War I as a capitalist war and, in 1916, helped spearhead a successful anticonscription campaign in Australia. Although initially he deplored the outcome of the Easter Rising in Ireland, he soon became, by reputation, a "rabid Sinn Feiner." When he left Melbourne in the summer of 1920, on the first stage of a journey that was meant to take him home to visit his "venerable mother," a crowd of two hundred thousand people gathered to see him off. He sailed for San Francisco and then took a train across the United States. Along the route, hundreds of thousands turned out to hear him speak at mass rallies. In New York the mayor honored him with the "freedom of the city," and fifteen thousand people cheered him at Madison Square Garden. But the climactic moment came on July 31, when he boarded the White Star liner *Baltic* at Pier 60, intending to continue his pilgrimage to Ireland. The ship's cooks and stewards threatened to go on strike if the archbishop was allowed to board the vessel; the coal passers, who were mainly Irish, threatened to strike if he was not allowed on board. As the *Baltic* prepared to depart, thousands of Mannix's supporters broke through police lines and gathered at the pier; the Fighting 69th regimental band provided musical accompaniment; dockworkers insisted on kissing the archbishop's ring as he approached the gangway; Sinn Fein leader Eamon de Valera, the "President of the Irish Republic," appeared by his side at the ship's railing; and policemen brandished their revolvers to prevent angry longshoremen from pummeling a British heckler. It was, according to the *New York Times*, a moment "marked by disorders rarely if ever equalled at an American transatlantic passenger pier."[50]

And the drama had just begun. Spokesmen for the British government had intimated that Mannix would not be allowed to land in

Ireland, and Prime Minister David Lloyd George reaffirmed that position after the *Baltic* set sail. But even allowing him free access to Britain seemed unduly risky, for with the ship scheduled to land in Liverpool, newspapers declared that the Merseyside was "ablaze with Sinn Fein flags and banners, and . . . tense with excitement." From Ireland, meanwhile, telegrams reported that welcoming bonfires were blazing all along the southern coast, from Mizen Head to Waterford. Finally, a British destroyer intercepted the *Baltic* as it approached England; naval officers removed Mannix from the ship and brought him ashore at Penzance. It was a clumsy act of repression that only fed the fires of Irish nationalism. "Up Mannix," declared the protest placards. "Down with the Pirates of Penzance."[51]

It was on the day the *Baltic* returned to New York Harbor, and a berth at Pier 59, that the Irish Patriotic Strike began. About thirty women, mostly Irish immigrants and Irish Americans who called themselves the American Women Pickets for the Enforcement of America's War Aims, established a picket line on the Chelsea docks and called on the *Baltic*'s coal passers to walk off the ship to protest Britain's treatment of Mannix and MacSwiney. According to the *New York Tribune*, about 150 of them answered the women's call, and the strike was on. They were joined, immediately, by Irish longshoremen working on Pier 59 and others nearby. Many of these dockworkers may have been recent emigrants from Ireland and refugees from rural smallholdings in the impoverished west. One veteran unionist recalled that as of 1920 longshore gangs in Chelsea were composed not only of men from the same country but, in the case of the Irish, of men from the same county. They were accustomed to supporting Irish causes; they belonged to their own chapters of the Ancient Order of Hibernians; they were, in many cases, adherents of "physical force" republicanism.[52]

That evening there was a euphoric "victory rally"—one newspaper called it a "tremendous burst of enthusiasm and wild Irish patriotism"— at the Lexington Opera House. Thirty-five hundred people jammed into the opera house; thousands more gathered outside. The assemblage took up a collection for the striking longshoremen that would help to sustain them in the days and weeks ahead. But the heroes of the evening were the coal passers whose walkout had triggered the wider strike. The crowd "howled" with joy when fifty members of the *Baltic*'s engine room crew entered the auditorium and took their places of honor on stage. Frank P. Walsh, former chairman of the Commission on Industrial Relations and a major American spokesman for Irish indepen-

Fig. 1.2. "A handful of brave young women": In 1920 Irish and Irish American women mounted an aggressive campaign in support of the struggle for Irish independence. Their picket lines on Manhattan's Chelsea piers triggered a three-week-long boycott of British shipping in New York Harbor. Credit: National Library of Ireland

dence, captured the spirit of the moment when he declared that the coal passers "symbolize the resistless force of labor in the world today." But equally significant, for Walsh and his audience, was the success of the Women Pickets in merging the "resistless force of labor" with the struggle of oppressed nations—above all, Ireland—for self-determination. "When a handful of brave young women today brought their banners to the ships," said Walsh, "they singlehandedly set in motion events which shall cause the downfall of that empire which has built up its great power upon crimes committed against weaker nations all over the world."[53]

These "brave young women" appealed with consummate skill not only to Irish (and American) patriotism but to the workers' sense of manhood. Ordinarily the waterfront was masculine space, and a group of protesting females on the docks would have been little more than an oddity. But in this instance the Women Pickets struck a responsive chord when they called upon "Every Red-Blooded Workingman" to take a stand against "England, the Common Enemy." Increasingly, it was women who manned the picket lines, in part because the strike was illegal and male pickets would probably have been singled out for retaliation, and in part because the women allowed, and even compelled, the men to "be men." "The men . . . count on the women not to fail them," wrote boycott leader Helen Golden, "for it is a great encouragement to them to see a strong picket, and it keeps the waverers from going back."[54]

The most remarkable feature of the Irish Patriotic Strike, though, was the participation of black longshoremen. The enmity between African Americans and the Irish American community in the United States—above all in New York City—was legendary. Indeed, the radical black journal *The Messenger* characterized the Irish as "the race which Negroes . . . dislike most." On the New York waterfront, Irishmen had seen to it that blacks paid "with their blood" for any gains they made, and in Chelsea they were excluded from most piers, especially those where the work was steadiest and the wages were highest. But on August 27, when the picketers approached the docks where several hundred black longshoremen were working, they walked off the ships and fell in with what had become a remarkably diverse and multinational line of march: Irish American women and Irish longshoremen, "British" coal passers, Italian coal heavers, and now black dockworkers—all of them apparently marching for the cause of Irish freedom. The women, at least, had thought carefully about how they would appeal to the black longshoremen. They came prepared with picket signs that read "Ireland's Fight Is Our Fight! Up Liberty, Down Slavery," "The Emancipation of the Irish Is the Emancipation of All Mankind," and "Ireland for the Irish. Africa for the Africans."[55]

Few if any developments in the entire history of the New York waterfront could equal, or explain, this extraordinary event and the convergence of class, nationalist, and racial slogans it generated. Partly it was a reflection of the moment—1919 had been an apocalyptic year in much of the world, and the currents of proletarian upheaval and insurgent nationalism that were its hallmarks continued to crest in many places for some time thereafter. In this case, "British" coal passers, many of them wearing small American flags on their coats, stopped work in support of the "Irish Republic"; and according to the *New York World*, black longshoremen shouted "Free Africa" as they joined the strike. When the boycott spread to the Brooklyn waterfront, rank-and-file spokesman Patrick McGovern declared that "three thousand stalwart men have stopped work to force . . . British troops out of Ireland. It's the Irish spirit—no use—England can't kill it." But McGovern went on to add, "[I]t's not simply an Irishman's fight. It is the fight of labor all over the world." Irish American labor activist Leonora O'Reilly developed this point more explicitly. "They can no longer divide us on religious lines or on lines of nationality," she told a mass meeting of strikers. "Labor is labor, the same the world over."[56]

But it is unlikely that labor internationalism alone could have motivated African American workers to go on strike proclaiming that "Ireland's Fight Is Our Fight." It appears, rather, that the key factor was the influence of the charismatic black nationalist Marcus Garvey, whose Universal Negro Improvement Association (UNIA) was headquartered in Harlem. Garvey had been, and would continue to be, inspired by the example of Irish nationalism. His ringing slogan, "Africa for the Africans at home and abroad," echoed an oft-repeated Irish slogan, "the Irish race at home and abroad." He may have named his Harlem headquarters Liberty Hall in conscious imitation of Dublin's Liberty Hall, the headquarters of the Irish Transport and General Workers' Union and one of the sites from which the famed Easter Rising was launched in 1916. Above all, he believed that the Irish struggle provided inspiration for the African diaspora, and that the many generations of martyrs for Irish freedom offered a model for the martyrs of the "Negro race" whom Garvey was calling to the "altar of liberty."[57]

For African Americans the previous decade had brought the hopes and disappointments associated with the Great Migration, the experience of fighting for democracy in a European war and returning home to face the frenzied hatred of lynch mobs and race rioters, and an unprecedented awareness of their own connection with the problems and aspirations of "darker races throughout the world." Black participation in the Irish Patriotic Strike suggests that, like their Irish counterparts, African American dockworkers were part of a much wider community—in this case, one that was nurtured by chain migration, by newspapers and agitational leaflets, and above all by the relationship of the longshoremen to an informal network of communication that reached from Harlem to the West Indies to London and other European ports and ultimately to various sites in Africa. Just as black Pullman porters and other railroad workers were vital conveyors of information within

31

Fig. 1.3. "The New Negro Has No Fear": Universal Negro Improvement Association parade in Harlem, 1920. Credit: Schomburg Center for Research in Black Culture, New York Public Library, Astor, Lenox and Tilden Foundations

Black America, so African American, West Indian, and African seafarers played an important role in developing the links that bound the "Black Atlantic" together. Claude McKay became part of such a community in London in 1920; it was composed mainly of seamen, former soldiers, students, petty professionals, and athletes. A few years later, in Marseilles, McKay encountered a more proletarian version of the same community. Some of its members were dockers; most were seamen—from West Africa, the West Indies, and the United States. According to his biographer, McKay found that all of the black seamen "had been touched in one way or another by the Garvey movement, by radical agitation in Europe, and by the growing movements of anticolonial protest in West Africa, India, and the Middle East."[58]

Garveyism, which reached its peak in 1919 and 1920, was critical to the development of this imagined community. The Jamaican-born Garvey had lived in Britain as well as in the United States; and he was determined to use the UNIA and above all its newspaper, the *Negro World*, to build a universal race consciousness among the children of the African diaspora. Thus he focused not only on events in Harlem, Chicago, and the American South, but also in Britain, the West Indies, and Africa. But apart from these formal channels of communication, black longshoremen and seamen were already accustomed to transmitting information about "the race" from one port to another, often by word of mouth but sometimes by passing newspapers and leaflets from hand to hand or simply by placing them in the hold atop a ship's cargo. Through these varied channels, black longshoremen on the Chelsea piers might well have known of the humiliating—and tragic—odyssey of the British West Indies Regiment (BWIR) during World War I. Like their African American counterparts, members of the BWIR eagerly enlisted in the armed forces, only to encounter a near pervasive pattern of segregation and discrimination.[59] Most of them were excluded from combat and consigned to menial labor under conditions that killed more than a thousand of them. Throughout their term of service they were "subjected to every kind of petty racial abuse" and were ultimately compelled to conclude that "we [were] treated neither as Christians nor as British citizens, but as West Indian 'niggers.' "[60]

Yet their ordeal did not end with the war's conclusion. When they were demobilized in port cities such as Liverpool and Cardiff, they confronted not a grateful British public but an escalating sense of resentment at their very presence, a resentment that exploded in Britain's own season of bloodletting in the spring of 1919. Liverpool witnessed an "anti-black reign of terror"; Cardiff, an organized paramilitary assault on the city's black community, led by armed "Colonial Soldiers" (in this case, Australians). News of these atrocities rippled outward, toward the Anglophone Caribbean and the growing West Indian enclaves in Atlantic seaboard cities such as New York. When veterans of the BWIR finally reached their Caribbean homes, they became the equivalent of burning embers in parched grassland. Their bitter stories fueled the fires of an enhanced race consciousness and at the same time strengthened the bonds of a militant working-class movement that launched an unprecedented wave of strikes in the islands of the Black Atlantic. The largest of these upheavals occurred in Port-of-Spain, Trinidad, and was led in part by ex-servicemen. It began, appropriately, as a dockworkers' strike and spread from there to rural Trinidad and the island of Tobago. According to local authorities, its leaders were "imbued with the idea that there must be a black world controlled and governed by . . . black people."[61]

In this context, insofar as the Irish Patriotic Strikers appeared to be merely "white," black longshoremen might well have felt little sympathy for their cause. But the news from the African diaspora also highlighted the role of Britain as an oppressor of colonized nations, thereby complicating the meaning of Irishness and offering two historic antagonists an unprecedented opportunity to discover how much they had in common. Both were, after all, uprooted peoples who—in many instances—believed that they had been exiled from their homelands. "We have been chained together in the same slave ships," an Irish immigrant wrote to *The Messenger* in 1919, "and sold into serfdom by the same tyrant—England." Although few blacks were prepared to acknowledge that the suffering of the Irish was comparable to their own, many of their leaders and most energetic propagandists were eager to hold up the Irish independence struggle as a model for Black America. Thus Claude McKay enthusiastically recounted his attendance at a "monster" Sinn Fein rally in London's Trafalgar Square in the summer of 1920. "All Ireland was there," it seemed; "all wearing the shamrock or some green symbol." McKay "wore a green necktie and was greeted from different quarters as 'Black Murphy' or 'Black Irish.' " "For that day at least," he wrote, "I was filled with the spirit of Irish nationalism." In fact, even though he was a Marxist who would join the American Communist party in 1921, soon after his return from England, McKay was deeply moved by Ireland's fight for freedom. "American Negroes hold some sort of a grudge against the Irish," he acknowledged. "They have asserted that Irishmen have been their bitterest enemies." But, he concluded, "I react more to the emotions of the Irish people than to those of any other whites; they are so passionately primitive in their loves and hates. They are quite free of the disease which is known in bourgeois phraseology as Anglo-Saxon hypocrisy. I suffer with the Irish. I think I understand the Irish. My belonging to a subject race entitles me to some understanding of them."[62]

The Afro-Caribbean intellectual Cyril Briggs also applauded "Heroic Ireland" in the pages of his journal, *The Crusader*. Briggs, the son of a colored woman and a white plantation overseer, was an "angry blond Negro" and a tireless agitator on behalf of "the sons and daughters of Ethiopia." Born on the island of Saint Kitts, he emigrated to the United States in 1905 and settled in Harlem, where—drawing on the example of the Irish Republican Brotherhood that had sparked the Easter Rising—he founded the African Blood Brotherhood in 1919. Like McKay, Briggs moved rapidly toward Marxism and membership in the Communist party, but he still regarded "the Irish fight for liberty" as "the greatest Epic of Modern History." He called upon African Americans to emulate the Irish and to learn from them that "he who would be free himself must strike the blow." "It should be easily possible

Fig. 1.4. Liberty Hall, Dublin, ca. 1916, the headquarters of the Irish Transport and General Workers Union and a symbol of the struggle for Irish independence. Inspired by the example of the Irish, Marcus Garvey named his Universal Negro Improvement Association's Harlem headquarters Liberty Hall. Credit: National Library of Ireland

for Negroes to sympathize with the Irish fight against tyranny and oppression, and vice versa," he concluded, "since both are in the same boat and both the victims of the same Anglo-Saxon race."[63]

To Briggs, it was self-evident that "two groups fighting the same enemy [should] act in unison and move in co-operation." But on the Chelsea waterfront, cooperation between Irish and African Americans was a rarity. In March 1920 coastwise longshoremen had struck for higher wages, and their strike dragged on into August. With the help of strikebreakers, some of whom were black, the employers finally succeeded in defeating the strike and breaking the union among the coastwise men. Although the coastwise longshoremen were a separate group from the higher-paid "deep sea" men in the foreign trade, they worked on piers that were not far removed from the transatlantic docks, and their fate could not have escaped their deep sea counterparts. Only a week and a half before the Irish Patriotic Strike began, a group of striking white longshoremen from the Morgan Line pier on Manhattan's West Side had ambushed about twenty-five black strikebreakers. In the ensuing battle two whites (named Curran and Kearns) suffered gunshot wounds and four Negroes were hospitalized with fractured skulls. The conflict on the Morgan Line dock continued throughout the boycott of British shipping and featured another melee in which the street adjoining the pier became a "mass of 1,500 fighting men" who attacked each other with cargo hooks, sticks, stones, and fists. More than a decade later, Caroline Ware found that the white longshoremen had long and bitter memories. "Negroes and Spaniards were violently hated," she reported, "for ruining a decent trade and undercutting wages which the union had achieved."[64]

The perception of African Americans as strikebreakers was reinforced when, two weeks into the boycott of British shipping, the employers sought to gain the upper hand by bringing in black longshoremen from other areas of the port to work the paralyzed White Star Line piers. These men were union members; they were recruited with the full support of the ILA leadership; the shipowners housed and fed them right on the docks. But in this instance there was no race riot. Garvey sent one of his chief lieutenants, Rev. J. W. Selkridge, down to the piers to "urge all the Negro longshoremen not to load British ships." The next evening a contingent of fourteen Irish Americans, including some longshoremen, journeyed to Harlem's Liberty Hall to seek a closer working relationship with Garvey and the UNIA. According to an undercover agent who was monitoring the UNIA's activities for the federal government, the visitors "spoke in high terms of Garvey and his movement and pledged their support." Garvey in turn assured them of his goodwill and affirmed that the quest for "Liberty was common to all mankind, irrespective of creed or color."[65]

On the following day a remarkable four-way conference took place. It involved Adrian Johnson of the UNIA, Helen Golden of the American Women Pickets, a representative of the striking Irish longshoremen, and the foreman who was supervising the work of the black strikebreakers. The foreman maintained that his men would consider joining "the Irishman in the strike for liberty by virtue of it being a Common Cause akin to that of the Aethiopian people," but they were also deeply concerned about their exclusion from the piers on which the "wages were highest." Thus they demanded that "some proper arrangements be made . . . to guarantee them a confraternal consideration with the Irish Workers in the Cause of Liberty which they conjointly are striving to attain." The spokesman for the Irish longshoremen acknowledged the justice of the black workers' concerns, but apparently the rank-and-file strikers refused to make any concessions with regard to Pier

60. Helen Golden explained their rationale. "Is it not understandable," she wrote on September 19, "that the Longshoremen of the Irish Race should at the present time take the stand that they have taken? The circumstances are peculiar. They have worked that Pier for many years. The *Baltic* (upon which Archbishop Mannix sailed; upon which he was insulted and spat upon by a Britisher; and from which he was forcibly removed by officers of the British Navy) has always docked there." No one had worked harder to ensure the success of the boycott of British shipping than Helen Golden, and, along with other leaders of the Irish independence movement, her belief that the Irish and African diasporas were engaged in a "Common fight for Liberty" was apparently genuine. Nonetheless, the argument that the Irish monopoly on Pier 60 represented a kind of natural order that had been rendered sacrosanct by the presence of Archbishop Mannix did not satisfy the black strikebreakers. Their decision to keep working sealed the fate of the strike, which was called off two days later.[66]

The Irish Patriotic Strike had little effect on Britain's decision to grant Ireland independence, which came more than a year later in a manner clothed in sufficient ambiguity that Eamon de Valera and other Sinn Finn partisans were moved to take up arms against the government their struggle had helped to create. Nor did the strike force the British to free Terence MacSwiney. He died on October 25 and was memorialized around the world, including New York City's Polo Grounds, where de Valera and New York governor Al Smith addressed a crowd of thirty-five thousand mourners and the American Women Pickets served as an honor guard. As for Archbishop Mannix, he was not able to visit Ireland until 1925, and it was hardly a triumphant return. Because of his unrelenting sympathy for Sinn Fein and de Valera, the Irish government and the nation's Catholic hierarchy virtually boycotted him throughout his visit. Meanwhile, on the New York waterfront, less than six months after the strike for Ireland, Irish longshoremen walked off a Hoboken pier, declaring that they would not work with "smokes." Indeed, as E. Franklin Frazier found, "One Irishman almost precipitated a race riot by striking a colored longshoreman with a piece of coal."[67]

But Frazier also discovered something quite remarkable in Chelsea. As a result of the momentous events of August and September 1920, he said, Negroes were now "permitted to work on the White Star piers." Thus for a brief moment two parallel nationalisms had converged to create genuine bonds of sympathy and a tangible redistribution of resources among workingmen who had long regarded each other with suspicion and even hatred.[68]

. . . . .

In the early 1920s, there were more than five thousand black long-shoremen in New York City. Their presence reflected the momentary needs of a tight wartime labor market but also the accelerating—and apparently irreversible—pace of black migration from the rural South to the urban North. In the two decades after 1910, the city's African American population increased by more than 235,000. Frazier inter-viewed eighty-two black longshoremen in 1921 and three years later published a richly documented portrait of them in the *Howard Review*. Seventy-two of the men he interviewed were born in the South, the great majority of them in Virginia and the Carolinas. Seventy percent had lived in New York City for more than seven years, a third for more than twenty years. Remarkably, few were young; in fact, no one appeared to be younger than twenty-five, and a clear majority were over forty. Sixty-nine of the men were married, and three were widow-ers. Thirty of their wives were employed, a far higher proportion than among white longshoremen, and several men acknowledged that "without the assistance of their wives they would not like to contem-plate their fate." In general, they were compelled to live in unsanitary and overcrowded tenements, and in many cases churches provided the only associational outlet for their families.[69]

Seventy percent of the men Frazier interviewed had been in long-shore work for more than five years; and nearly half for more than ten years. Apparently, they believed they were "unfit for any other form of employment," perhaps because of their lack of education. Twenty-eight reported no schooling at all, and thirty-five had gone no further than the fifth grade (in most cases less). Although Frazier found that a "dis-cussion of labor problems . . . was conspicuously absent" from the many conversations he observed, the men were nonetheless prounion. Eighty out of eighty-two answered an "unconditional 'Yes' " when Frazier asked whether they favored unions. A majority believed, however, that "the Negro was compelled to join the unions, primarily, for the conve-nience of white men." Outside the ILA he could "scab" on whites; inside it, he could "be controlled."[70]

Frazier also interviewed a number of "employing stevedores," and their responses yield important insights into the pattern of opportunity and discrimination that prevailed in the early 1920s. A Ward Line

stevedore employed an equal number of white and black men, undoubtedly in segregated gangs, and sometimes hired more blacks than
whites. Over a twenty-year period, he "found the colored men excellent workers especially under good leadership." "They sing as they
work," he concluded, "and abstain from [the] profanity that often
characterizes the discourse of other men." A White Star Line stevedore
told Frazier that he regularly employed "two gangs of Negroes, three
gangs of whites, and two gangs of Italians." This was a recent innovation, in the wake of the strike for Ireland and the negotiations that
had occurred at that time. The stevedore found the Negro workers "as
efficient as the others," and he tried to distribute the work equally
among the "three racial groups." Finally, a French Line stevedore acknowledged that he did not hire black longshoremen. He had attempted to on one occasion, when it became clear that the white longshoremen who monopolized the work were trying to "run him." But
when the whites found that he was planning to hire blacks, they went
over his head to French Line officials, and "the company put a ban on
the project."[71]

Frazier found, then, that the longshoremen themselves exercised a
not insignificant influence with the stevedores and foremen who hired
them, and thus they played an important role in determining the ethnic and racial complexion of the port's labor force. The hiring foreman,
in particular, developed a relationship with his gangs that was one of
"mutual fidelity." He agreed to provide them with as much employment
as possible, and they in turn worked with an "ardor" that solidified his
relationship with the steamship company. But because the manpower
requirements of the industry were not increasing, Frazier said, "these
foremen can take on colored men only by displacing their white following. . . . [T]his would be treachery, [and] in the eyes of those depending
upon the foremen for their livelihood, worthy of death. As the foremen
know this and are aware of the hardened nature of longshoremen, they
would not take such chances."[72]

What this signified was that apart from a few enclaves, black longshoremen would remain on the margins of the dock labor force. Apparently, they were achieving a near monopoly of the work of "coaling
the ships," but these jobs were among the dirtiest, heaviest, and most
debilitating in the industry. Beyond that, the most hopeful sign Frazier
could identify was that "in some cases the employers have conceded
the right of the Negro to appear at all the shapes and take chances of
employment *after* the regular white group has been selected."[73]

The port's ethnic and racial stratification became visible in ways that should have been obvious to even the most superficial observer. The "white" longshoremen—Irish, Scandinavian, and German—performed the most coveted jobs, as foremen, riggers, and winch operators, whereas the Italians started out performing the least skilled work and gradually pulled themselves up to a middling position in the occupational hierarchy. Blacks developed a few enclaves of relative security but more often were consigned to the dirtiest work or remained on the margins, as the most "casual" of the casuals. The stratification also became geographic as well as—perhaps more than—occupational, and certain piers and areas of the port became the preserve of particular groups. The Irish maintained their predominance on Manhattan's West Side; the Italians, in much of Brooklyn. Hoboken, once home to Germans and Scandinavians, gradually fell to the Italians. Indeed, well into the 1950s Italian remained the most common language on the Hoboken waterfront, and "ship jumpers" (illegal aliens) from a single village in Italy continually reinforced the New Jersey port's ethnic homogeneity.[74]

· · · · ·

Beyond New York, each city had its distinctive pattern. Boston remained an enclave of the Irish; one observer noted an "unmatched Irishness" among the longshoremen there. In fact, as Irish dockworkers used their control of the port's ILA locals to limit membership in the union and thereby marginalize rival groups, Boston replicated Hoboken's pattern of increasing ethnic homogeneity. There were 198 Negro longshoremen in the port in 1930, but only 78 in 1950 and 34 in 1960. Then, in the sixties, as a result of technological innovation, decasualization, and the declining competitive position of the port of Boston, the number of dockworkers in Massachusetts declined to only 766. As Irish Americans defended their embattled ethnic niche and preserved the few remaining jobs in the trade for their family members, blacks were virtually eliminated from waterfront work. In 1970 there were 4 black longshoremen in the entire state.[75]

From Baltimore southward as far as Lake Charles, Louisiana, the labor force was predominantly black. Here the pattern that prevailed in Boston was often reversed. African American slaves had once performed much of the dock work in the cities along the South Atlantic and Gulf of Mexico, and blacks continued to make up the overwhelming majority of the labor force in many of these ports. Not that their substantial presence necessarily translated into power. In Mobile skilled and relatively well paid whites handled timber and screwed cotton, whereas the black majority was relegated to unskilled labor, low wages, and harsh working conditions. In Savannah a larger black majority fared even worse. But the enduring black presence on the waterfront was a much needed consolation to an African American community that was steadily losing ground in the labor markets of the South. Although the black portion of the workforce among coal miners and railway trainmen fell precipitously, the percentage of black longshoremen in the South Atlantic and East Gulf ports continued to increase. In the West Gulf, especially Houston and Galveston, the work was divided "more or less equally" between whites and blacks. But on the Pacific Coast, until the 1930s and in some ports for much longer, African Americans were almost entirely excluded from the waterfront.[76]

In the early twentieth century, Philadelphia offered the sharpest contrast to New York's pattern of racial hierarchy and ethnic balkanization. As of 1910, there were about three thousand longshoremen in the port, and, remarkably for a northern city, about 40 percent of them were black. Poles accounted for 25 percent of the total; the rest were Lithuanians, Italians, Irishmen, and Jews. The open shop prevailed, and employers for the most part had their own way in shaping the Philadelphia waterfront's ethnoracial mix. But then, in 1913, organizers for the revolutionary Industrial Workers of the World (IWW) appeared on the waterfront and, with amazing dispatch, built a union that thrived for the next seven years. Local 8 of the IWW-affiliated Marine Transport Workers was self-consciously interracial; the IWW called it "the most striking example ever seen in this country of . . . working-class solidarity between whites and Negroes." The local achieved a remarkable degree of job control, and it was careful to share leadership in the union equally between whites and blacks.[77]

But gradually, perhaps inevitably, Local 8 fell on hard times. Its interracialism stood in stark contrast to the ugly racial conflicts that pockmarked Philadelphia's residential neighborhoods. And even on the waterfront, labor struggles sometimes exacerbated racial tensions, as black scabs played a prominent role in undermining several bitterly fought strikes. Finally, with the waterfront labor force swollen to seven thousand by 1920, the employers were in a good position to undermine Local 8, and they received a helping hand from the International Longshoremen's Association, which had its own reasons for wanting to displace its rival. Black workers became a special target of the ILA's organizing campaign, which sought—initially at least—to assign the men to separate "colored," Irish, and Polish locals. It may be that Garveyism and other currents of black nationalism also played a role in weaning blacks away from the interracialism of the IWW. In any case, Local 8 eventually collapsed and was succeeded by the ILA. According to a survey conducted in 1930, the union membership was "fairly evenly divided between colored and white, the white workers being predominantly Polish or of other Slavic nationalities."[78]

If Philadelphia offered the example of a proud and aggressive interracialism that eventually gave way to more muted forms of multiethnic accommodation, New Orleans achieved a pattern of biracial cooperation that was longer lasting and, in the context of the Jim Crow South, even more remarkable. Between 1880 and the early 1920s New Orleans dockworkers created what Eric Arnesen has called "the most powerful biracial labor movement in the nation." Although German and Irish immigrants were an important component of the Crescent City's labor force, race was the major motif in Southern society, and white supremacy was the norm. But black workers, as slaves and freedmen, had established a formidable presence on the riverfront, and employers had no interest in acceding to demands for their removal when to do so would only drive up the price of white labor. Gradually, the painful—and sometimes deadly—lessons of experience convinced workers of both races that competition had to give way to cooperation if either group was to achieve a modicum of security.[79]

The most advanced and innovative forms of cooperation developed among the screw men, the aristocrats of the riverfront, whose name derived from the jackscrew they used to stow giant bales of cotton in a ship's hold. After a disastrous round of competition in the 1890s, the white and black screw men's unions decided to share the available work equally, with the same number of blacks and whites assigned to each hold. Beginning in 1901, the New Orleans Dock and Cotton Council was built upon this foundation. Initially, it incorporated eight unions—three of them white, the rest black. Two decades later the council had expanded to include twenty-four unions with twelve to fifteen thousand members. Although it observed a pattern of segregated seating at its meetings, and although its constituent unions remained racially separate and by mutual agreement its president was always white, the council achieved a remarkable level of biracial accord at the very moment rigid segregation was becoming the norm throughout the South.

"We have had white supremacy and [. . .] black supremacy on the levee," declared a black union official in 1908, "and there was trouble in each case. Now, we have amalgamation and freedom and we are getting along all right." So well, complained a white state senator, that when the waterfront unions flexed their considerable muscle, New Orleans was "practically under negro government."[80]

This was, of course, hyperbole verging on hysteria. The leaders of the Dock and Cotton Council were motivated by pragmatism rather than a principled commitment to racial equality. Even black unionists readily acknowledged that their objective was not "social equality with whites" but "meat and bread." The screw men and longshoremen who dominated the council were unwilling to risk the organization's resources in gestures of support for the most vulnerable waterfront workers, the freight handlers and cotton teamsters and loaders who in most cases were black. And to the dismay of labor radicals, the council's leadership insisted on regarding collective bargaining agreements as "binding and sacred." There were, moreover, clear limits to black-white cooperation. The Dock and Cotton Council refused to support African American struggles against disfranchisement and segregation, and it insisted that foremen's jobs be reserved for whites. But for the most part black-white unity on the riverfront held until the 1920s, when the combination of technological innovation, regional economic competition, and the spread of antiunion ideology created the basis for a conflict between labor and capital that reduced the waterfront unions to an empty shell. The employers' principal concern was not biracial unionism as such but the stubborn control that the workers, especially the screw men, exercised over the pace of work on the docks. During a walkout in 1923 steamship operators succeeded in breaking the strike—and the unions—by mobilizing large numbers of strikebreakers from rural sections of the state and then relying on the municipal and state governments and the federal courts to run interference for their "open shop" offensive.[81]

With the defeat of the 1923 strike, a proud tradition of unionism came to an end. So did the era of interracial cooperation. Blacks soon outnumbered whites on the riverfront by a three-to-one margin, and African American longshoremen became increasingly concerned with defending their fragile turf against what they now regarded as white encroachment. Whites, meanwhile, complained that the riverfront had been "Africanized." For the next generation, racial competition

43

and conflict would take precedence over biracial cooperation in the Crescent City.[82]

. . . . .

New York, then, offered only one among many patterns of ethnic and racial accommodation. But New York was not merely one among many ports. With nearly fifty thousand workers, it was by far the largest in the nation. Indeed, according to the Bureau of Labor Statistics, the Chelsea piers alone supplied work "to more longshoremen than any other port on the Atlantic or any other port in the country." Moreover, as the International Longshoremen's Association became a national union, New York remained the principal source of its power and leadership and thus helped to define the character of longshore unionism in most of the nation's port cities. Above all, New York exemplifies the persistence of ethnicity as a medium through which class was experienced and the gradual but seemingly inevitable racialization of working-class identity.[83]

By forcibly displacing others, and then re-creating the waterfront as "white," the Irish dominated dock labor in New York for several generations. When the Italian "invaders" came, they were resented as economic competitors and despised as not yet "white." Although the Irish lost their near monopoly and ultimately their majority status to the Italians, they fought tenaciously to maintain control of their most prized possessions—the Chelsea piers, the upper echelons of the union, even the "longshoremen's rest" in the West Village. As late as the 1950s, the writer Budd Schulberg found that the Irish "have a better deal than [the] Italians, who in turn are a niche above the Negroes." For the Italians, then, the process of becoming "white" was slow and uneven; and the wages of whiteness were sometimes meager at best. But like the Irish, the Italians were also the beneficiaries of a "public and psychological wage." They had relatively untrammeled access to public space; above all, they were linked to neighborhoods, political networks, and criminal gangs that offered them psychic capital and avenues of mobility that barely existed for blacks.[84]

To be sure, African Americans also increased their presence in New York during the era of the new immigration. In 1890 only one in seventy people in Manhattan was a Negro; by 1930, the ratio was one in nine. Largely because the employers compelled it, blacks were begrudgingly accorded a place on the docks. But even though they appeared to become a critical mass, they were unable to achieve the standing—

the relatively secure niche—that their numbers should have afforded. As we shall see more fully in the next chapter, the distinctive character of waterfront employment in New York, and the unyielding determination of Irish and Italian longshoremen to defend their ethnoracial turf, would keep blacks on the margins.[85]

This was the key difference between New York and the southern ports. On the waterfronts of the South blacks could not be excluded or marginalized, and they were able to reap the reward when circumstances made durable organization and meaningful change possible. Sometimes organization served to consolidate a virtual black monopoly of longshore employment; at other times it meant a carefully constructed biracial accommodation.[86]

Even in New York, there were moments of solidarity when longshoremen found that common grievances made broader unity possible. In the strikes of 1907 and 1919, massive rank-and-file insurgency created tentative alliances that appeared to transcend the ethnocentrism of pier and neighborhood. In 1920 an even more remarkable strike created a common ground rooted in larger currents of nationalist insurgency. Indeed, the Irish Patriotic Strike opened access to jobs from which blacks had long been excluded. But apart from this significant concession, the end of the strike meant a return to older and more familiar patterns of localism that would endure for decades. The majority of New York's longshoremen continued to define themselves in ethnic terms, and even more so, perhaps, as members of family and neighborhood networks. And yet this localism was not incompatible with a larger transformation of their consciousness. Gradually and unevenly, they relinquished their status as "inbetween peoples" and laid claim to their inheritance as "white" Americans. In this regard, certainly, they made themselves as much as they were made. And their agency had enormous implications, not only for the lived experience of class but for the patterning of racial inequality, on the waterfront and in the society beyond it.[87]

New York: "They . . . Helped to Create Themselves Out of What They Found Around Them"

In 1951 journalist Daniel Bell characterized the New York waterfront as "an atavistic world more redolent of the brawling, money-grabbing of the nineteenth century than the ideological twentieth." Bell, the labor reporter for *Fortune* magazine, vividly captured the themes that Elia Kazan would explore more fully a few years later in his film classic *On the Waterfront*. "Cross the shadow line" that divides the docks from the rest of the city, Bell wrote,

> and you are in a rough, racket-ridden frontier domain ruled by the bull-like figure of the shaping "boss." Here brawn and muscle, sustained where necessary by baling hook and knife, enforce discipline among a cowed and exploited group of Italian, Irish, Negro, and Eastern European workers. Here one finds kickbacks, loan sharking, petty extortion, payroll padding, tribute on cargo, bookmaking, numbers, theft, pilferage, and that commonplace of longshore life, murder.[1]

As Bell portrayed them, the New York longshoremen were the passive victims of exploitation and intimidation, victimized less by the shipowners than by gangsters, hiring foremen, and their own union officials. Thanks largely to *On the Waterfront*, this view has become normative, even indelible. But the question that novelist Ralph Ellison asked about African Americans also applies to the longshoremen, white as well as black. In reviewing Gunnar Myrdal's classic *An American Dilemma*, Ellison expressed dismay at Myrdal's tendency to portray African Americans as if their lives constituted no more than a secondary reaction to the "primary pressures from the side of the dominant white majority." "Can a people . . . live and develop for over three hundred years simply by reacting?" Ellison asked. "Are American Negroes the creation of white men, or have they at least helped to create themselves out of what they found around them?"[2]

This chapter will examine the lives of New York's longshoremen in the context of the CIO and Civil Rights eras and will attempt to erase the indelible. One would never know from Bell's funereal portrait that thanks to this "frightened," "intimidated," and "dispirited" labor force, the port of New York became one of the most volatile arenas of strike activity in the nation in the decade after World War II. In spite of the formidable—and sometimes deadly—obstacles they faced, long-shoremen were not simply inert victims. Rather, they were multidimensional human beings who remained more or less quiescent in one historical setting but became formidable rebels in another. As Ellison understood, they acted in ways that reflected their own sense of the rational; above all, they "helped to create themselves out of what they found around them."[3]

The story of the New York waterfront in the twentieth century is also the story of the International Longshoremen's Association. The ILA first became a power in Great Lakes ports such as Chicago, Detroit, Cleveland, and Buffalo. Its origins can be traced to the 1870s and the founding of local unions of lumber handlers in Bay City and Saginaw, Michigan, and tugboat men in Chicago. The individual who succeeded in spreading the union gospel to one lake port after another was Dan Keefe, an Irish American tugboat man from Chicago. Keefe's initiative was instrumental in the formation of the National Longshoremen's Association of the United States in 1892. Following the affiliation of a number of Canadian locals, the organization changed its name to the International Longshoremen's Association and received a charter from the American Federation of Labor. Under Keefe's energetic leadership, the ILA succeeded in organizing grain shovelers, lumber handlers, tug-boat men, freight handlers, warehousemen, and other occupational groups. But Keefe was hardly a radical proponent of "One Big Union." He was a friend of Mark Hanna, the Cleveland industrialist who served as national chairman of the Republican party, and he joined Hanna in advocating a more cooperative relationship between labor and capital. Keefe persuaded many maritime employers to sign closed-shop agreements with the ILA, but the quid pro quo was that the union would police its ranks and prevent any strikes during the life of the contract, even to the point of supplying strikebreakers to defeat an illegal work stoppage.[4]

Gradually, the ILA was able to exercise jurisdiction in most of the port cities of the Atlantic and Gulf Coasts and, for a relatively brief time, up and down the Pacific Coast as well. The union was conservative, committed to the maintenance of friendly relations with waterfront employers, and relentlessly anti-Communist. Indeed, its anticommunism defined and legitimized the ILA and its president, Joseph P. Ryan. Was the union corrupt? Did it fail to represent the day-to-day interests of its members? Was it, as one of its many critics charged, "in no real sense of the word a labor union at all"? Perhaps, but at a time when the specter of communism loomed large in the minds of Americans, the ILA was unfailingly anti-Communist; and the waterfront was an arena where the Communists' alleged penchant for disruption and sabotage seemed to represent a real and immediate threat to the nation's security.[5] Thus, as AFL president William Green put it, "every loyal American . . . ought to thank Almighty God that there is an organization established among the longshoremen that is based upon American principles and American ideals."[6]

The antithesis of the ILA was not communism as such but a rival organization, the International Longshoremen's and Warehousemen's Union (ILWU). The ILWU was a West Coast union. Born in a dramatic coastwide maritime strike in 1934, it assumed its long-term organizational form in 1937, when the ILA's Pacific Coast District seceded from its embattled parent and affiliated with the CIO. The ILWU was avowedly radical, led by men who were widely alleged to be Communists and committed in theory and practice to the "class struggle." The polemical heat generated by the issue of communism obscured the fact that from a trade union standpoint the ILWU was clearly superior to its bitter rival. It was thoroughly democratic in form; its members actively fought to improve their working conditions, until they became, in effect, the "Lords of the Docks." Above all, the ILWU succeeded in ending the surplus of labor that had been the hallmark of longshore work. Through the combined instruments of decasualization and the operation of a union-controlled hiring hall that equalized work opportunities for its members, the ILWU won wages and conditions that became the envy of other workers up and down the Pacific Coast. The ILA, by comparison, was corrupt and undemocratic; its leaders sought to maintain a vast surplus of dues-paying labor; its members' annual incomes paled in comparison with those of their West Coast counterparts.

When it came to issues of race, the ILWU also appeared to be the more progressive union. Its leadership unhesitatingly identified with the struggle for black equality, and several of its largest locals were models of racial egalitarianism. The ILA, meanwhile, maintained a policy of "separate but equal unionism" long after the heyday of the

THE NEW YORK AND POR

Fig. 2.1. Shape-up, New York waterfront, early 1950s. Credit: *New York World Telegram and Sun* Collection, Library of Congress

age of segregation, and it was often accused of relegating its black membership to "Jim Crow auxiliaries." In this arena, however, the reality was complex. The ILA had many more black members than the ILWU, and they took the lead in forging and maintaining the "separate but equal" pattern that prevailed in many southern ports. Moreover, the ILA had numerous black officials, up to and including a vice-president "for life" of the international union. As the Civil Rights movement gained momentum in the early 1960s, the ILA proudly celebrated its own achievements. "For all the years that I have known . . . organized Labor," said ILA attorney Louis Waldman, "I don't know of any International Union where integration has gone [as] far as it has in the International Longshoremen's Association." And, he added, "this has not been the result of any demonstrations." The white and Negro members and officers of the ILA "have learned that they can break bread together in the same restaurants, and they have done so for years. . . . They have learned that they can take their drinks and enjoy them at the same bar. They have learned that they can sleep in the same hotels and that it doesn't do them one bit of harm." Waldman's self-congratulation obscured as much as it illuminated, and it was no doubt meant as a reproach to the civil rights activists who were troubling the waters of American society even as he spoke. But in a number of southern ports, and even as far north as Philadelphia, the ILA *had* achieved a biracial equilibrium that was remarkable. In comparison, the ILWU could claim a more aggressive posture on civil rights, but that stance obscured a grassroots reality that was often ambiguous and sometimes characterized by the unabashedly racist exclusion of African Americans.[7]

Because New York was the home of one-third of the nation's longshoremen, it was the ILA's great bastion. Boston, a smaller port with a much more homogeneous workforce, had achieved conditions that were far superior to New York's.[8] But New York continued to control the union and even to define it. The ILA went through four distinct but overlapping stages of development in New York. The first, the organizing era, began in the early years of the twentieth century and carried over into the 1920s. During this period rank-and-file longshoremen continued to exercise considerable leverage—through their unauthorized portwide strikes and through locally organized job actions that reflected the heterogeneous character of the port's occupational structure and labor force. At some point in the 1920s, though, an era of consolidation, and pervasive corruption, began. Joe Ryan emerged as the ILA's central figure in New York, and the union began its evolution toward the "corrupt kingdom" that Bell, Kazan, and other journalists and intellectuals called to the nation's attention in the early 1950s. The longshoremen remained more or less quiescent during much of this period, especially in the turbulent 1930s—in part because of the mob's ominous weight, but also because the dockworkers themselves were enmeshed in a cultural and institutional network that offered few openings to the forces of renewal. In the decade after World War II, however, the New York waterfront became a cauldron of conflict. This was the era of insurgency. A wave of wildcat strikes helped bring down the Ryan regime and shine a bright light on the layers of rot that the ILA president's many apologists had winked at for a generation. The fallout nearly destroyed the union in the nation's largest port, but it survived—shorn of its most corrupt elements but otherwise largely unchanged. Finally, the 1960s brought an era of mechanization that dramatically reduced the size of the dock labor force and transformed the remaining longshoremen into a kind of rough-hewn labor aristocracy whose working conditions and wage guarantees would have been unimaginable to the "cowed" and "exploited" dock wallopers of the Ryan years.

Through all four of these eras, ethnicity and race continued to structure the longshore labor force and add layers of complexity to the ILA's development. Ethnic identities proved to be remarkably persistent in New York, perhaps nowhere more than on the waterfront. Increasingly, however, race and ethnicity became intertwined in ways that reinforced the status of African Americans as the ultimate outsiders. For the most part, blacks did not live in the neighborhoods adjacent to the docks; they were not a part of the network of family, church, and parish school that funneled young men toward the neighborhood pier. And when, during the era of insurgency, they finally organized to demand greater access to waterfront employment, even the leading anti-Ryan insurgents showed little if any sympathy for their cause. "Blacks just didn't shape down there," said one insurgent longshoreman of the West Village piers that were at the heart of his, and his father's, working life. There were, to be sure, a few enclaves where African Americans found regular employment, often in the jobs that whites found least desirable. But beyond these enclaves black dockworkers remained marginal men, standing on the edge of the shape, knowing from long and bitter experience that "everybody [else] had to be hired before they went."[9]

· · · · ·

By the turn of the century, the ILA had tens of thousands of members on the Great Lakes, but the key to its development as a national union remained the port of New York. For the union organizer, however, New York seemed to present more difficulty than opportunity. First, there was the port's immense territorial reach, from Brooklyn to Manhattan's East and North River piers, which—by themselves—constituted two separate worlds of waterfront work, to Staten Island, and from there to Hoboken and other New Jersey sites. Second, there was the ethnoracial character of the longshore labor force and the mutual animosities that often made difference synonymous with division. Third, there was the extraordinary diversity among the employers. They ranged from the world's largest steamship lines (Hamburg-American, North German Lloyd, White Star, and Cunard—all of them European), to the American companies active in the intercoastal and South American trade, to the coastwise lines—many of them owned by railroad companies— that plied the ports of the eastern seaboard, to the complex network of stevedoring, trucking, and lighterage firms that hired dock labor and provided a vital link in the movement of cargo. Overall, in the port of New York, there were more than one hundred steamship companies, some sixty stevedoring firms, and as many as five hundred harbor craft operators. In this crazy-quilt environment, it was perhaps inevitable that "sectoralism" would be the norm, among workers and employers and in the relations between them.[10]

At the Commission on Industrial Relations hearings in 1914, two witnesses offered detailed, and contrasting, portraits of how the ILA functioned at that time. John Riley, an international organizer for the union in New York, clearly identified with the Irish stronghold on Manhattan's West Side, and with Chelsea in particular. Although Riley refrained from denigrating the Italians, he agreed with Barnes that the "better class of men" were found on the "better class of piers," and he identified Pier 60 as the best in the entire port. "The organized men are the best workmen always," he said, "because the organization helps to keep the men in line." Riley pointed out that the union did not permit any drinking on the job or any pilfering of cargo and concluded that "if he is an organization man he is a good man for the companies."[11]

But Charles Kiehn, a socialist longshoreman from Hoboken, had a dramatically different view of the union's role, and he went out of his way to challenge the widely accepted belief that for the longshoremen themselves, Pier 60 was the best in the port. On Pier 60, said Kiehn, "the work is so Taylored that they work a man's life out in ten years"; in fact, "the men are worked harder on the White Star [pier] than they are worked anywhere else." Although the ILA had achieved an informal working agreement with the employers at Pier 60, its representatives apparently did not try to interfere in any way with the speedup; all they asked was that the company hire union men. In Hoboken, however, the ILA locals placed limits on the number of consecutive hours a man could work (no more than twenty) and played a direct role in increasing the gang size and regulating the pace of work so that it was "considerably easier" than on Pier 60.[12]

The ILA signed its first portwide agreement with the employers in 1916. It stipulated that longshoremen would work a ten-hour day at 40fi per hour between 7 A.M. and 6 P.M. and at 60¢ per hour thereafter. There was no provision for overtime pay after ten hours, although the agreement specified that men who worked during their mealtime would be compensated at 80¢ per hour, and that those working munitions and explosives would be paid double time. The agreement also mandated that any disputes the parties could not settle themselves would be resolved by means of binding arbitration. The union agreed not to "uphold incompetency, shirking of work, pilfering or poaching of cargo"; any man who engaged in such activity could be fired, as could anyone who consumed "beer or other intoxicating liquors" on the job. Although union members were to have preference in employment, the contract specified that the employers could hire other men when the ILA could not furnish its own members in sufficient numbers. There was no other mention of hiring—no reference to the shape-up, no attempt to place limits on the size of the port's labor force.[13]

Over the years this would become one of the ILA's defining characteristics. The union prided itself on the wage rates it negotiated for its members. Between 1916 and 1945, the hourly wage increased from 40¢ to $1.45. But at the same time the ILA actively encouraged the oversupply of labor on the docks. More members meant more dues money, and besides, the employers had no interest in reducing the available pool of workers. Thus, the dynamics of the casual labor market resulted in the anomaly of high hourly wages and low annual earnings. In 1946, when Atlantic and Gulf Coast dockworkers received a week's vacation with pay for the first time, *if* they had worked a total of thirty-four weeks in a year, 70 percent of the men in New York did not qualify. By the end of the 1940s, 87.9 percent of New York's longshoremen were earning less than $3,500 a year, whereas in San Francisco, where decasualization and the union-controlled hiring hall prevailed, 74 percent of the men were earning more than that amount.[14]

Apart from negotiating hourly wage increases and providing an abundant supply of labor, the ILA's principal function seemed to be to "keep the lid screwed down tight." Remarkably, there were no authorized strikes in the port of New York between 1916 and 1948. As a corollary, there was no democratic procedure within the union, no grievance handling, and no effective advocacy of the members' interests. It appears that most ILA locals seldom met, and when they did it was only to ratify decisions made beyond the purview of the membership. How did this happen? There had been a long-standing tradition of local unionism on the New York waterfront.[15] In Hoboken, moreover, union members played an active and direct role in regulating the conditions of work on the docks. Even John Riley, who saw the union's function as helping to "keep the men in line," cared deeply about conditions on the waterfront. In his testimony before the Commission on Industrial Relations, he advocated a plan of decasualization in the port of New York, because it would "mak[e] better men of the longshoremen [and] give them more time to be at their homes . . . and certainly they would not frequent the saloons so much."[16]

John Riley, the Irish moralist, and Charles Kiehn, the German socialist, were transitional figures on the New York waterfront. As they passed from the scene, the ILA ceased to reflect their concerns. Instead, the union became an especially crude reflection of George Meany's dictum that the key to success was not winning the allegiance of workers but "organizing" employers and thereby establishing control of labor markets. "We didn't want the [workers]," said Meany, whose fifty-year career in the AFL and, later, the AFL-CIO made him an authority on the subject. "We merely wanted the work. So far as the people that were on the work were concerned, . . . they could drop dead." Although the union would demonstrate an especially callous indifference to the needs of its own members, its leaders proved skillful at forging an effective working relationship with forces that ranged from the cop on the beat (who often moonlighted as a longshoreman) to the most influential members of the city government to criminal elements that had a strong interest in horning in on the port's lucrative waterborne commerce. In New York, moreover, the ILA became bigger than the employers, whose sectoral interests and outlook made it difficult for them to unite for common objectives. "Unable to resist collectively," said sociologist Howard Kimeldorf, "individual [steamship] lines cultivated informal, often collaborative, relations with local ILA leaders."[17]

The man whose name became synonymous with the ILA, and whose career goes a long way toward explaining the idiosyncrasies of its development, was the portly and affable Joseph Patrick Ryan, who served as the union's international president from 1927 to 1953. Often described as "big" and "bulky," "barrel-chested" and "bull-necked," Ryan was also, by his own account, a man who "neither smokes nor swears, and more often than not goes to eight o'clock mass." He was born in 1884 to Irish Catholic parents—James Ryan, a gardener, and Mary Shanahan Ryan. Both parents died during his childhood—his mother at his birth, and his father when he was only nine. Thereafter, he was raised by his stepmother in the Chelsea district of Manhattan. Chelsea, which stretched from Fifth Avenue to the Hudson River between Fourteenth and Thirty-fourth Streets, was quintessentially Irish, Catholic, and working class. Economically, the waterfront was its center of gravity. According to the neighborhood's oral historian, "there was hardly a Chelsea resident who didn't have a connection to the waterfront in one way or another." It was a place where violence was commonplace, and, among men at least, toughness was almost universally respected. One resident recalled that his father became a shop steward in the teamsters' union because he could "kick the shit out of anybody else in that stable." Ryan himself was widely known as "handy with his fists," and it stood him in good stead on the docks. Even one of the neighborhood's great success stories, the multimillionaire businessman William J. "Big Bill" McCormack, was remembered as a "brawler." The son of an Irish immigrant wagon driver who never rose above poverty, Big Bill was "always ready to use fists to reinforce words" during his youth. When he was twenty, he owned three teams of horses. Three years later he bought out a trucking company that had fifteen wagons and thirty horses. On his way to becoming a stevedoring and trucking magnate, he never forgot where he came from, which made him something of an icon in a neighborhood whose expectation was that its sons would work on the docks or "bec[o]me a cop or a fireman or . . . [go] to jail."[18]

Culturally, the Catholic Church was the center of life in Chelsea and the arbiter of its values. To a constituency that demonstrated little evidence of economic mobility, it conveyed the promise of a blessed afterlife while preaching the necessity of discipline, hierarchy, and repression in the here and now. Along with Tammany Hall, Manhattan's Irish-controlled political machine, it placed a premium on loyalty and obedience and often portrayed those beyond its fold as denizens of outer darkness. Above all, the church demonized communism as the ultimate heresy. For the most part, the message took. Even in times of economic depression and social upheaval, most residents of Chelsea remained loyal to their faith, their clientist political network, and their own kind.

Fig. 2.2. "Next to myself, I like silk underwear best": ILA president Joseph P. Ryan. Credit: *Dispatcher*, International Longshore and Warehouse Union

In such an environment, insurgent politics and left-wing unionism encountered stony soil and worse. Chelsea native Peggy Dolan recalled that when Communist May Day marchers paraded along her street, heading toward Union Square, "us kids used to save garbage on the roofs," and "when those Communists came, we used to dump the garbage on them. They were splattered with everything."[19]

Ryan prided himself on being a "Chelsea boy," and he faithfully reflected its mores in the union and the political arena. Upon completing the sixth grade at Saint Francis Xavier School, he went to work, first as a stock boy, then as an employee of the Metropolitan Street Railway, until he joined the ranks of Chelsea's longshoremen in 1912. After working on the docks for about a year, he "strayed into the labor business" and built a fiefdom that would have been the envy of many a Tammany boss. His domain stretched along the Atlantic and Gulf coastlines from Maine to Texas, and—briefly—up the Pacific shoreline from San Diego to Seattle and beyond. In various ports along the way, he hobnobbed with mayors, developed "exceedingly close and friendly" relations with shipowners, and became famous for dispensing generous cash favors to longshoremen in need. They would line up outside his office at the union's international headquarters in New York, or approach him on the streets of Savannah and New Orleans, and "put the bite on Joe Ryan." Invariably, according to legend, he would "reach in his pocket" and honor their plaintive requests. At times he even mingled with his "boys" at the morning shape-up. But dinnertime would variably find him far from the world of the waterfront, at the most expensive restaurants in town. "I like good food of all kinds," he admitted, "and I think my longshoremen want me to have it."[20]

Ryan played a key role in transforming the ILA from a weak but legitimate union into one that seemed to exist for the benefit of shipowners, stevedores, and ILA officials—perhaps everyone associated with cargo handling except the longshoremen. In the process, he had plenty of help from a deeply entrenched network of gangsters and industrial racketeers who were a fixture in New York City. They flourished for decades in industries such as baking, construction, garment, and trucking, all of which were characterized by small-scale and decentralized operations, cutthroat competition, and local product markets. Trade unions sought to bring order out of chaos in these industries, but the employers often turned to gangsters to accomplish the same goal. In fact, organized crime proved to be a useful mechanism for keeping organized labor out. Even where unions sank deep roots, gangsters often managed to thrive nonetheless.[21]

But criminal activity was by no means confined to the workplace and the union. In the city's working-class neighborhoods, many adolescent boys and adult males lived on the edge of violence; gambling, legal and illegal, was a daily obsession; and theft served as a useful adjunct of making a living. To be sure, most amateur lawbreakers operated under the constraints of a widely accepted moral code. Brooklyn native Jerry Della Femina recalled that "stealing from your next-door neighbor was never allowed," but "stealing from the outside world (if it was done without a gun) was perfectly legitimate." Della Femina remembered longshoremen from his neighborhood who were "surrounded by corruption" and who "felt that the world owed them something beyond a ruined back after forty years of labor." (That "something" was the cargo they managed to purloin and sell to neighbors and friends at bargain-basement prices.) As for the real gangsters, they were often despised as predators and bullies but also grudgingly respected as local boys who had escaped the daily grind and made something of themselves. They were, said Della Femina, "our version of royalty."[22]

Joe Ryan grew up in a world in which toughness was power and crime in various guises was part of the fabric of life. Apparently, he viewed gangsters less as moral pariahs than as useful instruments in the service of his career objectives. In any case, it can hardly be a coincidence that the Ryan era in the ILA and the era of industrial racketeering on the New York waterfront were virtually synonymous. With its vast stores of valuable goods, its decentralized, often chaotic, system of moving cargo from truck to warehouse to ship's hold and back, its armies of workers, middlemen, and managers, the port seemed to offer unlimited outlets for bribery, extortion, and theft. And while employers and government officials proved to be remarkably accommodating partners in crime, no group was as eager to cooperate as Ryan and his cronies in the New York District Council of the ILA. Ryan created "paper" locals in New York and turned them over to the mob, which returned the favor by helping to solidify his power at the local and district levels. Fortuitously, he served as chairman of the New York State Parole Board in the 1930s, and thus a steady stream of parolees beat a path from prison to the waterfront, where some went directly onto the ILA payroll as "organizers" and others served as hiring foremen for employers who welcomed their ability to maintain labor discipline and get the "maximum work" out of the men. One of the most notorious of these "organizers" was Edward McGrath, who—according to labor reporter A. H. Raskin—had a record of "twelve arrests for crimes ranging from petty larceny to murder and two convictions for burglary." Together with his brother-in-law John "Cockeye" Dunn, McGrath ruled the Greenwich Village piers, until Dunn was electrocuted in 1949 for the murder of an uncooperative hiring foreman.[23]

As the ILA in New York became the prisoner of various networks of hoods, genial Joe served as their ostrichlike spokesman to the world beyond the waterfront. Although Ryan referred to his parolees as "poor devils" and applauded his own charitable instincts in offering them a second chance, it would appear that they controlled him more than he controlled them. This becomes stunningly evident in a letter that Charles Logan of the National Labor Relations Board sent to Louis Stark of the *New York Times* in 1953. Logan, who knew Ryan well, recalled that

> [o]ne night, many years ago, I walked the New York water front until dawn with Joe Ryan, who was visibly upset over the fact that a notorious criminal . . . had just returned from the penitentiary and was going to be immediately installed as the hiring boss on one of the most important piers. . . . I argued then that he should resist the action, not only in this one instance but in instances where men of the same stamp were already functioning as hiring bosses. He felt that he was helpless to resist. I know that he had attempted to persuade the employer not to make the move, but his persuasion was without effect.[24]

In this regard, and many others, Ryan was something of a contradiction. He appeared to rule supreme and to leave his distinctive mark on everything he touched. Although Italians had become a clear majority of the ILA membership in New York, the union's conventions were strictly an Irish affair. Thus, in 1947, Lieutenant William Farrell sang the "Star-Spangled Banner"; Monsignor John J. O'Donnell gave the invocation; James Quinn and John O'Rourke offered fraternal greetings on behalf of the New York City labor movement; and the Honorable William O'Dwyer, an Irish immigrant whose occupation was mayor of the city of New York, addressed the delegates. The air was redolent with Irish blarney, the genial fellowship of labor's old men of power, and the rituals that consolidated Ryan's ties to a wider world of authority and privilege. But the annual dinners of the Joseph P. Ryan Association were even more remarkable in this regard. The association was a monument not only to Ryan himself but to the intimate relationship between the New York Central Trades and Labor Council (which he headed for ten years) and the city's political establishment. Each year, at the Commodore Hotel or the Waldorf-Astoria, city councilmen, mayors, even governors, paid homage to the ILA president; union officials rubbed shoulders with employers; district attorneys and police officers tiptoed warily around the invited "thugs and murderers." In 1937, according to journalist Allen Raymond, Mayor Fiorello La

Guardia and Police Commissioner Edward P. Mulrooney "were listed as guests at Table 26," and Philip Mangano, "[a] murderer now gone to his reward but then a flourishing member of the Anastasia-Adonis mob, sat at Table 80."[25]

But although "King Joe" reigned over these proceedings, he did not rule. In order to keep his throne, he was obliged to give the gangsters a free hand; he had to allow the restless Italians to consolidate their control of a large, and increasingly autonomous, ILA fiefdom on the Brooklyn waterfront; he had to ask for the employers' permission whenever he sought to make any changes in the collective bargaining agreement. He became increasingly dependent on the advice and counsel of his old boyhood friend William J. McCormack, who was, by reputation, the shadowy "Mr. Big" of the port of New York. In many years of negotiating, said one waterfront employer of his experience with Ryan, "when the chips were down and a decision had to be made, he'd have to go to the telephone"—not to call his fellow unionists but to seek the approval of "father confessor" McCormack. Handcuffed by employers on one side and hoods on the other, Ryan, according to another observer, was "the only AFL international president who has no real power."[26]

But for years Ryan's gangster allies proved chillingly adept at keeping the union membership in line. Paul O'Dwyer, an Irish immigrant and long-time political activist in New York City, worked as a checker on the Brooklyn waterfront in the late 1920s. He recalled "a little gangster there, a fellow named John Spanish, who'd come down to . . . Pier 44, and he would stand outside while the men were shaping. He was dressed in . . . a derby hat, a pair of spats, a silk [scarf] between his Chesterfield coat and his suit, with a diamond stickpin on his tie." He selected "among these Italian fellows those whom he thought should go to work and reject[ed] the ones he didn't want. And they came there literally with hat in hand as they passed by him." John Spanish may well have operated independently of Joe Ryan on turf that Ryan knew well enough to leave alone. But O'Dwyer also remembered that Ryan employed strong-arm men to quell rank-and-file dissent within the union as early as 1927, the year he ascended to the ILA presidency. Over time this kind of intimidation became the norm. In most locals, said longshoreman Sam Madell, "it was a very, very rare thing to have a union meeting. Maybe you'd have two or three during the whole year. Even when they were held, they in no way resembled a union meeting." A small clique would gather and swap stories about baseball in the summer and football in the fall. "If anybody tried to inject some work-ing-conditions issue, they'd be hooted down. They'd be questioned. 'Who are you?' 'Are you a member of this local?' 'Where is your book?' 'Is your dues paid up?' If you were too persistent, they'd knock you down the steps."[27]

. . . . .

Could black workers find a comfortable niche in such a union? Remark-ably, the answer is at least a qualified yes. In *The Black Worker*, which appeared in 1931, Sterling Spero and Abram Harris noted that the ILA "prides itself on the position of official equality which the Negro enjoys in its ranks." Thirteen years later, labor economist Herbert Northrup pointed out that since its inception the ILA had "officially opposed racial discrimination. Negroes compose a large portion of its member-ship, and today four of its fifteen vice-presidents are colored." In fact, the ILA provided an enclave where black leadership not only emerged but flourished. The pattern of organization was generally biracial rather than interracial. For the most part, the goal of black longshoremen was a unionism that was genuinely "separate but equal." In the Hampton Roads District of Virginia, encompassing the ports of Norfolk, Newport News, and Hampton, there were nine ILA locals, seven black and two white. About two thousand of the organized men were black; about two hundred were white. The whites were mainly checkers and weighers (occupations from which Negroes were excluded); the blacks were gen-eral longshoremen and coal trimmers. "There are no mixed locals," Spero and Harris noted, "due, first, to the strength of the southern tradition of racial separation and, second, to the preference of the Ne-groes themselves for their own organization. They feel that they can control these themselves through officials of their own race without the necessity of sharing power with the whites." In the Hampton Roads District, perhaps because such an overwhelming majority of the work-force and the union membership was African American, there were few concessions to the imperatives of white supremacy that usually governed biracial interaction in the Deep South. Not only was the president of the district council a Negro, but all of the members of the district's arbitration committee were black; and according to Harris, this committee handled "all matters affecting the longshoremen, both black and white."[28]

But race relations among longshoremen varied considerably from port to port. And where there was accommodation it resulted less from a commitment to racial equality than from a recognition, based on many years of painful experience, that blacks could not be kept off the docks and therefore must be organized. In New York, of the eighty-two Negro longshoremen whom Frazier interviewed in 1921, only one did not belong to the ILA. The others were distributed among five locals, two of which were "colored" and the other three, "mixed." Frazier reported that the two "colored locals" had a combined membership of about a thousand, and one of the "mixed" locals, Local 968, had "800 colored and 300 white members." Spero and Harris pointed out that a decade later there were still "Irish locals, Italian locals, Hungarian locals, in fact locals of almost every national and racial group that plays an important role in the longshore work of the port." By that time, however, the two "colored" locals had disappeared, and 968 had evolved into the port's only "Negro local." None of these ILA affiliates was exclusive in its racial or ethnic makeup. Even Local 968 included about a hundred whites (although gradually their number would be reduced to a "handful"), and Spero and Harris noted that an additional "two thousand or more" black longshoremen were dispersed throughout the port in other ILA locals. "The Negro's presence in the port is now accepted by the white man," they concluded. "He has a right to be there; he has a right to work; he has a right to belong to the union. Yet he is by no means regarded as an equal."[29]

Interviews with ILA officials in 1935 give a clearer sense of white unionists' attitudes toward their black counterparts. In the case of a Manhattan checkers' local, the lone Negro among the six hundred members of the union had been a member since the local was formed in 1912. "We found him working then," said the local's officers, "and let him in." But by and large Negroes were denied jobs as checkers, and, just in case, the local set its initiation fee at five hundred dollars. The officers readily admitted that they made the fee high and required that it be paid in "one lump sum" in order to "keep out undesirables." As one officer put it, "Negroes don't do this kind of work. . . . [T]hey don't fit in." Often checkers working on the piers came in contact with ships' passengers, and "the passengers don't want to be bothered with Negroes." It was a classic case of defining the work in a way that virtually excluded blacks, and then blaming the outcome on an external force (in this instance, the passengers).[30]

In the longshore locals, the resistance to blacks was less sweeping, but their presence remained more or less marginal. General Longshore Workers' Local 791, in Chelsea, first accepted blacks as members in

1925. "We [have] never had over 150 of them," said local spokesman Gene Sampson, who readily acknowledged that the local's white—and overwhelmingly Irish—members would not "accept the Negro as their social equal" but recognized that they had to "accept him as their industrial equal." Otherwise he could undermine their wages and conditions and break their strikes. According to Sampson, this was a lesson that had been learned through bitter experience. Negro strikebreaking had caused "the greatest possible racial antagonism," he said, and in union meetings, when black men were candidates for membership in the local, whites would declare angrily, "We don't want niggers who scabbed on us"; "keep the . . . out." The same theme was articulated by the secretary of General Cargo Workers 1124, a local with twelve black members out of a total membership of six hundred. "When they are union men, they are good," said Tony Porto, "but when they are not, they are terrible. . . . We catch hell from the unorganized Negroes—the strike breakers." Both Porto and Sampson drew a sharp distinction between black union men and black strikebreakers, but the impression they left with their interviewers was that no blacks would have been admitted to their locals except for the threat that they posed to whites outside the union. It was a clear confirmation of the suspicion that black longshoremen had expressed to E. Franklin Frazier fourteen years earlier. "The Negro was compelled to join the unions, primarily, for the convenience of white men," they told Frazier. Outside the ILA he could "scab" on whites; inside it, he could "be controlled."[31]

In the process of conflict and accommodation through which jobs were allocated on the docks, black workers were at a severe disadvantage. First, their numbers in the labor force did not begin to approach those of the Irish and Italians. Second, white ethnics tended to work at piers, and belong to local unions, near their homes, which created a close relationship between neighborhood and workplace. But because of housing segregation, few black workers lived in close proximity to the docks where they shaped. In 1917 John T. Clark of the New York Urban League interviewed Negro warehousemen at the Bush Terminal on the Brooklyn waterfront. He found that virtually none of them lived near their place of work. The shortest commuting time was half an hour; the average, among forty-four men, was one and a half hours. And this problem became more acute over time. As the African American population grew, blacks were pushed from dispersed residential enclaves into the dense concentrations that were evolving into the classic twentieth-century ghettos. For black longshoremen this meant

63

a move away from the waterfront. More and more, they came to the piers bearing the mark of the outsider. To make matters worse, even the port's one Negro local did not have its own pier. Members of Local 968 were compelled to go to other piers and try to find work on turf that other men regarded as their own. Spero and Harris acknowledged that there were "many piers . . . which refused to employ Negroes," and, ironically, this trend would sharpen even during the Civil Rights era. When black workers asked their union to address it, they received verbal assurances, but nothing changed. When they mobilized to fight for change, they encountered hostile opposition from their fellow workers and, at best, dissembling from the ILA leadership.[32]

• • • • •

Remarkably, the great insurgencies of the 1930s largely bypassed New York's dockworkers. Their West Coast counterparts became famously militant; even the seamen with whom they shared the New York waterfront became swashbuckling ambassadors of insurgent unionism. But on the docks the New Deal and the CIO seem not to have mattered. Some have argued that repression was to blame. It is true that on the few occasions when rank-and-file insurgency in the ILA reached significant proportions, the hoods responded with uncompromising ruthlessness. This was most notoriously evident in 1939, when longshoremen and their allies launched the Rank and File Committee to challenge the abysmal conditions that prevailed among Italian dockworkers in Brooklyn. Although covert payment for the privilege of working was a common practice on the New York waterfront, Italian longshoremen complained that they had to "kick back" as much as 25 percent of their wages to hiring bosses and union officials and then purchase tickets for banquets, dances, and parties that never occurred. Aided by the overlapping forces of the CIO and the Communist party, and aggressively supported by Congressman Vito Marcantonio of East Harlem, the Rank and File Committee held a series of mass meetings that culminated in a protest rally of more than a thousand workers. But then Pete Panto, a refugee from Fascist Italy and the leader of the insurgency, disappeared. Although his body was found in a New Jersey lime pit eighteen months later, New York City authorities never indicted any of the mob-affiliated suspects whose names were linked to the crime.[33]

Murder was the ultimate weapon in a waterfront network of extortion and violence that was designed to enrich the few and keep the many in check. Italian laborers—in the building trades and other occupations that depended on physical strength and endurance—had once been under the domination of labor contractors, or *padroni*, who had exercised far-reaching control over their lives. During the Depression decade, mobsters and industrial racketeers extended a more ominous *padronismo* into the workplace and the union hall. In Brooklyn six "extraordinarily corrupt" ILA locals were controlled by Emil Camarda, the ILA's "Italian" vice-president and an alleged front man for the mob. (When Camarda was murdered in 1941, "Tough Tony" Anastasia, brother of the "chief executioner" for Murder, Incorporated, gained control of the Brooklyn waterfront.) In these circumstances, what is remarkable about Italian longshoremen is not their quiescence but the fact that they rose up at all. There was another flurry of activity after Panto's murder, but the campaign of intimidation gradually took its toll, and the Pete Panto Memorial Committee became the province of left-wing trade unionists and intellectuals. As these "strangers" continued to ask "dove è Panto?" ("where is Panto?"), the longshoremen and the larger Red Hook community turned inward, toward the familiar confines of family and neighborhood.[34]

But what about the Irish? By the thirties Italian longshoremen outnumbered the Irish in New York, but the Irish had the best jobs, the clearest ethnic affinity with the ILA leadership, and the closest links to an ethnically based political and social order that had long been dominant in the city. The CIO offered them the prospect of an insurgent and more democratic trade unionism; the Roosevelt administration promised and, to a great extent, delivered enhanced social security to Americans beset by the ravages of the Great Depression; and the mayoral administration of Fiorello La Guardia not only identified with Roosevelt's New Deal nationally but sought to implement similar reforms at the municipal level.

On several fronts, however, Irish longshoremen may have found these currents of reform disquieting or worse. First, no group had been more closely identified with the American Federation of Labor than the Irish. In the early twentieth century, sixty-two AFL unions had Irish Catholic presidents, and Irish workers were heavily represented in the building trades, transportation, and other sectors of the economy in which the AFL was most entrenched. Given the CIO's increasing determination not only to organize the unorganized but to challenge some of the most venerable enclaves of AFL power, it stands to reason that many Irish Catholics would have been ambivalent at best about the new unionism and especially wary about its alleged, and sometimes real, association with Communists.[35]

Second, there was the challenge to the Democracy of Tammany Hall. The Irish had long been the bedrock constituency of the Tammany machine, which provided them with numerous jobs, especially in the police, fire, and public works departments. Beyond the public sector, New York's "Irish" unions, of longshoremen, teamsters, and building tradesmen, prospered through their links with Tammany. And for a much wider constituency, Tammany's power and high visibility imparted a sense of belonging, of being Irish and fully American at the same time. But La Guardia's election in 1933 came at the expense of Tammany; it represented the triumph of a coalition of Italians and Jews over their Irish rivals. The resulting sense of displacement gave rise to an intense backlash that over time would have a profound effect on the cultural and political life of New York and other centers of Irish America.[36]

At the heart of this backlash was the Catholic Church, and nowhere more so than in New York City. Catholicism had long been at odds with many aspects of modernity. By the 1930s communism had become the church's special target, but in the eyes of Catholic leaders communism was only the most extreme of a broad array of secular ideologies that—in historian David O'Brien's words—signified "modern man's revolt against God, the Church, and civilization." Many Catholic spokesmen were wary of reform movements that sought to make "the state our mother and father," and the church hierarchy opposed some of the most important legislative initiatives of the Roosevelt administration on these grounds. Increasingly, it was not just the programmatic agenda of the New Deal that was objectionable, but liberalism itself. By 1940 Father Robert Gannon, the president of Fordham University, was warning that

> there is a swarm abroad in the land. They call themselves "liberals." . . . What they want is not so much our money as our children. They want our schools and colleges. They want the key positions in the civil service. They want control of relief and all the social agencies and they are getting what they want. Later they hope, when they have the youth of the nation in their power, to eliminate all religion and all morality that does not conform to their peculiar ideology.[37]

Since "they" were often Jewish and—allegedly, if not in fact— Communist, many Catholics tended to see Jews, Communists, and liberals as more or less synonymous and as a triple threat to a social order under siege. The *Tablet*, the weekly newspaper of the diocese of Brooklyn, declared its opposition to fascism but wondered "why it is so infamous to restrict certain liberties of 600,000 Jews in Germany and not at all obnoxious to hold in slavery millions of other people in Russia, Mexico, and Spain." The implication was that Catholics were more at risk than Jews but unlike their Jewish counterparts were victims of a conspiracy of silence. From the *Tablet*'s standpoint, the same complaint applied to the domestic scene. To those who were intent on combating anti-Semitism in the United States, *Tablet* editor Patrick Scanlan asked, "Why . . . not assail the discrimination against the Germans, Italians, Irish and other races of New York who are fast being reduced to the most inconspicuous places?"[38]

Nationally, the most visible symbol of this mindset was Father Charles Coughlin, the Radio Priest from Royal Oak, Michigan, who ultimately became infamous for his strident attacks on the New Deal, his blatant anti-Semitism, and his defense of Hitler's Germany as a bulwark against communism. In New York Coughlinism found its most devoted adherents among Irish Catholics, and no one defended the embattled Radio Priest with more zeal than Patrick Scanlan in the pages of the *Tablet*.[39] Coughlin and his followers came to see the thirties as less an age of domestic reform than an era of global confrontation between the forces of good and evil. The Spanish Civil War played a major role in crystallizing this perception. Where liberals saw a battle between democracy and fascism, conservatives—and many Catholics of various political persuasions—saw a Manichaean struggle between civilization and communism. To those who identified with the Spanish Nationalists, the New Deal seemed to be on the wrong side in this struggle; and so, above all, did the CIO. West Coast longshoremen engaged in symbolic strikes in solidarity with the Spanish Republic, and the CIO-affiliated National Maritime Union celebrated as heroes and martyrs the seamen who fought and died with the Communist-led International Brigades in Spain. Meanwhile, the Catholic Church and its allies sought to build support for General Franco's counterrevolution and to expose the awful fruits of the "Red" reign of terror on the Iberian Peninsula. The *Irish World* reported in December 1938 that Spanish Republicans had "profaned, burned or destroyed" more than twenty-five thousand church buildings, and it charged that "the [Roosevelt] Administration . . . has never once raised its voice in protest against the persecution of Catholics" in Spain.[40]

Of course, Irish America was not a monolith, and neither was the Catholic Church. Because the Irish were overwhelmingly Democrats, many Irish American politicians and their constituents benefited from the ascendancy of the Roosevelt coalition. The church hierarchy was generally supportive of the broad outlines of the New Deal, and some priests, notably John A. Ryan and Francis Haas, were closely identified with the Roosevelt administration. Although the CIO was mercilessly red-baited by its critics, some of the church's highest authorities supported the industrial union movement, and so, of course, did hundreds of thousands of Polish, Italian, and Irish workers. In New York, Irish Catholics were by far the leading constituency of the CIO-affiliated Transport Workers Union (TWU), whose president was Michael J. "Red Mike" Quill. Born into a Gaelic-speaking farm family in rural Ireland, Quill was a veteran of the Irish Republican Army (IRA) who emigrated to New York in 1926 and joined not only the County Kerry society but the Clan na Gael, the ultranationalist organization that supplied the "guns and money" that enabled the IRA to survive in the inhospitable climate of the Irish Free State. It was Clan na Gael members in New York who joined hands with a small core of transit industry Communists to lay the groundwork for the Transport Workers Union. The close association of Quill and other TWU leaders with Irish republicanism, and their roots in New York's Irish immigrant community, legitimized them in the eyes of the union membership. To be sure, the incessant accusation that their leading officials were Communists caused some discomfort among the TWU's Catholic rank and file. But given the many positive fruits of unionism, it proved possible for the average TWU member to conclude that "maybe they're reds, maybe they're not, but they're nice guys and they bring home the bacon, so I shrug my shoulders, I go home and I sleep well."[41]

There would be no Red Mike on the New York waterfront, however. In the 1920s and 1930s, Irish immigrants were drawn to the newer centers of Irish New York that were emerging uptown and in the Bronx. At the same time, the exodus of the socially mobile from the historic Irish enclaves in the West Village, Chelsea, and Hell's Kitchen meant that those who were left behind became even more insular and defensive in relation to the world beyond their terrain. It was not an environment in which new ideas and insurgent leaders were likely to flourish. And although transport workers faced repression for identifying with the CIO, the transit police were a minor irritant in comparison with the mobsters who fortified Joe Ryan's regime. When the CIO launched a sustained campaign to win the New York longshoremen to the new unionism, its cadres paid a heavy price. By October 1937 CIO spokesman Mervyn Rathborne was complaining that in the previous month more than twenty-five organizers had been "brutally assaulted" by Ryan's goons. Rathborne charged that "several of the victims have been so badly slashed and gored by [steel cargo hooks] as to have required long hospitalization."[42]

But New York longshoremen did not remain entirely passive during the thirties. Confronted as they were by the ravages of the Great Depression, as well as by other challenges to their economic well-being, white longshoremen took aggressive steps to maintain the racially unequal division of labor on the docks. The catalyst was the decision of a number of steamship companies to shift their operations to new piers. The most notable example occurred in Chelsea, the historic heart of the port where the major European steamship lines had docked for many years. In 1937 the new Trans-Atlantic Steamship Terminal opened farther uptown, and operations that had centered around Pier 60 moved to an area that encompassed Piers 84 to 90. Hamburg-American, North German Lloyd, and the Cunard, French, and Italian Lines all relocated on these piers. Meanwhile, several other steamship companies began new operations at sites in lower Manhattan. All of this activity required a renegotiation of the longshoremen's territorial rights, and in the process black workers faced the prospect of further marginalization. According to Thurgood Marshall of the NAACP, two Negro gangs that had worked on Pier 60 were denied employment on piers in lower Manhattan. The companies were willing to hire them, Marshall reported, but the ILA delegate "stated that it was his intention to keep all hands white on these new piers." When the Grace Line moved its operations from Brooklyn to the Chelsea docks abandoned by the major European steamship companies, however, blacks were unable to follow the work to the new site because, once again, white union members refused to allow it. This compelled black longshoremen to wander farther afield and enter unfamiliar territory in search of work. According to Marshall, "no Negroes are permitted to work at the deep-sea piers on the Jersey side, [and] if they attempt to seek employment they are beaten severely by other members of the Union and run to the Ferry Boat." These developments may go far toward explaining why the percentage of blacks in the dock labor force fell from 15.2 in 1930 to 9.3 in 1940.[43]

The economic crisis intensified feelings of insecurity all around, but the white longshoremen's actions undermine the contention that although they would not "accept the Negro as their social equal," they recognized the need to "accept him as their industrial equal." In the renegotiation of access to employment during the Depression decade, the Irish and other Euro-American ethnic groups were determined to use their hard-earned whiteness as a lever to marginalize their black fellow workers. Even though African Americans had worked on the West Side waterfront and had been loyal union members for decades, they remained outsiders. "They came down as strikebreakers," one longshoreman recalled of his youth in the 1930s. "If [the strikers] caught one runnin' up the street, . . . they'd open up the sewer and drop him down."[44]

In sum, the occupational and ideological position of the Irish in the New York waterfront hierarchy suggests something of vital importance about the complex reality of class and class consciousness in the turbulent thirties and beyond. Few workers were more classically proletarian than the longshoremen; few were more exploited. But when opportunity appeared to beckon in the form of the CIO, they remained anchored to the racialized parameters of family, parish, and neighborhood; of Tammany Hall's politics and the AFL's familiar unions; and of the volatile brew of ideas and aspirations, anxieties and prejudices, that historian Steven Fraser has identified as an "Irish-Coughlinite" worldview. To be sure, the repression they faced meant that any challenge to the status quo entailed extraordinary risks. But this was also true in varying degrees of Michigan autoworkers, Pennsylvania steelworkers, Alabama coal miners, and even New York transit workers. Each of these groups was able to mount a significant challenge to the semifeudal regime that had held them in thrall. But the New York longshoremen remained isolated—and, in the case of the Irish, alienated—from the forces of insurgency in the thirties. Without denying the power of the institutional nexus that reinforced the boundaries of their lives, one cannot escape the conclusion that the constraints they faced were primarily cultural and ideological and the choices they made were largely their own.[45]

· · · · ·

Taken too far, however, insights about the "passivity" and "extreme conservatism" of the Irish congeal into ahistorical dogma. Irish long-

Fig. 2.3. Longshoremen's wildcat strike, Pier 65, Manhattan waterfront, 1951. Credit: Daniel Nilva Collection, Tamiment Institute Library, New York University

shoremen had fought militantly for their rights in the past, and they would do so again. The Big Strike of 1887, which involved as many as fifty thousand men, was essentially an Irish affair; the Irish were solid participants in the major waterfront walkouts of 1907 and 1919 as well. And in 1920 they participated in the remarkable boycott of British shipping, which the *New York Sun* characterized as "probably the first purely political strike of workmen in the history of the United States."[46]

At the end of World War II, the New York longshoremen finally rebelled against Ryan's autocracy and the conditions under which they had labored throughout his presidency. In October 1945 a spontaneous and apparently leaderless walkout against the terms of a "phony contract" exploded into a portwide strike that lasted seventeen days and tied up three hundred ships. When Ryan attempted to address a mass meeting of strikers, he was "booed, hissed, and shouted off the stage." The longshoremen returned to work without winning any of their demands, but the appointment of an arbitrator led to gains that far exceeded anything Ryan and the ILA leadership had negotiated. The rank and file had learned that direct action could be an effective weapon, and as a consequence they struck again in 1947, 1948, and

1951—each time to protest the terms of an agreement negotiated by their "nickel and dime" president and to raise issues that their leaders had been stubbornly unwilling to address. Ryan declared the 1948 strike official four days after the longshoremen walked out; it was the first officially sanctioned portwide strike in the harbor since the shipowners recognized the ILA in 1916.[47]

Ironically, during this period the media continued to portray the longshoremen as "frightened," "intimidated," and "dispirited by oppression." But it was these "frightened" dockworkers whose recurring waves of rebellion helped to focus the attention of the city and the nation on New York Harbor and to expose the enormous scope of the crime and corruption in the port. The resulting outcry led to significant changes, and the first casualty was Joe Ryan. By 1945 it was becoming clear that he had lost his capacity to "keep the lid screwed down tight." But the shipowners, the American Federation of Labor, and major public figures stood by him for years, perhaps because he appeared to be the only possible alternative to the "Communist" ILWU. In 1950 Governor Thomas E. Dewey of New York, who had been the Republican party's presidential standard-bearer in 1948, congratulated and thanked Ryan for his role in "keep[ing] the Communists from getting control of the New York Waterfront." In 1951 George Meany could still praise him as "my friend, Joe Ryan," and declare that "every American can be proud of him, proud of the ILA, proud of its affiliation with the American Federation of Labor." Two years later, however, when the public outcry against the manifold crimes and misdemeanors of the ILA was reaching a crescendo, Meany's AFL expelled the International Longshoremen's Association on the grounds that it had "permitted irresponsible, corrupt and criminal elements" to destroy the organization's "integrity," "effectiveness," and "trade union character." Seeking to stave off the destruction of his union, and under criminal indictment for accepting a bribe from employers, Ryan resigned from the presidency of the ILA in 1953. He was subsequently convicted as charged, but a federal appeals court overturned the decision on a technicality, thereby sparing him the final indignity of a term in prison. Nonetheless, he became a "sick old man" and a gaunt shadow of the potentate who once had presided over the world's largest waterfront.[48]

Ryan faded away and died in 1963. But his embattled union managed to survive, in spite of its abysmal reputation and a well-financed campaign by the American Federation of Labor aimed at replacing it with a newly chartered rival, the International Brotherhood of Longshoremen. The National Labor Relations Board conducted representation elections in December 1953 and May 1954, and although the long-shoremen split their votes down the middle, the ILA came out on top by a margin of 263 ballots in the decisive second election. However, the union had become and would remain the target of draconian government intervention, which kept it on the defensive for the rest of the decade. Most notably, in the aftermath of a series of articles by Malcolm Johnson in the *New York Sun*, the state of New York launched an investigation of crime on the waterfront that elicited one sensational revelation after another. It turned out that some of the biggest steamship and stevedoring firms in the harbor were cooperating, often voluntarily, with a vast criminal network; that government officials from the local to the federal level were playing along; that, as Allen Raymond said in reference to the ILA, "one third of the so-called union leaders have merely been criminal racketeers in disguise." The investigation revealed that more than 3,000 ILA members had police records; 594 of them had "a combined total of 2,287 convictions and 702 additional arrests." Their crimes, said A. H. Raskin, "included murder, manslaughter, narcotics, smuggling, hijacking and just about everything else in the book."[49]

These revelations led to the creation of the New York–New Jersey Waterfront Commission. From the moment it became operational in December 1953, the commission played a vital role in the harbor's labor relations. It purged the ILA's membership rolls of men with criminal records and required that every prospective longshoreman be registered with and approved by the commission. It abolished the shape-up, ruled that hiring bosses could not be members of the same union as the men they hired, and mandated that hiring take place at thirteen waterfront employment information centers that were to be established throughout the port. An employer could engage regular gangs the day before they were needed at the pier, and these men would not be obligated to appear at the centers as long as there was work for them with that company. For casuals, though, and even for regular gangs looking for work, it was a case of moving the shape-up indoors and conducting it under government auspices. The hiring agents continued to have significant latitude in choosing from the surplus of men available, and the commission bent over backward to honor the seniority practices that had developed over time in various sections of the port.[50]

The longshoremen did not, by themselves, determine all of these outcomes. The shipowners, the state, the American Federation of

Labor, and the reconstituted but unrepentant leadership of the ILA all played a major role. But in the welter of contending forces, two separate reform movements command special attention. The first was made up mainly of young Irish Americans from the West Side of Manhattan; the second, of black longshoremen acting in tandem with a succession of allies that included the Communist party, the Urban League of Greater New York, the NAACP, and the Negro American Labor Council. Although they never joined forces, both movements offered a dramatic challenge to the status quo, and their actions demonstrate the continuing salience of race and ethnicity as factors shaping the consciousness of the waterfront workforce and the distribution of employment opportunities on the docks.

. . . . .

Two Irish locals on the West Side of Manhattan played the principal role in triggering the extended series of walkouts that helped bring about Ryan's downfall. Within these locals, much of the impetus came from younger longshoremen who had served in the armed forces during the war and who, in some cases, returned to the docks "ready to fight at the drop of a hat." Just as black veterans were at the center of the widening challenge to Jim Crow in the South, men like Staff Sergeant William Francis McMahon took the lead in exposing the lack of democracy in the ILA. McMahon was born and raised in the Greenwich Village of the Irish and Italian working class. At the age of eighteen, he became a professional boxer, and a few years later he joined the other men of his family on the waterfront. Following a stint in the Aleutian Islands during the war, he became one of the insurgents in Local 895. There he joined forces with John Dwyer, another veteran of the war in the Pacific, who would become the heart and soul of the rank-and-file rebellion. Born and raised in Greenwich Village, only a block away from the neighborhood pier, Dwyer was one of nine children of a longshoreman who worked on the docks for thirty-five years. "He told me to stay away from the waterfront," Dwyer said of his Irish immigrant father, but he ended up there anyway. Like Ryan, he was very much a product of the Irish Catholic West Side. Although he became a leading symbol of the rebellion that rocked the port and sent shock waves throughout the New York metropolitan area, the West Coast longshoremen and their left-wing leadership were never an option for him. "Harry Bridges . . . got a better [contract] for his men," he recalled in 1989, "but . . . I just don't like the Commies, whether they get a better contract or not." Instead, his hero was Father John Corridan, the Waterfront Priest, whom Dwyer characterized as a "young Jesuit who never spoke in anger [or] failed to love his enemies."[51]

In late 1945, with help from the Association of Catholic Trade Unionists and the intervention of a court-appointed mediator, the rank and file of Local 895 succeeded in electing a reform administration led mainly by young Irish Americans. Another major breakthrough came in August 1946, when the Grace Line threw its weight on the side of the insurgents and appointed Dwyer hiring foreman on Pier 45. His incorruptible regime was unique in the port of New York. He was unable to eliminate the shape-up, which was sanctioned by the collective bargaining agreement, but he encouraged the consolidation of regular gangs, favored men with reliable work records and families to support, and even managed to install a system of work rotation. It was an informal version of the West Coast hiring hall; but in the personal idiom of the dockside working class, a patron in a local gin mill observed that West Street finally had a "heart."[52]

Local 895 may have been the heart of the postwar insurgency, but its most combative and volatile component was Joe Ryan's own local— 791, in Chelsea. Its members were "staunch Irish Catholics." Their leader, insofar as they acknowledged one, was their business agent, John J. "Gene" Sampson. Although Sampson identified with, and often spoke for, the young dissidents in Manhattan's West Side locals, he was hardly one of them, for he had joined Local 791 in 1910 and had been a business agent since 1919. For all of those years, he had coexisted more or less peacefully with the ILA leadership, until he emerged as the principal spokesman for the opposition during the turbulent postwar strike wave. Thereafter, he assumed an increasingly visible profile and even engaged in some memorable public confrontations with his boss. Given the lack of democracy in the ILA and the fate of critics like Pete Panto, his outspokenness appears to have been courageous, perhaps even foolhardy. But Sampson was no ordinary insurgent. Not only did he cut as dapper and well-heeled a figure as "King Joe," but he was also the brother of one of the leading power brokers in Tammany Hall. Like his brother Frank, Gene Sampson was a "survivor of many compromises."[53]

The other pole of the anti-Ryan leadership differed dramatically from Sampson in style and substance. Its members called themselves the waterfront underground, and at times they operated like a revolutionary cell. The cadres from different ILA locals were linked mainly by their relationship to the indefatigable Father Corridan, who spoke— almost conspiratorially—of his determination to "infiltrate Christ's interest" into the labor-management relations of the port. Corridan's formal title was associate director of the Saint Francis Xavier Labor School, which was located—appropriately enough—in the heart of Chelsea. Unlike Sampson, Corridan wanted to bring about change from the bottom up, and like many of the longshoremen he served, he had started life at or near the bottom. He was born in 1911, "within earshot of hiring bosses' whistles," on the West Side of Manhattan. His parents were Irish immigrants. His father, a New York policeman, died when John was only nine, leaving his mother to raise five sons. He attended Ascension Parochial School and Regis High School and took night classes at New York University before applying for admission to the Society of Jesus. Accepted in 1931, he began fifteen years of rigorous training that involved stints as a teacher at Canisius College in Buffalo and the Crown Heights Labor School in Brooklyn. Arriving at Xavier in 1946, he trained men like John Dwyer and Billy McMahon in trade union principles and Catholic social doctrine. His extraordinary impact on the insurgents is captured in the words of Pete Laughran, a member of the reform leadership in Local 895, who recalled Corridan's appearance on the docks as a turning point. "We were being sold out by Joe Ryan and his council of stooges," said Laughran. "Muscle men were roaming the waterfront. City Hall looked the other way and most newspapers thought we were radicals. The mob called us Reds and the Reds called us Fascists. Then Father John came down to the docks. It was like a sword cutting a path for us, separating us from the Commies on one side and the mob on the other."[54]

Father Corridan embodied the broad-gauged effort of the Catholic Church to reach out to industrial workers and influence the direction of labor-management relations, with the ultimate goal of re-creating an "organic society in which human solidarity conquered class hostility." Drawing on the papal encyclicals *Rerum Novarum* (1891) and *Quadragesimo Anno* (1931), Corridan and other agents of social Catholicism sought a middle way between laissez-faire capitalism and socialist collectivism, one that would minister to the needs of workers without attacking the foundations of private property. In the pursuit of this middle way, the church created a hundred labor schools, which by the late 1940s were graduating seventy-five hundred men and women a year into the ranks of organized labor. Although Corridan once described himself as hard-boiled in his willingness to "choose between two or more evils," he regarded the waterfront crisis as essentially spiritual in character. He identified with—and perhaps found his own spiritual validation in—the suffering of the longshoremen, whom he characterized as "living on the fringe of society in the backwash of the city." "These men are our brothers," he declared, "redeemed in the precious blood of Christ, and one cannot rest secure if His dignity in them continues to be violated and outraged." But precisely because the waterfront crisis was a spiritual one, neither the ILWU nor any Communist-led union could meet the essential needs of Corridan's dockworkers. Like the influential church spokesman Fulton J. Sheen, he believed that "Christ's Gospel gives no support to extremists who would violently dispossess capital." Rather, "He taught us how to be capitalists without being exploiters, and how to be laborers without being communists."[55]

Historians of the American working class, especially of the CIO era, have often highlighted the conflict between Catholics and Communists in the labor movement. But Father Corridan's role on the waterfront and the longshoremen's response to his high-profile presence suggest that a major motif of the 1930s and 1940s was the struggle *between* Catholics for the soul of their church and the allegiance of its communicants. Many longshoremen welcomed Corridan's intervention; some eagerly heeded his recommendation to abandon the ILA and line up with the AFL. But others expressed strong reservations about the AFL's intentions and backed the ILA as "the lesser of two evils." Some even defended the shape-up and feared that the alternative might be far worse. "With that system I was at least getting three days work a week," a longshoreman wrote from Newark. "If I vote A. F. of L. and they win out I will have to go on relief or find other employment." "We did not starve," added the son of a dockworker who had raised seven children and sent all of them to Catholic schools. "My father worked under the 'Shape-Up' System and things were not as bad as stated in the papers."[56]

Some longshoremen went even further and said that Corridan was "either a liar or a dope." These critics had an alternative role model in the person of Monsignor John J. O'Donnell, the rector of the Guardian Angel Church and the archconservative Cardinal Spellman's official representative on the waterfront. O'Donnell was Joe Ryan's priest, and Guardian Angel was Ryan's church. He went to Mass there daily and helped sustain its activities with generous, and well-publicized, mone-

Fig. 2.4. "The Waterfront Priest": Father John M. Corridan, New York Harbor, early 1950s. Credit: *Jubilee*

tary gifts. O'Donnell, in turn, spoke regularly at ILA gatherings, where he announced: "I am not a labor expert. . . . I wouldn't think of trying to tell a man who grew up in labor . . . what to do in the field of labor, any more than I would expect that he would tell me what I should . . . say in the pulpit." "May I stick to my own business, which is the spiritual," he concluded, before leading a grateful ILA leadership in prayer.[57]

Cardinal Spellman could have silenced the outspoken Waterfront Priest (apparently he came close to doing so at one point), but even the harshest letters from his dockside constituents could not deter him. Corridan called on the longshoremen "to sign up with the AFL when the big moment comes." John Dwyer became chairman of the AFL's port committee in New York Harbor, and Gene Sampson, who perhaps had the most to lose, quit his post as business agent of Local 791 and agreed to serve as an AFL organizer. But he failed to carry his local with him. At a turbulent mass meeting in Saint Bernard's Hall, only twenty-one men voted to follow Sampson out of 791 and into the AFL. Hundreds more—according to some accounts as many as nine hundred—opted to stay in the ILA. Meanwhile, Local 791 passed a resolution calling on Father Corridan to "let us run our own Union the way we want to."[58]

Intimidation no doubt played a role in the ILA's stunning victory over the AFL, but other factors were more important. The ILA won because the AFL's campaign was often spearheaded by members of the Teamsters' and Seafarers' unions whom the longshoremen suspected—rightly, in some cases—of wanting to take away their jobs;[59] because the Central Trades and Labor Council, the voice of the AFL in New York City, sided with the ILA in covert defiance of Meany and the AFL Executive Council; because many employers demonstrated a surprising willingness to live with the "devil" they knew; and because important figures in the Catholic Church and the city's political establishment found it impossible to abandon old friends, allies, and communicants with whom they had worked and played side by side for decades. The reformers came from the same dense network. In essence, theirs was a family feud, and "outsiders"—the Communist and Jewish leaders of the local CIO, the Protestant "do-gooders" at the neighborhood settlement house, and even the nominally Catholic Puerto Ricans who were pouring into Chelsea as the more affluent Irish escaped—were not welcome. Perhaps nothing exemplifies the boundaries of their worldview more clearly than the fact that the rebels in Local 895 chose to call themselves the Committee of Longshoremen of St. Veronica's Parish. Although they showed enormous courage in bucking Ryan and the deadly power of the mob, they were no more open to the "rational-materialist posture" of New Deal–era reform than the waterfront generation of the thirties had been.[60]

These boundaries became vividly apparent when black longshoremen, most of whom were members of Local 968, staged their own rebellion and demanded an end to "Jim Crowism" in the ILA's employment practices. This time the Irish did not rebel. On the contrary, they aligned themselves with Joe Ryan in his campaign to suppress a "Communist-inspired" challenge to the racial status quo on the docks.

• • • • •

Local 968 had long been an anomaly in the ILA because its members had never been granted complete jurisdiction over a single pier. Before World War II the local's leaders had developed a working relationship

79

with a number of companies that provided employment on docks running from the Brooklyn Bridge to Atlantic Avenue. The vast increase in shipping during the war had led to the breakdown of the old patterns of access to employment, and thus African Americans had been able to work on piers throughout the port. But after the war Local 968 was the victim of a squeeze play. Gradually, six Brooklyn locals claimed exclusive control of the areas of the waterfront where Local 968 had exercised at least partial jurisdiction. In ethnic terms, this move was a power grab directed by Brooklyn ILA officials who turned over the work that had customarily gone to African American longshoremen to their Italian constituents.[61]

The squeeze play became all the more devastating because on other piers throughout the port ILA locals were reclaiming the jurisdictional rights they had exercised before World War II, and at times their assertiveness seems to have been directed at black workers in particular. Local 968 president Cleophas Jacobs reported that at the Bayonne Naval Supply Depot, where more than a hundred members of his organization had worked for the "entire duration of the war," members of the local with customary jurisdiction there had not only reclaimed their turf but had threatened "bloodshed" if the "colored gangs" continued to work in Bayonne. Similarly, in 1946, at Piers 13 and 14 on the East River, where, according to Jacobs, "Negro gangs had been working . . . for forty years or more," black longshoremen were prevented from working there any longer because they were not members of the ILA local in that area. Finally, at Piers 95 and 96 on the North River, Local 968 gangs that had worked for a full day on ships there, and had been ordered by their supervisors to return the next day, were prevented from doing so when members of the local in that vicinity demanded jurisdiction over these jobs. They did so, said Jacobs, "in spite of the well-established ILA rule that when a gang starts a job it must be allowed to complete the work." Given these circumstances, Jacobs complained bitterly that "the delegates of Local 968, deprived of any jurisdiction, are compelled to go around throughout the entire . . . Port of New York, seeking work for their members, trying to pick up crumbs here and there." His local had become the "stepchild of the ILA." No matter how long its members had worked on the waterfront, their status was little better than that of the "casual" newcomers with whom they were compelled to compete for jobs, and they bore the additional onus of being black men seeking recognition from white hiring bosses.[62]

By the summer of 1948, conditions for Negro longshoremen had become so bad that some of them contemplated the establishment of their own labor exchange in Harlem, where they would offer to work at "10 or 15 cents below the contract rate in order to get some of the jobs." Instead, in March 1949 they began picketing the international union headquarters to demand that they be "given piers . . . on which they would receive preferential treatment." Although the protest was not openly sanctioned by the leadership of Local 968, many rank and filers took part and maintained daily picket lines on the sidewalk outside Ryan's office in Chelsea. According to Jacobs, Ryan had encouraged Local 968 to "go out and create a crisis," because "that will force me and the District Council into the picture." But now the ILA president showed little disposition to respond sympathetically to the local's demands, especially since the only way to meet them would have been to take a pier away from the Italian power brokers in Brooklyn. Finally, in early June, with the active support and encouragement of the Communist-led Harlem Trade Union Council, thirty-eight members of Local 968 staged a sit-in in Ryan's office. The sit-in, and the presence of a group closely associated with the Communist party, gave Ryan the opening he needed. He declared that "every Commie in town is here in our offices or downstairs," and he appealed to ILA members to rescue their union.[63]

Ironically, it was the Manhattan longshoremen, including Irish Catholic members of West Side locals that had been leading the anti-Ryan insurgency, who answered his call. On the day after the sit-in, more than two thousand longshoremen working nineteen ships on the East and North River piers quit work and began a march toward the ILA headquarters. Upon reaching their destination, they joined two hundred ILA loyalists, some of them in military uniform, who had marched there from a nearby American Legion hall, carrying signs that denounced the protesters' "phony Commy show." Together, the two groups, which now numbered twenty-five hundred or more men, assaulted several hundred pickets on the sidewalk. Only the presence of a substantial contingent of New York City policemen, and their own "fleetness of foot," saved the protesters from a severe drubbing.[64]

Given the proto-McCarthyite climate of 1949 and the presence of the Harlem Trade Union Council, it was easy to present the issue at stake as communism.[65] After their victory at the union headquarters, the ILA loyalists—led by Ryan, the commander of the American Legion post, and two longshoremen carrying an American flag and a union banner—marched to a nearby park, where their president thanked them for their "loyalty and devotion as union men" and the American Legion official lauded their "spirit of Americanism." Meanwhile, the officers of Local 968 hastily issued a statement denying they were Communists. They declared that they were "ready to submit to loyalty tests at any time" and immediately tried to pass one such test by "repudiat[ing] the efforts of the Communists to capitalize on this issue."[66]

The real issue, however, was not communism; it was the undeniable reality of racial discrimination in the employment of longshoremen on the New York waterfront. All longshoremen had a stake in this issue, but blacks and whites found themselves on different sides of it. The Irish, above all, had something to protect. As a group they were far more likely than blacks, or even Italians, to be members of regular gangs, to earn a steady income, and to have access to skilled employment on the waterfront. But there was more at stake in this case than the defense of material interests in the face of a challenge to the racial status quo on the docks. For there are indications that the Irish, and other white longshoremen, were also determined to maintain a necessary psychological space between themselves and African Americans. To be sure, black longshoremen were accepted in the shape-up; they had even been granted representation within the councils of the union (an arena with which most longshoremen had little direct contact), up to and including a vice-presidency for life. But insofar as the black protesters seemed to be demanding substantive equality and full citizenship as fellow workers, they were seeking to cross a barrier that few whites were willing to see breached. Can it be a coincidence that at the very moment when members of Local 968 began picketing the union headquarters, ILA officials were circulating a petition among the membership asking them to oppose changes that could "break the morale of the union through the wholesale hiring of Negro longshoremen"?[67]

· · · · ·

Even at the peak of the Civil Rights era there would be no "wholesale hiring" of African Americans. In part this reflected the general decline of waterfront employment in New York, as technological innovation and competition from other cities resulted in a significant contraction of the port's labor supply. Within the framework of the options avail-

able to the men along shore, most black dockworkers remained confined to the margins of their trade, and the much heralded reforms in
hiring imposed by the Waterfront Commission tended to legitimize the
status quo. After nearly a decade of involvement with the complaints
of black longshoremen, the Urban League of Greater New York
charged in 1959 that the shape-up, with all of its inequities, had returned in "government-rented buildings," and that the new regime for-
malized a "pattern of discrimination that has existed on the waterfront
for years."[68]

Part of the problem was that the new seniority system reinforced the
localism and the patterns of exclusion that had characterized the port's
employment practices for generations, and it failed to address the
unique disabilities that black longshoremen continued to face as a result of these practices. One of the most egregious examples was the
luxury liner piers on the West Side of Manhattan. The "cream" jobs
on these piers—carrying passengers' baggage and earning generous
tips—had long been an Irish monopoly. The new regime simply ratified
the seniority of the men who worked on these piers and thus closed
the door to the potential competitors they had excluded. As late as
1964 Local 824, which exercised jurisdiction in this area, counted one
Negro among its two thousand members. Nonmembers could report to
the waterfront employment center that served these piers and take
their chances on the "extra" jobs that became available on occasion.
But hiring continued to reflect long-standing local practice, which
meant that African Americans were almost certain to be bypassed
when the hiring agent made his choice.[69]

The same problem was evident at another prime location, the Brooklyn Army Terminal. In September 1956 the Urban League of Greater
New York monitored hiring practices at the terminal for a week and
found that while "hundreds of casual white longshoremen" were hired,
black dockworkers were systematically excluded. According to the
Urban League, "forty-two Negroes," who were "experienced, skilled, and
licensed by the Waterfront Commission," presented themselves as candidates for employment every day and were bypassed every day. When
the Urban League complained to the military officer who served as the
official liaison with the terminal's civilian contractors, he responded
that his superiors had warned him against dealing with the issue, because
"the union might tie up the waterfront at any provocation."[70]

Insofar as Negro longshoremen found regular employment, it was
mainly as members of gangs that were consigned to handling lumber,

paper, or sugar. The men who worked in these gangs usually traveled from pier to pier, working for the same employer. They had no pier of their own, and they could accumulate seniority only in work that was regarded as the most "arduous and least desirable" in the port. For those who handled iron ore, it was even worse; silicosis and an early death were the likely results. "They gave that work to the black workers," Roy Saunders recalled. "They'd work 'em all day, day and night, the worst work."[71]

In the case of clerks and checkers, coopers and cargo repairmen, watchmen and hiring foremen, the exclusion of African Americans was nearly total. In 1959 the Urban League estimated that among 630 hiring agents in the port, only 2 were black; among more than 2,000 watchmen, none were black. In the mid-1950s all of the port's clerks and checkers were consolidated into a single "lily-white" local, headed by Teddy Gleason. Several years later the local accepted a consent decree that ordered the admission of two blacks to membership and mandated the consideration of other African Americans "without discrimination." However, the union simply failed to comply with the decree, until Gleason and other local union leaders were threatened with a contempt-of-court citation. Even then the outcome was the token incorporation of a few blacks rather than a step toward full integration.[72]

The demise of Local 968 serves as a metaphor for the fate of black longshoremen through most of the port. For years the leaders of the local had tenaciously defended its separate status. According to Spero and Harris, they believed that the maintenance of a separate organization afforded blacks a level of power and influence that they could not have had if they were scattered throughout the port in predominantly white locals. But in fact power and influence had not been forthcoming. Local 968's officers tried supplication and came away empty-handed. In 1949 they tried confrontation and suffered a humiliating defeat. Throughout the 1950s they continued to seek jurisdiction over their own pier, but their quest went against the grain of the political reality on the Brooklyn waterfront, where "Tough Tony" Anastasia was aggressively extending his empire through the mechanism of Local 1814. Founded in 1954, when Anastasia orchestrated the merger of nine small locals into one big one, Local 1814 continued to expand until it became the largest not only in the port of New York but in the entire ILA. Naturally, the leaders of Local 968 turned to Anastasia for help, but he could not meet their needs without taking jobs away from his Italian base. So he dissembled and warned that to grant Local 968 jurisdiction over a pier "would be immoral because it would only serve to foster and perpetuate segregation." Anastasia wanted to become president of the international union, however, and that meant cultivating the ILA's substantial black membership in the South. Thus, in 1959, he promised the members of Local 968 that they would finally be assigned a pier of their own, and on that basis they agreed to merge with Local 1814. It was a significant break with precedent and one that went against the grain of the racial pattern in the ILA, where, especially in the South, black longshoremen sought to maintain racially separate organizations. But Local 968 president Cleveland Robinson had a simple explanation for the change. "Anastasia is the big man in Brooklyn," he said, "and we don't get any help from the international." Noting that many former members of 968 had already joined Local 1814 on their own, Robinson concluded, "We figure that if we merge now, before we lose any more of our members, we can get the best possible deal for our people."[73]

What kind of "deal" did they get? Anastasia promised at least four years of official jobs, in positions ranging from business agent to assistant secretary-treasurer, for the thirteen officers of Local 968. Moreover, in spite of his gangster image and the contempt and fear his name engendered in respectable labor circles, Anastasia transformed his nine-thousand-member local from a semifeudal principality into a modern trade union in ways that benefited blacks as well as whites. Following the lead of innovative labor leaders like John L. Lewis and Walter Reuther, he negotiated a separate agreement with the shipowners to provide a medical clinic for the members of Local 1814. (By 1964 its doctors were treating four hundred patients a day.) More remarkably, after Anastasia died of cancer in 1963, his son-in-law and successor Anthony Scotto became an outspoken supporter of the Civil Rights movement. Local 1814 sent a contingent to the historic March on Washington in August 1963 and joined with the American Committee on Africa and the Congress of Racial Equality in October of that year in a boycott of South African ships in New York Harbor. When members of Local 1814 refused to unload the *South African Pioneer* at Brooklyn's Pier 6, Scotto justified their actions with the declaration that "we consider opposition to apartheid in South Africa to be a logical extension of the struggle for equality in the United States." To be sure, Scotto, like Anastasia before him, was engaged in a maneuver for power within the ILA, and black longshoremen were important pawns in the

game. But his alliance with left-liberal political activists and his force-
ful public denunciation of "racism and white supremacy" represented
a major break with the unionism of Ryan and the ILA's old guard.[74]

Although African American dockworkers and their families clearly
benefited from the development of Local 1814's private-sector "welfare
state," a pier of their own never materialized. No matter how impressive
the local union's commitment to civil rights in the larger society, patterns of employment on the waterfront were deeply entrenched and
resistant to change. Many of the stevedores and most of the hiring
bosses were Italian Americans, and they were accustomed to giving
priority to their ethnic compatriots. To them, any other course would
have seemed unnatural. And so most black longshoremen remained
outsiders seeking work on other men's turf. A. Philip Randolph charged
in 1961 that "only two Negro gangs have been allowed to develop as
regulars on the entire Brooklyn waterfront." For the most part, blacks
remained "casuals" and "extras" who, when they found work at all,
were assigned to the "hard, menial jobs . . . in the hold of the ship."
Thus many of the local's fifteen hundred black members—one observer
estimated more than half—gradually ceased paying dues and drifted
away, as disillusionment with their continued "casual" status on the
waterfront impelled them to seek employment elsewhere.[75]

Technological innovation and the gradual decasualization of the
labor force led to a dramatic decline in the number of longshoremen
in New York Harbor. In 1955 more than 50,000 men were employed
in the port. By 1971 the number had decreased to about 17,500. During
the transition period, the attempt to rationalize longshore labor continually came up against the localism that had long been one of the port's
hallmarks. For the most part, localism worked against African Americans, who had few bastions to defend. But in one significant case the
traditions of the port actually benefited black workers. Containerization and the obsolescence of oceangoing passenger liners helped to
undermine Manhattan's (and even Brooklyn's) place as a dynamic hub
of the port of New York. Gradually, the port's center of gravity shifted
to the New Jersey side of the harbor, to new and spacious facilities in
Elizabeth and Port Newark. For decades there had been two longshore
locals based in Port Newark, one predominantly black and one "white"
(Italian and, increasingly, Puerto Rican). Since Port Newark lacked
the finger piers that characterized the older sections of the port, neither
local had been able to establish control over a piece of turf; instead, a
"high-handed" ILA business agent had established a pattern of rela-

tively equal work rotation, and the tradition had stuck. Thus, when containerization and other factors eliminated jobs in Manhattan, Brooklyn, and Hoboken, longshoremen from those sections of the port were not able to transfer in large numbers to Port Newark, where the work was expanding. By custom and contractual agreement, they had to defer to the existing labor force, which in this case was nearly half black.[76]

· · · · ·

The experience of black longshoremen in Port Newark serves as yet another reminder that for well over a century employment networks on the New York waterfront were built upon the rock of race and ethnicity. Generally speaking, men worked on a single pier that was closely linked to the ethnic community adjoining it. For the most part, "strangers" stayed away, took their place at the outer edge of the shape, or worked on the dirty, heavy, and debilitating jobs that insiders no longer felt compelled to perform. Even the Waterfront Commission, which the Catholic journal *America* characterized as a "drastic and extraordinary act of government intervention," made major concessions to this pattern of localism, and it therefore helped to reinforce the social and institutional weight of ethnicity at a time when social scientists were inclined to dismiss the entire phenomenon as the quaint relic of a bygone era.[77]

At times black workers were able to build stable enclaves for themselves within the framework of this ethnic geography. They were a shadowy but real presence on the docks in the early years of the republic; they returned, through a "series of invasions," in the mid- and late nineteenth century and finally established their own piece of turf on the Ward Line piers. Indeed, so strong did their sense of entitlement become that they protested vehemently—and "a race riot was barely averted"—when the Ward Line hired large numbers of white longshoremen during the economic boom generated by the First World War. From this narrow base black dockworkers expanded their numbers and their territorial range. But far more than the Germans, or even the Italians, they continued to bear the mark of the stranger. Their presence on the margins was sometimes begrudgingly accepted, but at other times they were expelled by physical force from territory other men claimed as their own. As late as 1961, A. Philip Randolph complained of "race violence and intimidation" and a "climate of racial terror" on the piers of New York.[78]

Thus, while New York remains a monument to the enduring power of ethnicity, it also serves as a testament to the intractability of race. The very word *race* has denoted a complex reality, as in the years when Italians were not yet "white," and the even more remote era when a black servant could complain that his employer treated him like a "common Irishman." But gradually white ethnics seized upon their "whiteness" as an indispensable marker of economic entitlement and physical and psychological space. While the Italians and the Irish continued to compete for jobs and, increasingly, for control of the ILA, the struggle for black equality reminded them of how much they had in common. In the context of the Civil Rights movement and the aggressive rights consciousness of African Americans, one black worker recounted how the whites he knew on the job could still grouse among themselves about the "fuckin' guinea" and the "stinkin' kike." But, he said, "when I come into the room they're all white."[79]

Waterfront Unionism and "Race Solidarity": From the Crescent City to the City of Angels

FROM THE MID-NINETEENTH CENTURY until World War II, African Americans were barely visible in the American West. In 1910 Los Angeles, a city of 319,000, had only 7,599 black residents; as late as 1940, Portland had only 1,800. But although blacks were—relatively speaking—absent, race was omnipresent. The region was settled, after all, by Anglo-Protestant migrants who brought their whiteness with them and by European immigrants who found the West a congenial environment in which to negotiate their citizenship in the White Republic. In their westward trek, these newcomers encountered a heterogeneous lot of dark-skinned peoples who had never thought of themselves as a single group, and from these raw materials they created the artificial coherence of race. Indians and Mexicans were vital to the process of race making, but it was the presence of tens of thousands of Chinese immigrants that was most instrumental in shaping the racial fault lines and cultural contours of whiteness in the West. By 1870 sixty-three thousand Chinese were in the United States; most of them resided in California, where they constituted 9 percent of the population and perhaps 20 percent of the labor force. The Chinese lived in separate enclaves but often worked in occupations such as mining and railroad labor that whites claimed as their own. Although employers did not contest the regnant view of the "Heathen Chinee" as an "inbred race of miserable slaves," they were dependent on their labor and inclined to applaud their "steadiness," "aptitude," and "capacity for hard work." In contrast, white workers saw the Chinese as a threat to their economic well-being and to their status as white Americans. Thus they took the lead in demonizing them as "the most degraded and beastly of all human creatures" and in demanding an end to the "Asiatic inundation" of the West. In the mass mobilizations that led to a succession of exclusionary laws, white workingmen unashamedly defined class and the mission of organized labor in racial terms. As late as

1929, a leading California trade unionist warned that if the legislation restricting "mass migration from the Orient" were repealed, "the white workers will literally be crucified by the proletariat from Asia."[1]

Although they shared in the prevailing animus toward the Chinese and limited membership in their unions to white males, dockworkers on the Pacific Coast had never faced serious job competition from Asians. But as early as 1901 employers imported African Americans to break strikes on the waterfront. In the bitter labor wars of 1916 and 1919, black strikebreaking became one of the major motifs of the conflict. In Seattle there were as many as fourteen hundred strikebreakers in 1916, including four hundred black longshoremen imported from New Orleans, Saint Louis, and Kansas City. Horace Cayton, who grew up in Seattle, remembered white strikers boarding trolley cars and assaulting black passengers. Once Cayton witnessed a striker swing "his cargo hook and [catch a Negro man] in the neck just below the ear, pulling him to his feet like a half of beef." In San Francisco, too, employers recruited hundreds of black strikebreakers. When the shipowners defeated the Riggers' and Stevedores' Union in 1919 and imposed a company union in its place, some of these men were able to hang on to their jobs. But for the most part, wherever unions prevailed, black workers were excluded. Thus, in the early 1930s, John Pittman, the editor of the *San Francisco Spokesman*, complained bitterly that "for Aframerican workers in the Bay cities, union labor has been and still is the chief obstacle to employment."[2]

And yet things were changing on the labor front even as Pittman spoke. The International Longshoremen's and Warehousemen's Union, which emerged on the West Coast waterfront in the mid- and late thirties, was led by Communists and Communist sympathizers who were determined to put an end to the long era of white supremacy.[3] Indeed, the Communist party was unique among predominantly white organizations in its close identification with the struggle for black equality. In Alabama, Communists took up the cause of nine black youths who were accused of raping two white women and mounted an international campaign to save them from the electric chair. In Chicago and other northern cities, during the depths of the Great Depression, they built interracial organizations of the unemployed and fought to prevent the eviction of black families from their homes. In Kentucky coal mines and Detroit auto plants, they welcomed black workers into the trade unions they led and raised the slogan "Negro and White,

Unite and Fight!" All of this compelled even moderate black leaders to pause and, in some cases, to explain "Why We Can't Hate Reds." "Is there any other political, religious, or civic organization in the country that would go to such lengths to prove itself not unfriendly to us?" Robert Abbott, the publisher of the *Chicago Defender*, asked in 1933. Abbott, who in other respects remained proudly bourgeois, marveled at the "zealousness" with which Communists guarded "the rights of the Race." Pittman marveled too, but with less restraint. He eventually joined the Communist party and became the executive editor of its West Coast newspaper, the *Daily People's World*.[4]

With the formation of the CIO in 1935 the Communists gained an unprecedented opportunity to enter the mainstream of the labor movement, and they succeeded in playing a leading role in many CIO unions. Historian Michael Honey contends that the combination of black support and Communist leadership "proved the key to success in many of the places where the CIO excelled," especially in the South. In cities such as Memphis and Winston-Salem, the CIO-affiliated Food, Tobacco, Agricultural and Allied Workers (FTA) aggressively defended the job rights of black workers and played an important role in fighting for the rights of African Americans beyond the workplace. The initiative in this regard clearly came from Communists in the FTA leadership, who were, to an unusual degree, open about their party affiliation. According to historian Robert Korstad, a significant number of black tobacco workers in Winston-Salem joined the Communist party, largely because they viewed it as a "militant civil rights organization."[5]

Although to outsiders Communists seemed to be unified in their approach to issues, the practice of the party's trade union cadres often varied according to circumstance. Where party members and their allies controlled a union with a membership that was majority black, the union was sure to take an aggressive stand on behalf of racial equality. Where blacks were a minority of a Communist-led union's membership but still constituted a critical mass, the organization was likely to reflect their concern for racial justice. But what about a Left-led union with a membership that was predominantly white? Here the example of the New York–based Transport Workers Union (TWU) is instructive. Rhetorically, the TWU's leadership demonstrated a strong commitment to the struggle for black equality. But in practice the union's record was far more ambiguous, largely because its membership was overwhelmingly white and Irish. Given the legacy of conflict between Irish immigrants and African Americans, it is not surprising that one of the union's Communist cadres remembered the problem of fighting racial discrimination as "so overwhelming that you couldn't win."[6]

Few trade unionists more candidly acknowledged the constraints a Left-led CIO union faced in this regard than Ferdinand Smith, the secretary-treasurer of the National Maritime Union (NMU). According to a 1938 NAACP memorandum, Smith "made it clear" to the association's Thurgood Marshall

> that the [NMU] leadership stood 100% opposed to any kind of discrimination against its 10% Negro membership, and was fighting to break it up. However, he said that the Union was also faced with keeping its ranks together. . . . He was firm in his statement that while the Union leadership was going to fight the discrimination problem wherever possible, no intelligent person could defend the Union's fighting the problem to the extent of breaking up the Union over the issue.[7]

Smith was an African American and a Communist. His frankly expressed determination not to allow the issue of race to break up the NMU reveals a concern with organizational self-preservation that was common to all of the Left-led unions. Like other trade unionists, Communists confronted the need to combine political principle with practical necessity. But because they were more intensely political than most, they were more willing to take risks in the name of their beliefs. Ultimately, however, they too faced the question of how to fight for a principle that went against the grain of the white majority's sensibilities without jeopardizing the survival of the unions that were their most prized possessions.

This chapter will explore the working out of this complex dynamic on the West Coast waterfront—mainly, through an examination of race relations in Longshore Local 13 in the port of Los Angeles.[8] The ILWU was, from its inception, a Left-led union. Its membership was racially diverse, especially in Hawaii, but also in the warehouse and cotton compress locals in the San Francisco Bay Area, Los Angeles, and California's Central Valley. The heart of the union, though, was its longshore division, and until World War II its membership was overwhelmingly white. The San Francisco longshore local experienced a dramatic influx of black workers during the war, but most others remained predominantly—and, in some cases, defiantly—white. Thus the union's racial practice was complex and contradictory. At the leadership level, the ILWU was aggressively committed to the cause of racial equality; its widely articulated stance and many resolute actions earned the union much praise for its civil rights record. But the leadership was not entirely free to impose its will on a sometimes resistant, and famously unruly, rank and file. On the contrary, ILWU leaders were constrained by their principled commitment to local autonomy, by their belief in rank-and-file democracy, and by practical considerations that mandated the choice of institutional self-preservation over what may have appeared at times to be a quixotic attachment to principle.[9]

Through every twist and turn, however, ILWU leaders and many rank-and-file activists remained proud of their record on race and convinced that it was superior to the "checkerboard" pattern of the ILA, where segregation and racial discrimination allegedly prevailed. For that very reason, it is important to take a comparative look at the development of the nation's leading example of "separate but equal" unionism, the ILA's General Longshoremen's Local 1419 in New Orleans. In the late thirties, the ILWU had sought to become a national organization of dockworkers and had chosen New Orleans as the focal point of its campaign. In a vote that was as unexpected as it was disorienting, black longshoremen had opted—overwhelmingly—for Local 1419 over the ILWU's interracial alternative. Thereafter Local 1419 had evolved into the nation's "largest and most powerful all Negro union." In the process, some civil rights activists denounced it as a relic of segregation, but others praised it as a vital and enduring expression of the black community's preference for autonomy.[10]

Could it be that a "conservative," "Jim Crow" local affiliated with the AFL was more successful in winning the allegiance and in representing the interests of black workers than a "left-wing" and "integrated" local affiliated with the CIO? For the last two decades scholars have tended to focus on the affinity between Left-led unions and black working-class constituencies during World War II and the postwar era, to lament the expulsion of the CIO's Left-led unions as a disaster for black workers, and, more broadly, to see the rightward drift of the labor movement after the war as an indication of "degeneration and decline."[11] But New Orleans complicates that scenario. The persecution of the Crescent City's few left-wing unions and their Communist leaders was indeed cruel, even tragic, in its consequences.[12] But Local 1419—a "conservative" AFL affiliate—thrived during this period. Its record and leadership bear out Earl Lewis's contention that black workers acted "in their own interests" but in doing so chose to adapt strategies that were far from uniform.[13]

. . . . .

The birth of the ILWU can be traced to the Big Strike, which began on May 9, 1934, when members of the Pacific Coast District of the International Longshoremen's Association walked off the job in ports from San Diego to Seattle and points north. Within a week they were joined by seamen and other maritime workers; teamsters refused to handle scab-unloaded cargo; and in July a bloody confrontation between police and unionists triggered a general strike of more than one hundred thousand workers in San Francisco and Alameda Counties. The eighty-three-day waterfront strike became famous not only for these expressions of solidarity but for the disciplined militancy of its rank-and-file participants and the left-wing political orientation of some of its key leaders. Especially in the San Francisco longshore local, a small core of Communists and Communist party sympathizers, led by Australian immigrant Harry Bridges, played a vital role in directing the strike locally and influencing its character up and down the coast.[14]

Soon after the longshoremen and seamen returned to work, a presidentially appointed arbitration board issued an award that offered major concessions to the ILA, including union recognition, de facto union control of hiring, and a six-hour day (in practice, an eight-hour day with overtime paid after six hours). The award was an attempt to right the injustices that had prevailed on the docks for many years, but it also came in the context of a continuing wave of job actions and "quickie" strikes at the point of production. Before long the shipowners were complaining that union stewards "establish the manner in which, and the speed at which, work is to be performed on the waterfronts of the Pacific Coast." What the employers lamented the longshoremen themselves could only celebrate. An "Admiral Line Stevie" was convinced that he and his fellow workers had achieved "the finest conditions in the world." An "Oldtimer," who had first joined the ILA in 1915, exulted that "we are the most militant and organized body of men the world has ever seen." Another longshoreman was moved to express his newfound sense of pride in poetic terms.

> I'm called dock-walloper and wharf rat
> With many laughs and many knocks.
> In spite of that, I glory in my element
> I'm one of the Lords of the Docks.[15]

To be sure, in the 1930s there was plenty of job-related militancy among industrial workers, highlighted by the sit-down strikes that helped spearhead the organization of the auto and rubber industries in Flint, Detroit, and Akron. But the West Coast maritime unionists were unique among American workers in the way they extended their militancy from the realm of "pork chops" to the world of politics. They protested, and engaged in symbolic strikes, over political issues such as the Italian invasion of Ethiopia, Japanese aggression against China, and Republican Spain's desperate fight for survival against a counter-revolution supported by Hitler and Mussolini. Longshoreman Henry Schrimpf declared that the goal of the maritime workers was not just to win better wages and conditions for themselves but "generally [to] advance the human cause." Schrimpf, who was closely identified with the Communists at the time, could not have spoken for all of his fellow maritime workers, but his statement conveys a sense of the spirit and vision that animated many of them during the turbulent thirties.[16]

Was this vision broad enough to incorporate African Americans and others who stood outside the parameters of whiteness? Maritime workers on the West Coast were the inheritors of a tradition of white supremacy nurtured in the anti-Chinese movement of the late nineteenth century and the broader campaign for "Asiatic exclusion" in the early twentieth. In San Francisco the venerable Riggers' and Stevedores' Union had specified that membership in the organization was limited to whites, and in virtually every port on the coast strikebreaking had provided African Americans with their only access to waterfront work, and then—for the most part—only temporarily. Seattle proved something of an exception to this rule. In the aftermath of the bitter 1916 strike, the union decided to admit blacks. According to the Bureau of the Census, in 1920, in a total workforce of 2,120, there were 97 Negro longshoremen in Seattle. But even on the inside they remained outsiders. One African American unionist remembered that "blacks would sit on benches for up to two weeks in the union hall waiting for job assignments while whites went from one job to another." White dockworkers often refused to accept blacks in their work gangs, and "when work was slack," Horace Cayton recalled, "colored longshoremen were frozen out" altogether.[17]

Meanwhile, among the hundreds of blacks who had helped break the 1919 strike in San Francisco, only a few managed to find steady work on the docks during the open-shop era that followed. The Bureau of the Census recorded 4 black longshoremen in San Francisco and Oakland in 1910, 23 in 1920, and 57 in 1930 (compared with 3,375 whites). The recollections of veteran longshoremen sometimes reaffirm and sometimes complicate these statistics. Alex Waters, whose father and uncle were dockworkers in Galveston, Texas, came to the San Francisco waterfront in 1932 and found that Negroes worked on only two docks. There were, he recalled, "14 Negroes for each company—six dockmen and eight holdmen, a total of 28." But Germaine Bulcke remembered that the "black" workers were not necessarily African American. One "black" gang, he recalled, included Chileans and other "South American people," as well as a winch driver who was a "100 percent native Indian from the Hoopa reservation." Perhaps the most reliable observation came from African American economist Robert Francis, a Berkeley graduate student who was completing a doctoral dissertation on the history of waterfront labor in San Francisco. Francis estimated that in 1934 there were "not more than fifty black men working on the San Francisco waterfront." A few of them had joined the ILA, but on the eve of the Big Strike there were apparently only twenty-three black union members along the entire West Coast.[18]

In San Francisco, at least, this situation changed dramatically during and after the strike, thanks mainly to the growing influence of Harry Bridges and the Left. Bridges began working as a longshoreman in 1922. In the early thirties, he was the leader of a San Francisco caucus of longshore unionists that was closely (but covertly) identified with the Communist party. He and his allies argued that building a strong union necessitated the recruiting of black longshoremen into its ranks and ending the pattern of racial and ethnic segregation that prevailed in waterfront work gangs. During the 1934 strike, Bridges spoke at black churches and "implored blacks to join him on the picket line." Nearly a decade later he recalled, "I went directly to them. I said: 'Our union means a new deal for Negroes. Stick with us and we'll stand for your inclusion in [the] industry.' " And, he declared, "[a]lmost without exception, they stuck with us. They helped us. The employers were frustrated in their attempt to use them for scabs."[19]

With the formation of the ILWU in 1937 and its affiliation with the CIO, San Francisco's Longshore Local 10 quickly distinguished itself as a "haven of racial equality." The substantial presence of Communist party members and their allies in Local 10 was vitally important to this achievement, as was the fact that Bridges and other leaders of the international union were based in San Francisco and played an active role in the local's deliberations. A third factor was the in-migration of thousands of black workers during World War II, when the port

Fig. 3.1. ILWU Longshore Local 10 hiring hall, San Francisco, 1946. Credit: *Dispatcher*, International Longshore and Warehouse Union.

boomed and, according to some estimates, provided employment for as many as nine thousand longshoremen. More than two thousand of these workers were African American. Many of them became full members of the union and eventually constituted a critical mass that in alliance with the Left had a significant impact on the local's internal life. Although the union did not use race as a category in counting its members, informed contemporaries estimated that blacks made up about 25 percent of Local 10's membership in 1946 and about 45 percent by the mid-1960s.[20]

Within the black community, especially in San Francisco, the ILWU's record on race received high praise, and Bridges was given much of the credit. The president of the Baptist Ministers' Union called him "a Godsend among men." The *Sun-Reporter* declared that "minority people have fared better in the ILWU under Bridges . . . than they have in any other labor union in the United States." Carleton

Goodlet, a physician and civil rights activist, characterized the ILWU and the Marine Cooks and Stewards, another Left-led maritime union with a large black membership, as "the guardians of the Negro community and its economic backbone." Even the staunchly anti-Communist Wilson Record conceded in the pages of *The Crisis* that "whatever one may think of the left-wing tendencies of the Bridges-controlled [ILWU], the fact remains that through it Negroes have obtained a fair break in job opportunities and union participation."[21]

The ILWU's achievements in the realm of race relations reached far beyond Local 10. By 1946 the union's research director concluded, "[A]pproximately 22% of our longshore and warehouse membership consists of Negroes. This amounts to about 11,000 Negroes out of approximately 50,000 members in these two categories." Beyond these two categories, there was the union's extraordinary breakthrough in organizing sugar and pineapple workers in the fields of Hawaii. Here virtually the entire labor force was made up of "minority peoples." In 1946 Filipino and Japanese workers constituted nearly 90 percent of the ILWU members in the islands, and the emergence of Hawaii as the union's greatest source of growth meant that people of color soon accounted for nearly half of the ILWU's total membership.[22]

Given the increasing importance of this multiracial constituency, the union moved aggressively in 1945 to suspend the charter of the Stockton Unit of Warehouse Local 6 because its members refused to work with a Japanese American who had recently been released from a wartime relocation camp. Bridges told the press that "the position of the ILWU on the question of equality for all, regardless of race, creed, color, or national origin, is clear and unequivocal. We cannot and will not compromise on it for one moment, for to do so would be to pick up the banner of fascism where Hitler dropped it." When the vast majority of the Stockton rank and file refused to sign pledge cards affirming their willingness to abide by the union's racially egalitarian principles, the suspension went into effect and, according to historian Harvey Schwartz, "an angry Harry Bridges . . . tore the Stockton Unit charter off the wall and drove back to San Francisco."[23]

Summing up its history in 1955, the union declared proudly that "the ILWU banned racial discrimination and segregation twenty years before the United States Supreme Court found the courage to do so." Although this statement may be an accurate indicator of the leadership's intent, as a summation of the union's history it obscures as much as it reveals. Bridges's own commitment to racial equality must be seen in relation to other principles he embraced—especially seniority, local autonomy, and a belief in rank-and-file democracy. When the practical application of these principles clashed with the ideal of racial equality, the ILWU president was compelled to negotiate a course that, perhaps necessarily, compromised one principle while upholding another. In relation to the recurring fluctuations in the waterfront labor market and the consequent ebb and flow of job opportunities, Bridges's clearest commitment was to seniority, which he called a "fair and honest trade union principle" that "no fair-minded, honest union member can oppose." He was convinced, moreover, that dockworkers should be sharing abundance rather than scarcity. "We readily admit that . . . the peaks and valleys of demand for longshoremen will present problems," he told a congressional committee in 1955. "But we are not prepared to return to the jungle of the New York waterfront and the west coast of pre-1934 in order to have a permanent surplus of men available at each dock gate. That way is the way of sharing starvation."[24]

His strong opposition to "sharing starvation" led Bridges to propose on one occasion that a thousand longshoremen from his own Local 10 be laid off, even though he knew full well that black workers, because of their low seniority, would be disproportionately affected. He made this proposal in 1949, after San Francisco longshoremen had been working "short" weeks for well over a year and had, in addition, lost substantial income during a ninety-eight-day strike in 1948. According to the *Local 10 Longshore Bulletin*, Bridges declared that "many men on the front" had asked him to do something to "remedy the situation, as they could no longer make a living." But in this instance Bridges's allies on the Left deserted him, and so did the black longshoremen, who immediately recognized the serious problem layoffs would cause for them at a time when black unemployment in the Bay Area was very high. In fact, among the membership as a whole the solidaristic spirit that had prevailed during the 1948 strike reasserted itself, and Bridges's proposal was overwhelmingly defeated.[25]

As this incident suggests, Bridges and other union leaders were frequently constrained by the fact that they operated within the framework of a democratic organization whose members had minds of their own and a strong commitment to local autonomy. More often than not, the membership also demonstrated a strong tendency to favor "son, brother, neighbor, or friend" when jobs became available on the waterfront. The ILWU could, and did, incorporate the principle of racial equality into its constitution and insist that all of its affiliated locals abide by this ideal. But in practice the principles of local autonomy and seniority, and the "brother-in-law" system of allocating new jobs, often took precedence over the goal of racial equality. Moreover, when conflict arose over racial issues, the union was compelled to seek resolution in a larger context that became increasingly precarious. The glory days of maritime unity in the mid-1930s soon gave way to intercraft friction that was rendered more complex and bitter by the jurisdictional warfare between the AFL and the CIO. And when the ILWU was expelled from the CIO in 1950 on the charge of "Communist domination," it became even more vulnerable to raiding by hostile unions. The ILA and the Teamsters were waiting in the wings; and local unionists hostile to Bridges's agenda could use the threat of secession to keep the international union at bay.[26]

The classic example of this dynamic was Portland's Local 8, which along with its counterparts in Seattle, San Francisco, and San Pedro was one of four major longshore locals on the West Coast. Oregon had been a major outpost of the Ku Klux Klan in the 1920s, and the continual influx of white Southerners reinforced the native tradition of white supremacy. As late as 1947, in his encyclopedic *Inside U.S.A.*, John Gunther reported: "I heard more and more bitter anti-Negro talk [in Portland] than in any other northern city." In this context Local 8 became an acute embarrassment to the ILWU and a blot on its reputation for racial egalitarianism. According to a study by the Oregon Bureau of Labor, Local 8 had "an unwritten policy and system that kept Negroes from being employed as longshoremen." During World War II, when about 15,000 African Americans came to the city seeking employment and the local took in 557 newcomers in a one-year period, Local 8 remained "lily white." As late as 1961, when there were about 1,200 regular and probationary union members on the Portland waterfront, the local continued to exclude blacks. This situation improved slightly in the 1960s, but even Bridges was unable to persuade the members of Local 8 to change their ways. Several times, when he addressed local union meetings and raised the issue of race, he was "unceremoniously booed out of the hall."[27]

The ILWU's Northwest regional director expressed the leadership's growing frustration—and sense of powerlessness—in regard to Portland's exclusion of African Americans. "Sure, we talked about [the Portland situation]," said Bill Gettings in 1952. "I talked about it with Harry [Bridges] lots of times. The ILWU Executive Board talked about it. It worried the hell out of the whole International. We didn't like it one damn bit. But what could we do? We got sores from scratching our head about it." Gettings believed that "kick[ing] the Portland local out of the International because they discriminated" would drive its members into the arms of the ILA, which would weaken the ILWU and thereby "hurt the Negro longshoremen . . . as well as the whites. So we decided to live with the situation, bad as it was."[28]

Clearly, the ILWU leadership's commitment to racial equality was not, by itself, sufficient to shape the practice of the Portland longshore local. And the Portland example raises a broader question about the racial attitudes and practices of the union's white rank and file, including the famed "generation of the 1930s." During the thirties the issue of racial equality remained more rhetorical than substantive in the ILWU, because in the context of the Great Depression there was hardly any influx of new workers of any race or nationality on the waterfront. In San Francisco and Oakland, according to census data, the number of black longshoremen increased by 9 during the 1930s, from 57 to 66; but in other ports their number decreased—from 68 to 34 in Seattle, and from 13 to 7 in Tacoma. Los Angeles and Portland remained "lily white."[29]

Insofar as race affected the ILWU significantly in its formative years, then, it was not on the West Coast but in New Orleans, the famed Crescent City, where the union focused its campaign to become a national organization of longshoremen. Whereas African Americans constituted about 30 percent of the Crescent City's population, they made up a far greater percentage of the riverfront labor force. Virtually all of the clerks and checkers in New Orleans were white, but blacks accounted for nearly three-fourths of the longshoremen and an even higher percentage of the banana handlers, freight-car loaders, warehousemen, and cotton compress workers. In dramatic contrast to their West Coast counterparts, these workers labored in an environment where employer domination continued to be a fact of life, where waterfront unions were weak and sometimes tainted by scandal, and where, as one CIO organizer admitted, the race issue "is loaded with lots of dynamite and can cause us much grief and misery."[30]

• • • • •

In the summer of 1937 the Pacific Coast District of the ILA voted to leave the American Federation of Labor, form a new union, and affiliate with the CIO, whose "tremendous march" appeared to be "sweeping everything before it." Bridges and his allies viewed the ILWU as a dynamic—even "invincible"—organization that would easily displace the ILA as the national union of longshoremen. To aid in this endeavor, the CIO formed a committee of maritime unions that promised "all possible support" in "organizing Longshoremen on a National basis." The committee's spokesman even ventured the opinion that ILA members on the Atlantic and Gulf Coasts could "be moved into the CIO as a result of two or three months [of] intensive work."[31]

He was wrong, of course. The AFL fought back vigorously, even viciously, and met the CIO's challenge with an aggressive organizing campaign of its own. AFL partisans unhesitatingly relied on brute force to deter the CIO's "aggression"; and no AFL unionist had more force at his disposal than Joe Ryan. When the CIO Maritime Committee assigned some of its most capable and courageous organizers to the port of New York, they came up against the insularity of the city's waterfront communities and the cargo hooks wielded by Ryan's henchmen. It was a devastating combination, and it persuaded the committee to shift its focus from the North Atlantic to the Gulf of Mexico—above all, to New Orleans, the South's second largest city and one of the nation's busiest ports.[32]

The ILWU representatives who arrived in the Crescent City in December 1937 were courageous and seasoned organizers, but they had little familiarity with or appreciation of the rich institutional network and distinctive culture that sustained African Americans in New Orleans. Also they were apparently unaware that strong unions and a tradition of biracial unity had prevailed on the riverfront for nearly a quarter of a century before the triumph of the open shop in the 1920s. Thus they lamented the "backwardness" of the Crescent City's black longshoremen and, in a moment of supreme frustration, complained that "the southern negro is only one step removed from the primitive superstitions of the African jungle tribes." In spite of their commitment to militant working-class unity, the organizers from the West Coast failed to understand how bitter competition for jobs had rendered black longshoremen suspicious of whites, even well-intentioned whites who, consciously or unconsciously, saw the unionism of the CIO as the means by which "the white man will lead the negro out of the pit and show him the light."[33]

With the defeat of the Dock and Cotton Council in 1923, a proud tradition of unionism had come to an end in the Crescent City. Thereafter, New Orleans employers delegated overall control of hiring to a black labor contractor named Alvin E. Harris, who instituted "a comprehensive fingerprinting and photo-identification system," with the result that in most of the port a longshoreman suspected of union affiliation could not find work. The exception was the docks utilized by vessels operating under the aegis of the United States Shipping Board, which maintained a gentleman's agreement with the International Longshoremen's Association and thus provided employment for union men. In 1931, however, the board turned over its contracts to private operators, who locked out union members, withstood a strike of nearly four months' duration, and thereby succeeded in making the entire port a stronghold of the open shop.[34]

During the open-shop era, whites—whether they were union members or not—found it increasingly difficult to obtain employment. In 1927 a mayoral candidate charged that Harris had "Africanized the waterfront," and that blacks "were driving to work in automobiles while whites were starving." In the same year, a veteran white longshoreman named Terrence Darcy sought to rebuild the ILA and use it as an instrument for restoring the position of whites on the docks. For the most part he failed, but in the process he convinced many black longshoremen that the return of the ILA would mean the curtailment—perhaps even the end—of their access to employment. Black workers watched with apprehension as spokesmen for the white longshoremen campaigned openly as the "White Man's Friend" and promised a fight to "give more work to the white man."[35]

In 1933 the passage of the National Industrial Recovery Act provoked a flurry of organization in the Crescent City. Seeking to rejuvenate its white and black longshore locals, the ILA held well-attended mass meetings along the riverfront. But the union was quickly outflanked by the employers, who convened a meeting in the board room of the New Orleans Steamship Association and "requested" the formation of "independent" organizations among their employees. Thus the Independent Colored Longshoremen's Association and the Independent White Longshoremen's Association were born. Although Charles Logan, the outspoken regional director of the National Labor Relations Board, dismissed them as "a farce, pure and simple," Ryan proved eager to incorporate the "independents" into the ILA. Never mind the fact that ILA locals were engaged in a bitter competition with the independents for the allegiance of the city's dockworkers. Ryan's concern was twofold: increasing the flow of dues money and cultivating a local leadership that would subordinate the interests of the Crescent City to those of New York. On both counts, the independents clearly offered him a better deal. In the spring of 1936, he finally succeeded in pushing aside the old ILA locals and chartering the independents in their place. The white association became ILA Local 1418; the "colored" association, ILA Local 1419. The former claimed about 850 members; the latter, about 2,300.[36]

With or without unions, conditions on the riverfront were a scandal. The problems were familiar: a vast oversupply of labor, rampant favoritism and corruption in the hiring process, and the lack of effective protection against speedup on the job. A survey published by the Bureau of Labor Statistics in 1930 had concluded that the average earnings of the longshoremen were "very low," and that "working conditions in New Orleans were less satisfactory than those found in any other port." The New Deal and the national surge of trade unionism spearheaded by the CIO brought significant upward pressure on hourly wages, but the income of most longshoremen remained appallingly low. During a six-month period in 1938, Charles Logan found that six thousand men were employed as longshoremen, but only half of them worked as many as eight times. The twenty-five hundred men who were employed at least eighteen times were paid 95¢ an hour but averaged only $20.67 a week. In the meantime, every black dockworker was required to pay $2.25 in quarterly dues and 5¢ on every dollar earned to the ILA. (Whites paid $3.00 quarterly but no percentage.) The shipowners collected the money for the union, and men who protested the practice were threatened with loss of employment.[37]

The president of the black union was Paul Hortman, who had headed the Independent Colored Longshoremen's Association before its metamorphosis into ILA Local 1419. According to Logan, he was "one of the two key men who . . . controlled the riverfront for the [steamship] operators." (The other was the head of the white longshoremen's union.) Hortman's was a classic success story in the Ryan mold. When he testified before the National Labor Relations Board in 1938, he claimed that he had worked as a longshoreman for twenty-one years and had performed "every class [of labor], from the bottom to the top." He had been an officer in an ILA local before joining the nonunion ranks, and it was widely believed that T. Smith and Son, the port's largest stevedoring firm, had been responsible for his selection as president of the colored "independent" association in 1933. After assuming the presidency of Local 1419, he lived in an expensive home and drove a Cadillac, wore tailored silk suits and Panama hats, and operated two "tonsorial palaces." Clearly, his ILA salary could not have sustained such a lifestyle, and in 1940 an investigation conducted by the NLRB revealed that Hortman and his cronies had secretly used about two hundred thousand dollars of the "percentage" money they received from the employers to enrich themselves at their members' expense. Long before these revelations became public, however, there was widespread cynicism about the role of the ILA on the docks. Even the ILA's South Atlantic and Gulf Coast District leadership acknowledged "the stigma of company domination" that permeated the black and white longshore locals in New Orleans.[38]

ILWU organizers were thus confident—even certain—that they would win a National Labor Relations Board election and thereby replace the ILA as the representative of the Crescent City's longshoremen, but it was not to be. When the election was finally held in October 1938, the ILA won a stunning—and, from the standpoint of the CIO, totally unexpected—victory. For Crescent City longshoremen, there were separate elections at twenty different companies. The ILA won eighteen of them; the ILWU, only one. In one case, neither union had a majority. The totals were 2,054 for the ILA and 553 for the ILWU. Out of 3,394 men whom the NLRB declared eligible to participate, there were 706 nonvoters. Even if all of them had cast their ballots for the ILWU, the CIO union would have lost the election by nearly 800 votes, as the ILA piled up huge majorities at one company after another. At Coastal Freight Handlers, the margin was 170 to 11; at Ryan Stevedoring, 182 to 27; at United Fruit, 136 to 3; at T. Smith and Son, 376 to 111.[39]

Why did the ILWU suffer such a crushing defeat? The first and most obvious answer is intimidation and the fact that "the employers, the [city] administration, and the A. F. of L. joined in impressing on the workers that if the C. I. O. won [the election], they would lose their jobs." To make sure that the dockworkers got the message, the New Orleans police force and AFL goon squads launched a closely coordinated reign of terror against the CIO that led to numerous arrests, the raiding and wrecking of the CIO headquarters, and the brutal beating of a number of the ILWU representatives who had come from the West Coast to direct the organizing campaign. Bob Robertson, a warehouseman from the San Francisco Bay Area, had his spine fractured in two places; Burt Nelson, a Seattle longshoreman, suffered a ruptured liver; Felix Siren, a member of the Inland Boatmen's Union, was arrested, badly beaten while in police custody, and forced to leave the state. Female office workers, including the wives of several male organizers, were also arrested and subjected to sustained harassment. "We . . . were sentenced in a 'kangaroo' court to [a] $25 fine and 30 days in jail," Ruby Heide recalled, "and while they had us there, they treated us worse than they did murderers."[40]

It would be wrong, however, to attribute the vote against the CIO entirely to intimidation. Bridges reported at the time that "the only companies we won were those with white longshoremen." The black dockworkers, many of whom had signed ILWU pledge cards, clearly voted overwhelmingly for the ILA. Fear may well have played a role in their decision, but they seem to have been motivated also by a cautious pragmatism, a sense of racial solidarity, and a distrust of the motives of white outsiders who failed to transcend the legacy of interracial competition for a place on the docks. In important respects, ILWU organizers in New Orleans seem to have misunderstood the terrain on which they were operating. Since 1923, most waterfront occupations had become "Negro" jobs, and black longshoremen had come to believe that whites in the ILA were "scabs and finks" who were scheming to drive them from the docks. As a singular—and fragile—enclave of black advantage, moreover, the riverfront stood in sharp contrast to the larger pattern throughout the South, where African American labor force participation was even more marginal and restricted at the end of the 1930s than it had been at the decade's outset—not simply because of the general effects of the Great Depression but also because whites were aggressively laying claim to jobs that historically had been reserved for blacks. In this setting, the ILWU organizers' call for decasualization and equalization of employment opportunity struck a discordant note with many black longshoremen. For men who regarded themselves not as individual workers in a race-neutral labor market but as members of a besieged racial bloc, "equality" for whites could only have implied less work for blacks.[41]

There was no easy way to counteract this fear. But one necessary means would have involved a concerted effort to win respect and trust in New Orleans's African American community. Instead, the ILWU chose to wage its campaign on "a strictly trade union basis." Its out-of-town organizers made little or no effort to develop ties with the myriad black churches, fraternal organizations, and social clubs that permeated Black New Orleans; nor did they seek the support of the NAACP. (Local 1419, meanwhile, paid dues on behalf of its members to the NAACP's Crescent City branch, and Hortman served on its executive committee.) They also failed to understand that for all of its weaknesses as an economic organization, the ILA had deep roots in the community. Hortman himself embodied the mores of the "Big Easy." Brazenly self-aggrandizing behavior was considered normative among white politicians in New Orleans, and blacks who successfully emulated them won widespread respect among their own constituents. The ILWU denounced the Hortman regime as an "iron dictatorship," but he employed more than sixty men on the union's payroll, including ministers, "black-and-tan" Republicans, and others who reinforced the links between the city's largest "Negro union" and its multilayered black community.[42]

Thus the CIO was trying to dislodge something that was an integral part of Black New Orleans, or so its opponents claimed. While the ILWU organizers spoke the language of class, ILA partisans couched their arguments in the more familiar idiom of racial solidarity. On the eve of the NLRB election, a black ILA spokesman declared that "anyone voting for the C. I. O. tomorrow is a traitor to his race." And a "Colored Citizens Committee" addressed a broadside to "My dear Longshoremen," declaring that "a vote for the C. I. O. will be a vote to drive the colored longshoremen from the highest paid jobs enjoyed by colored men of the United States and replace them by unemployed C. I. O. longshoremen and other unemployed radicals from the West Coast." The Colored Citizens Committee concluded: "It is your duty to your race, your family and your God to vote in this election and to vote for the I. L. A."[43]

These racially tinged arguments clearly carried weight among black longshoremen, but African American workers in the Crescent City were by no means uniformly hostile to the CIO. Almost all of the cotton compress workers were black, and in a 1939 representation election they voted overwhelmingly for the ILWU. In five separate elections, Logan reported, "out of 800 possible votes, the AFL received a grand total of 12." At the same time, the New Orleans teamsters, the great majority of whom were African American, voted for the CIO by a ratio of three to one, in spite of a vicious AFL campaign of intimidation. A year later black shipyard workers responded far more readily than their white counterparts to the Industrial Union of Marine and Shipbuilding Workers and may well have been the key to the CIO's victory at the Todd-Johnson Dry Dock. But in these occupations there had been little prior history of unionism among African Americans; here, for the most part, the AFL had presented black workers with the unpalatable choice of Jim Crow subordination or outright exclusion.[44]

In the final analysis, the fact that the ILA had long offered black workers a place on the waterfront at wages that were among the best available to African Americans anywhere in the South was probably a major factor in the outcome of the election. Black workers in some Gulf ports had carved out a relatively secure niche for themselves. They were, in the words of one astute observer, "the aristocrat[s] of black southern labor," and they trusted—even revered—their union because, as a Negro leader in Port Arthur, Texas, put it, "we all know that the ILA got us where we are today." In New Orleans there was a good deal less security and trust than in the Texas Gulf ports. Indeed, it may be that the Crescent City's black longshoremen did not so much choose the ILA in 1938 as they opted to "bear those ills they have [rather] than to accept others which may be worse." After all, most New Orleans longshoremen had been members of the ILA only since the spring of 1936. Until that time they had believed, according to the Urban League's Robert Francis, that "if in control [the ILA] would attempt to give the black man the bad end of the bargain." But once in place, the AFL union represented a continuation of the relationship that had existed on the riverfront since the demise of the Dock and Cotton Council, a relationship in which employer domination was mediated by aggressive but self-serving black leaders who, in the face of a chronic oversupply of labor, played an important role in determining who worked and who did not. The corruption and favoritism no doubt alienated some members; in fact, in 1940 the Hortman regime was overthrown in a major housecleaning. But the leadership was indigenous and committed to maintaining black workers' advantage in the apportioning of jobs; a core of men managed to find relatively steady employment; and an even smaller group—the heart of the union— worked regularly and made good money as foremen, derrick men, and winch drivers. These workers symbolized what a longshoreman *might* become; and even the less fortunate majority of the waterfront labor force earned a better living than was possible in the surrounding rural areas. One CIO partisan admitted that "any condition here is far better than the dire poverty they know in the Country. . . . [T]hose having jobs hang on to them for dear life"; another acknowledged that "conditions for longshoremen [here] are bad in comparison with longshoremen on the West Coast, [but] *in comparison with workers in other industries in Louisiana . . . they are excellent.*"[45]

In the wake of their bitter defeat on the riverfront, most of the ILWU organizers packed their bags and prepared to depart from the fabled city that for them had been anything but the Big Easy. In assessing the outcome of the elections, some of them could not help but dwell on the issue of race and on the ways it had affected the campaign. Paul Heide, a warehouse organizer from the Bay Area, believed that fear—of the wrath of "white bosses," of loss of employment, of the police and the local political machine—was the common thread that ran through every explanation of the ILWU's defeat. But in discussing the roots of this fear, he moved from the specific circumstances of New Orleans to the sweeping declaration that the "negro of the South is steeped in superstition and religion" and "is only one step removed from the primitive superstitions of the African jungle tribes." This line of "reasoning" was by no means limited to outsiders. Richard Dowling, a local attorney and crusader for liberalism who worked closely with the ILWU throughout the campaign, informed CIO general counsel Lee Pressman that the union's organizers had simply failed to

> understand the Southern Negro. Most people, who have not lived among them, as I have here in the South, consider that the Neg[ro] is a White man with a Black skin. That is far from truth. The Negro is a distinct species, different in viewpoint, make-up and everything else from a white man. His whole outlook on the facts of Life and Living [is] entirely different. He must be won to a cause more by emotion than logic. He can feel, but follows instinct rather than reason. They treated him as a rational man with a black skin. They missed the point entirely.

Perhaps, in their shock and disappointment, the ILWU representatives were ripe for such an explanation. Perhaps Dowling's views, which he aired at length in an informal postmortem with "the boys" on the organizing staff, influenced Heide's summation of events, which were soon disseminated among maritime workers up and down the West Coast in the *Voice of the Federation*.[46]

By their own lights, of course, the ILWU organizers were staunch opponents of racism. Hadn't the Louisiana legislature condemned them as "alien imported radicals" whose work in the state was endangering white supremacy? Hadn't Crescent City police detectives declared that they had "no business coming down to New Orleans . . . [and] telling the 'niggers' about their rights"? Indeed, they *had* dared to approach black longshoremen as fellow workers who could be moved to share their belief in the transforming power of militant interracial unionism, and they had paid a heavy price for taking that risk. But in return many—perhaps most—black longshoremen had persisted in seeing the ILWU as a "white man's organization" and as a threat to the niche African Americans had created for themselves on the riverfront. Perhaps the most painful lesson for the ILWU men, more painful than the serious physical injuries they suffered, came in the recognition that insofar as the Crescent City's black longshoremen were determined to climb out of "the pit" and see "the light," it would be mainly by their own efforts, and in ways that reflected not only their rational assessment of the opportunities available to them but their ongoing defense of racially separate organization as "a matter of pride and preference."[47]

・ ・ ・ ・ ・

On the Pacific Coast, race began to have a dramatic impact on the development of the union with the coming of World War II, when the vast expansion of production on the home front required the hiring of many new workers on the waterfront, for the first time in a generation. Many of the new workers on the docks were African Americans, especially in San Pedro and San Francisco, where the pace of black migration far exceeded that in the Pacific Northwest. When World War II began, Longshore Local 13, in San Pedro, had about twenty-five hundred members. Although its ranks had always included Mexican Americans, no African Americans found regular—or even irregular—employment on the waterfront before the war. Al Langley, who began working intermittently on the docks in 1934 and became a full member of the union in 1938, recalled that "prior to the war there wasn't one black on the [Los Angeles] waterfront." According to Langley, there were only two black families in San Pedro during the 1930s, and the men of both households worked as janitors in downtown commercial establishments. Tony Salcido, a longshoreman who grew up in Wilmington (which together with San Pedro constitutes the port of Los Angeles), remembered only two or three black families in his community during the thirties. Because Local 13 had a strong tendency to favor local residents and, above all, the family members of working longshoremen in allocating new jobs, blacks were at a great disadvantage. But their absence from the longshore workforce was not merely the product of these apparently "natural" circumstances. Langley recalled that Local 13 included in its ranks "a kind of a vigilante group of ultra-conservative[s]"—men who "had never been around blacks, or else they were southerners," and who were determined to exclude African Americans from the waterfront. On the rare occasions when black longshoremen from San Francisco sought to exercise their right as union members to visit San Pedro and work there temporarily, the local "vigilantes" made it clear that the newcomers were unwelcome. "The [black] guys" got the message, said Langley, "and they [left]."[48]

In the first six months after Pearl Harbor, there was very little work for longshoremen in San Pedro, as the almost complete elimination of commercial shipping and the breathtakingly rapid development of San Francisco as the West Coast's principal military port of embarkation left the port of Los Angeles virtually defunct. Some members of Local 13 went into the armed forces; many others went to work in the ship-yards, or to San Francisco, where they worked on the docks under the auspices of Local 10. To Langley, who spent fourteen months in "Frisco," it seemed that "every second man up there was a Pedro man." But gradually shipping returned to Los Angeles, most of its longshore-men came home, and the demand for labor soon outstripped the capac-ity of Local 13 to provide experienced men. In these circumstances, the first two black longshoremen since the founding of the local were registered in November 1942. Both were experienced dockworkers from Galveston, Texas. They were followed, in the next two years, by hundreds of other African Americans. In January 1945, according to a "rough estimate" by the local union president, the "number of Negro members in Local 13" was "between 400 and 500"—less than 10 per-cent of a workforce that had more than doubled since the war began.[49]

In important respects, the presence of African Americans altered the working relationships among the men on the waterfront. Arthur Kaunisto shipped out on a Liberty ship in 1942 and came back to San Pedro in 1944. He recalled that when he returned to the hiring hall, "I didn't recognize many people. They was mostly strangers to me"— "a lot of colored people" and "a mixture that I'd never seen before." Corky Wilson, who also shipped out in the merchant marine in 1942 and returned to the docks in 1944, made the same point, although much more crudely: "I walked in[to the hiring hall]," he recalled, "and I didn't see a white guy anywhere—all niggers, all niggers. . . . We had never had a colored guy up until then, and then . . . the place was packed with colored guys."[50]

Although Kaunisto's and Wilson's recollections overestimated the percentage of blacks among the newcomers to the waterfront, they correctly implied that the transition to a multiracial workforce was not an easy one. Longshoring had always required close cooperation in the work process and therefore a sense of affinity among the men on the job. Some work gangs had been organized on an ethnic basis, and some—in part, at least—on a family basis. Thus for many whites the sudden presence of African Americans on the docks represented an unprecedented challenge to the sense of camaraderie and mutual respect that undergirded their working relationships. Langley recalled that "most of the whites were scared of the blacks, because we never had any around here and we never associated with them. . . . When they started to come in, the whites didn't want to work with them." And the blacks themselves were "more or less clannish."[51]

The way the hiring hall operated made it easy to establish a pattern of racial separation on the job, especially during the war, when work was plentiful and labor relatively scarce. A man who was dissatisfied with his partner or his gang, for any reason, could simply "replace" himself—that is, return to the hall, from which a "replacement" would be dispatched, and then wait for the next available job. Joe Stahl recalled that "a lot of [old-timers] wouldn't work with a black guy. [They'd] turn around and call a replacement." And Walter Williams remembered that "some of the regular 'longies' . . . would say, 'I'm going to call me a damn replacement,' if they saw a black guy coming down into the hold. And they would call a replacement rather than work with us."[52]

Williams first went to work on the docks in September 1943. Before that he had been an organizer for the CIO Industrial Union Council in Los Angeles and a welder at the California Shipbuilding Company, where he served as a leader of the opposition to the flagrantly racist practices of the AFL-affiliated International Brotherhood of Boilermakers. He recalled hearing about longshoring from fellow workers, who told him it was "great work"; besides, the pay was more than he was making as a welder, and he had been attracted to the CIO in the first place because of its progressive reputation on matters of race. So he eagerly sought employment on the waterfront. But forty-five years later, he still remembered with bitterness the reception he received there.

> I wasn't on any job [long] before I was reminded that I was a temp worker. [The white longshoremen would say,] "You guys are only here temporarily. What are you gonna do when the war's over?" And I promptly told them, "I intend to be here when the war's over. I'm gonna do everything I can to stay here."
>
> It's a strain on a person to have to work in an atmosphere where he knows that people have these racist feelings. From time to time you have

Fig. 3.2. Walter Williams, longshoreman and member of ILWU Longshore Local 13, San Pedro. Credit: *Dispatcher*, International Longshore and Warehouse Union.

to listen to racist remarks and control yourself, or try to control yourself anyway. . . . You had a lot of brawls. You had a lot of fights down there . . . over name calling [that] involved racism.

When Williams finally got into a fight with a white worker who had called him a "black something," he remembered the experience—above all the release of accumulated tension—as downright exhilarating. "It was like letting off a lot of steam. . . . I mean, it was just like somebody had lifted an elephant off my shoulders," he recalled.[53]

Over time, the interaction among black, white, and Mexican American workers bred friendship and respect as well as tension. But it would appear that among many, perhaps most, of San Pedro's founding generation, there was considerable resistance to working side by side with black newcomers, letting them become full union members, and promoting those who did become full members to head a gang. The issue came to a head in 1945. After a group of temporary longshoremen refused to work under the direction of a black union member who had been dispatched as a gang boss, representatives of Local 13 and the employers reached an agreement that henceforth no man could be a gang boss until he had worked in the industry on the Pacific Coast for

113

five years. The pact also applied to winch drivers, jitney drivers, and carpenters—in other words, to the most desirable jobs on the waterfront. Since no blacks had been members of Local 13 before November 1942, the agreement effectively placed a ceiling on their job mobility, and, according to Langley, "every one of them had to come back in and work in the hold or on the dock. . . . [Matters] had come to a head because the blacks had begun to get acclimated, and they knew their stuff. . . . They wanted to be part of the industry too. But the whites weren't ready for it."[54]

In 1946 another change of policy shifted the issue from containment to exclusion. In April, Bill Lawrence, who had just completed a term as president of Local 13, reported that "work in this Port has dropped to the extent that we have approximately 700 or 800 men too many for the industry." Lawrence estimated that if the waterfront's war-inflated labor force was not reduced, the union would face a situation in which some low-seniority men would be dispatched only about once a week and others, once every two or three weeks at best. Thus the local decided that its five hundred lowest-seniority members should be "deregistered" and "placed on an unemployed list." This decision was implemented on April 22, 1946, with the understanding that "no new men [would] be taken into the industry until the above 500 men were called back." (The group would become known, in the folklore of the union, as the Unemployed 500.)[55]

The initial call for a reduction in the workforce had come from the employer representatives on the joint Labor Relations Committee in the port of Los Angeles. But the local union leadership had readily agreed with this proposal, and so had the international union. Lawrence and other Local 13 officers discussed the matter with ILWU secretary-treasurer Louis Goldblatt and Northwest Regional Director Bill Gettings and reported that "[we] acted right along the lines that [Goldblatt] suggested." Bridges himself expressed the belief that the decision was not only "clearly legal, but founded on good trade union principles."[56]

When he penned these words in September 1947, Bridges could hardly have anticipated that the decision to deregister five hundred men in San Pedro would haunt the ILWU for the next twenty-five years. The problem was that nearly half of the deregistered men were black and, even more so, that the deregistration served to eliminate about 90 percent of Local 13's black members. Since the union followed the principle of seniority in determining who would be laid off, Lawrence believed that there were no grounds for complaint; apparently, the international union agreed. But for black workers, the decision rankled, not only because so many of them were laid off, but because, as Williams recalled, some of Local 13's white members openly boasted that " 'this union was lily-white before you guys came down here, and [now] it's going to be lily-white again.' They were just arrogant about it." In the immediate aftermath of the decision, Lawrence reported that "a few disgruntled colored brothers" had discussed the matter with Rev. Clayton D. Russell, a prominent civil rights activist who had led a campaign during World War II to expand job opportunities for African Americans in Los Angeles. Lawrence complained that Russell was "attempting to make a 'Big To Do' about the entire situation," and was, moreover, "inferring that there might have been some [racial] discrimination . . . involved." Under Williams's leadership, the ranks of the "disgruntled colored brothers" expanded dramatically. They built an informal group, which they called the Afro-American Labor Protective Society, and in the summer of 1947 about sixty members of the group approached an attorney and began discussing the possibility of achieving legal redress outside the channels of the union.[57]

The number of grievants multiplied, as it became increasingly obvious that Local 13 was violating its promise that "no new men [would] be taken into the industry until the . . . 500 . . . were called back." In all probability, the local had never intended to apply this resolution literally, for it was in conflict with a number of earlier ones that had given priority to longshoremen who left the docks to join the armed forces or serve in the merchant marine during the war. As these men returned to San Pedro, they were automatically reregistered. Moreover, the union's membership committee decided that other former members should also be reregistered ahead of the Unemployed 500. Thus Local 13 members who had transferred to other ILWU locals during the war or who had taken jobs in the shipyards were given the same priority as military and merchant marine veterans when they returned. In addition, the local continued to follow a policy of making jobs and union membership available to sons and other male relatives of longshoremen, even if these family members had never worked on the docks before. Here, perhaps, was the most flagrant violation of the rights of the men on the unemployed list, for Local 13 had voted "that no man be initiated into this Union" before its unemployed members were "called back."[58]

In practice, all of this meant that between the end of April 1946 and December 31, 1949, 613 returnees were reregistered and 60 new men were registered on the Los Angeles waterfront. During the same period, as a result of death, retirement, and other factors, 901 men were eliminated from the registration list. And yet over time work on the waterfront increased, and the need for men grew accordingly. As early as January 1947 the employers suggested that all of the Unemployed 500 be reregistered, but Local 13 refused. From the time of the original deregistration through the end of 1949, only 58 of the laid-off men were reregistered.[59]

The final ingredient that cemented the black workers' conviction that racial discrimination was at the heart of the union's practice was the fact that even when men from the unemployed list were called back for reregistration, Local 13 ignored seniority and privileged whites over blacks. The first man reregistered was a white worker who had been initiated into the union on April 4, 1946, only eighteen days before his deregistration! Overall, from April 1946 until July 30, 1947, only ten men were reregistered. All of them were white, and all had less seniority than many of the black longshoremen on the unemployed list.[60]

Facing the possibility of a lawsuit, the international union pressured Local 13 to follow seniority in reregistering men from the unemployed list, and this was done beginning in October 1947. Bridges advised the local that men who had left the waterfront and were now seeking reregistration should not be given "any priority" simply because they possessed a withdrawal card. Rather, the ILWU president proposed a formula for reregistering all men in accordance with their *real* seniority (that is, the actual amount of time spent on the Los Angeles waterfront), which would, he believed, win the acceptance of "any fair-minded working stiff." But the local ignored his advice and continued favoring virtually anyone who had withdrawn from the union before April 1946 over men from the unemployed list. It was not until the Korean War and the consequent expansion of work on the docks that most of the laid-off longshoremen had their active union status restored. When 138 men were reregistered in December 1950, it appeared that the saga of the Unemployed 500 was finally at an end.[61]

But it wasn't. In May 1965, during the heyday of the Civil Rights movement, twenty-four veterans of the Unemployed 500 filed a grievance against the shipowners, demanding the restoration of their full seniority. This time the international union actively sided with the grievants and tried to pin the entire blame for the discriminatory treatment of the Unemployed 500 on the employers. But this argument was simply untenable, for the decision to deregister five hundred men was a joint one, made by the local union and the employers together. In practice, the union exercised nearly full control of hiring (including the registration of new longshoremen), and the employers simply rubber-stamped the choices made by Local 13's membership committee. The conclusion seems inescapable that insofar as there was a pattern of discrimination, the principal responsibility in this case lay with the union rather than the employers.[62]

The fate of the Unemployed 500 tells us much about the character of Local 13, which in some respects seems to have functioned like an AFL craft union in the building trades. In these unions, there was a long history of reserving new jobs for the family and friends of current members. By this mechanism, and more formal ones such as the unions' control of apprenticeships and the dispatching of work, blacks and other people of color were relentlessly excluded from various trades, and local unions retained a high degree of racial and, sometimes, ethnic homogeneity. Local 13 had its own mechanism, "sponsorship," which served to maintain and reinforce patterns of racial exclusion. To be a successful candidate for employment on the Los Angeles waterfront, one had to be sponsored by a member of Local 13. The membership decided that priority in this regard should be given to the sons of deceased members, and then to the sons and brothers of active members. Generally, the right to sponsor was based on seniority, with the first choice given to men whose membership dated from 1933. Since the union assumed that a member would be likely to sponsor a "son, brother, neighbor, or friend," this practice "naturally" served to reinforce Local 13's pattern of racial exclusion. With the exception of a small number of Mexican Americans, all of the local's most senior members were white; and in the residentially segregated and racially polarized environment of Los Angeles, a Local 13 member's "son, brother, neighbor, or friend" was likely to be white as well.[63]

In an apparent attempt to solidify this pattern further, the membership voted in July 1951 that an applicant for employment on the docks must have been "a resident of Los Angeles County for ten years." In the short run, at least, the implementation of this resolution automatically excluded African Americans who had migrated to Los Angeles during World War II, along with those who continued the flow of black migration after the war. And this exclusion occurred at a time when the port of Los Angeles was booming and the longshore labor force was expanding. George Love, who served several terms as local union president in the fifties, recalled "beat[ing] the bushes" to find prospective longshoremen in 1955, because "the work was so damn good!" "We got everybody we could get our hands on," Love said. But "everybody" included very few African Americans. Prospective members of Local 13 still required a sponsor; high-seniority whites continued to favor their "sons and brothers" and, in any case, showed no interest in sponsoring blacks; and most of the African Americans in the local did not have enough seniority to be able to sponsor anyone. Thus Tony Salcido and John Pandora, both of whom were the sons of charter members of the local, recalled few if any blacks among the men with whom they were registered. According to imprecise estimates compiled by the ILWU's international and regional staff, there were about 250 black members of Local 13 at the end of 1946 (which must have included the blacks on the unemployed list) and "over 300 Negroes" in 1964, when the Los Angeles area's black population exceeded half a million. In a southern California variation on a common pattern of ethnic succession, Mexican Americans, who had accounted for a very small percentage of the local's membership in 1934, gradually became the majority within Local 13. But African Americans were unable to make the same inroads.[64]

The African American wartime pioneers who continued working on the waterfront remained outsiders who found it difficult to move up the occupational ladder and achieve acceptance as full members of the longshore community. There were, to be sure, black workers who simply tried to get along, and virtually all of them were grateful for the superior wages, conditions, and benefits that waterfront employment provided. Salcido recalled, however, that when blacks finally accumulated enough seniority to become gang bosses, they were "invariably . . . assigned to the worst hatches on the ship," and when men practiced driving winches during their lunch hour, in the hope of moving up to a better job, "it was easier for the Anglos and the Mexicans [to do this] than it was for the blacks. I actually saw blacks get run off the [winch] handles," he said, "whereas they would tolerate myself or somebody else." He also remembered occasions when men went out on a job, and if there was a "lone black" in the gang, "it was very, very out in the open that nobody wanted . . . him" as a partner. Inevitably, the accumulation of indignities took their toll. "It's a wonder," said Williams, "that I haven't died of a stroke."[65]

The AFL defended its racially discriminatory practices by pointing to the autonomy of its affiliated unions. The ILWU leadership also respected the right of its local unions to make autonomous choices on many issues, including the question of layoffs. In 1946 Bridges had informed an "old-time member of the ILWU" that "every Local has complete autonomy in these matters unless there [are] clear . . . violations of the International Constitution." In the case of the Unemployed 500, the international believed that Local 13 had made a decision that fell within its proper jurisdiction, and it asked only that the decision be implemented in accordance with the principle of seniority. It was not until nearly twenty years after the original deregistration that the international came to recognize how blatantly the rights of its black members, and the union's own principles, had been violated.[66]

· · · · ·

How, finally, does one explain the behavior of Local 13's white rank and file toward the Unemployed 500 and toward black workers in general? Was it pure-and-simple racism? Black workers certainly saw it in those terms, and with much justification. But for the historian, it is necessary to place racism in a specific historical context and to see it in relation to a larger pattern of habits and beliefs. Local 13's white rank and file shared a history of exploitation and powerlessness in the 1920s and early 1930s, of triumph in the Big Strike and its volatile aftermath, and of increasing pride and cohesion through the remainder of the decade. For them, "solidarity" became the watchword; and their slogan, "An injury to one is an injury to all." In their relations with other maritime unions, they learned the limits of that slogan. But within their own ranks, it continued to resonate powerfully, as they demonstrated in 1939, when an arbitrator ruled that sixty-one San Pedro longshoremen who had refused to load scrap iron bound for Japan were in violation of the collective bargaining agreement and would thus be suspended without pay for a week. The ILWU refused to accept this ruling, which came at a time when the union was aggressively seeking to mobilize public opinion and its own membership in active opposition to fascism and to Japanese aggression against China in particular. Bridges argued that commitment to the union's principles could not be subordinated to "the technical wording of an agreement," and the leadership of Local 13 distributed the suspended men among a large number of work gangs. When employer representatives prevented the penalized longshoremen from working, their fellow workers walked off the job, and a partial shut-down of Los Angeles Harbor ensued.[67]

By the time World War II began, then, the San Pedro longshoremen had accumulated a common experience of suffering, struggle, and triumph that marked them as the generation of the 1930s. The Big Strike, in particular, became the foundation of their identity as union men. All potential newcomers to ILWU locals were interrogated as to their whereabouts in 1934. If there was any possibility that they had served as strikebreakers during this epic confrontation, they were simply unwelcome. Mickey Mahon, who had joined the union during World War II, recalled: "I filled out the papers and went before [the Local 13] membership committee. They were all '34 guys, good, solid men. . . . They wanted to know where I was in the '34 strike. . . . Well, I was out here, all through it. But I was living off the land—bumming water, food, panhandling, you name it, washing dishes, whatever, just to make a buck. . . . You had to prove it to [the committee]. So I had to get verification."[68]

It was easy for Mahon to win acceptance as a member of the waterfront fraternity. He readily found a sponsor in Pat Hagerty, a fellow Irish American with whom he had worked from the time he came on the docks as a casual. ("We Irish got to stick together, you know," Mahon recalled good-naturedly.) But when the war economy brought large numbers of African Americans to the waterfront, the members of Local 13 responded in ways that revealed not only a specific identity as " '34 men" but a racialized class consciousness. Blacks were not only newcomers to the docks; they had not been on the picket lines in 1934; they had not worked side by side with the '34 men thereafter to transform conditions on the waterfront. Nor had they lived, as neighbors and friends, in the working-class communities of San Pedro and Wilmington. None of this was mere coincidence. African Americans had been excluded from work on the docks for a generation or more, and at the same time white Angelenos had been ruthlessly vigilant in protecting the racial homogeneity of their neighborhoods by means of restrictive covenants, the organization of aggressively exclusionist homeowners' associations, and—when necessary—vigilante violence. Whites accepted this pattern of exclusion and enforced inequality as natural and necessary. In the longshoremen's experience of life and work, whiteness merged with class; and in spite of all the changes that had occurred in the thirties, the specific group identity of the "Lords of the Docks" remained racialized.[69]

When World War II ended and employment opportunities on the docks declined significantly, many whites wondered how they could restore the comfortable working environment that the war had disrupted, how, in other words, they could make their union "lily white" again. Black workers' low seniority, together with the conscious policies of the union leadership, led to a dramatic reduction in the number of African Americans in Local 13; and the use of sponsorship as the means of entry to the union when jobs did become available only reinforced this pattern of racial exclusion. For blacks it was further evidence of racism. To whites, however, it was entirely natural that they would want their family and friends—men who were readily identifiable as "us"—to inherit the wages and conditions the union had won. Thus George Love remembered the Unemployed 500 controversy not as a conflict between blacks and whites but as an issue of "people who lived close" versus "out-of-towners."[70]

The way black workers responded to their deregistration and subsequent exclusion from Local 13 only reinforced whites' sense that African Americans were out-of-towners who operated outside the moral code that prevailed in the ILWU. In 1947 a sizable number of blacks—nearly a hundred—turned to the legal system for restitution. They did so, apparently, after exhausting all avenues open to them within the local union. Initially they sought assistance from an attorney in filing an appeal to the international executive board; and at this stage their lawyer hastened to assure Harry Bridges that the men who had sought his assistance were "not in any sense belligerent, but rather . . . their conduct in every respect and at all times has represented the highest type [of] loyalty toward Local No. 13."[71]

Eventually, however, the members of the Unemployed 500 sought to resolve an intraunion dispute by going outside the channels of the ILWU altogether. Some filed a complaint with the National Labor Relations Board; others sued the union for damages. They did so at a time when the passage and implementation of the Taft-Hartley Act called into question the legitimacy of the very institutional mechanisms that the '34 men had fought so tenaciously to win. Decasualization, union control of hiring, and the equalization of earnings among "regular" longshoremen—this was the legacy of the Big Strike. The hiring hall, in particular, had become the cornerstone of the union. Without it, said one observer, "the ILWU would cease to exist." But in outlawing the closed shop, Taft-Hartley made the legal status of the hiring hall tenuous at best and, in general, placed the union on the defensive. Especially after the onset of a Republican presidential administration in 1953, the NLRB appeared willing to embrace the notion that any man who had worked as a casual for a day or two could claim an "employment right in the industry," thereby undermining union control of hiring. "There isn't a waterfront local union today which isn't up to its ears in sessions with its . . . lawyers," said Bridges in 1955, "seeking out a formula which will meet port manpower needs without saddling us with Taft-Hartley charges and damage suits." "Over the past years," union attorney Norman Leonard added, "dozens of charges of discrimination have been filed against both the union and the employers" because of openings in this direction created by Taft-Hartley. The union "aimed at being fair to all concerned," said Leonard, but could not permit "a few casuals, 'free riders,' or disgruntled individuals to take advantage of the situation."[72]

The case of the Unemployed 500 had arisen before the passage of the Taft-Hartley Act, but those who went to "the law" did so afterward. In the minds of Local 13's overwhelmingly white membership, the blacks who sued the ILWU were disgruntled individuals and worse. Not only were they refusing to accept the union's authority, but they appeared to be aligning themselves with hostile forces that threatened the survival of the very instruments that the '34 men had won through blood sacrifice. Thus a Portland longshoreman expressed a sentiment that must have been shared by many of his fellow unionists in San Pedro when he declared that "anyone who is taken into this union and then sues it is an enemy of mine."[73]

· · · · ·

Although white and black workers defined themselves and each other in racial terms, the saga of Local 13 was not merely a story in black and white, for from the very beginning of the union's resurgence on the Los Angeles waterfront Mexican Americans were a part of the dock labor force. At least some of them were charter members of the San Pedro longshore local and had been active participants in the Big Strike. After the strike, 2,049 men were declared eligible for registration as regular longshoremen; about 80 of them—or more than 4 percent—were Mexican Americans. Most of these men worked in lumber gangs, because labor in the lumber mills and yards adjacent to the harbor had become the province of "Mexicans." Joe Uranga, whose father had become a longshoreman in the 1920s, recalled that "they had more Mexicans working lumber than on freight because freight jobs were a little more clannish with their Swedish and Norwegian gangs that worked steady for the stevedoring companies." Mexican Americans gradually made the transition from lumber to general cargo, in the thirties, but for some time thereafter they were excluded from key jobs such as driving lifts and winches. The existence of "segregated" gangs also suggests an element of discrimination. But Tony Salcido, who joined his father, the union pioneer "Chu Chu" Salcido, plus five brothers and several cousins on the waterfront, recalled that even after gangs became mixed Mexican Americans preferred to work not only with family members but with neighbors and friends of the same ethnicity. "The normal tendency, at least . . . for me," he said, "was to seek out another Mexican-American fella, because in the first place you grew up with him, and those were your friends."[74]

As the example of the Salcido family suggests, Mexican Americans gradually became a formidable presence in Local 13. They faced, and overcame, discrimination; in fact, numerically and politically, they eventually came to dominate the local, which makes it all the more remarkable that in the reflections of white and black longshoremen, and in discussions of the union's internal life well into the 1960s, Mexican Americans were rarely part of the frame of reference. The term *race relations* meant the relations between blacks and whites, and the Los Angeles waterfront was portrayed as "lily white" until African Americans appeared during World War II.

As the competition for place and preferment on the docks became a three-way affair, the dominant white majority saw Mexicans as far less threatening than blacks. For many whites, blacks represented the negation of the status and self-image they cherished. But Mexican Americans increasingly were regarded as an *ethnic* group—akin to Scandinavians, Italians, and even perhaps "hay shakers" from the Midwest—and hence as a legitimate presence on the docks and in the union's internal life. In such circumstances, Mexican Americans apparently saw no advantage for themselves in uniting with blacks to challenge the power of the white majority. On the contrary, such an alliance may well have appeared to be a path toward marginalization and exclusion. And relative to blacks, Mexican Americans had a number of distinct advantages. In 1940 they outnumbered blacks by about three to one in the city, and their margin increased over the years. Their community base was not only larger but much more cohesive. Indeed, despite the persistence of segregation and discrimination, Los Angeles was becoming the "Mexican capital of the United States."[75]

Above all, Mexican American longshoremen were on a mission to establish an ethnic niche on the waterfront, as a means to enhance the

Fig. 3.3. Cristobal "Chu Chu" Salcido. An immigrant from Mexico, Salcido began working on the Los Angeles waterfront in 1919. Eventually, six of his sons joined him as longshoremen and members of Local 13. Credit: *Dispatcher*, International Longshore and Warehouse Union

economic security of their families and *compadres*. In what became a de facto competition with blacks and perhaps—as Neil Foley argues— a "Faustian pact with whiteness," Mexicans mixed more easily with whites and in many cases shared some of their prejudices toward African Americans. Moreover, they used their greater seniority and greater access to the levers of power within the union to take care of their own. In the process, their very success contributed to the continued marginalization of blacks.[76]

. . . . .

Finally, there is the case of Walter Williams. The conspicuous failure of white rank and filers and the Local 13 leadership to accord him the recognition as a fellow worker that he deserved suggests that the containment and exclusion of African Americans was at the heart of their agenda. When he went to work on the docks, Williams was not an out-of-towner. He had already distinguished himself as a union activist and as a spokesman for a cause with which the ILWU as an institution was closely associated. Although born in Atlanta, Georgia, he had come to Los Angeles with his mother and brother as a one-year-old and had lived in the city ever since. He graduated from Thomas Jefferson High School and attended junior college for a semester before economic necessity forced him into the job market. Eventually, he worked in a foundry, where he encountered the CIO and became an organizer for its Industrial Union Council in Los Angeles. When he went to work at Calship, he was a leader in the fight against the Jim Crow auxiliaries to which the boilermakers' union consigned its black members. In fact, he served as chairman of the Ship Yard Workers Committee for Equal Participation.[77]

Here, then, was a man with obvious leadership qualities and experience in the trade union movement. So why not welcome him into the ILWU? Bridges himself recommended that "record and background" in the union and beyond should be a factor in deciding when to reinstate men who had withdrawn from Local 13. Indeed, the ILWU soon became famous as a "haven for heretics" and often applied political criteria in selecting registrants from among the enormous number of applicants for employment on the waterfront. But from the very beginning Williams identified with the aspirations and grievances of the black workers who came to the waterfront with him. He was, in other words, one of "them." In fact, he quickly became their leading spokesman. He took the initiative in organizing members of the Unemployed 500 to protest their treatment and eventually filed an NLRB complaint against the union. But as one who had a strong commitment to unionism, he refused to sue the ILWU for damages, and he sought to persuade others to join him in that refusal. "The black fellas were split on the matter," he recalled. "I influenced quite a few of . . . the guys—in fact, most of [them]—not to sue for damages. Because the union had to survive. The idea was to get back into the industry and to help build the union."[78]

Within Local 13, however, Williams remained an outsider, a spokesman for black longshoremen but not—in any formal or widely accepted sense—for the union itself. Finally, he and two other African Americans from San Pedro journeyed north to San Francisco to present their grievances to Harry Bridges and to ask for the ILWU president's assistance in fighting racial discrimination in Local 13. He recalled that during the discussion he had said to Bridges,

> "We want to know . . . what your position is going to be. . . . If you're opposed to [discrimination], we would like some assurance that you're going to help us fight it."
>
> He looked at us, had his legs crossed at his big desk there. And he says, "I'm not going to upset Local 13 over the race question."
>
> . . . Boy, that was a shock to me. . . . So I blinked and said, "Well," I said, "[w]e're not asking you to upset the local over anything! We're expecting support from you, that's all, if the [contract] language means anything. . . . You're obliged to join with the employers to enforce the no discrimination language in the contract! That's what the contract says and that's what it means!"
>
> And he says, "Well, I'm not about to join the employers to force Local 13 to do anything." So that just about knocked the wind out of our sails. We knew what the score was. So I said, "Come on, let's get the hell out of here!"
>
> [And] Harry says, "Well, . . . I guess you guys will go to the courts now." He says, "That's what you usually do."[79]

Was this the same Harry Bridges who was lionized in the San Francisco civil rights community and whom a black minister had called a "Godsend among men"? Of course, but for his seemingly contradictory stance to make sense it must be understood in the context of the ILWU's internal politics. In San Francisco, principle, practical necessity, and political expediency merged in a way that reinforced Bridges's commitment to the union's black members. He was, of course, an outspoken advocate of the goal of racial equality. Moreover, as the war in the Pacific theater heated to the boiling point, the frenetic expansion of the San Francisco labor market meant that thousands of blacks, and many whites as well, found employment on the docks. As a result, the relatively homogeneous membership of Local 10 gave way to a more diverse and ideologically fragmented body politic. In 1947 a "right-wing" slate won control of the local and immediately developed a program that in some respects was sharply at odds with that of Bridges and his allies on the Left. Under the new regime, the *Local 10 Longshore Bulletin* began displaying an American flag on the front page, with the words "God Bless America" emblazoned under it. In an implicit rebuke to Bridges, who was becoming increasingly critical of U.S. foreign policy in the escalating cold war, the bulletin's editor announced that he had no interest in "Saudi Arabia, Karachi, Pakistan or Moscow" but was concerned only with "seeing that the brothers make a few more coconuts." Since the new leadership had the support of many whites, old-timers and newcomers alike, Bridges looked for political allies and a solid base of support among the black segment of the membership. Black longshoremen became his loyal allies in the union's internal battles, and their substantial presence in Local 10 served to reinforce its progressive reputation.[80]

In San Pedro, however, the political situation was dramatically different, and it elicited a different response from Bridges. Al Langley believed that many of San Pedro's '34 men became "rather conservative, after they [got] what they wanted." But he also acknowledged their continuing militancy on the job, to the point where "we just said, 'This is the way it is.' And that's the way it was." Moreover, the *official* culture of Local 13 remained progressive during World War II and the immediate postwar years. Even as the local's white majority was seeking to contain and marginalize African American newcomers to the waterfront, the Local 13 *Bulletin* noted with pride that "our organization . . . has always been in the forefront of every labor battle and progressive movement." It reaffirmed the local's support for the *People's World*, the Communist party newspaper on the West Coast. It even denounced race hatred and declared that "we Trade Unionists must be the vanguard in fighting against discrimination." Indeed, only a week after the deregistration of the Unemployed 500, President L. B. Thomas informed Bridges that the Local 13 leadership had been "very successful" in encouraging members to take a day off from work on May 1 in order to participate in Los Angeles's May Day parade.[81]

Compared with Local 10, though, Local 13 had always been notoriously independent and was, by reputation, "very rebellious" and "anti-Bridges." In June 1934 it had been the only major longshore local to vote in favor of a compromise proposal that would have ended the Big Strike prematurely, with many of the longshoremen's key demands unmet; and in 1960 it was the only major local that voted against the

Mechanization and Modernization Agreement (M & M), this time by a substantial margin. Bridges may have had "a chip on his shoulder" in regard to Local 13, as some of its members believed, but he also recognized the necessity of maintaining lines of communication with a local that remained vital to the ILWU and its identity.[82]

Bridges's willingness to accommodate himself to the political realities in Local 13 was no doubt strengthened by the fact that the San Pedro leadership was made up of veteran longshoremen who in many cases had fought the good fight in 1934, and certainly had done so in subsequent conflicts with the employers. However much the ILWU president objected to policies that marginalized African Americans in Local 13, he regarded the leadership and white rank and file as fellow workers with whom he had shared much travail and triumph in building the union. But the blacks in Local 13 were not only newcomers, they were a politically insignificant force; and many of them had violated the ILWU's moral code by going to "the law" and suing the union. This pattern—of blacks as an alienated and marginal element who looked for allies outside the union to resolve their grievances—continued for many years in Local 13, and there was no political payoff for Bridges in aligning himself with such a force. Thus, at the same time that he was aiding and abetting the empowerment of black longshoremen in Local 10, he turned his back on Walter Williams and the legitimate grievances of black workers in Local 13. Fortunately for him, his union's reputation as an ally of the cause of black freedom was forged in the San Francisco Bay Area's longshore and warehouse locals. From the vantage point of San Pedro, however, there was good reason to question the ILWU's claim to be "known far and wide for its progressive outlook on civil rights."[83]

· · · · ·

In 1971, in the twilight of his long career, the irrepressible Bridges confounded ILWU members by recommending that they merge with the ILA to form one national organization of longshoremen. This had been Bridges's objective in leaving the ILA in 1937. The hope then had been to topple Joe Ryan from his throne by bringing ILA members on the Atlantic and Gulf Coasts into a new, CIO-affiliated union, with the ILA's rebellious Pacific Coast district at its core. Instead, two separate and often hostile organizations of longshoremen had developed, and over the years ILWU members had taken pride in the things that separated them from their dockside rivals. On the issue of race the

ILWU faced troubles of its own, but the union's left-leaning activists could take considerable comfort from the fact that the Justice Department had recently filed suit against the ILA, the union's South Atlantic and Gulf Coast district, and thirty-seven ILA locals in Texas, charging them with racial discrimination and seeking to compel the merger of the racially separate locals in order to bring them into compliance with the Civil Rights Act of 1964.[84]

The ILA had long been known for incorporating black workers into its ranks at every level, and in most ports—New York was a conspicuous exception—the union had managed to avoid litigation or even direct criticism from civil rights organizations. But as the struggle for black equality reached its peak in the late 1960s, accusations of racial discrimination came to the fore in many cities on the South Atlantic and Gulf Coasts. The Justice Department charged that in Baltimore blacks received "less work and less desirable work than white longshoremen" and were expected to handle "dirty" cargoes such as fertilizer and fish meal. In New Orleans litigants claimed that "Negroes are virtually excluded from work as carpenters, clerks, safety men, timekeepers," and "are denied equal promotional opportunities to . . . supervisory jobs." In Houston and other Texas ports, the Justice Department took the position that racially separate locals were inherently unequal and discriminatory. But as the *Baltimore Sun* acknowledged, the issues were "not completely black and white." In fact, much of the opposition to integrating the white and Negro locals came from black longshoremen.[85]

For the remnants of the ILWU's founding generation, this stance must have awakened bitter memories of their defeat in New Orleans in 1938, when they had been convinced that Local 1419 was a company union and "Jim Crow outfit" that was inferior in every respect to the organizations they had built on the Pacific Coast. They had not been entirely wrong in this judgment, but they had failed to penetrate the veil that separated the black and white communities throughout the South and to comprehend the "interior life . . . [that] permitted black Southerners to survive and endure." Much had changed since 1938. The South had modernized; Jim Crow had been toppled; blacks were riding at the front of the bus, voting, even running for sheriff. But in this new, unevenly desegregated environment, large remnants of the "veil" remained in place, and in the 1970s the interior life of African Americans remained almost as incomprehensible to whites as it had been in the 1930s.[86]

The evolution of the Crescent City's Local 1419 from "company union" to proud and persistent symbol of "separate but equal" unionism is a vivid case in point. Tracing the development of an institution that became the nation's "largest and most powerful all Negro union" offers the opportunity to compare not only the ILA and the ILWU but the relative benefits of two dramatically different answers to the question of how the interests of black workers could best be served in the volatile racial climate of the Civil Rights era. Of course, the New Orleans and San Pedro longshore locals reflected the different environments in which they evolved. There probably would have been no basis for the development of separate but equal unionism in Los Angeles; and the extraordinary virulence and longevity of McCarthyism in the Deep South undoubtedly precluded the survival of a Communist-led dock-workers' union in New Orleans. But for all of the ILWU's proud achievements in the realm of wages, benefits, and working conditions, Local 1419 ultimately offered black workers something that Local 13 did not—a solid rock upon which to stand and a place that was dis-tinctly their own.[87]

In 1942, two years after the removal of Paul Hortman from office, labor economist Herbert Northrup had observed that "charges of cor-ruption and graft at the expense of the colored longshoremen" were once again prevalent in New Orleans. But World War II and the Cres-cent City's postwar economic boom gave the embattled local a new lease on life. In 1948 *Business Week* declared with admiration that "in four years, this city has bolstered its port to an extent that would nor-mally take 25 years." The value of waterborne commerce totaled $1 billion in 1947 (up from $287 million in 1940) and approached $2 billion in 1952, as New Orleans dramatically expanded its imports from Europe, increased the flow of sugar, bananas, bauxite, coffee, fertilizer, and coal from the Third World, and became the world's leading ex-porter of grain. Suddenly, or so it seemed, a port that had been notori-ously inefficient emerged as the nation's second busiest. Situated at the mouth of "the richest river valley on earth," the Crescent City beck-oned to new customers "from the Alleghenies to the Rockies."[88]

In this heady atmosphere, Local 1419 expanded its membership to about thirty-five hundred, developed a network of businesses that of-fered many benefits to its members, and became a significant force in local and even state politics. At the heart of these developments was Dave A. Dennis, a veteran longshoreman whose experience as a sea-man and wartime shipyard worker in California had taken him well

Fig. 3.4. Members of ILWU Warehouse Local 2-7 during World War II. Although the ILWU campaign to organize New Orleans longshoremen ended in failure, the union succeeded in organizing an interracial warehouse local of men and women in the Crescent City. Credit: *Dispatcher*, International Longshore and Warehouse Union

beyond the insular precincts of the Crescent City's riverfront. Dennis was elected president of the local in 1948, and according to the *Louisiana Weekly*, he quickly emerged as "a powerful and nationally prominent civic and political figure." He claimed that more than three-fourths of the local's members were registered voters, and insofar as any African American citizen could, he negotiated on behalf of his constituents with some of the most powerful white politicians in the state. He also served as cochairman of the local NAACP's annual membership drive, played an active role in the Louisiana State Federation of Labor, and became an international vice-president of the ILA. During his presidency, Local 1419 employed twelve full-time officials and retained the services of a law firm, a pharmacist, and five physicians. The Dennis administration also invested in a life insurance company, a funeral home, and a recreation center that—in the context of the segregated South—it promised to make available to black "Mardi Gras visitors and summer tourists" as well as to its members. According to the magazine *Color*, Dennis was "looking forward to the day when Local 1419 will have its own chain of grocery stores, a bank and a clothing store to outfit the members and their families." "No other Negro labor local in the world can compare with th[is] outstanding record."[89]

In a sharp break with recent precedent, Local 1419 also became much more aggressive in defending the rights of black workers on the job. In 1953 employer spokesman Charles Harrington complained that because longshoremen were "so jumpy" and "quick on the trigger," "work stoppages . . . have hurt the port, and have cost us lots of business." He expressed the hope that in the future the unions "would sit more around the conference table, rather than knocking off a ship." On occasion, black longshoremen even struck over grievances that were not directly related to the job. In April 1952, for example, they shut down the riverfront after police arrested two of their fellow workers. "The word went down the levee that no ships would work that night," Harrington recalled, because "the police were pushing their men around." In this instance, members of the white longshoremen's union joined the protest and refused to report for work. When asked to explain this example of interracial solidarity, the president of the white local replied, "We don't want race prejudice or race riots and these are averted by the men working together."[90]

In spite of these impressive achievements, allegations of corruption continued to shadow Local 1419 and its president. Unlike Hortman, Dennis was free of the taint of "company-ism," but like Hortman his leadership style was imperious and self-aggrandizing. He drove a baby blue Cadillac, owned five rental properties in New Orleans and a house on the Gulf Coast, and even operated a detective agency while drawing a full-time salary from the local union. A larger-than-life figure with a reputation as a hothead, he carried a gun in his briefcase and showed little disposition to tolerate dissent in the ranks. In June 1953 a U.S. Senate committee charged with investigating "waterfront racketeering and port security" held hearings in New Orleans and focused on the "fabulous wealth" the Dennis administration had accumulated. The Republican senators who conducted the hearings made it clear that they were opposed to the 5 percent deduction from longshoremen's wages, that they believed there were "leeches at work" in Local 1419, and that Dennis was guilty of using the union's bulging treasury as his private preserve. They charged, specifically, that the union had failed to account for $287,000 of the "percentage" money collected during Dennis's tenure in office, and that the local president had misappropriated more than $12,000 in union funds to purchase property for himself and his family. Although the *Louisiana Weekly* argued that Local 1419 had made "amazing progress politically and financially" under Dennis and called on the black community to "give him our fullest moral support in this hour of need," the Senate investigation triggered a rank-and-file rebellion in the local that brought an end to Dennis's meteoric career. To stave off impeachment proceedings, he asked for a leave of absence from the presidency in July, and the ILA's South Atlantic and Gulf Coast district appointed a committee of eight trustees to oversee the affairs of the local. In August the Orleans Parish district attorney formally charged Dennis with embezzling union funds for his personal use. He was acquitted, but he never again played an active role in the affairs of Local 1419. Instead, he became a Baptist minister and eventually presided over two churches.[91]

When Dennis's term as president expired in 1954, he was succeeded not by one of the rebels who had driven him from office but by his right-hand man, Clarence "Chink" Henry. Under Henry's leadership, the union remained a powerful force on the waterfront and in the community. In fact, by virtue of their close ties to Mayor deLesseps Morrison, Henry and Local 1419 operative Avery Alexander allegedly were among the "three most powerful black leaders in New Orleans." (The third member of the triumvirate, Rev. Abraham Lincoln Davis, was, according to the mayor's political rivals, "a Baptist preacher that didn't preach nothing but Morrison.") When the local built a $500,000 office building and meeting hall in 1959, Mayor Morrison joined Henry in addressing a crowd of ten thousand at the opening ceremonies. But the Henry administration quietly sold off some of the local's business operations and instead negotiated an impressive array of welfare benefits through the more conventional channels of collective bargaining. The 1956 contract raised the base wage rate to $2.60 per hour and provided for a pension, welfare, and vacation plan at the employers' expense. Eligible employees received group life insurance, disability payments, and "liberal medical insurance benefits" for longshoremen and their dependents.[92]

Like the union insurgency of the 1930s, the Civil Rights movement of the 1950s and 1960s represented both promise and peril for Local 1419. Naturally, its leaders identified with the cause of civil rights, especially with the local branch of the NAACP, and they became aggressively involved in voter registration campaigns in New Orleans and throughout Louisiana. Dennis served as the first president of the Orleans Parish Progressive Voters League, a broadly based intraracial coalition founded in 1949. He resigned from the citywide organization in 1950 and formed the Crescent City Independent Voters League, which served as the political arm of Local 1419 and was controlled entirely by longshoremen. According to Dennis and his allies, Democratic presidential candidate Adlai Stevenson, who lost the national election to Dwight Eisenhower in 1952, carried Louisiana by a narrow margin only because the leadership of Local 1419 had been successful in mobilizing black voters on his behalf. Although the longshoremen may have claimed too much credit for themselves, the *Louisiana Weekly* hailed the statewide voter registration campaign spearheaded by Dennis as a "Herculean effort"; and Perry Howard, a longtime scholarly analyst of Louisiana politics at Louisiana State University, concluded that "the Negro vote (over 100,000 strong) proved the deciding factor in giving the Democrats a majority" in the state. But while they looked to Stevenson and the national Democratic party to reward their loyalty by supporting the struggle for black equality, the leaders of Local 1419 continued to maintain a close and mutually beneficial relationship with Mayor Morrison, even though he felt compelled to swear undying allegiance to segregation. It was a balancing act characteristic of the larger stance of Local 1419 and other black ILA locals in the Gulf— aggressively advocating black interests while accommodating themselves to the power of white elites and the realities of segregation.[93]

As the Civil Rights movement entered a more aggressively integrationist phase in the wake of the *Brown* decision and the Montgomery bus boycott, the ILA's commitment to racial separation appeared increasingly anomalous. Speaking at the AFL-CIO convention in 1959, A. Philip Randolph, the president of the Brotherhood of Sleeping Car Porters, called upon black advocates of separate but equal unionism to abandon their comfortable niche and embrace the cause of integration. Randolph, the nation's leading black trade unionist, acknowledged that "there are a few racially segregated local unions that are demanded and maintained by their Negro officials and members," but, he argued, such unions were "morally unjustifiable and indefensible" no matter who supported them. "I don't believe that . . . Negro members of a union have a right to maintain a Jim Crow local," he declared. AFL-CIO president George Meany responded by defending the right of black unionists to "think for themselves" and to choose racial separation in the process. The NAACP quickly weighed in on Randolph's side of the debate. Speaking for the association, John Morsell denied that Negro unionists were "entitled to special consideration" and stated unequivocally that if the black unionist "is for segregation, I am against him."[94]

In spite of the weight of this criticism, the Crescent City's black longshoremen stayed their separate course and remained an integral part of the African American community. In the context of the "Freedom Now" era, they may have appeared conservative to those who unreservedly embraced the goal of integration and the tactics of direct action. But the struggle for black equality was a multifaceted phenomenon, and the longshoremen were by no means out of step with its essential characteristics and goals. Insofar as it sought to dismantle the citadels of segregation and racist exclusion, the Civil Rights movement *was* integrationist. But at times it was also narrowly group centered and opportunistic, as many black leaders continued to operate on the premise that "we must 'play the game' just as others have played it" and sought concessions for themselves and their constituents within the framework of white control of the political and economic system. And in Louisiana, at least, some of the characteristic impulses and themes of Black Power became evident at a surprisingly early stage of the Civil Rights movement's development. In New Orleans the local chapter of the Congress of Racial Equality (CORE), which had embodied the racially inclusive spirit of "Freedom Now," suddenly changed direction in 1962 and expelled its white members on the grounds that uninhibited interracial fraternization was violating the mores of the Crescent City's African American community and threatening to isolate CORE from its natural base. Farther north, in the paper mill town of Bogalusa, segregationist violence sparked the formation of the all-black Deacons for Defense and Justice in February 1965. (A precursor of the Bogalusa group had emerged in Jonesboro in July 1964.) The gun-toting Deacons represented a sharp break with the movement's ethos of nonviolence. Together with the leadership of New Orleans CORE, they appeared to prefigure a shift "from integration to black nationalism."[95]

In important respects, Local 1419 represented each of the salient characteristics of the larger struggle for black equality. Its members had long been actively committed to enhancing black access to the resources of American society; its leaders continued their opportunistic practice of brokering deals with mayors and legislators, including those who felt obliged to reaffirm their belief in white supremacy. Above all, the union embodied the black community's enduring preference for autonomous, and racially separate, organization.

Significantly, two of New Orleans CORE's pioneering activists had close ties with Local 1419. Jerome Smith was the son of a merchant seaman and the grandson of a longshoreman. He remembered that as a child he had been surrounded by "all these men with these huge hands. I would stand with my grandfather, I could see all these big hands, these strong men, all these hands [would] run up and they would grab me." In the spring of 1960, Smith dropped out of Southern University in Baton Rouge and returned to New Orleans to join those "big hands" on the riverfront. He dreamed of "integrating the black and white longshoremen's unions," but also of strengthening Local 1419 as an "autonomous and controlling force on the docks." Soon, however, he was "bitten by this other bug" and became a Freedom Rider. Rudy Lombard was another son of the black working class. His father was a hospital orderly, and his mother a domestic. After attending the University of Michigan for a year, he returned to New Orleans and enrolled at Xavier University. While in college he worked as a longshoreman and even hoped to make the union his career. But like Smith, his "ambitions got bigger. I wanted to turn the whole country upside down," he recalled.

Both men left the riverfront to work full-time in the Civil Rights movement. However, both regarded Local 1419 not as a remnant of segregation but as a solid foundation from which to launch the campaign for "Freedom Now."[96] And with good reason. The local had played a central role in Black New Orleans's postwar political mobilization, but its achievements in its own bailiwick were even more impressive. Once derided as a company union—more famous for strikebreaking than striking—Local 1419 became a formidable player on the riverfront. Again and again in the postwar years its members demonstrated their capacity to "paralyze" shipping in the port. When they went on strike in 1962, the *Times-Picayune* claimed it was "the sixth in less than ten years." "Chink" Henry may have been engaging in self-promotional hyperbole when he declared that ILA officials in the Crescent City had negotiated "the best agreement for longshoremen anywhere in the country," but he was not far off the mark. And in comparison with other black workers in the labor markets of New Orleans and its hinterland, longshoremen were fortunate indeed. During

the postwar years, Louisiana remained one of the nation's least indus-
trialized states. Its number of manufacturing jobs declined during the
1950s, while mechanization reduced the farm population by more than
three hundred thousand. Many displaced farmers headed north; others
migrated to New Orleans and accentuated its character as a booming
city with a burgeoning black "underclass."

African Americans continued to account for about one-third of the
Crescent City's population but made up 0.015 percent of the phone
company's workforce and 0.054 percent of the workers in city government. There were no black firemen or bus drivers, and only a handful
of black policemen, who were assigned to plainclothes units and kept
well away from white citizens. In the private sector, craft unions of
skilled workers continued to bar African Americans from apprenticeships, and in shipbuilding and repair their numbers declined. Meanwhile, with the gains they had made during and especially after World
War II, the Crescent City's longshoremen were becoming an "aristocracy" of black labor. Significantly, one of the few home builders willing
to invest in the development of a "middle-class Negro market" in the
city found that "most of his buyers [were] longshoremen and postal
clerks" who earned between $60 and $150 a week and purchased
houses whose prices ranged from $10,000 to $12,500.[97]

But was the continuing pattern of separate but equal unionism a
necessary factor in the achievement of these gains, and were the relations between black and white longshoremen really equal? Although
it is difficult to disentangle necessity from pride and preference, it is
clear that the preference for racial separation was at least as strong
among blacks as it was among whites. Southern custom did not pre-
clude interracial unionism, but it had conditioned both blacks and
whites to expect racial separation where matters of voluntary association were concerned. And because unions were social as well as economic organizations, because Local 1419 was deeply rooted in the
Crescent City's African American community, the impulse toward separation remained strong on both sides. On the job, matters were more
complex, and the inertial weight of white supremacy was greater.
Whites continued to monopolize the clerks' and checkers' jobs and to
predominate among the foremen. But by an informal arrangement
blacks had conceded the clerks' and checkers' positions to whites as
long as whites allowed blacks to monopolize the lower-paying but much
more numerous freight-handlers' jobs. Blacks, moreover, made up
three-fourths of the longshore labor force, and they were steadily mov-

ing into the more desirable jobs on deck. Even when foremen wanted to favor whites over blacks, they were finding it increasingly difficult to do so, because the foreman's own position depended on the productivity of his gang and black workers would not "produce" when they believed they were being discriminated against. As an employer representative acknowledged, "It used to be that a white man could come out on the docks and get a deck job. Now the hold men would not stand for it. . . . The senior black men coming out of the hold insist that they get the deck jobs." By 1965, at nine New Orleans stevedoring companies, blacks constituted 61.4 percent of the forklift drivers, 69.5 percent of the winch men, and 94 percent of the derrick men.[98]

In spite of these gains, some black workers continued to press charges of discrimination against the New Orleans Steamship Association, and in 1971 a few filed suit to compel a merging of the black and white longshore locals. But the latter act, in particular, went against the grain of dockworkers' sentiments, for although they worked in integrated gangs on the riverfront, longshoremen continued to live and socialize in a world characterized by racial separation. Indeed, in important respects, their larger environment was becoming more segregated, not less, during the Age of Integration. Unlike many southern cities, New Orleans had not had rigidly segregated residential patterns during the first half of the twentieth century. The civil rights leader Andrew Young, who was born in the Crescent City in 1932, recalled his neighborhood as "a real jambalaya"—a racial and ethnic stew in which Irish, German, Italian, and Cajun whites lived in close proximity to blacks. But a more sharply differentiated pattern emerged after World War II, as the federal and municipal governments financed the development of racially separate public housing projects, the momentum of "massive resistance" impelled white politicians to reinforce the ramparts of white supremacy, and the growing reality of "white flight" darkened the demographic landscape. All of these factors made the city's African American citizens more aware of the separate dimensions of their experience and interests. And because the struggle for integration precipitated an ugly and unrelenting white backlash, more and more blacks began to question whether they wanted to mix with people who feared and despised them. This was especially true in relation to school desegregation, which was implemented in the late 1960s and early 1970s. For blacks in Louisiana, writes historian Adam Fairclough, "school integration was a massive disappointment, a painful, bewildering, and sometimes frightening experience that caused widespread disillusionment. . . . Throughout the state, . . . the creation of unitary school systems entailed the closure of black schools, the demotion of black principals, and the dismissal of black teachers." The treatment of black principals was especially humiliating. Between 1966 and 1971, their number declined from 513 to 362, whereas the number of white principals increased from 941 to 1,057. Although black principals "were *never* assigned to majority-white schools, white principals . . . were often placed in charge of majority-black and even all-black schools."[99]

In this context, the main question confronting black dockworkers in New Orleans and other South Atlantic and Gulf ports was, "How . . . can we survive?" Integration may have sounded good in principle, but most black longshoremen feared that the merging of the Negro and white locals would mean the displacement of black union leaders by whites and—at a time when mechanization was eroding the foundations of waterfront employment—that blacks' jobs would be placed at even greater risk. Local 1419 had its critics, to be sure; they accused its aging leaders of corruption and class collaboration. But for years these leaders had also demonstrated the capacity to work in close tandem with white longshoremen *and* to safeguard the separate interests of "the race." Thus the members of Local 1419 hung on to their creation, until a 1982 federal court order compelled them to merge with the white local.[100]

Meanwhile, in San Pedro, Walter Williams paused to reflect on a waterfront career that had begun during World War II and lasted into the 1980s. Although he and other black longshoremen in the port of Los Angeles bitterly resented the racism that had kept their numbers small and denied them access to the best jobs on the docks, they also recognized that they had achieved a level of economic status and security that was all too rare among black workers, for the ILWU was a union that "delivered the goods"; in vitally important respects its policies benefited its entire membership. The "low-man-out" system of job rotation through the hiring hall ensured that all longshoremen, no matter what their race or nationality, achieved equal access to work and relatively equal earnings, and the union won working conditions on the docks that remained the envy of other workers and the standard against which they judged their own conditions. Williams readily acknowledged this reality in oral history interviews conducted by the local and international unions in the mid- and late 1980s. He praised the ILWU for "being the kind of union it has been . . . because I don't know of any unions anywhere that can provide [their members] with the kind of working conditions, [and] the type of welfare coverage that we have." Being a longshoreman, he reflected, "was an experience I don't think I'd trade for anything."[101]

Had he looked eastward to New Orleans, Williams would have found that the Crescent City was the only major port in the nation that continued to dispatch jobs to longshoremen through an employer-controlled hiring hall; he would also have noted a wider disparity in the incomes of dockworkers than the ILWU's system of job rotation allowed. But no doubt he would have acknowledged too that African American longshoremen in the Crescent City had constructed a "home" they could call their own, that they had not only achieved equal standing with their white counterparts but had compelled white longshoremen to adjust to African Americans' majority status and, sometimes at least, to follow their lead. In comparison, the black members of Local 13 not only remained a minority but were relegated to the margins of an organization they had never been allowed to call their own.[102]

. . . . .

In the aftermath of the *Brown* decision, W.E.B. Du Bois had asserted that the historic Supreme Court ruling presented blacks with a "cruel dilemma." From his voluntary exile in Africa, he expressed the belief that African Americans "must eventually surrender race solidarity and the idea of American Negro culture to the concept of world humanity, above race and nation." Few blacks in the United States were willing to follow such a course—certainly not on the New Orleans waterfront, where race solidarity had remained the watchword among Negro dockworkers for generations, even in the face of sharp criticism from leading black integrationists in the trade union movement and the civil rights community. But, lest we forget, white longshoremen in the City of Angels also opted for "race solidarity," sometimes in crudely chauvinistic ways, as when—at the end of World War II—they bragged about making their union "lily white" again. During the Civil Rights era that unfolded over the next two decades, however, the hideous excesses of segregation's violent defenders and the moral idealism of the Civil Rights movement made such candid celebrations of white supremacy appear unsavory and anachronistic. Arguably, the movement's expanding presence made the great majority of Americans—white as well as black—more conscious of race, but quite unwittingly it also encouraged whites to represent themselves as "race-free" even as they defended privileges that were based on race. As African Americans demanded access to "more than a hamburger" and turned the centuries-old stain of blackness into a badge of pride, many whites became all the more inclined to "naturalize" their own racial identity and to speak the language of color blindness. Thus San Pedro longshoreman and Local 13 president George Love recalled the Unemployed 500 controversy not as a conflict between blacks and whites but as an issue of "people who lived close" versus "out-of-towners." "I never considered it racial," Love said in 1989. Rather, "it was a move . . . to go back to what [Local 13 had] always done. That to be a longshoreman, . . . number one, you [had to] be local and usually a relative." From Love's perspective, "you were some kind of guy if you *didn't* go to bat for your own family. And if you didn't have any sons or brothers, then [you'd] go for [your] fellow member's sons and brothers. That's what made it a good union."[103]

That is also what excluded African Americans from the ranks of Local 13 and served to keep them on the margins after they were admitted. But to Love and, apparently, many of his fellow longshoremen in Los Angeles, it was not "racial"; it was "natural." By such reasoning white racial privilege may not have remained unassailable, but for millions of white Americans it became invisible and hence deniable.[104]

PART TWO

STEELWORKERS

Ethnicity and Race in Steel's Nonunion Era

FOR NEARLY HALF A CENTURY, from the legendary Homestead Strike of 1892 until the United States Steel Corporation's recognition of the CIO in 1937, the iron and steel industry remained the nation's preeminent symbol of the open shop. The power of the masters of steel was legendary. They employed more than half a million men (and a few thousand women), and in doing so created the most heterogeneous and internally stratified workforce in American industry. There were 54 different "races" and nationalities employed at the Homestead Works of Carnegie Steel in 1919—including 5 "Arabians," 3 Belgians, 1 Brazilian, 6 "Hollanders," 4 Norwegians, 18 Puerto Ricans, and 53 Turks. But in spite of its extraordinary diversity, the bulk of the steel labor force was concentrated in three main groupings, each of which occupied a distinct layer in the mills' occupational hierarchy. At the top, filling the skilled ranks, were the dwindling numbers of old-stock Americans, along with tens of thousands of old immigrants: the Germans and the Irish, plus the English, Scots, and Welsh who in the language of the mills were lumped together as "Johnny Bulls." In the middle tier, by the hundreds of thousands, were the new immigrants from rural southern and eastern Europe. And at the bottom were black migrants from the American South who came in small numbers at first but established a significant presence during World War I and its aftermath. In confronting this heterogeneous mass of humanity, the employers used the tried and true methods of divide and rule to buttress their own position and to reinforce the powerlessness of those who labored in their vast domain.[1]

Clearly, there was no united working class in steel. Trade unionism's bitter defeats, especially in the Great Steel Strike of 1919, confirmed not only the power of capital but the deep contradictions among the workers. But why were workers divided? Were the fissures in their own ranks only a reflection of the employers' malice and power, or did they also reflect impulses toward fragmentation that operated independently of capital? How much, even in the dictatorship of steel, can we deny agency to workers in sustaining the hierarchies and rivalries that became so integral to their lives? The tendency of scholars has been to emphasize—and sometimes reify—the power of capital; and yet even in steel's company towns, where the ironclad regimen of the mills prevailed, workers gradually developed rich networks of cultural, fraternal, and religious life that served as vivid testaments to their own creativity. Likewise, within the mills, they helped to shape the occupational fault lines that further differentiated them from each other. Their own sense of a distinct and separate place in this hierarchy is evident in the comment of a skilled man who acknowledged that "we workers have our classes the same as other people."[2]

This chapter will examine the experience of African Americans and of the new immigrants from eastern and southern Europe during the long nonunion era. The Hunkies—a term that applied indiscriminately not only to Hungarians but also to Poles, Slovaks, Serbs, Croats, Italians, and other nationalities—were, in a very real sense, "inbetween" people. In steel's occupational ladder, they became the semiskilled component, below the skilled, old immigrants but above the unskilled blacks. In the larger society as well as in the mills, they were racially in between—not colored, to be sure, but not yet white either. Gradually, they became more American and thus ever more sensitive to the racial stereotypes and slurs that prevented them from reaping the benefits of citizenship, on the job and in the larger society. Ironically, becoming more American meant not only combating the ethnic stereotypes that marked them as Hunkies but appropriating the "system of signs, symbols, and layered racial codes" that marked blacks as inferior beings. In a very real sense, they ceased being Hunkies by becoming white.[3]

Over time, the immigrants, old and new, did achieve security for themselves and a measure of upward mobility as well. For the Germans and the Johnny Bulls, the path was relatively smooth. For the Irish, it was much rockier, but as a people the Irish ultimately prospered in their own distinctive ways. For the Hunkies, the material gains were less impressive but nonetheless real. Once derided as unassimilable, they became American and white and laid claim to the fruits thereof. That left African Americans as the "last of the immigrants." Or did it? In important—indeed, fundamental—respects, the answer is no. The ambiguous reality of racial indeterminacy did not apply to most African Americans; racially speaking, they were in no sense in between. Moreover, their experience in the steel industry confirms an essential truth of American history that goes directly against the grain of American myth, for by and large they did not experience incremental mobility in the same ways their fellow workers did. Not only were they locked into the lowest-paying and most hazardous jobs, but even where they had established enclaves of skilled and semiskilled employment, they tended to lose these advantaged positions over time. Their experience suggests that relative to the immigrants with whom they are often compared, African Americans lived history differently and, as one scholar has written, "in reverse."[4] How significant a factor was the agency of white workers, and their in-between predecessors, in creating and deepening patterns of ethnic segmentation and racial inequality in the mills and the communities that developed in their long shadow? What role did organized labor, and the new unionism of the CIO in particular, play in mediating interracial competition and institutionalizing racially based inequality? And what larger forces—from the power of capital to the unsteady but increasingly interventionist hand of the liberal state—constrained working people as they "made" themselves and their own history under conditions not of their own choosing? These are the central questions that part 2 will explore, with steel as the arena.

· · · · ·

The steel industry epitomized the meaning of the term *economy of scale*. Virtually everything in steel was huge—the amount of capital required to enter the business, the mills' physical plant, the instruments of production, and the size of the labor force. In the industry's heyday, contemporaries were overawed by the almost magical power emanating from the mills. Journalist J. H. Bridge declared that at the Homestead Works of U.S. Steel, "wonders are performed as amazing as those of the Arabian Nights. Here machines endowed with the strength of a hundred giants move obedient to a touch, opening furnace doors and lifting out of the glowing flames enormous slabs of white hot steel, much as a child would pick up a match box from the table." For industrial relations specialist John A. Fitch, it was "the very size of things [that] grips the mind with an overwhelming sense of power. Blast furnaces, eighty, ninety, one hundred feet tall, gaunt and insatiable, are continually gaping to admit ton after ton of ore, fuel, and stone. Bessemer converters dazzle the eye with their leaping flames. Steel ingots at white heat, weighing thousands of pounds, are carried from place to place and tossed about like toys." Indeed, steel was a fitting symbol of

147

the power and majesty of American capitalism. By the end of the 1890s, one American company, Carnegie Steel, was outproducing the entire British steel industry; and the formation of the United States Steel Corporation in 1901, with Carnegie Steel as the jewel in the crown, brought 213 manufacturing plants and transportation companies, 41 mines, nearly 1,000 miles of railroad, and a lake fleet of 112 vessels under one corporate umbrella. Capitalized at $1.4 billion, U.S. Steel was an enterprise that "far exceeded the imaginations of most contemporary citizens."[5]

For all of its size, however, steel was hardly representative of the Fordist technology that characterized the giants of the second industrial revolution. With its intricate assembly-line techniques and meticulously rationalized production, the auto industry became the preeminent symbol of the new industrial order. Increasingly, steel seemed archaic by comparison. Whereas everything in auto production appeared to be closely interconnected, a steel mill remained a vast network of semifeudal principalities. To be sure, from the coke ovens, where coal became coke; to the blast furnace, where coke, limestone, and iron ore became molten iron; to the majestic open hearth, where iron became steel; to the rolling and finishing mills, where red-hot ingots became rolls, coils, plates, and bars—everything *was* connected, most visibly by an internal railroad system. And yet each department in the mill appeared to be a separate world.[6]

The industry's internal labor market was equally balkanized. In auto the vast majority of workers were semiskilled and largely interchangeable. There were hundreds of job categories, but the occupational structure was essentially horizontal. It followed the assembly line, laterally.[7] In steel, however, the lines were mainly vertical. There were innumerable job ladders, with unskilled laborers at the bottom, highly skilled blowers, melters, pourers, and rollers at the top, and a bewildering array of semiskilled categories in between. Since steel's greatest expansion occurred during the four decades of the new immigration from southern and eastern Europe, its labor force became as diverse and segmented as the industry's occupational ladders. Initially, individuals came and found work in Pittsburgh, Aliquippa, Cleveland, Gary, and other steel towns in a geographical belt that stretched from Pennsylvania through Ohio to the Calumet region of Chicago and northwest Indiana. Then, the first wave of immigrants sent money and words of encouragement home, inducing family and friends to follow from villages in Galicia,

Bohemia, Croatia, Calabria, and a thousand other points of origin in the agricultural regions of southern and eastern Europe.[8]

This pattern of chain migration led right into the mills. Fitch, the keenest contemporary observer of the steel industry, characterized its labor force as "cleft horizontally into two great divisions." The upper stratum, he wrote, "includes what is known in mill parlance as the 'English-speaking' men; the lower contains the 'Hunkies' or 'Ginnies.' " Not that an "English-speaking" worker necessarily spoke English; nor was a Hunky necessarily Hungarian. A German or a Scandinavian could rank among the English-speaking men, whereas anyone from southern or eastern Europe was a Hunky. The jobs that were "too damned dirty and too damned hot for a 'white' man" became Hunky jobs, often at a very high cost to those who performed them. On the basis of news accounts from Steelton, Pennsylvania, historian John Bodnar provides a memorable portrait of the "grimness of life in the mills" for the new immigrants.

> Men lost arms, legs, and "were burned to a cinder." In 1902 five "Austrians"— Jurovic, Marovoich, Gatis, Muza, and Radjanovic—were burned to death "in a horrible manner" when molten metal from the open hearth poured on them. In 1906 Anton Picjac, a boy of sixteen, fell through the top of a gas oven and was cremated. The story was repeated frequently and became a way of life [and death]. Immigrants, working in the most dangerous jobs, were continually killed. The list of victims in 1907 speaks for itself: Tesak, Pajolic, Stifko, Knukle, Termer, Petruti, Pierce, Oconicke, Ukelic, Krameric, Szep, Peffer, Gross, Susic, Restoff, Trajbarico, Polanec, Turnbaugh, and Pugar.[9]

Sometimes the survivors' stories were almost as grim as the accounts of those who perished. Andrew Antonik, a Hungarian immigrant who had left a wife and five children behind when he came to America, worked at the Homestead Works of Carnegie Steel and ran a skull-cracker, a machine that broke up scrap metal so that it could be melted more easily. When he dropped the skull-cracker's iron ball on the scrap, metal would fly in all directions. One night, after working a twenty-four-hour turn the previous day, Antonik was hit by a piece of scrap weighing four to five hundred pounds; his leg was crushed and had to be amputated. Almost a year after the accident an investigator for the Pittsburgh Survey found him

149

sitting in his landlady's kitchen rocking her baby. That was Antonik's job now, to take care of his landlady's children in part payment for his board; that was all he was good for yet, for he had only a leg and a stump. He had been paid $150 by the company; of this he had sent $50 to his wife in Hungary and had used the balance to pay his board since he had left the hospital. Now nothing remained. . . .

He looked at the future blankly, helplessly. He had at first planned to bring his family here, but now he could not get the money for that. Nor could he go back to them. He would be more useless, more helpless, on a farm than here. The only solution Antonik could see . . . was for him and his family to remain indefinitely apart, he working at whatever poor job and at whatever low wage he could get, and sending a little to Hungary to help out, his wife to continue working on a farm at 12 or 15 cents a day.[10]

In the segmented world of steel, the English-speaking men showed little sympathy for the plight of a Hunky like Andrew Antonik. On the contrary, the gap between the two groups often seemed unbridgeable. The skilled, the native-born, and the old immigrants were "Americans" and "white men." Often they identified with shopkeepers, white-collar employees, and even mill management, rather than with their new immigrant fellow workers, who were stereotyped as "foreigners" and were somehow not yet "white." Over time, as the English-speaking men consolidated their hold on skilled employment in the mills, skill itself—as an occupational qualification and badge of status—became identified as American and white. Thus in Johnstown, Pennsylvania, the few new immigrants who achieved skilled jobs chose to remain aloof from their ethnic group; in the recollection of their fellow immigrants, they were anomalies, "neither here nor there." Likewise, in Chicago, long after a Mexican immigrant had become a skilled craftsman, he reported that "sometimes even now when people see that I am a machinist, they say to me, 'You are not Mexican.' "[11]

These highly charged signifiers of nationality, race, and status had potent implications not only for unionism in steel but for the development of the American working class. They deepened intraclass fault lines and gave some workers a vested material and psychological interest in separating themselves from others. A congressionally sanctioned survey reported in 1911 that while "immigrants of the [English, German, and Welsh] races are treated by natives on terms of equality[,] . . . the line drawn between the natives and the southern and eastern European races is very decided." Those who were unable to maintain

Fig. 4.1. Steelworkers, Hubbard Furnace (Youngstown area), early twentieth century. Credit: Youngstown Sheet and Tube Audiovisual Archives, Youngstown Historical Center of Industry and Labor / Ohio Historical Society

the appropriate physical distance sometimes felt compelled to redraw the psychological line all the more sharply. "Here I am with these Hunkies," a Scotch-Irish furnace boss complained. "They don't seem like men to me hardly." Likewise, a skilled heater found the newcomers "filthy in their personal habits and the very idea of working with them . . . repugnant to any man who wants to retain his self-respect." Another skilled worker distanced himself from the hardships a new immigrant had encountered in the mill with the declaration that "he was only a Hunky, and no decent American would have anything to do with him."[12]

In the face of an unfamiliar, and sometimes terrifying, environment, the newcomers naturally preferred to work with those who understood their language, shared their culture, and could help shield them from the sting of nativist prejudice. For their own purposes, the companies often encouraged ethnic segregation on the job, relying on strategically located intermediaries in the immigrant communities to provide a steady stream of reliable workers, and ultimately allowing supervisors and gang leaders from various nationality groups to hire their own countrymen.[13] But immigrants also remembered their own role in shaping these patterns. In Aliquippa a second-generation Slovak worker recalled that "it was only natural for an old-timer to favor his own kind.

151

If he was a Croatian and he saw a nice strong young Croatian boy that he kind of liked, he would try to get him [a job] as his helper. . . . Maybe he even had a daughter and wanted him to marry his daughter." And in Pittsburgh, a Polish immigrant remembered, "if a Russian got his job in a shear department, . . . he's looking for a buddy, a Russian buddy. He's not going to look for a Croatian buddy. And if he sees the boss looking for a man he says, 'Look, I have a good man,' and he's picking out his friends. A Ukrainian department, a Russian department, a Polish department. And it was a beautiful thing in a way."[14]

By 1910 the new immigrants made up 68 percent of the steel labor force in Pittsburgh and Allegheny County, and the very weight of their presence afforded them a modicum of upward mobility. David Brody, the preeminent historian of steel's nonunion era, concluded that after a decade "13 per cent of the recent immigrants in the industry held skilled jobs, and another 42 per cent semiskilled."[15] But contemporary observers and veteran workers remained more impressed with the persistence of the industry's discriminatory barriers. In 1919 the Interchurch World Movement found tremendous resentment on this score, especially among immigrants with five to fifteen years' experience. The bar that stood out strongest in their minds was "not being an 'American.' " Typical, perhaps, was the "Slavish" laborer in Homestead, Pennsylvania, who told an investigator that he had "no chance to get ahead," even after thirteen years in the mill. "The foreman kept people back because they were hunkies and brought in his relatives and those who treated him to booze to take the better positions." Even the achievement of American citizenship had little, if any, positive effect on the newcomers' chances. Thus a Lithuanian immigrant who had been a citizen for six years reported that "the foreigners are given the dirtiest and hardest jobs and are lorded over by the skilled American workers." "He is always told to wait by the foreman when he asks for a better job." While he waited, young Americans who had worked in the mills for only a short time were promoted over him, an experience so common—and so galling—that it became central to the immigrants' historical memory. "There was a time when I thought I'd surely get a good job sometime," Mike Dobrejcak, the quasi-fictional steelworker in Thomas Bell's *Out of This Furnace*, recalled after more than twenty years in the mill. "I worked hard. I did what I was told and more. . . . But I'm a Hunky and they don't give good jobs to Hunkies."[16]

. . . . .

The mill was, almost by definition, a "man's world." The noise, the dirt, the heat, the heavy lifting and constant danger—all signified an environment that appeared to be suitable for men only. But the industry did provide some jobs for women. In 1935 U.S. Steel listed 1,250 females among its 196,000 employees. Some were clerks and stenographers (although in the mills even clerical work was done mainly by men); some worked in plant hospitals; and a few were technicians in metallurgy labs. In production and maintenance, about the only place that employed women was the tin mill, where they worked as tin floppers, inspecting razor-thin sheets of tin plate for defects. At the Sparrows Point (Maryland) Works of Bethlehem Steel, about two hundred women per shift worked as tin floppers, under the direction of an eccentric martinet who dressed her foreladies in pink and her "girls" in navy blue uniforms and relentlessly sought to maintain an oasis of sanitized female space in an otherwise crude male environment. Tin floppers were paid the lowest wage at Sparrows Point, a penny less than the black male laborers, but more than twice as much as the women who worked in Baltimore's oyster canneries and garment factories.[17]

If steel was a man's world, it was not a place where manly virtues were often on proud display. True, there were locomotive engineers, machinists, and other craftsmen whose very skill seemed to symbolize manliness. But among workingmen the concept of manliness clearly implied independence from close supervision and the maintenance of an environment that reflected the values of autonomy and voluntary cooperation. In steel, however, the breaking of the unions had led to the imposition of an unusually repressive regime in which even skilled men were convinced that any open expression of dissatisfaction would lead to their discharge. Under such conditions, the mill became a manly environment primarily in the negative sense that only males could be expected to endure the hardships it imposed. The twelve-hour days, the six- and seven-day weeks, and the heat, dirt, and danger robbed the men of something vital and left them with scant time and energy for life beyond the job. They saw little of their children and had little energy for relations with their wives. As one worker recalled, "When I got home in the evening, all I would do is go to sleep. I couldn't even pick up a piece of bread, my fingers were so racked up from the steel mill."[18]

Women were largely absent from the mills, but they were the indispensable life force that held families and communities together. In the words of historian S. J. Kleinberg, they were "completely peripheral

153

but absolutely vital. Peripheral because, with a few exceptions, they did not hold industrial jobs, and vital because they undertook all the daily work in the home." Margaret Byington, the author of a classic book on the households of a mill town, marveled at women's capacity to manage family finances, nurture children, and—in the face of a nearly impossible schedule—create the underpinnings of a comfortable home life for their husbands. All the while, they fought off the inevitable dirt and smoke that gushed from the mills. One resident of Sparrows Point, who kept her windows closed and caulked, remembered that "as clean as you kept the place, you could still wipe that dirt off the windowsills." And "when it came to washing and hanging out clothes, you'd have to look to see which way the wind blew. If it came from the open hearth, you were going to get red clothes. . . . If it came from the east side, the clothes would be black. If you had a lovely high windy day, there would be people washing all over town."[19]

In keeping with the mill towns' near pervasive pattern, there were significant differences in the lives of native-born and immigrant women, and little, if any, sense of sisterhood across the boundaries of culture and ethnicity. In Homestead, Byington found an unwillingness "on the part of the English-speaking people to include 'Hunkies' in any organization which would bring them into social and personal contact." She also observed stark differences in the family lives of the Americans and the Slavs. The Americans were generally better paid; and because the work they performed was more skilled, their work environment was often less onerous, and they had more energy to expend on their wives and children. Byington vividly recalled one English-speaking family. At supper time the wife awaited her husband with a clean apron on, and her children stood on the porch with clean dresses. When the father appeared, the girls ran to meet him, "the older one to carry his bucket, the little one to take possession of his hand. After supper he smoked contentedly with a child on each knee and talked with his wife of the day's doings." But other skilled men told John Fitch that virtually all of their time was spent "in the mills or in bed." "No man who works twelve hours," said one, "has time or energy to do much outside of his work."[20]

In the case of the Slavs, Byington was struck by "the utter barrenness of the[ir] two-room homes." Even when they lived in single-family dwellings with gardens, the surrounding environment tended to be crowded, squalid, and unhealthy. Child mortality among the new immigrants was more than twice as high as it was among "English-speaking Europeans," and Byington described one relatively well off family in which the four children were "sickly" and the mother was overworked and unhealthy. And this family did not take in boarders. Where wives had to care for boarders as well as for their husbands and children, the hours of work appeared interminable—"from 4:30 in the morning to 9:00 at night," one observer recalled, "seven days a week."[21]

But women's home lives were not all drudgery and subservience to the demands of others. On the contrary, the household was the one area in which women exercised real authority. This may have been especially true in the steel towns, which offered few outlets for female employment. Some women, most of them unmarried and between the ages of sixteen and twenty-four, worked in the clothing, glass, and tobacco industries. Many more were employed in domestic service. And increasingly, some daughters of the working class found an outlet— even a way out—as clerical workers in the burgeoning corporate headquarters of Pittsburgh and Chicago. But in most cases, just as a boy looked forward to joining his father in the mill, so a girl would anticipate following her mother in marrying a steelworker and creating a home in the familiar confines of the local community. Such a course was not only expected of her; it also gave meaning and a sense of purposeful autonomy to her life. The greatest terror, perhaps, was that her mate would be killed or maimed on the job. Then she would have to leave the home to fend for herself and her children in a work environment that offered little in the way of security and self-respect.[22]

• • • • •

The ethnic segmentation of life in the mills and the surrounding communities remained a defining characteristic of the steel industry for many years, often until World War II, and in some places well into the postwar era. Youngstown steelworker Sam Camens painted a vivid portrait of the layering of the workforce at the Ohio Works of U.S. Steel. The plant, he said, "was divided up into ethnic groupings. The blast furnace was basically black. The machine shop was English and German. The open hearth was Irish and Scotch, with a sprinkling of . . . East Europeans. . . . The primary mills . . . were mostly East Europeans. The masons, bricklayers, were all Italians. . . . The riggers were all [Hungarians]. . . . That's the way the plant was. . . . It was all little islands of ethnic concentrations."[23]

Oliver Montgomery and Frank Leseganich offered a similar portrayal of the Campbell Works of Youngstown Sheet and Tube. Montgomery, a third-generation steelworker who was hired at the Campbell Works in 1948, remembered the mill as "like the United Nations. Every department was a different ethnic group." Leseganich, whose father emigrated from the Ukraine to Youngstown in 1914, recalled that "if you were a certain nationality, you ended up in a certain area of the mill. There was nothing unusual for . . . the track gang to be Italian, all of them. Dinky operators were mostly Ukrainian. . . . My father ended up in the tube mill, which had a lot of Ukrainians." When Leseganich followed his father into the Campbell Works, he was hired as a rigger in a department that was composed of "nothing but Slovaks. . . . [The other riggers] thought I was a Jew, and they wondered what the hell I was doing in the rigger gang. And I heard them [saying] in Slovak, 'What is that Jew doing here?' . . . I finally walked over to them—at that time I could talk a little Slovak—and said, 'I'm not a Jew; I'm a Ukrainian.' And they said, 'Oh, you're one of *us*!' "[24]

Leseganich's story suggests that by the 1930s ethnic identities had loosened sufficiently to allow Slovaks to regard a Ukrainian as one of "us." But Angela Campana, whose husband worked at Republic Steel's Youngstown Works, recalled how deep and abiding the obligations of ethnicity could be. She had emigrated from Italy to Youngstown in 1927. Interviewed fifty-five years later, she remembered her arrival in New York—alone, speaking no English, and wearing a badge that read only "Ohio." Her husband had preceded her by two years and found a job in the mill alongside compatriots who had been part of the same process of chain migration that brought him to Youngstown and Republic Steel. These men continued to speak Italian on the job. Even in the community it was rarely necessary to speak English. And when Frank Campana joined the famed Little Steel Strike in May 1937, he came home and informed his wife that he "had to strike for the union." Why? "Since the others, all from the same region and village in Italy, were striking[,] we had to strike."[25]

At first, new immigrants like Frank Campana had been grateful for the chance to labor in circumstances that few others would have countenanced. Driven less by ideas of freedom than by a futile quest to restore order and predictability in peasant societies that the commercialization of agriculture had torn asunder, they came mainly as "birds of passage" who hoped "to earn money and to return home to buy a farm bigger than my father's." Many, perhaps a third of them, did return to the old country. Those who stayed sought incremental mobility, or "a better life than [their parents] had." They became "a people apart" who succeeded in forging a remarkably durable network of ethnic enclaves. Sociologist Ewa Morawska found that in Johnstown during the interwar period there were "more than 140 ethnic societies, 3 foreign-language newspapers, 8 orchestras, 2 theatre groups, 4 choir and dance ensembles, and over 20 sports teams that competed in local and regional ethnic tournaments." As a rule, she concluded, "the 'foreigners' and the 'Americans' patronized different societies, halls, and recreational facilities . . . even when they shared the same class position."[26]

At the heart of many of these ethnic enclaves stood the church, most often the Roman Catholic Church. Catholicism played a vital role in giving cohesion to the lives of the immigrants. It was a familiar beacon in an otherwise strange land; it reinforced—and sanctified—parochial identities; it structured communal rites of passage and offered consolation in times of sorrow. It was the Church Universal—absolutist in its claims, hierarchical in its organization, and governed from a distant see by an infallible authority. But it was also, paradoxically, local, tangible, and eminently familiar—often created as the result of lay initiative and reflective of the mores of local ethnic communities. The church gave meaning to the lives of its parishioners, and they in turn made the church an instrument of their communal will.[27]

In industrial towns and cities where immigrants were concentrated in large numbers, the parish became synonymous with the neighborhood, and the church often became identified with a particular nationality. In Chicago's famed Back of the Yards area, there were eleven Catholic churches in little more than a square mile. Two were Irish, two Polish, and two German; the others were Bohemian, Croatian, Italian, Lithuanian, and Slovak. Thus even in the Church Universal religious life was local and particularistic; it reinforced the physical boundaries between groups and the separateness of their identities; it defined "our" neighborhood as "sacred space"; and it created a kind of separate but equal ethos that provided a Catholic rationale for the exclusion of outsiders. With the coming of the Civil Rights movement, this rationale would meet a theological test that it could not survive. But in the meantime, writes historian John T. McGreevy, each Catholic parish remained "a small planet, whirling through its orbit, oblivious to the rest of the ecclesiastical solar system."[28]

Scholars have generally portrayed the immigrants as men and women for whom a less than friendly host country and a harsh and precarious work environment reinforced an essentially conservative worldview that derived in large measure from Roman Catholicism's "culture of authority."[29] But in fact the "foreigners" were the backbone of the Great Steel Strike. Once celebrated for their docility and submissiveness, as men who "did the heavy and exhausting work, and never asked the reason why," the immigrants shocked their employers in 1919. This was especially true of those who had lived and worked in the steel towns for a while and had begun to sink roots in America. Longevity lessened their willingness to accept the "horse and wagon" routine of twelve hours a day in the mills; World War I, with its patriotic appeals and rhetoric of democracy, raised their expectations; the upheavals that swept across their native lands in the aftermath of the war stirred their imaginations. "They came from Eastern Europe and now Eastern Europe means to them mainly the overthrow of autocracy," the Interchurch World Movement reported. "They have a vague idea that big rich people who run things 'arbitrarily,' even in mills, are coming down in the world. . . . They have a vague idea that poor people who have been run for a long time, on farms and in mills, are coming up in the world and are beginning to run themselves."[30]

In communities where the immigrants remained a people apart, with their own ethnic institutions and sense of community, they proved to be the most committed unionists and resolute combatants in the bitterly contested organizing campaigns of the late 1930s. In Johnstown immigrants had picketed at the mill gates in separate national groups in 1919, whereas the "Americans" held back; and for the next generation the ethnic and cultural boundaries in and around the city's mills remained remarkably resistant to change. "Status plants" continued to provide employment mainly for old immigrants and native-born Americans, and the "foreign plant," the giant Franklin division of Bethlehem Steel, employed mainly Hunkies. According to Morawska, the Little Steel Strike of 1937 only accentuated the "deep chasm dividing the 'foreign' and 'American' labor force." A survey of men supporting the back-to-work movement revealed that they were overwhelmingly of American and western European background, whereas 70 percent of the strikers were new immigrants and their sons. This time, however, the sons were imbued with a rights consciousness far beyond anything their fathers had felt in 1919. They too were Americans now, and they recalled telling their oppressors, "You are not going to call us 'Hunky' no more."[31]

The combined force of the New Deal and CIO unionism eroded the lines that separated the "foreigners" from their American and old immigrant counterparts. World War II, and the cornucopia of veterans' benefits that flowed from the GI Bill, dramatically hastened the process. Union members reaped the expanding rewards of the "private welfare state" that collective bargaining agreements created. Men once derided as Hunkies or dagos became the leaders of United Steelworkers' locals and the mayors and city councilmen of steel towns.[32]

But there was another key dynamic in the process of acculturation. For years the immigrants had been "inbetween peoples," whose racial status—in their own minds and in the eyes of the larger society—was in flux. Although eastern, and even central, European immigrants were sometimes condemned in the most vicious terms as "filthy Huns" and "ignorant animals," the greatest antagonism was reserved for the often darker-skinned peoples of southeastern Europe—especially Italians, Greeks, Serbs, and Croats. An African American worker at the Clairton Works of Carnegie Steel remembered that Serbs and Croats "were treated almost like blacks"; and an Italian steelworker in nearby Aliquippa commiserated with blacks, who were "one step lower than the Italians." Actually, mill owners in Alabama characterized southern Italian laborers as one step lower than blacks. The federal Immigration Commission encountered the "practically universal opinion among employers that South Italians are . . . the most inefficient of all races, whether immigrant or native." In the North as well as the South, they were described as "olive-tinted," "swarthy," and "kinky-haired," often called "guineas" (historically, a reference to African slaves and their descendants), and sometimes characterized as "white Chinese" and even "white-skinned negro[es]."[33]

The mixing of whiteness and nonwhiteness is vividly evident in the latter terms, but often the naming process hinged less on color than on attributes such as servility, unmanliness, and poverty that in the minds of the WASP majority were indissolubly linked with certain races and nationalities. African Americans could escape neither their color nor the symbolic legacy of slavery; their alleged deficiencies of character and temperament made them complicit in their own enslavement. Likewise, the cultural characteristics of Chinese immigrants merged into "Coolieism," which stood in stark—and ominous—contrast to "American manhood." And finally, in comparison with the mythic Teutons and Anglo-Saxons of nativist imagination, southern and eastern Europeans were "persons of a lower moral tone," or "beaten men of beaten races, representing the worst failures in the struggle for existence."[34]

In steel, John Fitch perceived a fundamental distinction between the "white men" and the "foreigners" in the mills. He might have quoted the skilled heater who said that working with the "coarse, vulgar, and brutal" newcomers to the industry was "no place for a man with a white man's heart to be." But gradually and unevenly, the foreigners did become white, which meant they bridged the skill and status gap between the Americans and themselves and claimed the "wages of whiteness" as part of their own inheritance.[35]

. . . . .

Although most African American workers followed the English-speaking men and the foreigners into the mills, they were by no means the "last of the immigrants." On the contrary, theirs was a race-specific journey, from the beginning of the steel industry to its near demise as a source of employment in the 1970s and 1980s. Initially, they performed slave labor in the ironworking establishments of the South. On the eve of the Civil War, more than two thousand slaves labored in the iron mills of Tennessee's Cumberland River Valley. At the famed Tredegar Iron Works in Richmond, Virginia, Joseph Anderson was employing more than a hundred slaves as ironworkers by 1848. When white workers, most of them migrants from the North, went on strike that year to "prohibit the employment of colored people in the . . . Works," he increased his use of African Americans and moved some of them to skilled positions. Anderson became the "ironmaker to the Confederacy," and the scarcity of free white labor during the war compelled him to rely on hundreds of black slaves to man a far-flung enterprise that included coal mines, blast furnaces, rolling mills, and a fleet of canal boats. Overall, the South had only twenty thousand white tradesmen in 1865, but approximately one hundred thousand slaves worked as blacksmiths, cabinetmakers, stonemasons, and a variety of other skilled crafts.[36]

By the 1880s black iron puddlers were working in Richmond (where they remained a significant component of the Tredegar workforce), Atlanta, Knoxville, and even Pittsburgh. For the most part, however, they confronted white employers who were inclined to exclude them from the industry except in times of emergency and white workers who were determined to keep them out at all times. Thus in 1875 black iron puddlers from Richmond found employment in Pittsburgh during a bitter lockout of the Sons of Vulcan, a union of skilled workers that denied membership to African Americans by constitutional provision. In what would become an all too familiar scene, the black strikebreakers required the protection of a company of soldiers as they ran the gauntlet of an angry crowd of strike supporters. Apparently, these were "the first Negroes to enter the steel industry in the North."[37]

In 1876 the Sons of Vulcan merged with several other unions to form the Amalgamated Association of Iron and Steel Workers. At first the new organization continued its predecessors' policy of racial exclusion. But in 1881, recognizing that it lacked the power to keep black workers out of the mills, the union changed course and voted to admit "colored lodges" to full membership. Soon after, African Americans established lodges in Pittsburgh and Richmond, and the new policy paid quick dividends. When a representative of the Black Diamond Steel Works journeyed from Pittsburgh to Richmond seeking to lure black strikebreakers northward, he found no takers, because, as a black union member exulted, "the true gospel of the A. A. of I. & S. W. had been preached, and all the darkeys of any account had been converted, baptized, and received the right hand of fellowship in the union."[38]

In spite of this evangelical expression of solidarity, many white unionists still refused to work with blacks, and some who accepted them did so only for pragmatic—and narrowly self-serving—reasons. As early as the Baltimore congress of 1866, where the short-lived National Labor Union was founded, a delegate had warned that "Negroes will take possession of the shops unless we take possession of the Negroes." More than forty years later, a delegate to an Amalgamated Association convention offered up the same warning. The question, he said, was who would "use" the black worker, the white unionist or the employer? If the former, it would be to maintain the wages and conditions of whites; if the latter, it would be to lower white workers' standard of living. (In either case, blacks were regarded not as fellow workers but as instruments in the hands of others.) The union's greatest mistake, said this delegate, was to allow black strikebreakers to concentrate in the struck iron mills and then "teach [other African Americans] the iron and steel business." The solution was to encourage blacks to become union members, in which case "they would be scattered about"—in effect, surrounded and controlled by whites.[39]

The defeat of the Amalgamated Association in the epic Homestead strike of 1892 led to the rapid decline of an organization that had once been among the largest and most powerful of American trade unions. From then on the steelmasters would exercise full control of employment in their burgeoning industry. In times of acute labor shortage, especially during the two world wars of the twentieth century, they offered African Americans access to jobs from which they had historically been excluded. But access to employment in steel, even in the lowest-paying and most disagreeable jobs, came slowly and unevenly. A survey conducted in 1907 revealed that African Americans made up 39.1 percent of all steelworkers in the South, but only 1.5 percent in the East and 0.5 percent in the Midwest. In 1910 there were 789 black workers in the Pittsburgh area steel industry, whereas only 37 black men were employed in Chicago's blast furnaces, rolling mills, and iron foundries. Overall, African Americans made up 4.5 percent of the steel labor force in 1910 and were most heavily concentrated in the mills of the Tennessee Coal, Iron and Railroad Company (TCI) in the Birmingham-Bessemer area of Alabama.[40]

With 253 iron and steel plants in 1906, the greater Pittsburgh area was by far the most important steel-producing region in the nation. Richard R. Wright's interviews with Negro employees of Carnegie Steel's Clark Mills offer a fascinating portrait of black steelworkers in Pittsburgh. Initially African Americans had gained access to employment in this plant during a strike in the 1880s, and in 1907 110 blacks were working there. Forty-seven of them had been in the mill for more than five years, and most of these men had moved up to semiskilled and even skilled jobs. In fact, 2 had reached the top job in the plant. These "chief rollers" were each in charge of 10 to 18 employees, white as well as black. Wright found that "in one furnace the chief heater was a Negro and his assistant was white; in another the chief was white and the assistant a Negro; another had a Negro heater and Negro assistant, and a white boy to open doors." Clearly, in this plant at least, it was "possible for a [black] man of ability to work up to a good position."[41]

Most of the men Wright interviewed had been born in the South. Of the 94 who specified a birthplace, 61 were from Virginia, 9 from Tennessee, and 7 from Alabama; only 5 were from Pennsylvania or other northern states. Generally they had had little schooling (some admitted to less than two years), and many had worked in agriculture, the railroads, or hod carrying before their employment in steel. One of the rollers, however, "claimed to have started in the mills in Virginia at eleven years of age and to have continued in the work for forty years." Wright estimated that he was "probably the highest paid Negro workman in the Pittsburgh District."[42]

The percentage of married men among these steelworkers was much higher than among the Negroes of Pittsburgh as a whole. Of the 89 men reporting in this category, 67 were married; 7 were widowed, di-

Fig. 4.2. Steelworkers, Clark Mills, Pittsburgh, early twentieth century. Credit: *Wage-Earning Pittsburgh* (Russell Sage Foundation, 1914)

vorced, or separated. But their family size was remarkably small. Among the 74 men who were or had been married, nearly three-fifths had no living children; and few of the sons of these steelworkers followed their fathers into the mills. Moreover, none of the men owned his own home. The great majority lived in frame buildings on unpaved streets or alleys, but many of their houses had "neat sitting rooms or parlors containing pianos or organs." In general, they ate "substantial and abundant" food, and away from work Wright found them "well, even stylishly, dressed," in clothes that gave no indication of their proletarian calling. Many belonged to fraternal organizations such as the Knights of Pythias, the Odd Fellows, and the Masons. But less than half were members of a church, and most of those who were members attended only occasionally.[43]

Altogether, then, Wright's portrait is of a group of men whose work was "well up to the standard" of the industry, who could—and often did—ascend to semiskilled and skilled positions in the mills, who coexisted easily with whites on the job, who lived reasonably comfortably, and who appeared for the most part to have stable family lives. Statistics from the Pittsburgh area at the time indicate that weekly earnings among black workers in steel were higher than those of many of the new immigrants. In a 1910 survey, 493 black steelworkers averaged $14.98 a week, more than the Germans ($14.55) and not much less than the Irish ($15.85), but substantially more than the Rumanians ($11.24), Croatians ($11.46), Greeks ($11.85), Poles ($12.21), and Russians ($12.47). But there were clear danger signs as well. The number of African Americans was small—only 493 of 47,469 workers in the survey, and among the newcomers the Slovaks alone (7,633) vastly outnumbered the blacks. Clearly, chain migration was working for virtually all of the European immigrant groups but not for black migrants or even for African American men who had lived in Pittsburgh for years. As the older cohort of black steelworkers left the industry, their sons and nephews were not replacing them, or they were not sinking roots in the mills when they did. Employers who had once welcomed blacks' antiunionism were now celebrating Slavic workers for their "habit of silent submission, their amenity to discipline, and their willingness to work long hours . . . without a murmur." And European ethnic networks had become the channel through which nearly all lower-level jobs in the mills were filled. Except in a few enclaves such as the Clark Mills, blacks were being inundated and marginalized.[44]

But in the second decade of the twentieth century a world war and recurring labor conflict precipitated another round of changes, dramatically increasing the number of black workers in steel and shifting their concentration from south to north. The prevailing stereotype was that African Americans entered the iron and steel industry mainly as strikebreakers during the Great Steel Strike of 1919; it was estimated that about thirty thousand blacks were recruited for this purpose. But the tight wartime labor market and the virtual cessation of immigration from southern and eastern Europe during the war actually played a far more important role in creating opportunities for blacks. In fact, much of their employment preceded the 1919 strike. In Indiana the number of African Americans at the huge Gary Works of Illinois Steel jumped from 66 in 1909 to 1,295 in 1918. In the Pittsburgh area, Carnegie Steel employed "only a handful of Negroes" in 1910 but about 4,000 by 1917. Overall, job opportunities for African Americans increased dramatically between 1910 and the mid-1920s. In western Pennsylvania, blacks constituted 3 percent of the steel labor force in 1910 and 21 percent in 1923. At the Gary Works, blacks made up less than 1 percent of the workforce in 1910 but 20.5 percent in 1923. Black employment paralleled the Great Migration from south to north. In 1910, 62.6 percent of the African Americans in steel worked in southern mills; but in 1920 only 32.7 percent of them were employed in the South. They remained a critical component of the southern labor force, but increasingly their destiny was the northern mills, where they mingled uneasily with the "foreigners" and the "English-speaking men."[45]

The Great Steel Strike of 1919 was the first major test of the capacity of the industry's multilayered workforce to merge into a relatively unified whole. In the organizing campaign leading up to the strike, the American Federation of Labor brought twenty-four separate unions that claimed jurisdiction in steel under one umbrella and awarded practical leadership of the campaign to William Z. Foster, a seasoned organizer who would soon become a leading member of the Communist party. Foster recognized the need to appeal to black workers and bring them into the unions, but most of his associates did not share his concern. John Fitzpatrick, the chairman of the National Committee for Organizing Iron and Steel Workers, recalled that "there was no campaign to organize Negroes at that time, and they were given no special consideration as a group."[46]

On the other side of the battle lines, the employers were quick to recognize the value of African Americans as an antiunion contingent within the larger mill workforce. The acute labor shortage of the World War I era required the employment of large numbers of black workers anyway. But as the strike approached, the companies recruited additional African Americans for the sole purpose of undermining it. Not that blacks were necessarily antiunion. Those born in the North responded to the appeal of unionism about as readily as white workers did. But virtually all blacks were at least aware of the racist policies of the unions affiliated with the AFL and the railroad brotherhoods. And black migrants from the South, the key constituency in the expanding industrial labor force, were acutely conscious of the fact that the companies and not the unions were providing them with employment that offered far more remuneration than sharecropping and agricultural labor had afforded. Most southern migrants took their cue from other African Americans—ranging from middle-class adherents of racial uplift to fellow workers on the shop floor—who were skeptical at best about the sincerity of the AFL's appeal. "They didn't have no unions where I comed from," said one migrant to Chicago. He had not joined a union, he admitted, because "these other folks . . . ain't joined and I reckon they know more about it than me."[47]

When the walkout began on September 22, black participation was uneven. In Cleveland African Americans were virtually unanimous in their support of the strike. In Chicago, at the South Works of Illinois Steel, 85 percent of the black workers joined the walkout on the first day, but their commitment to the cause proved weak, and most of them drifted back to work at the first opportunity. In Gary few blacks joined the ranks of the strikers, and racial tensions were high. In Pittsburgh, the critical district where 70 percent of steel production was concentrated, black participation was virtually nil. According to labor economists Sterling Spero and Abram Harris, there were 1,737 Negroes among the 14,687 employees at the Homestead Works of Carnegie Steel. "Of these Negroes only eight joined the unions and but one struck, while 75 percent of the white unskilled workers joined the unions and 90 percent struck." The pattern was essentially the same in Braddock, Clairton, Duquesne, and other Pittsburgh-area steel towns. Overall, said Foster, "in the entire steel industry, the Negroes . . . gave the movement less cooperation than any other element, skilled or unskilled, foreign or native."[48]

Black workers did not play the key role in undermining the strike, however. That responsibility belonged to the "English-speaking men," whose skill and experience were essential to the running of the mills. "They were the ones that went back first and began to scab," Fitzpatrick recalled. "None of the Negroes from the South could have replaced these skilled men if they had continued to strike." Nonetheless, it was widely believed in the steel towns that the "niggers did it." In a moment of bitterness, even Foster asserted that "the colored worker . . . seems to feel that the best way he can solve his problem is to break down the white working man. He acts as a scab at all times." And the Interchurch World Movement expressed the fear that the steel companies were "deliberately attempting to turn the Negroes into a race of strike-breakers, with whom to hold the white workers in check."[49]

But blacks were no mere pawns in the employers' game. They had their own motives—usually the opportunity for steady employment in better-paying jobs—and their own vivid recollections of how the aggression of white workers had helped structure their marginal access to industrial labor markets. In the folk memory of African Americans, it was the old immigrants who had been most virulent in their antagonism toward the black southerners who came north looking for work in factory, mine, and mill. One observer recalled how, in the 1890s, "the Irish and Welsh employed 'Direct Action' . . . with a vengeance in keeping Negroes out of the crowds of job seekers at steel mill gates." The "Slavs," by comparison, had not been "personally hostile." But the Great Steel Strike created a new—and lasting—antagonism. The "foreigners" were now inclined to view blacks not only as "scabs" but as thuggish allies of the local authorities in the reign of terror they had visited on immigrant strikers and their families. In accounts of the strike's bitter defeat, more than a few stories focused on the brutality of "negro deputies." Blacks in turn saw the strikers as obstacles to their right to have a job and provide for their families. "All I am interested in is to make a living," a veteran steelworker recalled many years later, "and no 'hunky' has a right to keep me from working."[50]

As a result of this spiraling antagonism, some black workers took special pride in breaking strikes, undermining unions, and taking revenge on those who had greeted them with "rebuff and refusal of admission." When western Pennsylvania was again convulsed by industrial conflict in the mid-1920s, black strikebreakers in the coal fields around Pittsburgh taunted white union miners with the cry: "You would not work with me before the strike. Now I have your job and I am going to keep it." By the late 1920s the National Urban League was reporting from Pittsburgh: "Negro men are not kindly disposed to the unions— not because they do not believe in unionism but because they feel that one of their greatest enemies is the white union man."[51]

World War I and the Great Steel Strike created a permanent place for African Americans in the steel labor force. Their numbers grew especially rapidly from 1917 to 1919 and soared again in 1922 and the succeeding boom year, when the industry rebounded from a severe postwar depression. Overall, the number of iron and steelworkers in the United States increased from 401,039 to 620,894 between 1910 and 1930. The increase among blacks during the same period was from 18,220 to 52,956, or from 4.5 to 8.5 percent of the total.[52]

Black workers' gains seem impressive, especially when measured against the jobs—in agriculture and domestic service and on the margins of the industrial economy—that were most readily available to African Americans at the time. But a closer look at the statistics suggests how limited their advances really were. In 1910, 73.6 percent of black steelworkers were laborers; in 1930, the figure stood at 73.5 percent, an improvement of one-tenth of 1 percent in twenty years. In this respect blacks differed sharply not only from native-born whites but from the "foreigners," who had legitimate grievances about their relative exclusion from skilled jobs but nonetheless demonstrated significant movement from the unskilled to the semiskilled sectors of the workforce. Unlike the immigrants, blacks became more concentrated in the heaviest, most dangerous, and lowest-paying jobs; and more than any other group they were victimized by technological innovation, at both ends of the occupational scale. In Alabama black employment plummeted by 40 percent during the 1920s as industrial modernization eliminated many unskilled jobs and quadrupled the number of semi-skilled positions, which went mainly to whites. In Pittsburgh, whose share of the nation's steel output declined in the 1920s as the industry's center of gravity moved westward toward Gary and Chicago, blacks lost ground not only in the unskilled sector but in the skilled one as well. In 1910 more than one-quarter of the black steelworkers in the area had held skilled jobs, and some had worked in the highest-paying and most prestigious jobs in the industry. But apparently these very occupations were among the most vulnerable to technological innovation. Thus, although African Americans made up more than 20 percent of Pittsburgh's furnacemen, smelters, heaters, and puddlers in 1910, they accounted for less than 2 percent of these jobs in 1930. Overall during this period, the percentage of black steelworkers who were unskilled jumped from 66 to 90.[53]

In the nation as a whole, the black percentage of the skilled and semiskilled labor force in steel did increase slightly during the 1920s— from 2.9 to 4.0 percent in the former category and from 4.3 to 6.5 percent in the latter. But even where there were gains there was un-evenness. Thus the number of blacks at the Gary Works of Illinois Steel peaked at 3,181 in 1923 and would not reach that level again until World War II. By 1929 the number of African Americans in the plant had fallen by more than six hundred, even though employment had increased by nearly a thousand. The superintendent of industrial relations at the Gary Works later admitted that this change was the result of a conscious policy on the part of management to stabilize Negro employment at 15 percent of the workforce and to confine blacks to unskilled labor. Perhaps to compensate for the smaller number of blacks, the Gary Works dramatically increased its hiring of Mexican immigrants in the 1920s. By the middle of the decade Mexicans constituted 8 percent of the workforce at the plant (and a remarkable 34.6 percent of the labor force at Inland Steel in nearby Indiana Harbor). Overall, from 1919 to 1928, the number of Mexican workers at Inland Steel, the Gary Works, and Illinois Steel's South Works in Chicago increased from 104 to 4,081. Meanwhile, the number of black workers at the three plants fell from a high of 4,096 in 1924 to 3,203 in 1928. Both groups were concentrated at the bottom of the job hierarchy, where, apparently, they were consciously pitted against each other. In 1928 the superintendent of a large steel products plant told economist Paul Taylor that "it isn't good to have all of one nationality; they will gang up on you. . . . We have Negroes and Mexicans in a sort of competition with each other." The growing number of Mexicans, he admitted, reflected a policy "decided by malice aforethought."[54]

The testimony of black steelworkers illuminates the human dimensions of their subordinate status in ways that statistics can barely fathom. To be stuck at the bottom of steel's occupational hierarchy meant a constant exposure to heat, dirt, and danger that was always debilitating and sometimes deadly. Although blacks were dispersed throughout the mills in laborers' jobs, they were disproportionately concentrated in the coke ovens and blast furnaces, where the heat was most intense and the conditions were most hazardous. Work in the coke ovens, said an African American laborer in Gary, "burns your clothes" and "cooks [your] blood. . . . The men who work in the acid have their clothes eaten up daily. . . . And when the acid touches them it leaves a scar." In Clairton a black worker lamented: "[O]ur lives are short. The reason I say so is that the last few persons that worked [in the coke ovens] was not out but a short time before they died. You get hot on the job, your heart beats way too fast, you suffer from cramps." From Birmingham, a worker at the Sloss-Sheffield Steel and Iron Company remembered his job as a "man-killer." The heat around the blast furnace was so great that "you'd be wet from the time you hit the clock."[55]

Even in "black" departments like the blast furnaces and coke ovens, skilled and supervisory positions were generally reserved for whites. It was not uncommon for black workers to train whites for jobs and then watch them ascend the ladder into occupational terrain that was off-limits to blacks. When a black worker in Birmingham expressed the desire to move up to one of these positions, his supervisor replied, "We ain't going to give niggers no white folks' jobs." At Sparrows Point, Bethlehem Steel's massive complex in Baltimore, black workers recalled that even asking about a "white" job could get a man fired. And these indignities were by no means confined to the Deep South or to a border city like Baltimore. In Clairton a black worker recalled how in hard economic times Negroes would be bumped from the machines they had been tending in the coke ovens. "They take a white man right out of the street and make you teach him and after you teach him they give him your job or make you your foreman." Perhaps the ultimate humiliation occurred around the furnaces where blacks customarily labored—and suffered from the extreme heat—in the summer months.

In winter, when the heat of the furnaces offered consolation from the bitter cold, Pittsburgh area bosses routinely "transferred the black men to outdoor jobs . . . and gave the furnace jobs to white workers."[56]

Although some of this testimony suggests that the boundaries between black and white jobs were not absolute, the overall tendency toward race-based segmentation was clear. In Gary a black middle-class observer declared that "wherever you see mills that are dirty, dusty, noisy and hot you'll find plenty of colored men working. Wherever you see buildings fairly clean with machinery doing most of the work you'll find very few Negroes." Black workers put it more simply but no less eloquently. In Clairton: "There are jobs that whites won't touch. We get them." In Gary: "The Negro's job is any job that the white man cannot stand." In Birmingham: "the [N]egro had his job, what he was doing, and the white man had his."[57]

· · · · ·

The employers, who had beaten the Amalgamated Association in 1892 and crushed the Great Steel Strike of 1919, were largely responsible for this occupational hierarchy and for much of the regimen in the mills and the surrounding communities. Outside observers, and the workers themselves, were almost sure to comment on both the power of the companies and the dirt and oppression that seemed omnipresent in the steel towns they created. An immigrant from Galicia remembered that "my disappointment was unspeakable when . . . I [first] saw the city of Johnstown: squalid and ugly, with those congested shabby houses, blackened with soot from the factory chimneys." Farther west, on the Monongahela River, journalist Mary Heaton Vorse observed that "all of Braddock is black. The soot of the mills has covered it." Vorse lamented the generations of children "born where no green thing grows" and "reared under the somber magnificence of the clouds of smoke which blanket the sky and obscure the sun." But she also paid tribute to the wives of steelworkers, who against all odds insisted on hanging white curtains in their windows. Wherever you go in the steel towns, she said, "you will find courageous women hopefully washing their white curtains," which became "a flag of defiance against the dirt."[58]

These curtains were exceptional not only because of their whiteness but because they were symbols of defiance in communities that ordinarily tolerated no such thing. According to Edward Wieck, an astute and widely traveled contemporary observer, the steel companies "control public opinion, the city and county administrations, the financial institutions of the towns, the church, the press, the business and professional men, and also the radio where such exists. Their spies are everywhere in all these towns; they find out everything [that] goes on or is contemplated." Aliquippa, a few miles west of Pittsburgh on the Ohio River, was the home of the Jones and Laughlin Steel Company (J and L). Nicknamed Little Siberia, it was perhaps the most notoriously anti-union steel town in the nation. Dominic Del Turco, who went to work there in 1924, recalled that "when we were first organizing the union in Aliquippa, the police department was against us, the fire department, every governmental group was against us. . . . You couldn't even breathe in there without somebody stooging on you." More than forty years later Del Turco still remembered vividly how, in 1935, a huge company goon beat up an "aggressive little Serbian" union activist named Mike Kellar, while police stood by and watched. "He busted his ear drums, kicked him in the head, kicked him in the stomach so bad. . . . And the police were standing right there, and they wouldn't move, because they had orders not to interfere."[59]

Through its control of the Republican party, J and L also dominated the political life of the community. According to steelworker Joe Periello, "If you wanted to work, if you wanted to eat, if you wanted to have something, you had to be a Republican." Another steelworker, Mike Zahorsky, recalled, "I don't know how I was registered [to vote]. . . . [T]he company took care of all that for you; saved you the trouble." Zahorsky estimated that J and L controlled 95 percent of the votes in the mill, and he concluded, "There was no such thing as challenging [the company's power]. . . . You were declared an anarchist just because you raised your voice." Not surprisingly, before the emergence of the New Deal and the new unionism of the CIO, there were precious few "anarchists" in Aliquippa.[60]

But even in Little Siberia Jones and Laughlin did not rely entirely on force and intimidation to maintain its hegemony. Rather, like other steel companies, it invested heavily in what it called welfare work to reconcile workers to their powerlessness and to reduce labor turnover and increase productivity. During the fifteen-year reign of legendary executive Tom Girdler, J and L combined welfare work and repression to create a domain that some steel masters admiringly characterized as the "perfect company town." But the real pioneer in this kind of activity was U.S. Steel, the industry's behemoth, which by the mid-1930s employed 35 percent of the nation's steelworkers. The Corporation, as it was widely known, created a welfare department in 1911, and by 1935 estimated that it had spent $295 million on behalf of its employees. U.S. Steel built and maintained 24 churches, 17 schools, 34 clubhouses, 96 athletic fields, and 120 playgrounds. It offered its employees the services of 9 hospitals; it paid the salaries of 406 doctors and 199 nurses. By 1935 it was paying pensions, averaging $55.90 a month, to approximately 12,500 of its employees, who were eligible to retire at the age of sixty-five after twenty-five years of continuous service.[61]

Corporate welfare work was initially aimed at the "English-speaking men"; gradually it was expanded to include "foreigners" and blacks. In fact, even before the organization of U.S. Steel's welfare department, the Corporation had invested millions in its employees at the Tennessee Coal, Iron and Railroad Company, most of whom were African American. According to *Fortune*, when U.S. Steel took over TCI in 1907, "it drained swamps around its twenty-two company towns, built hospitals, established schools, sent out visiting nurses to educate the wives of Negro employees in the rudiments of domestic hygiene." Thus relative to other black workers in the Birmingham-Bessemer area, and even more so to those who engaged in sharecropping or agricultural labor in rural Alabama, TCI's African American workers made good money and had access to superior schools and housing.[62]

But for black steelworkers in general, corporate welfare was a separate and unequal proposition. It conferred real benefits but failed to address underlying issues of racial discrimination in employment and in the residential and social life of the steel towns. Moreover, in the North, for a number of critically important years, the companies' welfare expenditures utterly failed to keep pace with the needs engendered by accelerating black migration. In 1924, when Abram Harris was writing his master's thesis, "The New Negro Worker in Pittsburgh," he found African American families concentrated in badly overcrowded boarding houses and single men confined to bunkhouses and camps that were even more congested. "Almost invariably," he wrote, "the rooms of the average boarding house are so small as to barely afford bed space. Ventilation is poor and bathing facilities inadequate." In the bunkhouses in particular, the lack of recreation facilities created a vacuum in which gambling and trafficking in bootleg liquor flourished, with the attendant "brawls, shootings, cuttings and murders." Health conditions were even worse. Black men who migrated without their families, and without the clothing to protect them against the severe northern winters, succumbed to pneumonia, influenza, and tuberculosis at an alarming rate. Although they constituted only 6 percent of Pittsburgh's population, blacks accounted for as many as 25 percent of tuberculosis cases, 20 percent of deaths from influenza, and a near monopoly of recorded cases of pneumonia at a number of industrial plants. In one steel mill that employed about 800 Negroes, all but 6 of the 118 patients treated for pneumonia in 1923 were black, as were 71 of the 76 patients treated in the first three months of 1924.[63]

Gradually, some companies took steps to deal with the needs of African American workers. Carnegie Steel built a community center for black workers in Homestead as early as 1918, helped underwrite a "colored community chorus" in Clairton beginning in 1921, and sponsored baseball, basketball, track, and boxing programs in Braddock and many other communities. These corporate welfare programs no doubt had a positive impact on the lives of black workers and their families, but many steel towns also exemplified the uglier side of American race relations in the Age of Segregation. Thus in Aliquippa, Jones and Laughlin built housing for its employees in separate sections, or "plans," designed for each major group in the mill. According to John P. Davis, "Negroes live in 'Plan 11' and nowhere else." In Homestead blacks could not swim in the pool at the Carnegie Library; they had to sit in the balcony at the local vaudeville and movie theater; they could not enter through the front door or drink at the bar in most of the town's taverns. In Clairton the company deducted one dollar from every worker's pay to finance the construction of a swimming pool and then prohibited black workers from using it. In Gary the superintendent of U.S. Steel's Gary Works, who also served as head of the city's park board, not only insisted on segregating recreational facilities but threatened to fire black steelworkers if they—or their children!—dared to use the "white" parks. There was at least some "integration," however. Buck Leonard, a member of the Baseball Hall of Fame who lived in Homestead for seventeen years, vividly recalled the town's red-light district. "They had forty-five women in one block—forty-five women doin' business with men. And what was so queer about it to me, it was black women doin' business with white men. All the women were colored, but all the men were white."[64]

Within the context of exclusion and inequality, African Americans managed to develop a diverse array of institutions and activities that served their needs, gave expression to their own distinctive culture, and softened the rough edges of life in and around the mills. Black churches flourished, often with the encouragement of the steel companies and their welfare officers, who recognized that religious exhortation could help inculcate the virtues of industrial discipline and domestic containment among footloose southern migrants. Sometimes the companies offered buildings and land for aspiring congregations and provided employment in the mills for the workers who often pastored these churches. In Johnstown the Reverend J. H. Flagg was the founder and minister of the Bethel AME Zion Church, which held its worship services in a building donated by Cambria Steel. Flagg had been a blacksmith in Enterprise, Alabama, until a fire destroyed his shop and home. Then, as his son recalled, "the boll weevils flattened us out, too." He came to Johnstown in 1916, went to work in the mill for thirteen cents an hour, and became a prototype of the worker-preachers who were an integral part of black working-class communities. In Aliquippa, Rev. Theodore Roosevelt Snowden, a native of Portsmouth, Virginia, and graduate of Lincoln University, was a blast-furnace worker at J and L's Aliquippa Works and the minister of the First Missionary Baptist Church in nearby Leetsdale. In Duquesne Rev. Fletcher Williamson worked as a chipper at the Carnegie Steel works and pastored a storefront congregation.[65]

Many black preachers became so dependent on the companies for their economic well-being that they remained tactfully silent about racial discrimination in employment. Indeed, one clergyman in Gary acknowledged that "the churches have become subsidiaries of the steel corporation and the ministers dare not get up and say anything against the company." But it would be a distortion to see the black church only as an instrument of social control imposed from above. The main impetus toward religious activity came from within the community, and from black women in particular. Excluded as they were from all but the most menial employment, and relegated to homes in the most dilapidated sections of the mill towns, many women found redemption in the social and spiritual life of the church. Due in significant measure to their initiative, black migrants to Homestead organized twenty-three new churches between 1915 and 1939; and Abram Harris acknowledged that black congregations in Allegheny County were planning to spend a million dollars on new buildings in a single year, with most of the money coming from the pockets of church members. Harris, a highly educated man with an essentially secular outlook, lamented the absence of a comparable commitment to social welfare spending in the black community; and Lockhart Iron and Steel welfare officer William Young, a graduate of Lincoln University, complained that the Baptist church that black steelworkers attended in McKees Rocks was characterized by a lamentably "low intellectual level." It has "served [as] little better than a shouting station," he said, "a place where men and women get ready to die." More likely, the "shouting" that went on there provided much needed release and renewal for "the man who makes his hard daily turn in the mills and the woman who makes her hard daily turn in the home."[66]

In the 1930s and 1940s, some black churches became incubators of unionism. In Duquesne Rev. Williamson helped organize an Amalgamated Association lodge in 1933, and in the late 1930s he became a strong partisan of the Steel Workers Organizing Committee (SWOC) and an officer in his local union. Even many of the full-time pastors who had been closely aligned with the companies gradually transferred their allegiance to SWOC and the United Steelworkers. The CIO cultivated them as potential allies of great value in the black community and often asked them to deliver the invocation and benediction at union meetings, but it could not offer the kinds of material benefits the employers had provided. Nonetheless, as the members of their congregations went over to SWOC, the clergy had little choice but to go along. By 1946 Horace Cayton could declare that "few Negro preachers, whether they have large or small churches, whether in Gary or Pittsburgh, would dare to come out openly against the United Steelworkers of America. Any preacher foolhardy enough to do so would soon lose his congregation."[67]

In Birmingham gospel-singing groups provided a vital—and immensely popular—form of cultural expression. Initially, many of them were organized in and around the workplace and sanctioned by the companies, as in the case of the TCI Sacred Singers, TCI Women's Four, and TCI Section Crew. But with the coming of industrial unionism, at least one group announced proudly, "We want you to know we belong to the CIO." Another group, the Sterling Jubilee Singers, was transformed by ex-prizefighter, local radio disk jockey, and steelworker Perry "Tiger" Thompson into the CIO Singers. In their song "Satisfaction," biblical themes provided the foundation for the injunction to "stay in union."

175

Well you read in the Bible,
You read it well.
Listen to the story,
That I'm bound to tell.
Christ's last Passover,
He had his Communion.
He told his disciples,
Stay in union.
Together you stand,
Divided you fall.
Stay in union,
I'll save you all.[68]

Even more famous as an expression of the steel towns' racially separate culture were the athletic teams that, like the gospel quartets, often had their roots in company-sponsored activities. Hosea Hudson, a left-wing union activist who worked as a molder at Stockham Pipe and Fittings, recalled that "ball games and singing" were central to the social life of Birmingham's black community in the interwar years. Even after he became a Communist, Hudson remained a church member and sang in gospel quartets. But long hours on the job kept him from playing baseball for the Stockham team. "Ball game was over when I got out the shop," he remembered. "It was a real mess, I tell you, cause I love ball games." On occasion, especially when Stockham played a strong opponent, Hudson would miss an entire day's pay to attend the game. Nationally prominent teams like the Birmingham Barons and Homestead Grays drew heavily from the pool of talent provided by the industrial leagues in their areas; in fact, the Grays were originally made up of black workers at the Homestead Works of Carnegie Steel. By the 1920s they had become an independent and highly successful commercial enterprise that featured some of the best black ballplayers in the nation and provided a popular source of entertainment for African Americans in the Monongahela Valley steel towns.[69]

Ultimately, though, corporate welfare programs for African Americans achieved a good deal less than their architects intended, mainly because athletic leagues and colored community choruses could not compensate for the fact that the steel companies continued to limit most black workers to the "jobs 'no white man would keep.' " That this was true demonstrates how much corporate policy in this regard was driven by racist assumptions. Part of management's rationale for constructing elaborate occupational ladders was its recognition that dead-end jobs tended to breed discontent among workers. As early as 1918, one industrial manager had warned of the danger of "work of a character which leads to nothing in the way of further interest, opportunity, acquisition of skill, experience, or anything else which makes an appeal to normal human intelligence and ambition." But this was precisely the kind of work that employers reserved for blacks, apparently because they refused to credit them with "normal human intelligence and ambition." In the 1920s steel company officials were still arguing that "handling molten and white hot metal affords the kind of intensive work and alternating rest periods which . . . Negroes are peculiarly adapted to." According to John T. Clark of the Urban League, a corporate survey conducted in Pittsburgh "gives the Negro the highest rating in hot and wet work, as helpers to skilled workers, and especially recommends Negroes for work requiring speed."[70]

Trapped as they were in dead-end jobs, some black workers responded in ways that served to reinforce the stereotypes that haunted—and further circumscribed—their existence. Initially, black migrants from the South were concerned mainly with making as much money as they could in the shortest possible time. In their minds, the mills were a stepping-stone toward that goal but not necessarily a final destination. Some planned to return home as soon as possible; others were eager to test the boundaries of the labor market. Thus in the booming economy of the war years and the early 1920s, turnover rates among black workers became legendary. According to Clark, the average length of Negro employment during the war was one month; by 1923 it had improved to three and a half months. In that year, the A. M. Byers Company of Pittsburgh hired 1,408 black migrants to maintain an average southern black labor force of 228 men.[71]

In his investigation of the condition of African American workers in the Pittsburgh area, Harris found a ready explanation for these statistics. "Where the Negro was said to be un-industrious," he concluded, "incentive to better his lot in the plant was absent. Here, Negro workers were confined wholly to unskilled work and were not promoted as in some other plants where they had made favorable impressions upon their employers." Harris found that in places where black workers had achieved positions such as foremen, riveters, machine operators, time-keepers, and shipping clerks, there was little labor turnover among them. Twenty-one years later, when the Urban League was asked to conduct a study of "the reasons for excessive absenteeism among Negroes" in the coke ovens of Jones and Laughlin's South Side Works, its investigators reached essentially the same conclusion as Harris had in 1924. They found a problem rooted first and foremost in the company's long-standing policy of concentrating black workers in the most hazardous jobs and refusing to promote them. According to the Urban League's report, "practically all of the men claimed that the heat, smoke and gases made it necessary for them to stay away from the plant periodically for three or four days 'to get some fresh air.' " But above all, in a plant where "no Negro had ever been granted an apprenticeship or ever been promoted to any job above that of a laborer," the men in question "showed no feeling of loyalty to the company." On the contrary, "they were unanimous in their statement that . . . the company cares nothing about them and that, as a result, they feel no sense of responsibility in 'doing the company a favor' by working full time."[72]

· · · · ·

With the onset of the Great Depression in 1929, black workers found that their status as a permanent part of the steel industry remained unchanged, even in the most trying of circumstances. They also found, however, that relative to the "Americans" and the "foreigners," their vulnerability increased. Like many industries, steel was devastated by the collapse of the American economy in the early thirties. With the mills running at a small fraction of their capacity, layoffs and sharp reductions in the workweek ravaged the steel towns. In 1929 U.S. Steel had 224,980 full-time employees. By April 1933 more than half of them were laid off, and not a single hourly worker was employed full-time. Of course, all workers and their families suffered during the Depression. But in steel the sharply differentiated internal labor market meant that some workers suffered far more than others. Ethnic and racial factors accounted for the difference. Overall, the "native whites" fared best, as companies needed their skill and found it natural to reward their "loyalty" and "efficiency." The "foreigners" came next in the hierarchy, although Carroll Daugherty, an economics professor at the University of Pittsburgh, observed that within this vast and highly differentiated group employers demonstrated "very definite preferences for certain nationalities among them." Mexicans, the latest comers to the industry, proved to be the most vulnerable group of all. The Mexican population of Chicago was reduced by nearly half in the 1930s; the number of Mexicans at Illinois Steel's South Works declined from 1,900 to 300 in only two years. In Gary the repatriation of Mexicans, at first by voluntary means and then by coercion, became a civic crusade. The steel companies contributed their part by demanding that workers produce citizenship papers in order to keep their jobs.[73]

The extreme vulnerability of Mexican workers is a clear indication that the relationship between race and nationality was complex and subject to renegotiation as historical circumstances changed. Mexicans in the steel towns of the Midwest had been an "inbetween" people, and had even been regarded by some personnel managers and by many of their fellow workers as "white." In his pioneering ethnography of Mexicans in Chicago and the Calumet Region, Paul Taylor found that color was very much an issue in the hiring of Mexican immigrants. "We take the light-colored ones," said a management representative at a textile factory; "we want to avoid anything that isn't first-class and looks as though it might be colored." The employment manager of a steel mill said essentially the same thing. "When I hire Mexicans at the gate I pick out the lightest among them," he admitted. "It isn't that the lighter colored ones are any better workers, but the darker ones [look] like the niggers." Another employer spokesman put the matter in even balder terms. "Our Mexicans," he said, "are white." But foreign nationals who had emigrated from homes just south of the U.S. border, and who were in many cases dark skinned, could not lay claim to anything approximating the "wages of whiteness" in the crisis that engulfed American society in the early 1930s. African Americans may have been irrevocably "colored," but they were also citizens of the United States. Mexicans, by and large, were not, and they paid the price.[74]

Relative to "native whites" and "foreigners," however, blacks were laid off in disproportionate numbers, and generally they had fewer resources to fall back on in a time of sustained unemployment. Daugherty, who conducted extensive research in the nation's steel-producing regions, found "rather general agreement" that large numbers of black workers were so demoralized by this experience that from the employers' standpoint the "wisdom of re-employing them" became questionable at best. Quite apart from this observation, African Americans were vulnerable for other reasons. They were concentrated in the least skilled and most expendable jobs. In Alabama continued corporate investment in new technology led to a further "whitening" of the labor force; and when government pressure via the National Recovery Administration led to increased wages for steelworkers in 1933, employers—in the South at least—"preferred to employ whites rather than increase the wages of Negroes." Also, in the eyes of the companies, blacks were beginning to lose their value as a loyal bulwark against unionism, for after more than a decade in which their fidelity had gone largely unrewarded, they were suddenly suspected of *disloyalty* and therefore rendered all the more vulnerable. Overall, as far as African American employment in steel is concerned, the statistics for the Depression decade tell a simple story. Black workers constituted 8.5 percent of the industry's labor force in 1930 and 6.8 percent in 1940; during the decade, their numbers fell from 52,956 to 39,660.[75]

But statistics do not tell the whole story. A closer examination of Gary, Indiana, will provide a more nuanced portrait of the Great Depression's impact on the lives of black workers and on their attitudes toward employers and unions. The fabled Steel City was a segregated city—in its housing, schools, parks, and even cemeteries. When blacks migrated northward in search of employment at Illinois Steel's Gary Works, they were concentrated in several areas of the city and lived alongside European and Mexican immigrants, apparently with remarkably little friction at first. Gradually, however, a clear pattern of residential segregation emerged. Gary's black population more than tripled during the 1920s, even though employment in the mills could not begin to keep pace with the rate of migration, and black employment at the Gary Works actually declined after 1923. As migrants continued to pour into the central district and whites moved out, the area evolved into a ghetto and a slum. Overcrowding became a major problem, and death rates from pneumonia, tuberculosis, and homicide skyrocketed. Meanwhile, many restaurants and downtown businesses displayed Whites Only signs; schools were rigidly segregated, even where neighborhoods were not; and parks were "Jim Crowed." As late as 1944, a study conducted by the National Urban League found that Gary displayed many of the characteristics of "a typical community in the deep south."[76]

This was the city in which Claude Barnett, a Chicago-based journalist, entrepreneur, and apostle of racial uplift sought to implement an ambitious plan that he hoped would improve the condition of black workers and, at the same time, rekindle their sense of loyalty to management. Barnett's saga was an African American version of the Horatio Alger story. Like Alger, his was not exactly an ascent from rags to riches, but he did become a successful businessman whom *Ebony* magazine ranked among the one hundred most influential black Americans.

He was born in Florida in 1889 but raised in Chicago, mainly by his mother, who supported herself and her son by working as a domestic servant. While in high school, Barnett also worked part-time as a housekeeper in the home of Richard W. Sears, of Sears, Roebuck and Company. In 1904 he left Chicago to attend Tuskegee Institute, where he finished the advanced course in only two years. There he developed an intense admiration for Booker T. Washington and black capitalism. After a stint as a postal clerk back in Chicago, he founded the Associated Negro Press, the black counterpart of the white-run major news services, and directed it for the rest of his long working life.[77]

Barnett shared the antiunion animus that had long been prevalent among sections of the black bourgeoisie. He believed that although black workers' experience with unions had been "disastrous and discouraging," employers had generously provided them with jobs and, in some instances, community welfare programs aimed at improving their standard of living. Now, with the CIO reaching out to black workers in ways that the AFL had rarely done, he calculated that the steel companies, and U.S. Steel in particular, might be willing to make a major investment in the well-being of African Americans in return for a reaffirmation of their traditional hostility to unions. "My interest . . . is with the mass of Negro workers," he told a U.S. Steel official in October 1936. "I want to see their condition improved," by "striking a bargain" with capital.[78]

According to the terms of this bargain, "colored men . . . [would] follow their traditional instincts of remaining loyal to their employers," and management, in turn, would give black workers greater access to skilled jobs in the mills. Barnett presented himself as the broker who would oversee the implementation of this accord. He volunteered to conduct a survey of the attitudes of black workers in the steel-producing areas of Pennsylvania, Ohio, and Alabama. But above all, he focused on Gary.[79] The survey, he believed, would be beneficial to the employers in at least two respects. It would let them know what black workers were thinking, especially about the CIO, and it would be conducted by people who, without resorting to overt propaganda, would impart their antiunion views to the workers. In addition to the survey, Barnett suggested plans for expanding black home ownership, building housing projects, and developing a broadly based "community improvement program." The goal in each case would be to "tie the Negro close to management."[80]

181

After months of consultation with U.S. Steel executives, Barnett received the go-ahead to initiate what became known as the Gary Project. But the Corporation signed a landmark agreement with the Steel Workers Organizing Committee in March 1937, just after he and his staff had completed their recommendations. Although the Gary Project thereby became expendable, its survey data provide important material for understanding the lives of black workers and their attitude toward the company and the union on the eve of the SWOC era.[81]

The project's interviewers found that "approximately 80% of the Negroes now working in the mills came directly to the city from the South." About 90 percent of them had lived in Gary for more than six years, and 70 percent for more than ten years. Generally, the length of residence corresponded closely with the length of employment in the mills. Two-thirds of the men had at least a sixth-grade education, and almost one-fourth had "some high school or college training." This educational level, the interviewers hastened to point out, compared favorably with that of foreign-born whites and should have resulted in "considerable progress" for Negro workers.[82]

But the interviewers found very little evidence of progress or optimism in Gary's black community. Although many workers apparently were eager to become home owners, relatively few had been able to do so. Beyond the home, interviewers portrayed a "disorganized community without any really effective . . . institutions of social control." The churches, in particular, appeared to have declined in influence. Although two-thirds of the black steelworkers indicated a church affiliation, most admitted that they attended only occasionally, and "many did not even know the name of the church they professed to attend." Overall, interviewers encountered the near pervasive feeling that "Gary isn't much better than . . . the South." Many African Americans had lived in the city for twenty years or more but had not found the promised land. Barnett and his staff detected instead "an attitude of discouragement, resignation, and underlying resentment," and a communitywide consensus that "the men who control the company are not interested in the Negroes and their problems."[83]

The issue that engendered the most resentment was job discrimination. Men who were otherwise reticent about talking to interviewers, especially when asked about their attitude toward the CIO, were unusually forthright on this question. According to an early summary of the survey data, "It is apparent that Negroes can work only in certain jobs—which, for the most part, are the hardest, hottest, and dirtiest jobs in the mills. They recognize the fact that in most instances they cannot advance out of the common labor bracket—and are denied the opportunity of moving into skilled jobs." Interviewers reported that the workers were "almost unanimous" in this belief.[84]

Actually, there were—or at least had been—some skilled workers among the African Americans at the Gary Works, and the details of interviews with seven individuals reveal the painful fact of their downward mobility during the Great Depression. All of these men were from the South; most had come directly to Gary from there and had lived in the city for more than ten years. All were married; three were home owners, and in virtually every case the interviewers identified their homes as "neat" and "clean." Two did not attend church; the other five did. Altogether, then, these men were not only more skilled but may also have been more stable and prosperous than the group as a whole. They were precisely the kind of men Barnett and, presumably, the leaders of the Corporation were counting on to act as the most reliable counterweight to the CIO.

Instead, the harsh reality of job discrimination was driving them toward unionism. A laborer in the tin mill had begun as a semiskilled worker and become a skilled roller in four years. Then, when new machinery was introduced in 1935, "a white man was given his job and he was put back to common labor." A chipper in the sheet mill recounted how "after the strike in 1919 he was given a job as a skilled worker operating a machine, but when the depression came they gave his job to a white man." An individual with sixteen years' seniority, now a laborer in the sheet mill, had previously been a skilled worker in the tin mill. But with the introduction of new machinery, "the white men were transferred to other departments on jobs paying the same or better. The colored were shifted to common labor in the sheet mill." And so it went.

The men reported that the company had stopped hiring blacks but continued to hire whites, that the introduction of machinery invariably meant the displacement and demotion of blacks, and that experienced black workers were compelled to "break in" inexperienced whites, who then moved up the job ladder to positions from which the men who trained them were excluded. To be sure, one man among the seven remained a skilled worker. He had been hired as a laborer, then became a blacksmith's helper, and then a foreman. At the time of the survey he operated a machine and said he did not think "the colored men would derive any benefit by going into the CIO." Another man, who belonged to the company union, told his interviewer that he would not join the CIO until he had "talked with his Superintendent." But the other five were clearly moving toward at least a tentative affiliation with SWOC. One declared that "the CIO is the best thing for the colored worker." Another, who did not believe that the union would "keep [its] promise to give colored an even break," said nonetheless that the "only alternative for the colored men is to join the CIO." A third said he had joined the CIO and was "going to see if they will do what they say." In almost every case, these men believed that by signing up "things could not be any worse and the union might make them better."[85]

On the whole, black workers in Gary felt that the Corporation had "double crossed" them. "Even though they stood with the company in the strike of [1919]," read one summary, "they did not benefit." To be sure, "a few men were kept in good jobs," but over the years most of them had been displaced by whites. With the coming of the Great Depression, and the consequent reduction in employment, blacks were—apart from Mexican nationals—the first to be laid off or demoted to less skilled jobs. This was even true, Barnett admitted, for "many of the oldest and most faithful Negro employees." Then, with the introduction of new machinery in the mid-thirties, black workers found themselves "bumped" again, usually without regard to seniority. And for those who remained in the mills, segregation appeared to be increasing, as, for instance, in "the separation of White and Colored in the wash rooms." The general sense, then, was that time had not served blacks well, and the company had not rewarded their loyalty. Now the CIO beckoned. How would they respond to the gospel of industrial unionism? And how would the Americans and the foreigners in the union respond to them?[86]

"Regardless of Creed, Color or Nationality": Steelworkers and Civil Rights (I)

AMONG THE AXIOMS guiding the study of the CIO era, few have been more reflexive than the belief that the Steel Workers Organizing Committee (SWOC) and its successor, the United Steelworkers of America (USWA), were uniquely centralized, hierarchical, and immune to rank-and-file influence. SWOC was launched, with much fanfare, in June 1936; the USWA held its founding convention six years later. According to labor economist Frederick Harbison, writing in 1940, SWOC's "centralization of authority in the hands of experienced and capable leaders" was responsible for much of its "stability, strength and unity." In 1944 *Fortune* characterized the USWA as, "in the best sense of the word, a business union[,] . . . a compact, hard-hitting phalanx ready to face employers with no sabotaging or ideological sass from the rear ranks." The image popularized in the 1940s has endured virtually intact. In 1986, on the fiftieth anniversary of SWOC's founding, historian David Brody wrote that not only were SWOC and the USWA "highly centralized," but "there was no factionalism, scarcely any dispute over union policy or political issues, and no challenges whatever to the national leadership."[1]

Examining the development of steel unionism from the angle of race and civil rights, however, renders several of these assertions fundamentally untenable. From the outset, SWOC's stated policy was one of "absolute racial equality in Union membership,"[2] but the leadership's attempts to implement this policy met with active resistance from the white rank and file. It would be an oversimplification to portray a liberal leadership pitted against a conservative membership. The leadership *was* liberal (in ways that mirrored both the strengths and the shortcomings of liberalism on issues of race); and the USWA became an important component of the broad civil rights coalition that emerged during and after World War II. But union officials were more given to rhetorical flourishes than aggressive deeds when it came to their policy of "absolute racial equality." Meanwhile, at the local level, some white unionists joined with black workers in a protracted campaign against discrimination. Overall, however, the unwillingness of the white majority to countenance more than token changes in steel's occupational structure pushed USWA officials toward glacial incrementalism and hollow declarations of good intent. In the final analysis, the historical record suggests that "sabotaging" and "sass" from the ranks did more to shape the union's practice on race than the policy statements that emanated from its "highly centralized" leadership.

$$\cdot \quad \cdot \quad \cdot \quad \cdot \quad \cdot$$

In important respects, though, SWOC's reputation was richly deserved. It was, after all, the creation of John L. Lewis, the charismatic but dictatorial president of the United Mine Workers of America (UMW). Coal miners had long been an unusually independent and contentious lot, and it is a testament to Lewis's ruthlessness and skill that he could create order out of chaos and forge a centralized and disciplined organization where a loose confederation of local and regional unions had once prevailed. But the cost of his victory was inordinately high. There were schisms, rival unions, rank-and-file rebellions, and the expulsion of a succession of internal challengers until it appeared that only craven yes-men and Lewis's family members remained to implement the UMW president's orders. When Lewis engineered the formation of SWOC, he placed United Mine Workers' vice-president, Philip Murray, in charge of this vital arm of the CIO and staffed it mainly with organizers on loan from the UMW. Like his boss, Murray spoke the language of "centralized" and "responsible" unionism. One of his first acts as SWOC chairman was to establish the organization's national headquarters on the thirty-sixth floor of Pittsburgh's tallest building, where he could literally look down on the offices of the steel barons and remind them that SWOC was "no fly-by-night effort but a well-financed movement of labor union professionals."[3]

As he surveyed the Monongahela Valley and its omnipresent mills from his lofty vantage point, Murray must have paused on occasion to contemplate how far he had traveled. He was born in Blantyre, near Glasgow, the son of an Irish immigrant who had become a coal miner and union activist in Scotland. At the age of ten young Phil joined his father in the mines, and at sixteen he emigrated with him to the United States. They arrived in New York on Christmas morning of 1902 and headed for Pennsylvania's Westmoreland County, where once again they labored together in the mines. "In Scotland we were union men," he later recalled, but "in America we had no union. One night as I came out of the pit, I complained at the weighman's office that I was being short-weighted and thereby losing money every day. Words led to a knockdown, dragout fight, and the next morning I was fired." Six hundred miners walked out in solidarity with Murray's "fight for honest pay." They held a strike meeting, voted to join the United Mine Workers, and elected the eighteen-year-old rebel president of their local. The strike was eventually broken, and its young leader was expelled from Westmoreland County by the infamous coal and iron police. From that moment, his friend Patrick Fagan recalled, "as soon as they seen or heard of Murray, the dogs of war were after him." From that moment, unionism became his calling.[4]

Murray found an additional haven of camaraderie in the Ancient Order of Hibernians and demonstrated his penchant for self-improvement by enrolling in a math and science course through the International Correspondence School. But most of his education came via his long apprenticeship as the loyal associate of the legendary "John L." It was Lewis who placed him at the head of the steel-organizing campaign. There he would remain—through the battles that led eventually to the development of a million-member union, through a painful break with Lewis in the early 1940s and his own presidency of the CIO, through the turbulence of World War II and the equally volatile postwar era, until he had become a figure of legendary proportions in the steel towns. Like Lewis, Murray was an autocrat. But unlike Lewis, he was a benevolent autocrat—"the Good Man of the labor movement," Irving Bernstein called him—whose devout Catholicism, personal warmth, and plain lifestyle bred a fierce loyalty among the rank-and-file unionists he led. "He became like a god to the members of this union," one activist remembered. "You couldn't say anything about him. Say anything about Philip Murray and you'd probably be killed."[5]

In the western Pennsylvania coal fields, Murray had entered an extraordinarily heterogeneous world where the impulse toward class solidarity was often overwhelmed by the weight of ethnic and racial loyalties. William H. Crawford, an Ohio miner whose son and namesake would become a district director in the United Steelworkers, once complained that "an Irishman has no confidence in an Englishman, an Englishman no confidence in a Welshman, a Welshman no confidence in a Dutchman, a Negro no confidence in a Yankee and a Yankee no confidence in the Negro, and *vice versa*, all around." The great achievement of the UMW in this context was that it forged an enduring organization by teaching the miners that "in union there is strength." As the UMW developed, new immigrants and African Americans made up an increasing percentage of the coal-mining workforce, but the leadership of the union fell mainly to native-born whites and British and Irish immigrants. Lewis was the son of a Welsh miner who emigrated to Iowa in the late 1870s; Murray was a Scotsman and, at the same time, "Catholic Irish clear through." David McDonald, who served as Murray's assistant in the UMW and SWOC, was the son and grandson of Irish immigrants. (His grandfather served as financial secretary of the Sons of Vulcan.) Patrick Fagan, who succeeded Murray as president of United Mine Workers District 5, was yet another son of the Irish diaspora. His father emigrated from Scotland to Ohio's Hocking Valley in 1880 before settling in Westmoreland County and joining the UMW.[6]

In steel, too, the leadership of the organizing campaigns came from old immigrants and those who, by the 1930s, were identified simply as American. Clarence Irwin, a skilled worker from the Brier Hill Works of Youngstown Sheet and Tube, recalled that almost all the leaders of the rank-and-file movement that shattered the catatonic calm of the Amalgamated Association in 1934 and 1935 were "middle-aged family men, well paid, . . . of Anglo-Saxon origin[, and] . . . far better off than the average steel worker."[7]

Similarly, among the steelworkers who became leaders of SWOC, often after playing an active role in the company unions or employee representation plans (ERPs), it was the Americans who predominated. John J. Mullen, the "fighting Irishman" of Clairton, was the son of an Irish immigrant coal miner. A high school graduate and apprentice glassworker who was fired for trying to organize his fellow apprentices into a union, Mullen got a job at Carnegie Steel's Clairton coke works in 1926, eventually becoming a heater. ("It's considered skilled work," he told labor economist Robert R. R. Brooks, "since it takes from eight to ten years to make a good heater.") Like Mullen, Elmer Maloy was the son of a coal miner and UMW member. He began working at Carnegie's Duquesne Works as a water boy in 1911 and over the next seven years worked his way up to crane man and millwright before taking leave to fight in World War I. He returned to the mill after the 1919 strike and eventually became an electrician, one of the most skilled jobs in the industry. As he ascended the occupational ladder, he also tutored himself in accounting, stenography, and business English through the International Correspondence School. George Patterson, who was born "about a mile" from Murray's birthplace in Scotland, emigrated to the United States at the age of sixteen and found employment as a roll turner's apprentice at Illinois Steel's South Works in Chicago. After working ten hours a day at his trade, he attended classes for four hours in the evening until he earned his high school degree. Eventually, he became not only a highly skilled worker but a church deacon, Sunday school superintendent, and scoutmaster.[8]

Patterson and Maloy were fired by U.S. Steel for trying to transform the ERPs into bona fide unions and for drawing close to SWOC in the process. Mullen quit before he could be fired, but the company then evicted him and his family from their home as a warning to other workers. All three were appointed to SWOC staff positions in 1936. A year later, Maloy was elected mayor of Duquesne, and Mullen, mayor of Clairton (a position he held for the next sixteen years). The experience of such men—their relatively high levels of education, their location in the upper echelons of steel's occupational hierarchy, and their reflexive confidence in their rights as American citizens—made the exercise of leadership seem natural to them. At times, they were remarkably successful in forging a broad united front of the diverse elements that constituted the steel labor force. But for decades steel unionism continued to bear the mark of the ethnic rivalries and patterns of succession that were so integral a part of working-class experience in the United States. Len De Caux, the CIO's publicity director, remembered SWOC as a "Catholic setup." Apparently, this identity became more pronounced and more distinctively Irish over time. As late as the mid-1960s, labor journalist John Herling found widespread resentment in the ranks over the fact that "the leadership elite was largely confined to a single religious and ethnic sector of the union."[9]

The ties between coal and steel had always run deep. Many steelworkers were the sons of coal miners, and many had begun their working lives "underground," often before they reached their teens. Beyond these organic links at the grassroots, Lewis and Murray saw to it that the union they so carefully nurtured in steel would bear the mark of the UMW. Four of the top five officials in the Steel Workers Organizing Committee—Murray, David McDonald, Van Bittner, and William Mitch—were also officials of the United Mine Workers, and as late as 1940 two-thirds of SWOC's district directors continued to draw their salaries from the miners' union. The imprint of the UMW was especially evident in SWOC's peculiar mix of rational corporatism and quasi-feudal rule. But the miners also bequeathed another, quite differ-

189

ent, legacy to SWOC, for in the American labor movement few organizations had a better reputation for fairness on issues of race than the United Mine Workers. From its beginnings in the 1890s, the UMW had proclaimed its commitment to racial equality; it had painstakingly built interracial unions in Alabama and other southern coal fields during the heyday of Jim Crow; it had placed Negro organizers on its payroll and worked out a "UMW formula" to ensure black representation in the leadership of local unions. To be sure, the Mine Workers' formal commitment to racial equality masked a more complex reality. Black miners were concentrated in lower-paying jobs that were especially vulnerable to mechanization, and as late as 1919 a veteran black unionist charged that the great majority of the mines in Indiana and Illinois "deny colored men the right to work." During the 1920s large numbers of Indiana and Ohio miners, including some who were revered as union pioneers, belonged to the Ku Klux Klan, and in the coal fields of southwestern Pennsylvania white union members were largely responsible for the relative absence of blacks from the mines and surrounding communities. Even so, experienced black miners remained strongly committed to the union, and influential black voices continued to laud its "excellent record of racial fairness."[10]

The fact that the UMW was behind the formation of the CIO only accelerated the prestige of the new unionism in the black community. The National Urban League announced hopefully that "the plans are to model the new steel workers' union along the same lines as the Mine Workers." The NAACP declared that insofar as the CIO followed the racial policies of the UMW, "Negro workers ought to flock to the CIO unhesitatingly, for the UMW is known far and wide for their absolute equality, regardless of color." Even Claude Barnett, who regarded Negro workers' experience with organized labor as "disastrous and discouraging," acknowledged that the UMW "has been notably fair in its treatment of its colored membership."[11]

Perhaps no one was more euphoric about the coming of the CIO than John P. Davis, the executive secretary of the National Negro Congress.[12] Although he was a graduate of Bates College and Harvard Law School, Davis was also a sharp critic of capital, a deeply committed partisan of organized labor, and if not a Communist himself, then a close and willing ally of the Communist party, which played an increasingly dominant role in the National Negro Congress. He welcomed the rise of industrial unionism not only because he believed in the class struggle and the cause of labor, but also because he saw the CIO as an instrument that held out renewed hope for the full emancipation of African Americans. By September 1936 he was telling black workers that they faced a clear and momentous choice "between joining the union with their white fellow workers and taking the side of their slave driving employers." "Not for themselves alone," he declared,

but for all Black America, will Negro steel workers strike a telling blow for economic freedom by organization. For them it will mean the end of intolerable wage slavery. But 85,000 Negro steel workers with union cards will signal the beginning of the organization of all Negro workers. They will mark a start toward the liberation of hundreds of thousands of Negro sharecroppers, of hundreds of thousands of Negro women sweating away their lives as domestics. This will mean the winning of powerful allies in our struggle for democratic rights and civil liberties.[13]

Although he did not share Davis's soaring optimism, Murray no doubt welcomed the prospect of "85,000 Negro steel workers," or any fraction of that number, "with union cards." He announced a policy of "absolute racial equality in Union membership" and expressed his determination to "secure the active cooperation of all organizations of a racial character." But in the language of the day "racial" could refer to ethnicity and nationality as well as color, and Murray's priority in this regard was clearly the myriad fraternal organizations of the foreign-born. He was especially aware of the broad reach and strategic location of the International Workers Order (IWO), a Communist-controlled benefit society with more than sixty thousand members. In many steel towns where European immigrants remained a vital component of the labor force, the ethnic fraternal orders were deeply rooted in the community, and they offered a haven where unionism could be discussed openly and without fear of reprisal. Murray assigned IWO and Communist party leader Bill Gebert the task of building a close working relationship between SWOC and the ethnic associations. In October 1936 Gebert chaired and Murray gave the keynote address at a Fraternal Orders Conference in Pittsburgh, where organizations such as the Croatian Fraternal Union, the National Slovak Society, the Lodge of Lithuanians of America, the United Ukrainian Toilers, the South Slavonic Catholic Union, and the Greek Workers Educational Federation came together to endorse the steel campaign.[14]

In comparison, SWOC placed a lower priority on organizing black workers. In November 1936 Murray acknowledged that "we have not made satisfactory progress in getting [Negro] workers enrolled," and he expressed the belief that the organization of black steelworkers would "follow, rather than precede, the organization of the white mill workers." Nonetheless, SWOC leaders went out of their way to develop friendly ties with the black community. In February 1937, with SWOC's full cooperation, the National Negro Congress sponsored a well-attended National Conference of Negro Organizations in Pittsburgh, at which delegates from black churches and fraternal orders joined with rank-and-file workers to pledge their support for the steel drive. In an impassioned keynote address, Murray declared that "there is no industry where there is greater discrimination against the Negro than in steel," and—to a standing ovation—he pledged "complete equality for the Negro worker in the shop and . . . the union hall." Soon, leading black organizations and spokesmen for the race were broadcasting their support for the cause of industrial unionism. The National Urban League lauded the "tremendous effort . . . the CIO is making to enroll Negro members," and the NAACP declared that blacks had "everything to gain and nothing to lose by affiliation with the CIO." In Chicago a clergyman acknowledged that he had "always been against the A. F. of L. and organized labor, but I am convinced that this C. I. O. move is the only thing for my people. I want every steel worker of my church to sign up in this Union. And more than that I want you to go out into the by-ways and hedges and sign up every steel worker you come in contact with."[15]

More than any other "race" organization, the National Negro Congress threw itself into the fray with unqualified zeal. Davis promised to find—and, in some cases, fund—black organizers for the steel drive, and a month after SWOC's formation he reported that he had secured the appointment of three Negro organizers in the Pittsburgh area, two in Chicago, one in Cleveland, and one in Birmingham. By July 1937 there were fifteen black organizers on the SWOC staff. Some were from the United Mine Workers, but most had come to steel via the National Negro Congress and were closely associated with the Communist party. Although the well-funded SWOC operation recruited hundreds of organizers, few of them could match the credentials of African American Communists Ben Careathers and Henry "Hank" Johnson. Careathers, the son of a Tennessee sharecropper, played a key role in the organizing drive at Jones and Laughlin and later claimed that he had personally signed up nearly two thousand steelworkers in the union. Johnson, the ninth of eleven children from a Texas farm family, had lived a remarkable itinerant existence that included stints working in a Detroit auto plant, organizing longshoremen in Baltimore and Norfolk, and studying for a bachelor's degree at the City College of New York. When SWOC assigned him to Gary, he quickly became one of the best-known and most effective CIO organizers in the Chicago area.[16]

In SWOC's early days, because of the desperate need to find men and women with the experience and fortitude to confront the steel companies and their powerful allies, the leadership recruited numerous Communists, perhaps as many as sixty, onto the organizing staff. In Ohio, a Communist party leader claimed, the "entire staffs of the Party and the Young Communist League were incorporated into the steel drive." But as SWOC solidified its base, the "Reds," black and white, became expendable. Len De Caux, a "Party liner" in the CIO, recalled that every Communist in the steel drive was a "marked man, watched closely at all times, and dispensed with as soon as possible." Partly for this reason, De Caux called SWOC "as totalitarian as any big business."[17]

Totalitarian or not, SWOC was hardly the juggernaut it claimed to be. At the beginning of 1937, David Brody reminds us, it was "essentially a paper organization, a mountain of membership cards plus an indefinable reservoir of good will." Much of its energy had been focused on reelecting Roosevelt and breaking the Republican stranglehold on the municipal governments in the steel towns. Certainly its leadership had no reason to believe that SWOC could have won a representation election at any of the major steel companies. But on March 2 U.S. Steel signed a collective bargaining agreement with SWOC. The agreement meant that the long era of repression and suffocating corporate domination that had begun at Homestead in 1892 was finally over. It also meant that tens, and soon hundreds, of thousands of steelworkers would become members of an "outside" union that many of them continued to regard with a mix of apprehension and hope.[18]

With Big Steel under contract, SWOC's first great test in the trenches came with the Little Steel Strike that began on May 26, 1937, and ended in a crushing defeat for the union several months later. The Little Steel companies—American Rolling Mill, Bethlehem, Inland, National, Republic, and Youngstown Sheet and Tube—in reality were major corporations; they were little only in comparison with U.S. Steel. But their leaders were rabidly antiunion. Big Steel's willingness to recognize SWOC only strengthened their determination to resist any further encroachment on the industry's open-shop tradition. The strike's most volatile focal points were the plants of Republic Steel

Fig. 5.1. The union comes to "Little Siberia": SWOC picket line, Jones and Laughlin Steel, Aliquippa, Pa., 1937. Credit: Historical Collections and Labor Archives, Penn State

in Chicago and the industrial cities of northeast Ohio. In Chicago contemporaries estimated that the great majority of black workers at Republic joined the union; many of them were active on the picket lines and in the constant round of strike-related activities. But some blacks remained loyal to the company, and in the daily confrontations between pickets and strikebreakers their presence among the latter threatened the racial harmony that SWOC had worked hard to develop. The union overcame this danger to the strike's solidarity by sending a large corps of black activists out to do battle with Negroes who were menacing the picket line. The sight of black unionists thrashing black strikebreakers quickly undermined the perception that the conflict was about race. To Dan Burley, of the *Chicago Defender*, it appeared that "Mexicans, blacks, Polish, Italians, Germans, and Irish [were] all being poured into the pot and . . . moulded into American citizens."[19]

Burley's view was shared by other contemporary observers who believed that the unionism of the CIO was overcoming a generation of racial antagonism in steel. In Pittsburgh a *Daily Worker* reporter attended a mass meeting where hundreds of Negro and white workers "were packed close together in the union headquarters, . . . chatting together, talking over problems of strategy, their arms around each other." In Cleveland, George Schuyler of the *Pittsburgh Courier* observed black and white strikers eating and conversing together in "a perfect picture of labor solidarity and social equality." In Chicago, Schuyler told the story of Joe Cook, an African American who had been elected president of the Steelworkers' local at Valley Mould and Iron even though the overwhelming majority of his fellow workers were white. Cook was not only the president of the local union, Schuyler reported, but its "moral and spiritual leader" as well. When the Ku Klux Klan threatened to run him out of town, white unionists escorted Cook to the picket line to ensure his safety. "Not only that but they made the bartender in a saloon serve him although no Negro had ever been served there before."[20]

But the situation was dramatically different in the northeast Ohio steel towns of Canton, Massillon, Warren, and Youngstown, where Negroes formed a small percentage of the labor force, the black bourgeoisie was closely tied to the companies, and there were few liberal or left-wing forces that could provide alternative leadership in the black community. In Canton no more than half a dozen black steelworkers joined the strike, and many of those who scabbed "forced their way into the mills with guns." Republic Steel and Timken Roller Bearing not only hired large numbers of Negro strikebreakers but also offered wages that black men had never been paid before. "Negro Canton has not seen such prosperity in a long time," Schuyler reported. "Pimps, gamblers and 'stables' of loose women have descended upon the town to garner the pickings." Schuyler worried that the "jeering of white pickets, clashes at mill gates, and flaunting of new 'scab cars' by suddenly enriched black workers augurs ill for future race relations in these communities."[21]

In Johnstown, where blacks made up only 2.5 percent of the population, the strike against Bethlehem Steel began on June 11. Although the main dividing line continued to be the one that separated "Americans" from "foreigners," Schuyler also found "clashes between white and Negro workers." He estimated that of the four hundred African Americans employed at Bethlehem's Cambria Works, no more than half a dozen had joined the strike. There *were* many blacks on the picket lines, but they were coal miners, and members of the United Mine Workers of America, who had marched on the city from surrounding communities in solidarity with their fellow workers. They expressed shock at the failure of black steelworkers to join the walkout. But Schuyler was less surprised. He recalled a traumatic episode in 1923, when, following an altercation in which an African American migrant killed two white policemen, Johnstown's mayor had ordered every Negro who had lived in the community for less than seven years to "pack up his belongings and get out." To reinforce the mayor's ultimatum, the Ku Klux Klan had burned crosses on the hills surrounding the city. But Bethlehem Steel, which had attracted most of the Negro migrants to the city, had refused to implement the mayor's order. Thus, Schuyler concluded, "the workers of foreign extraction who are the backbone of the CIO strike do not . . . have as much claim on the Negroes' allegiance as the . . . mill bosses." They "have never helped the local Negroes in their struggle for citizenship rights. Nor have they ever insisted the Negroes be given a wider variety of employment in the mills. Their attitude has been almost identical with that of the American whites, and Negroes recall that twice the Ku Klux elements have sought to banish them from the community."[22]

The Little Steel Strike was a major setback for SWOC and the CIO, but the devastating impact of the Roosevelt recession created even greater problems. The nationwide economic downturn of 1937–38 caused a 70 percent drop in steel production and made workers' employment prospects uncertain at best. The problem was compounded by the companies' increasing reliance on technological innovation, in part to offset the increased labor costs that unionization brought. No sooner had major steel companies signed agreements with SWOC than workers found that mechanization was undermining the economic security they thought they had achieved. In August 1938 a unionist in Aliquippa complained to John L. Lewis that for eleven months he and fifteen hundred J and L workers had been "doing practically nothing," because "strip mills have taken our jobs [and] the contract drawn up by the CIO stops us from working in any other department." By 1940 U.S. Steel's brand new "Silvery Monster," the Irvin Works, had displaced eleven thousand employees of the Corporation in western Pennsylvania, and steel union officials expressed alarm that this "great engineering success" had become a "social flop."[23]

With SWOC unable to protect steelworkers' jobs, the number of paid-up union members fell precipitously. Often, in mill departments that had been SWOC strongholds, no more than a handful remained loyal to the union; in giant plants with thousands of workers, only a few hundred continued to pay dues. To remain solvent and maintain its authority in the mills, SWOC resorted to "dues picket lines," where staffers and loyal union members surrounded the plants and refused to let any hourly employees go to work until they paid their monthly dollar. Alex Powell, a black worker at the Duquesne Works of Carnegie-Illinois, recalled that Duquesne's mayor, SWOC official Elmer Maloy, even called out city fire fighters to reinforce the picket lines. He ordered the firemen to "turn the water on people who were trying to enter the mill," Powell declared. "We were forced to join the union."[24]

In fact, there were good reasons to join the union voluntarily. Black workers in particular benefited in clear and tangible ways from the unionization of steel. The signing of collective bargaining agreements in the industry meant not only a general raise in pay but also wage increases that served to narrow the yawning gap between higher- and lower-paid workers. That most of these agreements recognized the seniority rights of black workers meant that men who had worked many years for a company could no longer be discarded arbitrarily as they so often had been during the leanest years of the Great Depression. The very presence of the union on the shop floor encouraged black workers to be conscious of their rights in a way that had never been possible before; no longer would they have to rely entirely on the whims of front-line supervisors and other "good white people" in the ranks of management. In 1940, after asking whether "the CIO [has] played fair with us Negro workers," Joe Cook offered an unequivocally positive response. "Look at the new clothes our children wear," he declared, and "the homes that we are paying out since the SWOC enrolled us and showed us how to wage a successful fight for decent wages and better working conditions."[25]

On the picket lines in Cleveland, Indiana Harbor, and Chicago during the Little Steel Strike, and in more formal interviews with workers who were reflecting on what unionism had come to mean in steel,

Schuyler, Horace Cayton, George Mitchell, and other observers detected something deeper than the issue of wages and working conditions. They perceived the tender shoots of a new consciousness that appeared to transcend ethnocentrism and even color. A black worker in a small plant told Cayton and Mitchell that before the coming of the CIO, "everyone used to make remarks about 'that dirty Jew,' 'that stinkin' black bastard,' 'that low-life Bohunk,' but . . . I never hear that kind of stuff any more." A white steelworker acknowledged how much he had learned from the charismatic black organizer Hank Johnson, who "woke a lot of us up by showing how the company built up race hatred by playing on our sense of superiority." He also acknowledged that he had reflexively accepted the exclusion of black workers from his department, "until I began attending union meetings." Another white steelworker admitted that he would not want to work for a Negro foreman but added hopefully that "the CIO will get us away from thinking so much about color." Even at union-sponsored dances, there were forays across the great divide. One steelworker reported on the "mixing of the groups" and the "intermixing between both races and sexes in the dancing" at events sponsored by his local union. The Negroes "socialized with the others," he concluded, "and seemed to feel that we're all one race."[26]

Given the close and volatile connection between sex and race in the popular imagination, this "mixing" on the dance floor was even more remarkable than the fact that working men who had long been separated by color and ethnicity were greeting each other as "brother" at union meetings. Sex was "the principle around which the whole structure of segregation . . . is organized," Gunnar Myrdal observed in 1944. More than a decade later a veteran trade unionist acknowledged that with the "mingling of the sexes, anti-Negro sentiment reaches its wildest and most fantastic levels. Intermarriage, free love and rape become common scare words repeated over and over again." When the CIO promoted social "mingling," and no riot ensued, it was the occasion for wide-eyed commentary. Thus, Schuyler reported, "the Negroes [at a CIO-sponsored picnic in Akron, Ohio,] declared they were 'never so well treated' and 'didn't know they were colored.' White girls vied with each in dancing with the Negro men and expressed regret that there were no more Negroes to dance with than those present. No one was shot, cut or insulted," Schuyler concluded, "which was unique for a picnic anywhere, but especially for an interracial one in Akron, O[hio]."[27]

All of this ferment did not go unopposed, however. Because insurgent unionism challenged long-standing power relationships and cultural norms, it was bound to provoke a backlash, not only from recalcitrant employers and their allies in government but among working people themselves. The CIO presented itself as the vanguard of a unified working class and as a "people's movement" that spoke to—and on behalf of—the broad American majority. But to many Americans, it appeared that the CIO not only stood for industrial chaos and contempt for property rights but also embodied a secular-rationalist value system that was at odds with their own deepest beliefs. Many Roman Catholic and evangelical Protestant spokesmen strongly criticized the direction of the New Deal and the CIO in the late 1930s, and Father Coughlin maintained a devoted following in many of the same ethnic neighborhoods that the CIO depended on for support.[28]

Cayton and Mitchell were by no means unaware of the strength of this backlash and the danger it represented for the new unions. Their interviews with workers, black and white, reveal many instances of timidity, ambivalence, and hostility toward the CIO and its interracialism. Among the examples they recorded, perhaps none is more remarkable than the reflections of the "Italian president" of a SWOC women's auxiliary, who commented that if

> you give [Negroes] a foot . . . they'll take a yard. If you ask them to your dances they'll come and they don't just dance with each other but some of them will try to dance with white people. If they do, the white women will just stop going to the dances. There's something about colored men that just makes you *afraid*. I don't know what it is, but you have a certain *fear*. I don't feel that way at all about the girls, but the men are different. . . .
>
> I know that Negroes *are* workers, and I suppose that, really, they *are* human, but there's just something about them—that black skin[.] I guess the trouble with us is really that we're not liberal enough.[29]

Clearly, the speaker viewed black males through the lenses of ancient—and deadly—myths that ultimately reduced them to beasts and rapists. But insofar as "that black skin" evoked "a certain fear," only the men seemed to threaten. The speaker's divided consciousness is evident in her belief that black women were different—or, rather, were *not* different—as well as in her begrudging acknowledgment of African Americans' humanity and her sense of guilt that she was "not liberal enough." Alone, apart from the suffocating mores of the larger society, she felt she could "be nice to them." But "with the eyes of everyone" on her, it seemed impossible. Here, then, was a person who was no longer content to give unqualified expression to the hoary clichés and dogmas of white supremacy. SWOC had created the social space and cultural ferment that made her ambivalence and inner turmoil possible.[30]

But how far could the CIO go in contesting the mores of the larger society and transforming the consciousness of its expanding ranks? It had begun as an insurgent social movement whose grassroots leadership consisted disproportionately of left-wing cadres with a principled commitment to working-class unity and racial equality. For the "sparkplug unionists" who joined the cadres on the picket lines in battle against a formidable, often vicious, corporate adversary, there was a natural tendency to respect the commitment of anyone who stood by the union. In such circumstances, the color question could seem irrelevant, or nearly so. But the strikes of 1937 gave way to the uncertainty of the Roosevelt recession and the long, uneven process of broadening the organization's base plant by plant. When the CIO's victory was finally secured with the coming of World War II, it became apparent that the fence-sitters and newcomers who swelled the union membership rolls were far more likely than the "sparkplug unionists" to reflect the white supremacist reflexes of the larger society. Among the broad ranks of the CIO's new immigrant constituents, there was little receptivity to an agenda that threatened to disrupt insular communal norms. Their resistance to racial change was augmented during the war by the growing presence of white migrants from the hardscrabble farms of the rural South who found it strange or—more likely—subversive that anyone could "think a Negro is just the same as they are."[31]

From an organizational standpoint, however, steel unionism triumphed decisively in the context of a booming war economy. All of the major independents, except ARMCO and National, signed contracts with SWOC in 1942. Then, with the AFL still nipping at its flanks, SWOC called for a representation election at U.S. Steel and won by more than one hundred thousand votes, a margin of better than eleven to one. Although Murray continued to regard his no longer new creation as a "crawling, sprawling sort of an organization, which is just in its infancy," even he recognized that the time had come to transform SWOC into an international union. In May 1942, at the Public Music Hall in Cleveland, seventeen hundred delegates gathered to give birth to the United Steelworkers of America.[32]

• • • • •

During the war Philip Murray embraced the cause of racial equality as a "holy and a noble work . . . that all right-thinking citizens should dedicate themselves to." He became a member of the NAACP's national advisory board, and he helped make the CIO an important voice in support of fair employment practice and a wider civil rights agenda. Indeed, he was so proud of the industrial union federation's commitment and achievements in this regard that he told the 1944 CIO convention, "God help the Negro in America, and God help the minority groups of America, were it not for the splendid work that is being done by this great institution of yours and mine. We don't confine ourselves to the mere adoption of resolutions in meetings of this kind; we make those resolutions effective and workable."[33]

In embracing the cause of African American equality as noble and holy, however, Murray and most CIO leaders continued to understand race in essentially economic and "class-essentialist" terms.[34] They believed that aggressive government intervention to bring about "full employment" and "permanent prosperity" would create the climate that would make equal opportunity and racial harmony possible. In December 1945 Murray warned that the "need for a full employment program must be satisfied *before* we can answer the question of what will happen" to the Negro in the postwar economy. The key was the "size of the pie," said Walter Reuther of the United Auto Workers. "We had better plan for a bigger pie, enough for all." In the meantime, those who advocated special measures such as "super-seniority" to address problems of racial discrimination in the workplace were "confused," selfish," and a danger to labor solidarity as Murray and Reuther defined it.[35]

CIO leaders celebrated their organization as a "people's movement . . . [that] does not ask questions of race or color or creed or origin." Compared with the AFL's racism, this aggressively inclusive—and color-blind—stance represented a huge step forward. But it led Murray to conclude that racial equality could be achieved within the framework of conventional trade union goals and practices, and that the "emancipation of the colored people" was contingent on their "willingness to associate themselves" with organized labor. "The colored people have to be here," he told a black USWA official; "it is their only hope; they have nowhere else under God's sun to go but to the CIO labor movement."[36]

As a long-time trade union administrator who had gained access to the highest echelons of power and privilege in American society, Murray emphasized education, legislation, and negotiation via well-established channels over mobilization at the grassroots level as the best means to accomplish the goals he sought. "In the field of prejudice," he once said, "we go about our work steadily and quietly. We hold to the theory that we can get more done in that fashion." Because he believed in the essential "decency of the majority," he also believed that appeals to the best instincts of white Americans would lead to changes in their attitude and behavior toward people of color. Again, he envisioned no special—and costly—measures to rectify the long-standing grievances of African Americans, nor did he anticipate that the implementation of the seniority principle in the workplace would often give contractual sanction to the continued subordination of black workers.[37]

Above all, Murray was determined that control of the unions' civil rights agenda should remain in his own hands and those of his trusted associates. In 1942, when black delegates to the United Steelworkers' constitutional convention demanded the election or appointment of an African American to a position in the international union, he responded by choosing Boyd Wilson to serve as his "special envoy," with the nebulous responsibility of "developing the proper kind of human relations that ought to exist between colored and white workers." A native of Missouri and a high school graduate with two years of college, Wilson had been working at Scullin Steel in Saint Louis when SWOC launched an organizing drive at the plant in 1940. He was hired as a staff representative soon after he joined the union, and he became part of the informal network that approached Murray at the Cleveland convention. The black delegates had recommended the selection of Joe Cook as their representative, and compared with Wilson's credentials, Cook's were impeccable. Whereas Wilson had worked in steel only briefly before joining the SWOC staff, Cook had been a foundry worker since 1917 and a pioneer in the building of the union not only at Valley Mould and Iron but throughout the vitally important Calumet region. Schuyler called him the "moral and spiritual leader" of his local union, where he had earned the respect of black and white alike. But Cook was apparently too close to the "Reds"; he had been active in the National Negro Congress for years and was even featured on occasion in the pages of the *Daily Worker*. Wilson recalled being approached by a SWOC staffer close to Murray who informed him that "while Joe Cook is a good man, he is associated with Communists and is therefore unacceptable." When he asked "Who is acceptable?" the reply was, "You."[38]

In 1948, again in response to pressure from black activists, United Steelworkers' convention delegates authorized the creation of a permanent committee on civil rights. Murray appointed five district directors to the committee, with Thomas Shane, of the USWA district headquartered in Detroit, as chairman. The president and recording secretary of a Chicago local had publicly accused the international union of racial discrimination in its hiring practices, and they and other black workers dared to hope for the appointment of an African American as executive secretary of the committee. But instead Murray chose Tom Shane's brother Frank for the position. It was a bitter moment, Wilson recalled, because "Frank knew absolutely nothing about the Negro problem and had no interest in it."[39] In Detroit, moreover, many African Americans were serving on the staff of the United Auto Workers, but none on the United Steelworkers' staff. According to Wilson, "Tom insisted he could not find a single Negro worthy or competent to be a staff man."[40]

The issue of black representation erupted on the floor of the USWA convention in 1950. When several delegates raised questions about the makeup and agenda of the Committee on Civil Rights, Murray called on Tom Shane to offer a defense of the committee's record. Shane reminded black delegates that although the committee had existed for only two years, "it is 1,950 years ago that Christ was crucified," and that even he spent "33 years" preaching the doctrines of Christianity before his crucifixion. In response to calls for the greater involvement of African Americans in the committee, he declared that "where minorities are discriminated against, it falls upon those who are not among the minorities to be in the foreground of the fight." But he reserved his sharpest words for the resolutions submitted by four locals advocating the appointment of a "Negro Vice-President" of the international union. To Shane, this was simply "Jim Crowism" and "the type of thing that we are fighting against." He received immediate support for this position from several black delegates who came forward to defend the leadership's record on civil rights. "I am a trade unionist and a good trade unionist," declared Jimmy Jones of Philadelphia, "and although I would love to sit up there at [Phil Murray's] right or left hand, . . . I don't ask anybody to appoint me to any executive position in this Union because I am a Negro." Alex Fuller, from Detroit, followed and, even more than Jones, framed his remarks in a way that meshed almost perfectly with the leadership's perspective. "We have confidence in our International Officers and in our Chairman of this Committee," Fuller said, "and we, as the little people, know . . . they will continue to do the job."[41]

The United Steelworkers' leadership did make occasional concessions to black demands. In 1952 Murray assigned Joseph Neal, a black staffer from Baltimore, and Gilbert Anaya, a Mexican American from Los Angeles, to the Committee on Civil Rights. (Wilson would join them in 1956.) But the leadership's principal concern—and constraint—in approaching issues of race was the union's white majority. In deference to the ethnoracial character of this majority, the committee defined civil rights in terms that were broad enough to incorporate a wide variety of issues and groups, including "so-called 'minorities' " such as Japanese Americans, Puerto Ricans, the "large Hebrew population of New York City," and even Scandinavians in Wisconsin and Minnesota. Although the committee acknowledged that the "greatest degree of racial discrimination has been directed . . . against the American Negro," Murray himself argued that "we could not have a . . . singular civil rights program" that was too closely identified with the cause of African Americans. "It must be the type of program," he said, "that is dedicated to serv[ing] the interests of all groups, whoever they may be, that are subject to persecution or discrimination." Over time, the committee referred less to civil rights than to "human rights," "human relations," and "inter-group relations"; and its leaders rarely, if ever, mentioned combating racism as an objective. Instead, they spoke in vague generalities about the need to "create a better economic and social climate in which to live."[42]

In its own way, however, the committee played an active and highly visible role in the struggle for black equality. Within two years of its founding, it had issued more than one hundred thousand pieces of literature to USWA locals, supplemented by many feature articles in the union's newspaper, *Steel Labor*. In conjunction with academicians and civil rights spokesmen, it held numerous "human relations" conferences and seminars on college campuses and in various steel towns across the nation. It also worked closely with the Leadership Conference on Civil Rights, the NAACP, the Urban League, the Jewish Labor Committee, and the National Conference of Christians and Jews to lobby in support of a broad-gauged legislative agenda, and it was the recipient of generous praise for its efforts. In 1954 the executive director of the Pittsburgh Urban League acknowledged that the USWA was one of a handful of organizations seeking to eliminate employment discrimination in Pennsylvania. In the same year, Herbert Hill of the NAACP declared that "in city after city Steelworkers are in the active leadership of the fight for civil rights." Speaking to the delegates at the USWA's biennial convention, Hill applauded the "long history of joint activity and cooperation between our respective organizations."[43]

The union was especially effective in lobbying for the passage of fair employment practice legislation in Pittsburgh, Youngstown, Gary, and other urban areas where the steel industry predominated, but it also looked inward and sought to educate its own membership in the "principles of democracy." Echoing Murray, the union affirmed that "most humans are basically decent" and argued that an "appeal to the decency of the majority of workers" would suffice to "wip[e] out the last remnants of injustice" in the steel industry. Where there was resistance from white rank and filers, said one USWA official, it represented the lag between "intellectual understanding" and "actual practice." In such instances, patience and a "continuing . . . educational program" would solve the problem.[44]

When workers united under the banner of unionism, USWA leaders argued, all of them would reap the economic benefits; and thus "organizing the unorganized" became the best program for the "protection of civil rights." United Steelworkers secretary-treasurer David McDonald offered an especially crass version of this view in a speech he delivered at a USWA-sponsored civil rights conference in February 1950. "The very root of the evil," he said, "runs to the denial of economic rights to certain of our people." Attacking the problem at its roots meant focusing on the "economic base," and for McDonald the denial of decent wages became the denial of civil rights. By this sleight of hand he made the struggle for black equality synonymous with CIO campaigns to achieve better wages and benefits for all industrial workers. "Civil rights would not have improved," he concluded, "had it not been for the existence of the United Steelworkers of America. It took the United Steelworkers of America to bring our members the civil rights I am talking about. It took the United Steelworkers of America to bring to all our members, not just our colored members[,] these civil rights in the form of improved working conditions and security."[45]

Tactically, of course, it made sense for the union to define civil rights in broad terms that resonated in the life experience and historical memory of its new immigrant constituency. Such an approach may have made the very existence of the Committee on Civil Rights more palatable to the union membership. But it also tended to obscure the special character of the oppression of African Americans and to reinforce the comforting illusion that they were merely the "last of the immigrants," who would achieve their rightful place in the American social order by following the immigrants' presumed path of storing up communal resources and waiting their turn at the table of opportunity. In addition, the union's economic and class-essentialist perspective was wrong on at least two major counts. It was wrong, first, in assuming that the struggle for black equality could be subordinated to the conventional agenda of the trade union movement. Increasingly, African Americans were determined to wage that struggle as an end in itself and to take leadership of the struggle into their own hands. But equally important, the argument that racial discrimination imposed an economic cost on black and white workers alike contradicted the experience of many steelworkers. In an industry where the income gap between the skilled and the unskilled was unusually large, many whites must have known all too well that genuine equality for blacks, based on their ability and seniority, could impose an economic cost on *them*; it could mean giving up their privileged access to the skilled jobs, higher pay, and better, safer working environment that the wages of whiteness proffered.

· · · · ·

The leadership did remind the members periodically that "any collective bargaining contract which either by its terms or its actual operation permits discrimination on account of race, creed, color or nationality violates the policy of this union." And there were more than a few instances where the forthright application of this policy at the local level led to the expansion of opportunity for African Americans. In Lorain, Ohio, for example, Local 1104 confronted a "racial problem" in 1947, when three Negro workers were scheduled to move up from their jobs as bricklayers' helpers to the apprenticeship training that would allow them to become skilled tradesmen. Even though this move was clearly sanctioned by the local seniority agreement that had been in effect since 1940, the company balked, claiming that the attitude of the white bricklayers made it impossible. When the union threatened to take the case to arbitration, and the company agreed, white workers in the department went on strike for five days. But the union leadership stood firm, the strike collapsed, and, the local president reported in

1950, "we have not had any trouble since then," even though several other Negroes had become apprentices in the meantime.[46]

Another case in which aggressive intervention by the union leadership resulted in concrete gains for black workers occurred in Monessen, Pennsylvania. Here, according to the local union president, "sanitary accommodations such as showers [and] toilets . . . proved to be a very sore spot." In this case, the local officers insisted on "one large shower room for all," and when some white workers complained, the leadership took the position that "the individual whose prejudice don't allow him to wash with his fellow workers just has to go home dirty."[47]

Sometimes, the combination of union policy and tight wartime labor markets led to quite remarkable changes. Prior to the unionization of the giant Inland Steel complex at Indiana Harbor, blacks and Mexicans had worked only in the "lowest paid jobs in the lowest paid departments." But during the war minority workers were promoted to positions they had never held before, not only in "black" departments such as the blast furnace and coke plant, but in a "lily-white" department such as the tin mill as well. At the nearby South Works of Carnegie-Illinois Steel, Local 65 succeeded in opening seventy-one positions to black workers above the level of janitor and laborer, including jobs such as boilermaker, rigger, inspector, and crane operator, which traditionally had been defined as "white." At Valley Mould and Iron, Joe Cook reported that although skilled jobs such as machinist, millwright, carpenter, and electrician remained closed to blacks, their access to semiskilled positions had increased considerably.[48]

For the most part, however, the USWA acquiesced in the continuation of long-standing patterns of racial inequality in steel industry employment. The situation at TCI's Ensley Works was typical of the practices that prevailed over a long period of time in the Birmingham-Bessemer area of Alabama. According to Herbert Hill, black workers in the Ensley Works blast furnace were concentrated in a racially segregated labor pool and had separate, and limited, seniority rights only within its confines, whereas whites were "automatically promoted on the basis of seniority, skills and job vacancies into a variety of production and craft operations." Hill concluded that as a result of these separate seniority lines, which were negotiated by the company and the union at the local level, "Negro workers are permanently locked in menial and unskilled job classifications."[49]

At times these local seniority agreements not only limited opportunity for blacks but also hardened the lines of racial separation and subordination in the workplace. Writing on behalf of a "group of colored workers" at the U.S. Pipe and Foundry Company in Bessemer, the local union president complained in 1950 that "we hold no skill[ed] jobs and are losing semi-skilled jobs every year." Before the organization of the plant by the United Steelworkers, Charles Alford reported, "the Negro held many sub-foremen jobs and many skill[ed] jobs." But now "he is restricted to common labor and semiskill[ed jobs] the white[s] do not desire to fill." This pattern was also evident, on a much larger scale, at Pullman-Standard's railroad-car manufacturing plant in Bessemer. After the signing of a collective bargaining agreement in 1941, the number of "one-race" departments at Pullman-Standard actually increased; and in the mid-1950s, when the local union proposed a change from occupational to departmental seniority, seven new "one-race" departments were created. Attorneys for the NAACP Legal Defense Fund estimated that by 1964, "96% of the employees in the Bessemer plant were located in racially identifiable departments."[50]

Although the most egregious examples of racial segregation occurred in Alabama and other southern states, there was no Mason-Dixon line in steel. In keeping with the larger pattern nationwide, segregation in southern mills was de jure—that is, openly sanctioned by collective bargaining agreements—whereas in the North it was "merely" de facto. Jobs and lines of progression were not openly designated as black or white in northern mills as they often were in the South. But the combination of long-standing company hiring practices and union-negotiated seniority agreements essentially had the same effect in the North that the more explicit forms of racial identification had in the South. Because seniority was occupational or departmental rather than plant-wide, black workers were, in Herbert Hill's words, "locked in" to specific departments or lines of progression, in Buffalo as well as Birmingham. Even when they won the right to transfer to a new and better department or job ladder, they could not carry their accumulated seniority with them. As long as seniority agreements were negotiated locally, and as long as white rank and filers were determined to maintain their racially based advantages in the mills' occupational hierarchy, the contracts negotiated by the USWA would tend to "freeze" African Americans into low-paying, dead-end jobs.[51]

The observations of a local union official at the Bethlehem Steel plant in Steelton, Pennsylvania, cast a bright light on the pattern of racial discrimination in northern mills and offer tantalizing suggestions about the change from a multitiered pattern of collective identity and job segmentation to one in which "Negro" and "white" became the only fault line that mattered. Joseph Bazdar, the local union president in Steelton, observed in 1950 that "prior to the organization of our plant the range of jobs open to minority groups was very limited. In many departments it was necessary for workers belonging to the 'wrong' group to curry favor with their foremen by plying them with material gifts, including cash, or by the old fashioned method known as 'boot-licking[,]' in order to retain even the lowest paid and most menial of jobs." In Steelton the "wrong," or "minority," groups included not just "workers of the colored race" but "recent immigrants or sons of immigrants, workers of the wrong religious denomination, workers who did not belong to certain fraternal lodges and even workers who did not live in the same neighborhood as their foreman." By 1950, however, there had been an "appreciable change in the status of the majority of these workers." Apparently, the divisions between Hunkies and Americans had diminished significantly, and even the recent immigrants had left their minority status behind. In the process, the long-standing barriers to their upward mobility within the plant's occupational hierarchy had been "largely wiped out."

For black workers in Steelton the old barriers remained in place, but Bazdar's portrait of the relations between blacks and whites in the workplace was anything but simple. He asserted that "a definite ceiling exists on job opportunities for the majority of our negro workers slightly above the floor." At this level blacks and whites were "continuing to work in perfect harmony." It was at the higher levels that problems existed, and he blamed them on the company; on the local union, which had been "lackadaisical in its approach to this problem"; and on white workers who on one hand were dependent on the day-to-day assistance of "negro helpers" but on the other hand were fearful that these same workers would "encroach" upon jobs that whites wished to safeguard as their own. In a statement that marked him as a rarity among white members of the United Steelworkers, Bazdar admitted that the problem of racial discrimination was "becoming more acute with each passing day."[52]

. . . . .

Bazdar made his observations as part of a survey that the Committee on Civil Rights conducted in February and March 1950. Tom Shane's letter announcing the survey asked all local union presidents to describe the range of jobs open to minority groups and to discuss what steps the locals had taken to overcome problems of racial discrimination. Numerous respondents claimed that such discrimination simply did not exist. From Johnstown, Pennsylvania, came the report that discriminatory practices were "a thing of the past"; from Montvale, Virginia: "We have not had any trouble at all"; from South San Francisco: "We have nothing we can put our finger on here"; from Sterling, Illinois: "If we did have any discrimination it was so small that it was possible we did not notice it"; and from Saint Louis: "The membership has been nothing but a happy family of all for one and one for all."[53]

Many locals noted the absence—even the exclusion—of African Americans from their plants and managed to conclude that this signified the absence of racial discrimination. There may have been some basis for such an assertion in the union's geographically remote areas. The president of a local representing iron ore miners on Michigan's Upper Peninsula wrote that he had "worked in the mines for over 16 years and [I] have never seen a colored person or a Jew underground." But even in Memphis, Indianapolis, Youngstown, and several Pennsylvania steel towns there were statements to the effect that "our local union . . . has never been confronted with a racial discrimination problem inasmuch as there have never been Negroes employed at the . . . Plant." In Elwood, Indiana, a local union representative wrote, "Possibly you have heard that Elwood does not have any Negroes. They have not been able to get a foothold here. Not that I believe we are so opposed to the colored race, but . . . years ago something happened (I don't know what) and there has been a tradition that Negroes were not wanted here[;] so you see it is something that we can't help."[54]

Fortunately, some locals were much more candid in acknowledging problems of discrimination and reporting on the mixed outcome of efforts to achieve racial equality. The recording secretary of a Donora, Pennsylvania, local admitted that "there are four or five departments in our plant where white workers will not work with negro employees." A "year or two ago" a grievance committeeman had tried to "correct some of these evils, but he was cited for starting [a] racial disturbance, and he gave up." And at Inland Steel, where during the war black workers had been able to secure jobs in what had long been "lily-white" departments, local union president Harry Powell acknowledged that the end of wartime labor conditions had meant the erosion of these gains. In recent years, said Powell, "we not only have not gone forward but have been forced back"; in part, because "the Union on the departmental level has lost its drive to open all jobs . . . to all people."[55]

In Youngtown, Sam Camens, the president of Local 1330 at the Ohio Works of U.S. Steel, stated that overall the problem of discrimination in hiring and upgrading at the plant stemmed from "[c]ompany hiring practices"; and, he added, "there is nothing in our contract that can force the employment office to change these practices." Camens readily acknowledged, however, that the union's task was complicated by the fact that there was active rank-and-file resistance to the entry of blacks into certain departments and to their upgrading in other departments where they were concentrated in the less skilled jobs. "The broad gauge [railroad] is strictly discriminatory, with only white employees," he said. "There is definite resistance on the part of management, and even our union membership, to breaking down this Jim Crow set-up." Similarly, the rolling mills were "strictly Jim Crow"; and "all the [craft] shops in our plant, as elsewhere throughout the district[,] are Jim Crow outfits, due to the hiring practices of management" and the "strong" acquiescence of white union members in this discriminatory pattern.[56]

The conscientious and meticulously detailed reports from Joseph Bazdar in Steelton, Harry Powell in Indiana Harbor, and Sam Camens in Youngstown gave the Committee on Civil Rights ample indication of the problems in the steel industry. Perhaps the many denials of discrimination and the fact that hundreds of locals—including many in basic steel—did not bother to respond to the survey should have offered even more cause for concern. But the committee chose to take every glib and myopic letter at face value and thus to present a summation that was almost entirely self-congratulatory. "Approximately 99 per cent of all local unions participating in the survey," read the report, "report a wide range of jobs open to any worker, regardless of race, creed or color." The remarkable example of the South Works of Carnegie-Illinois Steel in Chicago, where Local 65 had succeeded in opening seventy-one jobs above the level of janitor and laborer to black workers, became—in the committee's summation—"typical" of the local unions' achievements. And in the relatively few cases where the committee acknowledged that "some form of discrimination still prevails," these were judged to be "largely a matter of company discrimination on the hiring level—a situation beyond the effective control of the union."[57]

· · · · ·

Fig. 5.2. Philip Murray, president of the United Steelworkers of America, speaking in Duquesne, Pa., 1949. Credit: Historical Collections and Labor Archives, Penn State

In retrospect, it is clear that the top leaders of the United Steelworkers were sitting on the edge of a smoldering volcano, with little apparent awareness of the dangers that confronted them. Over time, events would demonstrate that the union possessed neither the understanding nor the will to deal effectively with the festering problems of racial discrimination in steel's occupational structure and racism in the USWA's own ranks. But in 1950, and for a number of years thereafter, there was a moment of racial equilibrium within the union that convinced the leadership that its policies were achieving the objectives of maintaining institutional stability and advancing the cause of civil rights. This moment of equilibrium was made possible by the convergence of several factors, which included Philip Murray's continuing reputation among black workers as a man of honor who cared deeply about the goal of racial equality; the union's incremental gains in securing promotion rights for African Americans; the booming economy of the late 1940s and early 1950s; the favorable position of black steelworkers relative to their counterparts who labored in the service sector and on the margins of the industrial economy; and, finally, the relative calm that accompanied the larger struggle for black equality in the period between the Dixiecrat rebellion of 1948 and the Supreme Court's 1954 decision in *Brown v. Board of Education*.

Murray died, suddenly and unexpectedly, in November 1952. In the outpouring of affection for the man whose name and persona had been synonymous with steel unionism since the founding of SWOC, perhaps none could match the reverence an African American gospel group in Alabama expressed. According to the CIO Singers,

> The Congress Industrial Organization assembled.
> The whole world began to tremble.
> Men, women, and children cried,
> When they heard the sad news Mr. Murray had died.
>
> He was the CIO's loss, but he's Heaven's gain.
> In the day of Resurrection we'll see him again.
> Good God Almighty our best friend is gone.
> I want you boys to help me, just sing this song.[58]

The CIO Singers were based in Bessemer, which in the late 1940s was the site of a violent confrontation between the United Steelworkers and the rival Mine, Mill and Smelter Workers, one of the unions expelled from the CIO on charges of Communist domination. Throughout this conflict, black ore miners remained loyal to Mine Mill, which had won impressive material gains for them and had vigorously opposed racial discrimination in the process. For this very reason, white miners had never been entirely comfortable in Mine Mill. They accused it of fighting for "social equality" and trying to "change our way of life"; they took offense when visiting Mine Mill officials made a point of shaking hands with black miners; they threatened to "form a white party line in the union" to counteract the alleged influence of the NAACP and the Communists. But with the encouragement of key regional and national leaders of the CIO, they ultimately opted for secession instead. After a bitter and sometimes violent electoral campaign, in which the Ku Klux Klan openly supported the secessionists, the CIO (acting as a surrogate for the USWA) defeated Mine Mill by a vote of 2,696 to 2,233 at TCI's iron ore mines. To black miners it appeared that Murray had betrayed them and that, as their union newspaper put it, the CIO and the United Steelworkers were "ten times worse than the giant corporation we have to fight."[59]

Black ore miners lived in communities that overlapped in many ways with the world of their counterparts in steel. Some—perhaps many— of them drank in the same taverns, attended the same churches, belonged to the same fraternal orders, and were members of the same extended family networks.[60] And yet, in spite of the USWA's unsavory role in the destruction of Mine Mill, Negro steelworkers remained loyal to their union and apparently shared the CIO Singers' reverence for "Mr. Murray." In an environment characterized by rigid adherence to the norms of segregation, the United Steelworkers offered black workers a significant measure of protection and respect. On occasion at least, the union even defended their job rights against the competing claims of hostile white workers. At TCI's Fairfield Wire Works, for example, African Americans had moved into "white" jobs during World War II, with the result that after the war their accumulated seniority placed them higher on the occupational ladder than some whites in the same lines of progression. In a letter to President Murray in July 1946, eleven white unionists had complained that "as it stands now no young white returning veteran can work himself up to a job of Wire Drawer without first helping a negro operator, and gentlemen that will never happen." But union officials at the local and district levels responded by defending the existing arrangement as contractually sanctioned, thereby breaching the walls of white supremacy and inviting the accusation that they had fallen prey to "communistic ideas."[61]

The loyalty that the USWA engendered among blacks was strengthened when Murray appointed Howard Strevel, a white Tennessean, to the District 36 staff in 1951. Strevel won the respect of many white steelworkers by aggressively and intelligently prosecuting their grievances. At the same time, he proved unusually sensitive to the concerns of black workers. On one occasion he even persuaded white union members at TCI to go on strike in support of what were in essence black demands for improved conditions in the coke plant. Although Strevel found it necessary to accept some of the institutional trappings of segregation, he openly transgressed the boundaries of southern racial etiquette in his relations with black workers. When whites reminded him that "we don't shake hands with blacks in Alabama," he replied, "Well, it's a good thing I'm not from Alabama." In 1953 a union official in East Texas reported on an influx of white steelworkers from the Birmingham area who claimed that they had left Alabama "because . . . Strevel was making it too tough for them."[62]

Herbert Hill offered an eloquent testimonial to the effectiveness of Strevel and other union officials who recognized the need to build an organization that offered more effective shop-floor representation to blacks as well as whites. Hill joined the staff of the NAACP in 1948

214

and became labor relations assistant to NAACP executive secretary Walter White. As a teenager in New York City he had been drawn to black culture and to leading black intellectuals on the anti-Communist Left. At Harlem jazz clubs he met Duke Ellington and Richard Wright; in Greenwich Village he had long discussions on the "Negro Question" with the brilliant and charismatic C.L.R. James and other Trotskyists, black and white. Although he was a graduate of New York University, he also worked briefly at a Crucible Steel plant in New Jersey and on the staff of the United Steelworkers before joining the NAACP. Michael Harrington, who became the leading spokesman for democratic socialism in the United States, remembered Hill as "one of the first people to . . . educate me out of my sophisticated Marxist ignorance" on issues of race. "Hill had originally entered the fight against racism as a socialist doing 'mass work' in the NAACP," Harrington recalled. "But in the course of organizing militant demonstrations against police brutality in Harlem, Hill's basic loyalty began to shift . . . to the NAACP itself. . . . Indeed his identification with the cause was so strong that he sometimes passed as a Negro. Dark-haired and swarthy, his knowledge of black argot was so impressive that he sometimes confused even Negroes about his racial identity."[63]

Ultimately Hill became famous for his criticism of organized labor's failure to live up to its declared commitment to racial equality. Indeed, one unionist would characterize him as "completely anathema to almost everybody in the trade union movement." But in the early and mid-fifties he played a central role in strengthening the alliance between CIO unions and the emerging Civil Rights movement. When he came to Alabama in May 1953 to investigate relations between the NAACP and the CIO in the state, Hill reported that among NAACP leaders and black steelworkers in the Birmingham-Bessemer area, "there was general agreement that the staff representatives and local union officials of the Steelworkers Union had done an excellent job on behalf of Negro workers in the processing of grievances against management." He found significant black representation in the leadership of local unions and concluded that "on the level of day to day trade union operation in enforcing the union contract, officials of the Steelworkers Union vigorously defended the job rights of Negro workers."[64]

There were similar signs of progress in other areas of the South. In District 35, which covered Georgia, the Carolinas, Tennessee, and Virginia, director William Crawford had developed a well-deserved reputation for racial liberalism. A former coal miner and UMW activist in his native Ohio, Crawford went to work as a skilled roller in TCI's Fairfield, Alabama, sheet mill in 1926. During the early New Deal, he served as district president of the Amalgamated Association, and he claimed to have been the first person to sign a union card when SWOC began organizing in the South. In 1942 the Steelworkers assigned him to Atlanta, where he won widespread respect as a man of "genuinely Christian spirit." Shortly before his death in 1954, he told the CIO convention that all of the locals in his district, "without a single exception," had eliminated every manifestation of segregation in their union halls. He reported that in Chattanooga, Tennessee, "following one of our enthusiastic meetings the members of the local union went down [to] the plant themselves, tore down all of the signs that had to do with discrimination, and . . . threw them away." What he left unsaid was that in this plant the workforce was overwhelmingly black; that even in a district where many locals had a black majority, Negroes had achieved only token representation on the district staff and then were assigned only to organize black workers; that in the larger plants in the district the conflict between black aspirations and white resistance portended "real trouble" ahead (as Crawford himself acknowledged in a more reflective moment). But in 1954 it was still possible to believe that the union and the nation had embarked on a relatively straight, evolutionary path toward the promised land of racial equality.[65]

A National Urban League study of employment opportunities for African Americans in the early 1950s provides another angle of vision on the gains that black steelworkers had achieved through unionism. This was a time when the economy was booming and labor market participation by African American males was at an all-time high. Among black men in their early twenties, 93 percent were in the labor force during the peak of the Korean War boom in 1953. Even so, employment in the unionized industrial sector was uneven and sometimes severely limited. In Cleveland, for example, African Americans made up 13.6 percent of the workforce in basic steel in the spring of 1952; but in the automobile industry, General Motors employed no blacks at its diesel engine plant in the city, and only 120 "nonwhites" in a workforce of 2,000 at its Chevrolet assembly plant. Throughout Ohio, at Ford as well as General Motors, the Urban League found very few African Americans employed in the auto industry, and most of them were in custodial and other unskilled jobs. In other industries the situation was even worse. National Cash Register employed 10,000 workers in Dayton; only 140 of them were African American, and no blacks were employed as production workers. At the Radio Corporation of America plant in Cincinnati, there were 2 black workers in a labor force of 1,500.[66]

For steelworkers, regardless of race, the USWA succeeded in negotiating wage increases and fringe benefits that compared favorably with the more widely heralded achievements of Walter Reuther and his United Auto Workers. The USWA won company-paid health care and pension plans in 1949 and negotiated wage increases every year from 1950 to 1955; during this period real hourly wages for steelworkers rose by 20 percent. For southern workers, black as well as white, they rose even more in 1954, when the union succeeded in eliminating the industry's long-standing north-south wage differential. The myth of the blue-collar middle class was, to be sure, overdrawn, even when applied to members of the UAW and USWA. In 1953, a very good year in steel, average annual earnings reached $4,542, less than $300 above the amount the Bureau of Labor Statistics estimated that a family of four needed to achieve a modest standard of living. Nonetheless, in comparison with their fellow workers who remained on the fringes of the industrial labor market in casual and low-wage employment, African American steelworkers must have regarded themselves as an aristocracy of black labor.[67]

In these circumstances, the great majority of black steelworkers proved to be loyal but not particularly active union members. In Baltimore, Joe Neal, one of the few black staffers in the USWA, complained that "his greatest problem was the lethargy among union members in general and Negro members in particular." In Youngstown district director James Griffin also expressed concern about black workers' lack of participation in their local unions. When an Urban League representative responded that this problem was not "particularly racial," Griffin readily agreed but argued that Negro workers had "more at stake" than whites and therefore had more reason to make use of the union apparatus. In Atlanta, Crawford admitted that he became "discouraged" because "the colored workers themselves do not grasp the opportunity as they should." He pointed out that in the largest local in his district, Local 309 at the Aluminum Corporation of America plant in Maryville, Tennessee, the union bylaws provided that there must be a Negro on the executive board. But "not one of these colored workers" had attended enough meetings to be eligible for election to the board. "I would like them to take better hold of it than that," Crawford concluded. "I would like them to attend the Union meetings and show that they appreciate the wonderful things the Union has done for them."[68]

Black workers had no monopoly on inactivity when it came to the affairs of the United Steelworkers. Although hemmed in by management's prerogatives and the bureaucratic encumbrances of the rule of law, the union remained a vital presence on the shop floor, and many workers continued to believe that it took "a little violation" of the contract to make it serve their purposes. But for men whose lives beyond the world of work were enmeshed in family, community, and—increasingly—the culture of consumption, the union as institution was becoming more distant and less relevant, an arena frequented mainly by blue-collar "lawyers," penny-ante "politicians," and a diminishing Left cadre. As paid functionaries of the USWA, Neal, Griffin, and Crawford were deeply invested in *this* union, but rank-and-file workers, black and white, increasingly tended to ignore it except in moments of crisis.[69]

All of these factors contributed to an equilibrium that USWA leaders dared to hope would become the norm in race relations within the union. But this equilibrium was necessarily fragile and short-lived, constructed on a foundation of sand, and subject to pressures that union leaders could not contain. In spite of their best hopes, the larger forces of civil rights and white backlash would not "blow over"; nor would conditions "return to normal." Within the mills, moreover, black workers found their separate and unequal status increasingly intolerable. As early as 1953, Crawford warned that the leadership would soon be "placed in the position of being 'Damned if you do and damned if you don't.' " In the same year, Hill concluded that black union members were keenly aware of the gulf between the CIO's official statements on civil rights and "the every day realities within the plants and . . . local unions." In Alabama, he said, "many Negro workers indicated a sense of despair and futility because the one important institution operating in the South that they hoped would provide the bridge across the divide of color was not doing so."[70]

"We Are Determined to Secure Justice Now": Steelworkers and Civil Rights (II)

CRAWFORD'S AND HILL'S warnings about the fragility of the USWA's racial equilibrium stand as a necessary counterweight not only to the union's energetic public relations machine in the 1950s but to those scholars and public intellectuals in our time who long for the "good old days" of working-class unity and broadly based solidarities before the emergence of "identity politics."[1] These intellectuals look back on the CIO and the political currents associated with the New Deal as the place where "common dreams" were forged, dreams that allegedly transcended race and the messy divisiveness of the new politics of identity. In this rendering of the past, the CIO becomes the embodiment of "working-class interracialism," and the Civil Rights movement of the 1950s and 1960s bears the burden of "produc[ing] . . . divisive effects" among industrial workers.[2] Thus, according to one labor historian, "the unions that had done the most to advance the cause of minority workers . . . suffered most grievously from internal conflicts generated by the civil rights movement and the burgeoning of black consciousness."[3]

It is undeniable that the early CIO featured moments of interracial unity and hopes for a new unionism that would "get us away from thinking so much about color."[4] But quite apart from the question of whether the experience of class *can* transcend other forms of identity,[5] we know that the insurgent unionism of the CIO rapidly came up against the hard realities of *white* racial consciousness and the backlash that black migration generated during World War II. We know, too, that the divisions the Civil Rights movement allegedly caused were already there, rooted in the occupational structures of basic industry and, more broadly, in the very fabric of American life. But the Civil Rights movement did demonstrate, once again, that racial harmony in the United States has been premised on black acceptance of a subordinate place in the social order. When African Americans made it clear that such acceptance was no longer possible, massive resistance became the order of the day.

This chapter examines the unraveling of the United Steelworkers'—and the nation's—moment of equilibrium on matters of race, as the *Brown* decision, the Montgomery Bus Boycott, and, in general, the quickened pace of the struggle for black equality demonstrated the limited reach of the much vaunted "American Dilemma." The second half of the 1950s was characterized not only by massive resistance to racial change but also by the shift from an era of black economic progress to one in which ambiguity, foreclosed opportunity, and major setbacks deepened the sense of apprehension and urgency among African Americans. In this context, the move toward black self-organization in the mills and other industrial workplaces was as inevitable as it was necessary. It was rooted in the growing disillusionment of a generation of black industrial workers and in their emerging recognition that justice for them would come not by following but by challenging the leadership of organized labor. In taking this momentous step, they were often accused of violating union solidarity. But they were learning the painful lesson that where issues of racial justice were concerned, union solidarity and the fading myth of working-class interracialism were chains that bound them to an increasingly intolerable status quo.

It is true that white steelworkers in the South recognized the necessity of biracial unionism, that black voting in the United Steelworkers was "uncontested" at a time when it engendered violent opposition in the political arena, and that blacks could even, in some instances, "represent whites." But most whites were determined to maintain their privileged position in the mills; they insisted that collective bargaining agreements reflect and ratify their caste interests.[6] Although they accepted certain practices within the union that were anathema in the larger society, they made it clear that "outsiders" and "idealists" would not be allowed to undermine the foundations of Jim Crow. Indeed, even in the early 1950s, a time when the struggle for black equality was not encountering massive backlash, white steelworkers demonstrated their determination to reinforce the boundaries of racial separation and caste privilege.[7]

This became painfully clear in Birmingham in the spring of 1950, when Philip Murray's order calling for the desegregation of all CIO facilities and events generated an avalanche of resistance. White unionists were outraged, and threats of secession were widespread. District 36 director Reuben Farr informed Murray, "Yesterday I was notified that there was a petition for decertification being circulated [at] Fairfield Steel. It was also reported to me that practically every employee that this petition has gone to has signed." Farr reported that at Stock-ham Valve and Fitting Company, where a collective bargaining agreement was scheduled for imminent renewal, a large number of white employees were actively seeking to terminate their membership in the union via a fifteen-day escape clause in the contract. Overall, he concluded, Murray's order "has had a very unfavorable reaction, especially in the Basic Steel companies, among our Local Union offi-cers, grievance committeemen and [the] rank-and-file as a whole. . . . It looks as though our union is completely torn asunder."[8]

Murray also received a letter from seven local union presidents in the Birmingham area warning him that continued tampering with the "feelings, wishes, customs and beliefs" of southern white workers would "sound the death knell of the Union in the South." In language prefig-uring themes that George Wallace, Richard Nixon, and Ronald Reagan would later articulate at the national level, the local union presidents exalted their own common sense and sanctified their own interests in the face of "moralists" who were trying to engineer unwanted changes in their way of life. "We are greatly concerned about the action of some of the Union representatives sent into the South from the North," they said. "These men too often try to drive us instead of lead us. . . . [T]hey act as if we were backwoods people who only recently were run down and shod and who do not know what is good for them. We want good advice for the good of our Union but we resent being 'talked down to.' " "We of the South know that our people will not be moved by 'moralist[s]' and 'idealists' such as these Northern people believe them-selves to be," they concluded. "We need no one nor do we want anyone who is more concerned with changing our way of life than he is with the problems of bettering our economic conditions and settling . . . our grievances."[9]

Murray got the message. In September 1950, when he delivered a Labor Day address to thousands of steelworkers in Birmingham, Com-missioner of Public Safety Bull Connor and his men strung a heavy piece of rope down the center of the hall. Whites sat on one side, and blacks on the other. Although Murray continued to insist that Jim Crow signs be removed from all offices and meeting halls of the United Steelworkers, Herbert Hill reported that "white and colored" signs for toilets and drinking fountains remained in most local unions and that a pattern of segregated seating prevailed in "all union membership meetings." Clearly, the volatile situation in Birmingham and much of the South made the international union exceedingly cautious about challenging the segregationist mores of its white membership, even during the brief era when equilibrium predominated.[10]

The USWA Committee on Civil Rights had been planning to hold a conference in Birmingham in 1950, to educate and mobilize the union membership in support of fair employment practice legislation. Similar events had been held in Philadelphia, Pittsburgh, Chicago, and Los Angeles earlier in the year, but in the wake of Murray's ill-fated desegregation order, Farr warned that it would be "impossible at the present time for us to give much support to this program in this District and maintain our Organization." Murray immediately forwarded a copy of Farr's letter to Committee on Civil Rights secretary Frank Shane. Acknowledging the importance of avoiding issues that would "in any way jeopardize the present and future growth of our union in the South," Shane postponed the event indefinitely. Three years later he cautiously approached Farr about the possibility of holding a "small[,] informal[,] non-publicized conference" on civil rights in the Birmingham area. The meeting was finally held in April 1954, more than four years after it had originally been scheduled.[11]

But then, in May the historic *Brown* decision hit the Deep South like a bolt of lightning and precipitated the era of massive resistance. In Alabama, which became a major stronghold of the White Citizens Council and of the new, mass-based Civil Rights movement, many white workers deepened their commitment to segregation. According to a leader of the Citizens Council, Tuscaloosa rubber workers and Birmingham steelworkers were "the backbone of the council movement in Alabama." Even a USWA official acknowledged that "doubtless many members of the United Steelworkers, as well as members of other labor organizations, are members of these Councils." Estimates from within the Steelworkers ranged from "10 percent of the membership to 50 percent." In Atlanta, an alleged "oasis of tolerance" that proclaimed itself to be "too busy to hate," several locals of the United Auto Workers became bastions of the Ku Klux Klan; one of them even boasted the Georgia Klan's grand dragon as a member. When former USWA official Morton Elder visited the city in 1956 to conduct a race relations survey for the Southern Regional Council, he found that although other industrial unions in the area had managed to avoid the insurrectionary backlash that had engulfed the UAW, their leaders admitted to "rather strained relations on the job, with communication between the races becoming less and less frequent."[12]

Steelworkers' officials responded to the escalating racial conflict by trying to keep issues of civil rights off the union's agenda in the South. They were well aware that the White Citizens Council was active among USWA members on the shop floor and that petitions endorsing segregation were circulating in the mills. They recognized that the union was powerless to prevent such activity. But according to one USWA official, "only Steelworkers business is to be considered in the local union meetings . . . the racial issue has no place there." When, on occasion, international union officers in Pittsburgh tried to apply the USWA's civil rights program throughout their jurisdiction, even the most liberal spokesmen for the union in the South were quick to sound the alarm. "I cannot undo overnight the work of years of prejudice," said John Broome, the president of Local 309 in Maryville, Tennessee. "The rights of minorities are very important, but they cannot be obtained or even preserved by action that might destroy our Local Union." In Alabama, Howard Strevel sounded exactly the same note. "We can be heroes," he said; "we can jump up and down and say we're going to follow the International Office, but I'm not sure Dave McDonald or anyone else would want me to destroy what we've done and set us back maybe ten years."[13]

· · · · ·

Strevel was right about David McDonald. Even more than Murray, whom he succeeded as USWA president in November 1952, McDonald did not want to jeopardize the USWA's institutional stability by aggressively promoting civil rights. Once hailed by *Fortune* as a "sharp accountant who directs [the USWA's] financial affairs with the scrupulous efficiency of a state bank auditor," McDonald became obsessed with the access that the presidency of a major union provided to the wealthy and famous. Although civil rights and other currents of social reform did not interest him, he was deeply concerned about a "revival of the spirit of brotherly love" in the relations between union leaders and corporate executives.[14]

Like Murray, McDonald was a holdover from the United Mine Workers, although he had never been a coal miner. The son and grandson of Irish immigrant steelworkers, he recalled that even when his father was incapacitated by an injury in the mill, "My mother kept her head high, and it never occurred to [her children] to do otherwise. She let us know that we weren't 'shanty Irish' and she never let us forget

223

the importance of school." McDonald earned his high school diploma at Pittsburgh's Carnegie Institute of Technology, played for a sandlot football team organized by his parish priest, and in 1923 was working as a typist at Wheeling Steel when Murray hired him as his secretary. With Murray, he made the transition from coal to steel and became SWOC's secretary-treasurer. His reputation in the CIO was that of "a boy in a man's job," "the kid who got Phil's tickets and carried his valise." But he was a handsome, hearty fellow who could strike an impressive public pose. According to a fawning biography published in 1954, he looked "like a college football coach, big, broad shouldered, blue-eyed, handsome with wavy silver-white hair." President Eisenhower, who liked football coaches, found him to be "a man of great judgment and common sense." Steel executives were eager to strengthen his position within the USWA and to promote him as a counterweight in the CIO to the more aggressive and reputedly "socialistic" Walter Reuther. McDonald despised Reuther and bitterly resented his election to the presidency of the CIO after Murray's death. "Don't call him Reuther," he instructed an aide on one occasion. "Refer to him as that no good red-headed socialist bastard Reuther."[15]

During McDonald's presidency, the Human Relations Committee, a widely touted labor-management innovation, circumvented the normal channels of collective bargaining in steel and placed a premium on the rhetoric of cooperation.[16] Another McDonald innovation was his high-toned tours of the U.S. Steel mills with company president Ben Fairless, a reflection of his belief in "mutual trusteeship" and in the obligation of labor leaders to place themselves on the same social level as their corporate counterparts. "This man of steel dresses to fit the occasion," said his publicists. "Although favoring sports outfits and tweeds with bow ties, he wears 'Brooks Brothers' business suits when conservative clothes are in order." His critics had a field day, charging that the Human Relations Committee represented a descent from "collective bargaining" to "collective begging," that McDonald's sartorial splendor served only to expand the frontiers of "tuxedo unionism," and that his goal in life was "to be, think, and act like any corporation executive."[17]

The differences in personality between the austere, social-democratic Reuther and the self-indulgent and unashamedly bourgeois McDonald made it easy to conclude that the UAW and the United Steelworkers formed the poles of liberalism and conservatism in the post-Murray CIO. But in important respects, McDonald did not run his own show.

6.1. United Steelworkers president David McDonald, with Democratic presidential nominee John Fitzgerald Kennedy, Democratic National Convention, Los Angeles, 1960. Credit: Historical Collections and Labor Archives, Penn State

In historian David Stebenne's words, he "lacked the skills and intellect needed to function as the chief strategist for a major industrial union." Aware of his deficiencies, and wanting in any case to concentrate on the banquet and nightclub circuits, McDonald turned to USWA general counsel Arthur Goldberg to make many of the key decisions and conduct most of the time-consuming and often thankless negotiations with management. Goldberg, a product of the West Side of Chicago and Northwestern Law School, *was* a quintessential liberal, but in the 1950s mold. Like John F. Kennedy, whose administration he would join in

1961 as secretary of labor, Goldberg viewed the prospect of change through mass mobilization at the grassroots level as anachronistic and positively dangerous. His goal was to depend on the managerial skill of technocrats like himself and the cooperation of the corporate elite to achieve the sustained economic growth and expanded social security that were vital to the maintenance of society's equilibrium. Goldberg was pro–civil rights, but only insofar as the issue could be managed from the top and kept within the framework of an ideological consensus that emphasized the incremental evolution of Black America toward the social mainstream. This was also the approach and outlook of the USWA's Committee on Civil Rights; and although McDonald showed little interest in the committee's work, Secretary Frank Shane recalled that "he never put a roadblock in our way."[18]

During McDonald's presidency, the USWA lobbied aggressively on behalf of civil rights legislation, but for the most part the union's record combined cloying self-congratulation, even outright fabrication, with increasingly lackluster performance. On one occasion, Frank Shane told the editor of the *Pittsburgh Catholic* that the Steelworkers' "efforts in behalf of Negroes, both in and out of the union, have brought not a whisper of dissatisfaction, not even from US[W]A Southern members. 'All we hear are words of commendation and pledges to suport the policy of the union.'" The reality became clear when in 1959 the union attempted to conduct a second civil rights survey. Boyd Wilson mailed out questionnaires to 2,612 local unions but received only 509 replies. In the South there was 1 response from District 35 (Atlanta) and none from District 36 (Birmingham). There were 25 responses from District 26 (Youngstown), a more impressive figure, to be sure, but one that represented no more than 20 percent of the local unions in the district. Reluctantly, Wilson concluded that the material in hand was insufficient to proceed with a statistical evaluation of the United Steelworkers' record in combating racial discrimination. Shane later admitted that less than 25 percent of the local unions had even bothered to form a civil rights committee, in spite of the fact that the USWA constitution made it mandatory to do so. In a private memorandum to McDonald in December 1964, he pointed out that "we have only 632 such committees out of approximately 3000 local unions."[19]

In regard to the employment of African Americans as staffers and as clerical workers in Pittsburgh's high-rise headquarters, the union's record was even worse. This had been a source of friction from the very beginning, when an informal black caucus had pressured Murray to appoint more Negroes to responsible positions within the international and district unions. But the results had been meager at best, and the reassurances to outsiders that "we have many Negro members of the union who are working as Staff Representatives" were little more than a public relations ruse. Many districts, even some with a substantial African American membership, had no black appointees; others seemed to impose a quota of one.[20]

Ironically, the black unionists who were most concerned about these issues kept appealing to McDonald to change a situation that he was reluctant even to acknowledge as a problem. Pragmatically, they may have calculated that only the president had the power to change the union's direction. They may also have perceived McDonald in the Murray mold, as a less majestic but still benevolent autocrat who could be persuaded to override the resistance of his subordinates. In any case, a group of black unionists appealed to the USWA president in 1960 to strengthen the Committee on Civil Rights by becoming its cochairman. They also asked him to select an African American to serve as cochair of the committee with him and to appoint Negroes to its paid staff. Only this, they said, would put an end to "sneering and . . . sniping" and to the widespread perception that "the Steelworkers' approach is . . . the oddest and most contradictory in the field of civil rights."[21]

· · · · ·

By 1960 black workers had many reasons to be angry and disillusioned. For just as the first half of the 1950s had been a period of tenuous equilibrium in the realm of race relations, the second half of the decade was far more volatile and far more mixed in the signals it conveyed to African Americans. Most liberals continued to believe that the American Dilemma would soon be resolved in favor of racial equality, that poverty had become an afterthought in the Affluent Society, and that the rising tide of postwar prosperity would combine with the experience of northward migration to improve the economic circumstances of blacks, who would then be in a position to play their assigned role as the "last of the immigrants." In 1962 Anthony Lewis of the *New York Times* voiced several of these assumptions when he wrote that "in almost every aspect of American life it is possible to point to dramatic improvements in the status of the Negro." In the economic realm, in particular, he noted "striking progress."[22]

But many African Americans did not share this optimism, in large measure because persistent racial discrimination and far-reaching but largely unforeseen economic developments limited their opportunities and clouded their horizon. Gary, Indiana, became an outstanding example of the combined sense of hope and uncertainty that was growing in African American communities across the nation. By the 1950s blacks held one-third of the jobs at the huge Gary Works of Carnegie-Illinois Steel, and according to an Urban League report, their conditions had "improved 100 percent" since the unionization of the industry. Beyond the mills, three members of the city council, including its president, were African Americans; blacks held more than 20 percent of the jobs in city government; and their rates of home ownership were high. Indeed, their circumstances appeared so favorable that *Ebony* magazine selected Gary as the American city where "the Negro comes closest to first-class citizenship." Nonetheless, said Warner Bloomberg, a steelworker turned university teacher, "to walk from an average all-white precinct into an average all-Negro precinct . . . is to step off an economic cliff." Family income was 30 to 40 percent lower in the black community; black wives were compelled to work for wages far more often than the wives of white workers; and, according to the local Urban League director, they were restricted to "the usual menial jobs involving washing dishes, sweeping or cleaning." Ninety-five percent of Gary's Negro population lived in only six of the city's twenty-seven census tracts; and *after* the formal desegregation of the city's educational system, more than four out of five African American students attended all-black schools. "Keep looking around," said a black steelworker in 1956, "and you'll see more disintegration than integration."[23]

According to Bloomberg, many white workers had achieved a remarkable level of economic security by the mid-fifties, and more than a few were supplementing their mill earnings by renting out property, selling insurance, and running small trucking firms, grocery stores, or luncheonettes. During the monthlong steel strike of 1956, Chicago and Gary newspapers printed photos of white strikers fixing up their homes and working in their yards, and fishing trips were the order of the day for many. Black steelworkers, by comparison, had far fewer economic resources and were neither as comfortable nor as confident as their white counterparts. Many more of them had suffered layoffs recently; many lived from paycheck to paycheck. And these were the better-off black workers. For those who continued migrating from the rural South to the urban North in search of industrial employment, cities like Gary offered less and less opportunity, and the mills offered none at all.[24]

Gary was only one small piece in a much larger puzzle. Although blacks made up 21 percent of the U.S. Steel workforce nationwide in the early 1950s, they remained concentrated in occupations that were most likely to be eliminated by mechanization. As jobs became better—that is, more skilled and less hazardous—they also became "whiter." Thus, in Birmingham, the number of African American steelworkers declined by more than a thousand during the decade, whereas the number of white workers in steel increased by more than three thousand. The same trend prevailed at Bethlehem Steel in Johnstown. African Americans had worked in Johnstown's mills since the early twentieth century and had accumulated many years of seniority in departments "where the work was heavy and awkward or extremely hot or very dangerous." Veteran black workers recalled that there had been approximately sixty-five Negroes employed in Bethlehem's Wheel Plant in 1925. Over the years, however, the jobs they held were mechanized, with the result that where scores of Negroes used to work only five remained by the mid-1950s, and all of them were above the age of fifty. Even as the number of jobs in the Wheel Plant increased, the number of black workers steadily decreased. Similarly, at Bethlehem's Lower Cambria Division, African Americans had worked as manganese unloaders for more than three decades. "When this work was . . . done with sledge hammer, crow bar, shovel, and wheel barrow, it was [done] predomina[ntly] by Negroes," said Ben Cashaw, an NAACP activist and veteran of forty-four years at Bethlehem Steel. But when the job was mechanized, no more blacks were hired as manganese unloaders. Cashaw identified several other departments where the same process was unfolding and concluded that "there are generations of Negroes born within the shadow of these Mills and educated in the Johnstown Schools [who will] never have an opportunity to work at the jobs where their fathers have been worn out."[25]

Larger economic and demographic factors also had a major impact on the constraints and opportunities that African Americans encountered in the labor market. During World War II and the Korean War, the booming economy pulled millions of blacks from the rural South to the urban North, and the push provided by the mechanization of cotton agriculture in the Mississippi Delta turned the widening flow of migrants into a torrent. The journey to the promised land engendered great expectations—of better-paying jobs, decent housing, good schools, and a place where oppressed people could breathe free. In 1942 Uless Carter, a twenty-five-year-old black man from Clarksdale, Mississippi, visited his sister in Chicago. He had been in her apartment for less than an hour when he was offered a job in a restaurant at four times the wages he'd been earning in the Mississippi Delta. He stayed, of course. Although washing dishes in a restaurant did not offer anything like the money a black man could earn in steel or meatpacking, even casual and low-wage employment in Chicago's secondary—and largely black—labor market was a vast improvement over most "Negro" jobs in the Deep South. Over time, however, the pace of migration outran the opportunity. By the mid-1950s, there were many more unskilled laborers than unskilled jobs, but the migrants kept coming, for the process of chain migration had developed a momentum of its own, and, increasingly, a ticket to Chicago or Detroit was the best that Mississippi had to offer.[26]

In the meatpacking industry, economic restructuring and automation cost more than thirty-eight thousand workers their jobs between 1956 and 1964. Chicago, where blacks had constituted 40 percent of the packinghouse labor force at the end of World War II, was hit hardest. Wilson and Company began phasing out its killing operations in 1955 and completed the process two years later. Armour and Swift followed suit, and soon the Windy City's famous stockyards became "an eerie open space filled with the crumbling remains of packing plants." In Detroit the Ford Motor Company had once employed half of Detroit's black male workers, and for years Ford's giant River Rouge complex in nearby Dearborn was a dynamic center of black employment and militant trade unionism. But after the war the auto manufacturers' policy of deconcentration imposed a devastating cost on the Motor City, above all on its rapidly expanding black community. In 1945 the River Rouge employed 85,000 workers; by 1960, that number had fallen to 30,000. Overall, between 1947 and 1963, the number of manufacturing jobs in Detroit declined from 338,000 to 201,000. As unemployed industrial workers mingled with newly arrived migrants from the rural South in the inner cities of the North, the black unemployment rate began to grow, in absolute and relative terms. By 1962, according to labor economist Matthew Kessler, "nonwhite men in both the 25–34 and 35–44 brackets . . . recorded unemployment rates about three times as high as for white men." [27]

African Americans confronted not only a precarious economic environment but a growing backlash that incorporated broad segments of the white population in the South and in several key areas of the North. In Chicago's bungalow belt, where white workers from Carnegie-Illinois Steel and International Harvester's Wisconsin Steel Works were an integral component of the ethnic neighborhoods that surrounded the mills, fear of an African American "invasion" became a major motif of community life. When in 1953 the Chicago Housing Authority moved several black families into the Trumbull Park Homes in the South Deering neighborhood, recurring waves of violent protest lasted for a decade. Black tenants were compelled to barricade themselves in their apartments, as mobs gathered nightly to hurl bricks, stones, and fireworks through their windows. They had to travel to and from their place of residence with a police escort, which often meant riding in a paddy wagon. On the streets beyond the housing project, cars driven by blacks were subjected to sporadic attack, and black employees at the nearby Wisconsin Steel Works were assaulted by angry crowds as they walked to work. Even attempts to worship in local churches incurred hostile, and sometimes violent, outbursts from white parishioners.[28] CIO unions deplored this racist backlash, and some, like the United Packinghouse Workers, played an active role in defending the rights of black tenants. But a Packinghouse Workers' spokesman acknowledged that "some of our own union members are the people who are throwing those stones"; and according to a United Steelworkers activist from Republic Steel's South Chicago Works, the fireworks, or "bombs," that terrorized the black residents of Trumbull Park were "crudely manufactured by employees in the steel plants."[29]

What is most remarkable about these northern conflicts over residential and recreational space is that white ethnics dared to defend themselves as "a community welded together by an intense race consciousness" at a time when the social sciences were affirming the virtues of color blindness and civil rights advocates were calling for the "striking down of race" in the realm of public policy. The *South Deering Bulletin* declared that from the welter of European nationalities that had forged South Chicago's ethnic neighborhoods "a real American white has been evolved and should be allowed to evolve further." The *Bulletin* offered a racialized narrative of American history that lauded the contributions of the "foreigners" who "built this country" and demeaned the role of African Americans as inconsequential or worse. In the minds of these besieged white ethnics, there was far more at stake than housing values or the maintenance of a near monopoly of jobs at Wisconsin Steel. They interpreted attempts by African Americans to swim at public pools as acts of sexual aggression that were designed to promote interracial marriage. They saw the historic *Brown* decision as evidence that the government was riddled with Communists whose goal was to compel "race mixing" and thereby send the "whole white race . . . downhill."[30]

Meanwhile, in the labor movement, the center of gravity at the national level shifted decisively toward the more conservative AFL after its merger with the CIO in 1955. ("The CIO is a sorry mess," said a disillusioned Horace Cayton in November of that year; "that's why they are going back into the AFL.") The new AFL-CIO president was George Meany, an Irish American plumber from the Bronx. Meany's social attitudes mirrored those of the old immigrants and labor aristocrats who predominated in the building trades, and his long experience as a trade union administrator inclined him to rely on lobbying and backroom deals to achieve incremental change from the top down. On Meany's watch at the helm of the AFL-CIO, as on McDonald's at the head of the United Steelworkers, organized labor would find it increasingly difficult to relate sympathetically to a militant Civil Rights movement that challenged the existing relations of power through mass mobilization at the grassroots. Although AFL-CIO leaders spoke the language of racial equality, they were simply unwilling to launch a frontal assault on the deeply rooted patterns of inequality in trades and industries where labor's strength was greatest. What had begun as a historical moment of great promise for blacks—who greeted the *Brown* decision as a "second Emancipation Proclamation"—thus became tinged with bitterness, as more and more African Americans experienced the sharp disparity between the rhetoric of change and the reality of tokenism and backlash.[31]

In these circumstances A. Philip Randolph, the president of the Brotherhood of Sleeping Car Porters and the nation's preeminent black trade unionist, spoke out with uncompromising clarity about the failure of the AFL-CIO to set its house in order and received in return George Meany's taunt, "Who the hell appointed you as the guardian of all the Negroes in America?" For thousands of black trade unionists in the trenches of the struggle against racism, the brickbat that Meany launched against Randolph in 1959 served only to enhance the reputation of a man they already revered. He understood their disappointment and frustration; he spoke for them; and they flocked to his banner when he formed the Negro American Labor Council (NALC) in 1960. "We are in rebellion," Randolph bravely declared. "The NALC reflects within organized labor the same rebellion that finds its expression in the student lunch counter demonstrations in the South."[32]

The growing perception that the NAACP was at war with organized labor intensified when the association brought formal charges against two large and powerful unions—the United Steelworkers and the International Ladies Garment Workers Union (ILGWU)—that had been closely associated with the cause of civil rights. Historically a predominantly Jewish organization that took pride in its socialist heritage, the ILGWU's constituency had changed dramatically since World War II. Blacks and Hispanics made up a significant minority of its membership, especially in New York City, the union's heartland. But Jews continued to dominate the leadership of the ILGWU and the ranks of the skilled cutters' locals. As early as 1953, one scholarly observer had detected a "crisis of leadership" in the union that reflected the "cleavage between two membership generations, differing very considerably in composition, background, and outlook." By 1957 there were mass picket lines of black and Hispanic workers at the international union headquarters, protesting "sweetheart contracts." In the same year ILGWU members who worked in garment shops in the Bronx filed a decertification petition with the NLRB, apparently without any encouragement from the NAACP.[33]

But the association was bound to offer the hand of solidarity to workers of color in their fight against racial discrimination. Thus, in 1961, with the active support of the NAACP, African American garment worker Ernest Holmes filed a complaint with the New York State Commission for Human Rights, charging that the union had blocked his attempt to join Cutters Local 10 and learn the cutters' trade. In 1962, at the behest of Harlem representative Adam Clayton Powell, a congressional subcommittee held public hearings to investigate "nefarious practices" in the garment industry and heard accusations, from Herbert Hill among others, that the ILGWU was partly responsible for the industry's pattern of "de facto racial segregation."[34]

Trade union leaders and representatives of the Jewish community rushed to the ILGWU's defense. ILGWU vice-president Charles Zimmerman called Hill's charges "demonstrably untrue, . . . malicious and tinged with anti-Semitism." ("The fact that Mr. Hill is white and Jewish," said Zimmerman, "does not mitigate this in the least.") The *Jewish Daily Forward* accused the NAACP labor secretary of a "racist assault" on the ILGWU and of spreading "anti-Semitic poison." Emanuel Muravchik of the Jewish Labor Committee also raised the specter of anti-Semitism and questioned whether "it is any longer possible to work with the NAACP." Finally, the president of the AFL-CIO weighed in.

Fig. 6.2. NAACP labor secretary Herbert Hill addressing the New York State CIO Convention, Buffalo, 1952. Credit: Herbert Hill

In a speech to the Negro American Labor Council, Meany denounced Hill's "smears" and "falsehoods," defended the ILGWU as "a union whose record shines like a beacon in the history of human progress," and dismissed the NAACP's case against the United Steelworkers as "fantastic." According to the *New York Times*, his words were "blunt, bitter and scornful."[35]

But NAACP executive secretary Roy Wilkins refused to blink. The association's forty-eight-member national board had already come to Hill's defense and concurred publicly with his charges against the ILGWU. Now Wilkins himself defended Hill against the "baseless allegation" of anti-Semitism and the accusation that he was an "irresponsible individual" whose conduct threatened to "destroy" the alliance between the labor and civil rights movements. Unlike Muravchik and other liberal allies of labor, Wilkins said, Hill was "not for trade unions first and Negro workers second." His sole job was "to serve the interests of the Negro worker through the NAACP." If, in carrying out this task, he jeopardized the kind of "unity" advocated by Muravchik, this was

234

no "calamity" but rather a "blessed clearing of the air." As for Meany's barbs, Wilkins simply pointed to the "disgraceful" pace of "desegregation in the labor movement" and reminded the AFL-CIO president that "a Negro worker needs the patience of Job, the hide of an elephant plus a crowbar to get into Mr. Meany's own union—the plumbers."[36]

· · · · ·

The ways in which this larger context of ambiguity and disappointment affected the local level became dramatically evident in the case of Atlantic Steel. From 1957 to 1962, this Atlanta-based plant was a cauldron of conflict that highlighted the agency of an increasingly frustrated and assertive black rank and file, a local union committed to the defense of entrenched patterns of white privilege and black subordination, a labor leadership that was ill equipped by temperament and outlook to cope with the growing demand for racial change, and a national civil rights organization that was prepared to jeopardize its historic alliance with organized labor in order to honor its commitment to black workers. For African Americans at Atlantic Steel, it would become increasingly clear that the NAACP was keeping the faith while their own union and its most visible black spokesman appeared to be playing a game of charades. What the case of Atlantic Steel demonstrates most clearly, though, is that even when the United Steelworkers finally sought to address the problem of racially separate lines of progression, the solution it negotiated served only to highlight the gulf between black workers' demands and the union's sense of what was possible.[37]

Incorporated in 1901 to make steel bands for cotton bales and hoops for turpentine casks, Atlantic Steel dramatically expanded its production over the years, and by the early 1950s it was turning out more than two hundred thousand tons of steel ingots and a wide variety of steel products annually. At that time it employed two thousand workers, about 90 percent of whom were members of Local 2401 of the United Steelworkers of America. When Glenn Gilman and James Sweeney, from the School of Industrial Management at the Georgia Institute of Technology, conducted an in-depth study of labor relations at Atlantic Steel in 1953, they characterized the company as an outstanding example of labor-management cooperation and mutually beneficial collective bargaining. They also concluded that Atlantic Steel had "no race problem." According to Gilman and Sweeney, Local 2401 was working toward a solution of "the Negro problem in the South . . .

within the framework of southern tradition and custom, rather than by attempting revolutionary action." This meant that the local accepted "the policies of segregation that are practiced at the plant in deference to southern mores" but was also willing to "put the entire resources of the union behind an employee who has been subjected to individual discrimination because of his color."[38]

The fact that Gilman and Sweeney could reach such a conclusion suggests that they spent very little time talking to black workers, or perhaps that black workers did not yet feel free to express their growing dissatisfaction with the racial separation and inequality that continued to characterize the plant's employment pattern. But the weight of external events soon revealed that Atlantic Steel had a race problem after all. The catalyst was the Rev. Joseph Rabun, a Baptist minister who had been employed at the plant since 1949, first as a production worker and then, briefly, as a foreman. In the aftermath of the lynching of fourteen-year-old Emmett Till (whose grandfather was a Chicago steelworker) and the acquittal of his murderers in Mississippi, Rabun wrote a letter of protest to the *Atlanta Constitution*. Published in October 1955, under the heading "Atlanta Preacher Calls Till Trial a Lynching," it declared: "With what humility and shame we 'supreme' whites should bow our heads and implore God's mercy when we think of our own share of responsibility for the outrageous murder and the jury's cowardly verdict." "As long as we remain silent and inactive before the corruption of justice," Rabun concluded, "all of us are criminal."[39]

As his letter suggests, Rabun was hardly a typical employee of Atlantic Steel. He had lost his pulpit in McRae, Georgia, in 1947, after speaking out against the racial policies of the congregation's most famous member, Governor Eugene Talmadge, one of the Deep South's most virulent and outspoken segregationists. At the urging of the USWA's Bill Crawford, he had made an unsuccessful run for governor in 1948. Then, with no church and no prospect of one, he had turned to Crawford, who helped him secure employment at Atlantic Steel. He was, by his own account, a "faithful member of 2401," until he had the opportunity to become a foreman in the wiredrawing department in September 1955.[40]

After a little more than a month on his new job, Rabun recalled, "lightning struck without warning." The cause was his letter to the *Atlanta Constitution*. When he came to work the next evening, he noticed immediately that someone had posted his letter on a bulletin board and had written, "Why the hell don't you go to Mississippi and tell them this?" Soon agitated workers were calling him a "nigger lover," and several of the men under his supervision went to other departments to spread the word of his heresy. Before long there was a work stoppage, and, when confronted by the local union president and the company's director of industrial relations, the strikers announced that they would not return to work as long as Rabun remained their foreman. He was told to go home, allegedly to allow matters to cool down, and then was removed from his job on the grounds that he "did not get along with the employees under his supervision." Rabun appealed to the United Steelworkers, including President David Mc-Donald, for help. But taking the position that as a foreman he was not a member of the bargaining unit, the district and international union leaders washed their hands of the matter. It was not, after all, a "union problem."[41]

In the narrowest and most technical sense, perhaps it was not. But the combination of external stimuli and internal grievances was pushing black employees of Atlantic Steel in a direction that would make Local 2401 one of the most contentious in the United Steelworkers' jurisdiction. In April 1957, after concluding that the local leadership was unwilling to address their concerns, eight black workers met with the Labor and Industry Committee of the Atlanta NAACP and unveiled a long list of grievances. They complained that blacks received a maximum wage of $2.13 per hour, whereas the maximum among whites was $4.95; that even black workers who did the same work as whites received lower wages; that whites with low seniority were upgraded to more skilled and better-paying jobs and high-seniority black workers were bypassed; and that there were no black union officials in Local 2401. Blacks paid the same dues as whites, they said, but had "no voice" in the union. Soon the national office of the NAACP—above all, Labor Secretary Herbert Hill—became deeply involved in the case. After a lengthy investigation that included extensive correspondence with black workers at Atlantic Steel, with the director of District 35, and with members of the international union's Committee on Civil Rights, Hill painted a clear portrait of racial segregation and discrimination at the Atlanta facility, which by the late 1950s employed twenty-five hundred workers, about nine hundred of whom were African American. He reported that there were "separate lines of progression for white and Negro employees." Blacks were "hired exclusively into a classification designated as 'common laborer' " and did not enjoy seniority or promotional rights in the higher-paying and more skilled classifications. Whites, meanwhile, were hired into production and craft positions that were "completely closed" to blacks.[42]

A subsequent investigation by the U.S. Commission on Civil Rights not only bore out Hill's observations but added additional detail to what would become a searing indictment. The commission found that in a sample department with thirty job classifications, only whites held occupational seniority in nineteen of the classifications, and only blacks held seniority in the rest. Within the department, the pay grades ranged from 1 to 26. None of the black workers had attained a pay grade above 8, and more than half of the sixty-four blacks remained at pay grade 4 or lower. The commission concluded that "a similar picture prevails throughout the plant."[43]

In the summer of 1957, Hill met with black steelworkers in Atlanta and then sought to inform Boyd Wilson of the urgency of the situation. He warned that because of the local leadership's "continuing indifference" to the pattern of racial discrimination in the mill, "a number of Negro workers are desirous of quitting the Steelworkers Union under the Georgia 'Right to Work' law." Together with the president of the Atlanta NAACP branch, Hill spent several hours persuading them not to abandon the USWA, but he also promised that in return representatives of the international union would meet with them and seek to resolve their grievances.[44]

Hill acknowledged that the company was "at least equally responsible" for the maintenance of Jim Crow seniority lines. And indeed, at management's initiative, many forms of segregation were operative in the plant. The company maintained separate time clocks for black and white employees, with a partition between them. There were also separate water fountains, rest rooms, bathhouses, and locker rooms and a segregated cafeteria, which the company eventually abolished and replaced with vending machines. But the local union also bore some responsibility for this situation. Industrial relations specialists Gilman and Sweeney had observed in 1953 that collective bargaining between the company and the union was informal, continuous, and remarkably broad in scope. One union official informed them that "the company has never yet refused to bargain with us over any issue we've brought up." In a letter to the USWA staffer who serviced Local 2401, a company vice-president expressed willingness to bargain over issues of race and insisted only that "measures to correct any unfairness to any of the negro Employees be initiated by your Union." This may have been a subterfuge or a simple passing of the buck. Given the general climate of massive resistance in the late 1950s and the potential for disruption on the shop floor and in the union hall, it is likely that both management and the union were reluctant to confront these issues.[45]

In this situation, it became the responsibility of the international union to act, and Hill was convinced that only forthright intervention by Wilson and other international representatives would prevent the aggrieved black steelworkers from quitting the USWA. But Wilson's response was bound to disappoint the NAACP and Atlantic Steel's black rank and file, for although he was the most visible African American in the United Steelworkers' hierarchy, his high visibility only accentuated the fact that his position was largely symbolic. (When asked in 1992 about the extent of Wilson's authority, his former secretary responded, "His authority? Well, he didn't have any.") His alleged role was to serve as the USWA's ambassador to the black community and to represent the interests of the union's African American membership. But at Atlantic Steel he was caught between his obligations to the international union on one hand and to an increasingly restive rank-and-file constituency on the other. While black workers demanded that he be an agent of change, USWA officials insisted that he be an instrument of containment. Whatever his sentiments may have been, Wilson knew where his bread was buttered and acted accordingly. In this case, his goal was to fend off the NAACP and keep black protest within the channels of the union. As relations between the USWA and the association became more acrimonious, Wilson informed black workers that he resented "Hill's interference" and warned that "too many cooks spoil the brew." Hill, in turn, became increasingly incensed at Wilson's failure to "take a prompt and honest stand" and concluded, after more than a year of NAACP involvement in the case, that "absolutely no progress has been made."[46]

Stymied by the white majority in Local 2401 and frustrated by the district leadership's acquiescence in the status quo, black rank and filers raised the money to send veteran unionist Nathaniel Brown to Pittsburgh in the summer of 1960 to plead their case with the international union. According to the *Pittsburgh Courier*, he was "refused admission to a meeting . . . where the race problem was being discussed." Afterward, a clearly disillusioned Brown told the *Courier* that racial discrimination at Atlantic Steel was "the fault of the union." "The company has been willing to eliminate the discriminatory practice," he said, but union officials continued to insist that "employment be 'within the framework of tradition and custom.' " Brown charged that McDonald was "aware of the situation and has done nothing about it," and that Wilson was "sitting on his fingers" and offering little, if any, cooperation to his aggrieved constituents. Thus he and his fellow workers developed a new protest strategy and planned "to take the[ir] case to the courts" as soon as they had exhausted all avenues within the USWA. The clear implication was that the union, rather than Atlantic Steel, had become the target of their wrath.[47]

Actually, members of the Committee on Civil Rights had been meeting with the bargaining committee of Local 2401 since April 1960 in an attempt to develop new contract language that would alleviate the problem of racially separate lines of progression. Specifically, the international union took the position that "no line of progression should be composed exclusively of either white or colored workers." Negotiations with the company on this matter and others dragged on for well over a year, and a new agreement incorporating this principle was ratified in the summer of 1961. The contract appeared to create unprecedented opportunities for black workers. By June 1962 seventeen African Americans were employed in jobs that formerly had been closed to them—thirteen in one department and four in another. This was a modest beginning, to be sure, but Frank Shane informed Hill that "the present local union officers are determined to make the new pattern work and we are certainly going to give them the fullest opportunity to do so."[48]

For many black workers, however, incremental gains of this kind represented no improvement at all. The problem, or a large part of it, had to do with the way the principle of seniority was applied in the steel industry. Seniority had long been occupational or departmental rather than plantwide. The more seniority a worker earned in one department or line of progression, the less likely he (or, occasionally, she) would be to transfer, even to a higher-paying job in another department or line, because such a move meant giving up one's accumulated seniority and starting over again. To create the necessary freedom of movement, the principle of retroactivity, and a broadening of the bases of seniority, would have to prevail. But lower-seniority workers who held desirable jobs were overwhelmingly opposed to any changes in the seniority system that would make them vulnerable to downgrading and layoffs. In practice, not only at Atlantic Steel but throughout the industry, this meant that the white majority was opposed to contractual innovations that would facilitate black mobility, and the union leadership was seldom willing to jeopardize its own security by siding with the minority. When new, nonracial lines of progression were created at Atlantic Steel, the international union took the position that "retroactivity could not be enforced" in upgrading employees into jobs from which they had been excluded.[49]

What the union saw as half a loaf black workers saw as sham and betrayal. Many of them bitterly opposed the ratification of the 1961 contract and its renewal in 1962. Without the protection of retroactivity, few black workers, especially the high-seniority men who had been among the founders and most faithful members of the union, were willing to sacrifice decades of seniority for a higher-paying job in which they would be vulnerable to layoffs. The fact that the steel industry was still mired in a sustained period of stagnation when the 1961 contract was signed undoubtedly contributed to their concerns, as did the fact that as racial polarization at the plant intensified, Atlantic Steel simply stopped hiring black workers.[50]

Apparently some African Americans—especially younger and lower-seniority workers—joined the union in seeing the new regime as a step forward. But others were so disillusioned that they were ready to quit the United Steelworkers. Speaking to Hill, Brown poignantly and compellingly articulated his own sense of grievance and that of his fellow workers. "When the union first came," he said,

> most of the whites were afraid, but we Negroes . . . wore the CIO button. We were the first to come out for the union. We helped get it started here. . . . But now they—the whites—get all the benefits and we are left behind again. Turned out CIO meant one thing for the whites and another thing for us. The union don't handle our grievances, we are stuck with Jim Crow seniority, back-breaking jobs and we get less pay than they do. . . . White boys just hired off the street get treated better than we do after twenty years. That's what we get for bringing in the union here.[51]

After the ratification of the 1962 contract, black workers met with representatives of the NAACP and decided to petition the National Labor Relations Board for a decertification election. This was an extraordinary step. It meant that some of the men who had been most loyal and active in building the United Steelworkers were now prepared to dismantle it. In taking this step, Brown and his fellow workers had the full support of the NAACP, which had authorized such an initiative at its annual convention in 1960. On October 30, 1962, accompanied by Georgia field secretary Vernon Jordan, Hill filed a decer-tification petition on behalf of thirteen members of Local 2401.[52]

Union representatives reacted with surprise and dismay. General Counsel David Feller complained that the USWA had not been warned of this move, in spite of a long-standing agreement between the two organizations to consult before acting on discriminatory prac-tices of "mutual interest." After reviewing the history of the case from the union's perspective, Feller offered the by-now familiar refrain "we have, perhaps, not been able to do enough but we have continued to make progress." But Wilkins disagreed. He countered with an eloquent summary of the nearly six years of frustration that had accumulated in the Atlantic Steel case. "The conditions existed long before they were brought formally to our attention," he said. "Every possible method (short of NLRB proceedings) has been employed to try to redress the grievances. . . . Piles of correspondence with the USWA have accumu-lated. Numerous conferences have been held, high-level, low-level and in-between." And yet, in all that time, "Nothing has produced a mean-ingful change."[53]

• • • • •

Had there been no meaningful change? From the standpoint of Na-thaniel Brown and many black workers, Wilkins's assertion was unam-biguously true. From the vantage point of the United Steelworkers, however, the union had succeeded in dismantling the segregated lines of promotion at Atlantic Steel, and this was only one among many positive examples of the USWA's commitment to civil rights. Earlier in 1962, the international union had signed a collective bargaining agreement with United States Steel, which, for the first time, included the statement that "the provisions of this agreement shall be applied to all employes without regard to race, color, religious creed or national origin." The union leadership regarded this agreement as historic, called it a "non-discrimination policy which can be rigidly enforced," and sought to duplicate it in contracts with other steel companies.[54]

In the pages of *Steel Labor*, black workers offered testimony to the USWA's many achievements. In a feature article entitled "The Old Members Won't Forget! . . . The New Members Shouldn't Forget!" Bartow Tipper, who had worked at Jones and Laughlin for thirty-five years, remembered the "early days" of SWOC in Aliquippa and de-clared that "I often thank God for this great union of ours." Eddie Longshore, a twenty-two-year veteran of Republic Steel in Massillon, described his experience in the USWA as "most satisfying"; sixty-four-year-old Anthony McCann called the union "the greatest thing that ever was." "Used to be that a man didn't know when he had a job," McCann said. "Now we have protection and security." Even Joe Cook added the weight of his voice to this carefully orchestrated self-congratulation. Now retired after forty-two years at Valley Mould and Iron, Cook recalled that "fifty years ago my wife and I came to Chicago carrying our lunch in a bag and riding in a Jim Crow car. In 1956 we went to the Los Angeles union convention in a Pullman car, slept in a nice clean bed and woke up and ate our breakfast in the dining car. This is what the CIO and the Steelworkers' Union did for me."[55]

There was no denying the validity of Cook's heartfelt testimony; it is all the more impressive as a testament to the generosity of a man whom the leadership had shunted aside as too "Red" to be a member of the international union staff. But Cook was measuring the union mainly against his experience in the long nonunion era, and no doubt he remembered with pride that his fellow foundry workers had honored him as their local union president for more than twenty years. For many black workers, however, the days before SWOC were a dim memory at best, whereas the unfulfilled promises of the previous generation were vividly engraved in their consciousness. They had experienced the ambiguities and disappointments of the 1950s. Now, in the early 1960s, a powerful Civil Rights movement was quickening their sense of urgency and allowing them to imagine—and demand—a new regime. As they found their own voice and articulated their long-suppressed aspirations, more conflict and polarization were inevitable.

This became clear at a meeting of the USWA's international executive board in October 1963, an extraordinary year in the annals of the black freedom struggle. In April and May a massive wave of nonviolent direct action in Birmingham had rocked the cradle of Jim Crow as never before; the sickening spectacle of an embattled power structure that responded to marching schoolchildren with snarling police dogs and high-powered fire hoses had triggered the creation of a northern white consensus on behalf of sweeping racial change in the South. The United Steelworkers had put up large amounts of bail money to win the release of demonstrators from Birmingham's jails and lobbied aggressively on behalf of the civil rights bill that the Kennedy administration introduced in June. But like most unions, and the AFL-CIO executive council, the USWA had not endorsed the March on Washington in August; and only two of the union's twenty-nine district directors had bothered to attend this historic event on their own. Now, in October, the entire leadership met in Chicago to take stock.[56]

In the spirit of the moment, McDonald and other leaders of the union were concerned about issues of civil rights, and facing pressure from black steelworkers and community leaders, they were willing to entertain reasonable proposals to address what clearly had become a national crisis. But at the same time they wanted "the Negro" to remain orderly, to defer to duly constituted authority, and to act in ways that were consistent with the USWA's sense of propriety and principle. McDonald reported that recently he had met with African American leaders in the Pittsburgh area who were concerned about job opportunities for Negroes and also, he admitted, about "lack of opportunity for advancement in the union." "These Negro leaders were a bunch of real nice guys," McDonald said, "very well dressed, very mannerly and very orderly. Of course, they came in with a few ideas which were rather in outer limits. [But] we had a very nice visit with them, and that night I got an idea—what to do about this problem?"[57]

The solution, he decided, was to expand the role of the union's extensive network of community services committees to include job training for black steelworkers and for their sons who were entering the labor market. He first discussed the idea with staff members in the union's Pittsburgh headquarters, then appointed himself chairman of a committee to pursue it and broached the subject with two top officials of U.S. Steel in the hope that the union and the Corporation might undertake this endeavor together. "It is my thought," said McDonald "that this will take the heat off the union and the companies in this field of job opportunities for our colored brothers."[58]

In the discussion that followed, five district directors, including Joe Germano of Chicago, spoke in favor of the plan. When McDonald asked Germano whether black union members in the Chicago-Gary area would be willing to participate in such a program, he responded, "I think they would welcome it. There's quite a few of mine that would welcome it, because you would be giving them more recognition." He admitted that "for some reason" the union had been "reluctant to give the Negro member an active role in things," and concluded, "Hell, put them on. We have got some fine, intelligent Negro people. In fact, I have got a few on my staff that I am damn proud of."[59]

Finally, Charles Younglove of Detroit added a disquieting note to the conversation. Detroit was a cauldron of racial conflict where black activists had organized the Trade Union Leadership Council to pressure the United Auto Workers and other unions to narrow the gap between promise and performance on issues of race. Younglove had clearly been feeling the heat. "I think your idea . . . is good," he told McDonald.

Although I don't think this is what the Negroes are going to buy. I think they are going to brand it as puny. . . .

I am looking at it from my district. I have had quite a few meetings—Frank Shane knows that I have had quite a few. I have tried to cope with this situation and have tried to be quite fair with them.

I had a group in my office last Friday for five hours, consisting of about 17 in number. They are demanding another staff man, period; whether the district can afford it financially or not they want a staff man. . . .

I have had several calls about the International putting money up for moving expenses or subsidizing Negroes to move in[to] all white neighborhoods. I have had a lot of pressure put on about super seniority.

"I am for anything . . . that will help this situation out," Younglove concluded. "I think that we ought to be fair and we ought to stand up and be counted when they are not treated right, but at the same time I think when they go too far . . . we ought to stand up and be counted too and tell them in plain English where we stand."[60]

Frank Shane shared Younglove's anxiety. He had been executive secretary of the Committee on Civil Rights for fifteen years and, by his own lights, had worked tirelessly to advance the cause of racial equality. For the first four years of his tenure, he later recalled, "I had no secretary, I had a desk." In effect, he *was* the Committee on Civil Rights. The five district directors who were members of the committee did little, and one of them openly grumbled about having to participate in its activities. Meanwhile, from black union members, there had been constant sniping about "color" and about the need to have African Americans in positions of authority. Shane apparently believed, with much of the labor establishment, that when whites were elected or appointed to union office they were chosen entirely on their merits and were acting as trade unionists without regard to race. But for veteran black workers to demand a leading role for themselves, even in relation to issues of civil rights, was to ask for "special preference." He reminded the union leadership that "from the first [USWA] convention I recall that our stand was that we were for equal opportunity for all those we represent. . . . Today there is a hue and cry for preferential treatment and compensatory hiring. In the light of what we have done in our Conventions and the stand we have taken down through the years, we cannot afford to compromise our position." Above all, he concluded, "we cannot give in to the idea that we are going to give special preference to any particular group." Not a single member of the executive board dissented from Shane's remarks or offered even the hint of an alternative perspective. The complete absence of blacks from these deliberations, in which issues of civil rights were discussed at great length in terms of "us" and "them," no doubt made greater candor possible. It also made the leadership's self-serving paternalism and intellectual stasis all the more vivid.[61]

. . . . .

Given the union leadership's glaring deficiencies and the grassroots backlash against black demands for full equality, it was inevitable that African American steelworkers would organize as an autonomous force on behalf of their own agenda. There was, however, a moment of hope for interracial unity in 1965, when USWA secretary-treasurer I. W. Abel defeated McDonald for the presidency of the United Steelworkers. Abel's narrow victory came in part because he offered black union members a new deal and won their support on that basis. He followed through by reorganizing the Committee on Civil Rights as a department of the international union and appointing a black union veteran as director of the new department. But in the context of the mid- and late 1960s, it turned out to be too little, too late. Of the 625 staff men assigned to the union's twenty-nine districts, only twenty-seven were Negroes; they constituted "less than one-half of one percent" of the union's employees in 1967. Under Abel, moreover, the USWA leadership continued to argue that black demands for greater representation within the union constituted a request for "special privileges." In 1950 Tom Shane had called the campaign for a Negro vice-president of the union "Jim Crowism." In 1968 Abel took the same position, declaring, "I didn't hold office all these years as a Welshman but as a steelworker." Blacks knew full well, however, that it was ethnoracial status as much as ability that had propelled many old immigrants into leadership positions within the union, and that unconscious assumptions of white supremacy were giving way to a conscious effort to render the wages of whiteness invisible.[62]

Thus, of necessity, they organized black caucuses—within plants and local unions and at the national level—and developed an ongoing alliance with civil rights organizations, above all the NAACP. Although much of this activity was new, it was not without precedent in the experience of black industrial workers. On the contrary, many African Americans who joined the CIO in the 1930s had done so because of the work of black union organizers and the influence of churches and other institutions in the black community. In 1945 St. Clair Drake and Horace Cayton pointed out that "while [Negroes] accept the overtures of the labor movement they still do not dismantle their *racial* organizations," because "they believe that their bargaining power *within* the labor movement will be strengthened if they stick together." Drake and Cayton were still willing to characterize the CIO as a "crusading movement," but Cayton's brother, Revels Cayton, was already moving toward a more sober assessment. A Communist party member and maritime union activist, he was no longer willing to take slogans about black-white unity at face value because, too often, "unity" meant "whites leading blacks and putting the interests of whites first." By the late 1940s, Revels Cayton was advocating the creation of black caucuses even within the most progressive CIO unions. When a leading African American member of the Communist party accused him of "petit-bourgeois nationalism," he exploded, "The white working class is supposed to be leading us, and where the hell are they going? . . . They're not doing a goddamn thing for blacks!"[63]

Black caucuses emerged, then, out of a combination of pragmatism and hope on one hand and disillusionment and angry self-reliance on the other. In Los Angeles, Walter Williams spearheaded the formation of the Afro-American Labor Protective Society soon after the deregistration of the Unemployed 500 in 1946. (Williams's use of the term "Afro-American" at this time was no accident. Influenced by the popular journalist Joel A. Rogers, an immigrant from Jamaica who used his writings to instill a sense of black pride and African heritage among his readers, Williams recalled that he "had been doing some reading about who I was, [so] I just suggested the name, and the fellas accepted it.")[64] At approximately the same time, in the San Francisco Bay area, members of ILWU Warehouse Local 6 formed the Frontiersmen, a black caucus that "discussed grievances we thought were not being handled properly" and fought for African American representation in the union leadership. In the early 1950s, at the Gary Works of U.S. Steel, black workers in the coke plant organized the Sentinel League and launched a series of wildcat strikes to improve the abysmal health and safety conditions in their department. From the coke plant they built a plantwide organization, the Eureka Club, which (like the Frontiersmen) drew on long-standing social networks in the community to

247

create an effective power base in the local union. In 1957 workers in Detroit and Chicago launched the Trade Union Leadership Council, an independent Negro protest organization, to compel recognition of black aspirations for greater representation within the United Auto Workers. Its leaders pointed out that blacks constituted less than 1 percent of the skilled labor force in Detroit's auto plants and blasted the UAW and other CIO unions for staking out a "good public posture on the question of 'civil rights and fair practices' while they resist with every means at their disposal any effort to change the 'lily-white' character of their own international executive boards." Then, in 1959, Randolph's famous confrontation with Meany at the AFL-CIO convention sent shock waves through Black America and triggered the formation of the Negro American Labor Council.[65]

At Republic Steel's South Chicago Works, black workers had played an active and important role in the blood-soaked Little Steel Strike of 1937. Indeed, the example of the South Chicago Works had demonstrated to Drake and Cayton that "in a time of crisis white workers would not only struggle side by side with Negroes, but would also follow them as leaders and honor them as martyrs." The authors of *Black Metropolis* had also recorded the sentiments of a black activist with fourteen years' experience at Republic who had been acutely aware that even high-seniority Negro workers remained stuck in the lowest-paying and most hazardous jobs at the plant. "That's why I wanted organization," he said at the time. "I understand that without organization a person can't get anyplace." The implication was that organization would mean a resolute fight against racially based inequality in the mills' occupational structure. "I believe from the way they talk," he said hopefully, "that there is no discrimination in the CIO."[66]

But nearly thirty years later that hope remained unfulfilled. In August 1966, the month United Steelworkers Local 1033 celebrated its thirtieth birthday, black workers at Republic's South Chicago Works presented a litany of grievances that sounded ominously reminiscent of the bad old days of the nonunion era. They pointed out that "Negroes and Spanish speaking members of our union are confined to the worst and lowest paid jobs" and that " 'integration' in employment has been less than tokenism." They backed these charges with devastating statistics. As of May 1, 1966, they said, there were no Negro employees in the carpenter shop, the electric shop, or the pipe shop. In fact, in the entire plant there was not a single black apprentice in training for the skilled trades, even though "there are scores of Negro employees in the mill who are *good* electricians, carpenters, painters, pipefitters, etc." What were these men doing? "Pushing brooms, chipping, working in the labor gang or just common labor." Beyond the skilled trades, in the sections of the plant that required no apprenticeship training but still offered the opportunity for skilled, high-paying work, the racial disparity was almost as glaring. In the rolling mills, where most of the jobs were skilled and semiskilled, whites tended to outnumber blacks by a margin of fifteen to one. But in the coke plant, which one African American worker characterized as the "gateway to Hell," there were 145 blacks and 2 whites.[67]

Black workers at Republic placed much of the blame for this situation on management, but they were also highly critical of their union. Weeks and months after they filed grievances or brought their complaints to higher levels of the union, they continued to hear the old admonitions and excuses: "wait," "it takes time," "go through procedure." "We have heard this for nearly thirty years," they said, "and we are still waiting." Their response was to organize a black caucus within the plant to fight on behalf of their own agenda. And they warned that if their union failed to support them in that fight, "we will be compelled to seek help from other groups in the civil rights field[,] for we are determined to secure justice now."[68]

In their determination to "secure justice now," these Republic Steel workers were reflecting not only the dynamics of a historical moment of unprecedented black insurgency but also the specific experience of a generation of African American industrial workers. From Birmingham to Buffalo, and Atlanta to Chicago, black steelworkers had long since begun to recognize that—in Nathaniel Brown's memorable words—the CIO had "meant one thing for the whites and another thing for us." As this recognition crystallized and deepened, it created a new set of alliances that pitted black workers, civil rights groups, and federal courts and administrative agencies against white workers, unions, and corporate management. Not that most blacks became antiunion. In fact, public opinion polls and their response to organizing campaigns revealed that as a group they were more prounion than whites. What is tragic, however, is the disillusionment of veteran workers who, in many cases, had been "the first to come out for the union." They had taken great risks to build the CIO and had taken its leaders at face value when they announced their commitment to racial equality. Many of them had developed a sophisticated awareness of the need to defend and strengthen their unions *and* to fight against them when they served as instruments of white privilege. But there were also many veterans of the CIO era who had come to believe that their unions were part of the apparatus that kept black Americans down. "Looking back," Youngstown steelworker James Trevathan recalled, "the union helped only when it was backed into a corner. . . . The union did just what it had to for us blacks. No more. That's all. The least possible."[69]

To focus entirely on the shortcomings of the United Steelworkers' leadership, however, is to ignore the very real constraints the leaders faced. In attempting to address racial discrimination in the mills, they came up against a union majority that had little commitment to change and—often—a vested interest in the survival of the old regime. Again and again, the determination of white workers to maintain a narrowly defined seniority system and—more broadly—to invest whiteness with the status of property reduced the United Steelworkers' stance on racial equality to little more than pious platitudes. The leaders could—indeed, should—have done more. But they understood that in doing so they would have jeopardized their own job security and, perhaps, the institutional equilibrium of the union. So they temporized, passed more resolutions, and nibbled at the edges of the system of white privilege, until the union and the companies became the joint target of black steelworkers' demands for justice and restitution.[70]

"The Steel Was Hot, the Jobs Were Dirty, and It Was War": Class, Race, and Working-Class Agency in Youngstown

TODAY YOUNGSTOWN is a steel mausoleum, but it was a working steel town for nearly a century, and for many years the Mahoning Valley of northeast Ohio—from Warren, through Youngstown, to the Pennsylvania border—constituted the third-largest steel-producing area in the United States. Iron manufacturing had begun in the Mahoning Valley as early as 1804, and although overshadowed by Pittsburgh, it continued to expand throughout the nineteenth century. In the 1890s the area's pig-iron producers made the transition to steel, and in 1900 the valley's future as a major center of steel production was secured with the formation of Youngstown Sheet and Tube. Over a period of two decades, Sheet and Tube's founder, James Campbell, built it into one of the nation's largest steel companies. Specializing in seamless pipe for the oil industry worldwide and sheet steel for Detroit and other centers of automobile manufacturing, Sheet and Tube became the largest employer in a city whose population tripled between 1900 and 1920 and peaked at 170,000 in 1930. The company's principal production facilities were the Campbell Works, in the community that bore James Campbell's name, and the Brier Hill Works, on Youngstown's northern border. Because the Republic Steel Corporation also maintained two major mills in the area, *Iron Age* characterized Youngstown as the "capital of the independent steel industry."[1]

In addition to the "independents," U.S. Steel had two production facilities in the Youngstown area—the Ohio Works, within the city, and the McDonald Works, in the northwestern suburb of McDonald. To the east, just across the Pennsylvania border, the Shenango Valley was also an important production center, anchored by Sharon Steel in Sharon and a U.S. Steel complex in Farrell. By 1960 the nine major mills in the Mahoning and Shenango Valleys had a capacity of 12.4 million tons, which nearly exceeded that of the rest of the nation west of the Mississippi.[2]

These impressive figures, however, masked a number of problems that placed Mahoning Valley producers in an increasingly precarious position. By the late nineteenth century they were compelled to import coal and iron ore from as far away as the Mesabi Range in Minnesota, and their reliance on rail rather than cheaper, waterborne means of transportation only accentuated their disadvantage.[3] Finally, when plans to develop an interconnecting waterway from the Great Lakes to the Ohio River failed to materialize, U.S. Steel and Sheet and Tube shifted their production priorities away from Youngstown and decided not to modernize their facilities in the area. One by one, the Mahoning Valley's mills were eliminated, until only Republic's Warren Works remained.[4]

• • • • •

The massive shutdowns, and the destruction of a way of life based on the rhythm and material benefits of steel production, engendered a desperate struggle to save the mills. At first, steelworkers argued that because "we put our lives into the valley," the steel companies were obligated to invest in the regeneration of their Youngstown-area plants. When it became clear that such investments would not be forthcoming, steelworkers and their allies developed a sophisticated legal strategy to challenge the companies' prerogatives in court and crafted innovative plans to reopen the mills under worker-community ownership. They also mobilized at the grassroots level to fight for their jobs. In January 1980 they occupied U.S. Steel's headquarters in Youngstown. The catalyst for the occupation was a speech by Ed Mann, a veteran steelworker and local union president who reminded his fellow workers that "every day you put your life on the line when you went into that iron house. Every day you sucked up the dirt and took a chance on breaking your legs or breaking your back." Mann quoted at length from a speech by the famed black abolitionist Frederick Douglass:

> Those who profess to favor freedom and yet discourage agitation are men who want crops without plowing up the ground. They want rain without thunder and lightning. They want the ocean without the awful roar of its waters. This struggle may be a moral one [and you've heard a lot about that, Mann interjected] or it may be a physical one [and you're going to hear about that] but it must be a struggle. Power concedes nothing without a demand. It never did and it never will. Find out what people will submit to and you will find out the exact measure of injustice and wrong which will be imposed upon them.

"This was said in 1857," Mann told his audience, "and things haven't changed much. U.S. Steel is going to see how much they can put on you." Gesturing toward the Corporation's local headquarters, he declared, "I'm going down that hill and I'm going into that building." Hundreds followed (estimates ranged from five hundred to seven hundred), broke through the locked glass doors, and entered the building.[5]

Mann was a socialist—not a member of a political sect who had come to colonize the mill and its embattled workforce, but a man with deep roots in the Mahoning Valley whose family members joined him in occupying the U.S. Steel building. ("My daughter Beth changed her baby's diaper on the executives' pool table," he later recalled.) Mann was hired at the Brier Hill Works in 1952 and labored for more than twenty years in the shadow of the open hearth, until he was elected president of his local union in 1973. His aggressive and eloquent leadership, his left-wing politics, and his appeal to a legacy of struggle that highlighted the words of a legendary African American hero signified far more than the desperate circumstances he and his fellow workers faced. Rather, they reflected a tradition of militant unionism that dated from the formative years of the CIO in Youngstown and that—in some form—had found continuous expression there since World War II. Mann's history, indeed the broader history of the USWA in the Mahoning Valley, suggests that the conventional portrait of steelworkers as "conservative," "traditionalist," even "petit bourgeois," needs to be redrawn.[6]

There were conservatives and traditionalists among Youngstown's steelworkers, of course, and the USWA in the Mahoning Valley had its share of business unionists, heavy-handed bureaucrats, and self-serving functionaries who lacked "social vision." But contrary to the received wisdom, the union was hardly a monolith, and every stage of its history was hotly contested by a diverse cast of characters. The Little Steel Strike of 1937 and the signing of collective bargaining agreements with Republic and Youngstown Sheet and Tube in 1942 were the first great moments, but the wartime wildcats that crested in 1945 revealed a higher level of organization and a militant leadership with deep roots in steel. Carl E. "Jerry" Beck, the steelworker who stood at the forefront of that insurgent wave, represented a tradition of solidarity and shop-floor militancy that flourished in the early CIO but was often driven to the margins as the new federation "matured." The wildcats Beck led were crushed—by the combined force of the state, the employers, and the top leadership of his own union—and Beck himself was exiled. But a tradition of independence and militancy continued at the local level.

253

John Barbero, who began working at Brier Hill in 1948, recalled that "in the early days . . . we had many shutdowns. . . . We had a no-strike clause in the contract. But Pittsburgh would be called by the company, and they were always told that Murray would be out of town for two or three days: just enough time for you to settle your problem." Likewise, Oliver Montgomery, who came to Brier Hill in 1950, remembered that "we used to strike so much, particularly in the mason department, around the open hearth, that when you came to work in the afternoon, on the three to eleven turn, you didn't know whether the [day turn] guys were striking or whether they were going home."[7]

For the next three decades, the mills of the Mahoning Valley continued to generate many forms of activism and grassroots leaders who ranged from ethnic politicians to Trotskyists and independent socialists to African American workers who took their inspiration from the model of black self-organization developed by A. Philip Randolph. These tendencies came together most clearly in two local unions— Local 1330 at the Ohio Works of U.S. Steel and Local 1462 at the Brier Hill Works of Youngstown Sheet and Tube. The history of race relations in these plants and local unions is the principal focus of this chapter. It is a history marked by small triumphs and persistent ambiguity; a history in which working-class agency often meant both grassroots initiatives to achieve racial equality *and* determined rank-and-file defense of the wages of whiteness; a history that highlights the complex and increasingly volatile convergence of a racialized democracy, a militant minority, and the "liberal state."

· · · · ·

Like many of the production centers in the nation's industrial heartland, Youngstown was an ethnic city. It had been settled at the end of the eighteenth century by Anglo-Protestant migrants from New England, and in the course of the nineteenth century Welsh and German immigrants broadened the city's ethnic mix but reinforced its Protestant culture. This ethnocultural regime remained in place in some of the mills until as late as World War II. At Sheet and Tube's Campbell Works, for example, the foremen and skilled workers tended to be English, Scottish, and Welsh, along with smaller numbers of Irish and Germans. Even after World War II, most of the workers in the electric shop at Campbell were "Johnny Bulls"; and in the boiler room "nearly everyone"—that is, workers and their supervisors—belonged to one of two Protestant churches: Brownlee Woods Presbyterian and Third Reformed Evangelical Lutheran.[8]

But these were shrinking enclaves. Beginning in the late nineteenth century, new immigrants from southern and eastern Europe had poured in to fill many of the jobs in the expanding steel industry. By 1920 the foreign-born and their children accounted for 59.8 percent of Youngstown's population, and 69.9 percent of the foreign-born were from southern and eastern Europe. Nativists railed against the newcomers, and in the 1920s a born-again Ku Klux Klan sought to vanquish the "deviant" strains of immigrant Catholicism and secular modernism. But the immigrants were here to stay, and SWOC's victory in the Mahoning Valley greatly accelerated the process through which they became full citizens in the political arena and achieved a new level of self-respect in the workplace. In Youngstown, however, as in much of the nation, it was the older immigrant nationalities and the exceptional groups among the newer ones that benefited most from the opportunities for mobility that the CIO offered. Thus James Griffin, the son of an Irish father and an Austrian mother, became the United Steelworkers' district director. The Irish American Charles Carney became the CIO's state senator and, ultimately, a member of the U.S. House of Representatives. Sam Camens, the son of a Jewish shopkeeper, went from local union president to the district staff and, finally, became the assistant to the president of the international union in the early 1980s. The experience of the more typical new immigrant groups—the Czechs, Slovaks, Hungarians, and Italians—demonstrates both the resilience of ethnic subcultures in the industrial heartland and the opportunities for incremental group mobility that the New Deal and the CIO offered. In spite of layoffs and a shrinking labor market, the real income of steelworkers doubled in the course of a generation, thanks in large measure to the benefits the USWA negotiated on their behalf. And for some individuals there were significant opportunities for leadership within the CIO locals and municipal administrations of the Mahoning Valley.[9]

For African Americans, there were also significant gains. Blacks in Youngstown were able to build a niche for themselves in steel that lasted, in some cases, for three generations. But in comparison with the trajectory of the "foreigners," their experience was one of ambiguity and frequent disappointment. Even in the legendary years of postwar prosperity, steel offered a shrinking foundation. Steel employment in the Mahoning Valley peaked at 53,793 in 1950 and declined by 25,000

Fig. 7.1. Coke plant workers and supervisors, Youngstown Sheet and Tube, 1940. Credit: Youngstown Sheet and Tube Audiovisual Archives, Youngstown Historical Center of Industry and Labor / Ohio Historical Society

in the next two decades. The number of black workers fell by nearly 1,000 in the fifties—from 5,909 to 5,015—and by more than 1,500 in the 1960s. The eventual collapse of steel industry employment meant the relegation of a large segment of the African American population to economic marginality and greater social isolation. Indeed, black unemployment in the city was higher in 1980 than it had been at the end of the Great Depression forty years earlier.[10]

Blacks had come to work in the mills in the second decade of the twentieth century, and by 1930 they constituted 10 percent of the operatives in Youngstown's blast furnaces and rolling mills and 23 percent of the laborers. Employment plummeted during the Great Depression, for blacks and whites, and some Mahoning Valley residents recalled that in the context of mutual deprivation Negroes and "foreigners" mixed easily and amicably on a day-to-day basis. Steelworker Sam Donnorumo, who grew up in the Brier Hill section of Youngstown in the 1930s, remembered his neighborhood as "one big happy family." Brier Hill was mainly Italian at that time, but it included a generous smattering of other European nationalities and some African Americans. "Them were the good old days," Donnorumo said. "People baked bread [in outdoor ovens]; you'd come over and sit down out in the backyard—

eat bread, pizza, baked sausages." In the crime-ridden and racially polarized 1990s, he was—understandably—nostalgic for that "mixed neighborhood [where] we all got along well," where "you never had to lock your doors," where "[you'd] leave your doors open all night long." But African American memories were sometimes less roseate. Steelworker Jim Davis recalled Brier Hill as a place characterized by "very strong ethnic ties" and persistent conflict between black and Italian youth. It was, he said, "the melting pot that never melted."[11]

Insofar as there was racial harmony during the Depression years, it was sorely tested by the dramatically different response of African American and "foreign" workers to the Little Steel Strike. Unlike the foreign-born and their children, black workers generally remained loyal to their employers during the bitter conflict that convulsed the Mahoning Valley in the spring and summer of 1937. A SWOC official stated that only about 2 percent of the Negro workers in Youngstown had joined the strike. The rest, he said, had "flocked back to the mills." Likewise, in Warren, a union official reported that of about two thousand men out on strike, "only ten . . . were Negroes." A representative of the Urban League spoke with several white workers in front of the union headquarters in Warren and painted a depressing portrait of racial polarization. "All of [the whites] trenchantly denounced the Negro," he wrote. "In fact, quite a few colored men ha[ve] been beaten." According to George Schuyler, black strikebreakers who were drawing higher pay than ever before openly jested about owning "scab cars," whereas "the whites have become impoverished and many [have been] forced to move from their homes." Not surprisingly, he concluded that racial prejudice in the Youngstown-Warren area was on the rise.[12]

・・・・・

Nonetheless, when Archie Nelson, a black worker from Montgomery, Alabama, arrived in Youngstown during World War II, he came with great expectations. After a few weeks repairing track for the Pennsylvania Railroad, a friend from Montgomery helped him get a job at the Brier Hill Works. He recalled: "As I looked around there, every job I saw that was a decent job, it was held by whites. And all the greasy, nasty, cheap jobs was held by blacks. And I went to thinking. I said [to myself], 'Now these folks been tellin' me this is God's country. But so far as discrimination is concerned, I don't see no difference.' " Nelson went on to describe the racial employment pattern at Brier Hill in greater detail. "You take the coke plant. They got nasty, smoky jobs

257

down there where you live in that smoke and fumes and stuff. Well, that's where the black man was. And you take a place like . . . the plate mill. It was cheap jobs and nasty work. It was *loaded* with blacks." But in the machine shop, where the jobs were skilled, the pay was high, and the working conditions were relatively good, there were no blacks. In fact, he maintained, so great was the taboo against their presence in this white enclave that blacks did not dare set foot in that part of the plant.[13]

Nelson's anger and disillusionment remained vivid nearly fifty years after his arrival in Youngstown from the South. But his description of the job structure at Sheet and Tube was borne out by others, black and white, who were from the North and had no expectation of finding "God's country" when they entered the mills. Mann recalled that "blacks got the worst jobs. They worked in the coke plants, blast furnaces, track labor, plate mill, scarfing yard. . . . Even in the 'black' departments, the top job was usually held by a white man." James Trevathan, who was employed at Sheet and Tube for thirty years, echoed Nelson. The masonry department was "predominantly black," he said of the Campbell Works. "Coke plant, predominantly black; tube mill, predominantly black. . . . It was the same way in the blast furnace. . . . Wherever you found dirty, hot, and nasty work, you found your black workers. . . . Low pay, that's where you found 'em. Bad working conditions, that's where you found 'em."[14]

With a few minor variations, conditions at U.S. Steel's Ohio Works mirrored those at the Brier Hill and Campbell Works. Camens, who served as local union president at the Ohio Works from 1945 to 1957, believed that the problem of discrimination in hiring and upgrading stemmed first and foremost from company hiring practices, but he knew all too well that the union's task was complicated by active rank-and-file resistance to the entry of blacks into certain departments and to their upgrading in others where they were confined to the less skilled jobs. Even in the blast furnace and the masonry department, where blacks were concentrated in large numbers, the better jobs were denied to them because black workers had been accumulating seniority only in dead-end lines of progression.[15]

Camens was a former Ohio State University student who had been influenced by his father's social-democratic politics and further radicalized by the Great Depression. For him, entering the mills was a political act and an attractive alternative to running the family grocery store. Along with other "Depression babies" such as Marvin Weinstock and black workers such as Harry Green and Nathaniel Lee, he mounted an unusually determined campaign aimed at "eliminating th[e] evil" of Jim Crow in the plant. Their strategy was, first, to fight for departmental seniority and then, in occupations where access came only through apprenticeships, to open these lily-white programs to blacks. Thus Camens was able to report that in the blast furnace "every job in this department [has been] filled by strict seniority, regardless of race, color or creed. Our Union has wiped out discrimination in this Department." Likewise, in the steam and power department, where about 20 percent of the workers were black, "Discrimination has been completely wiped out . . . due to the work of our Grievance Committee."[16]

One of the focal points of contention was the open hearth. At both the Ohio Works and Brier Hill, this department illustrates the intractability of a shop-floor culture that was hostile to racial equality. The Ohio Works open hearth had more than a thousand workers, laboring in the shadow of huge furnaces that held two hundred tons of molten metal. Ethnically, it was dominated by old immigrant groups, even though the work was notoriously hot and heavy. According to Weinstock, "The open hearth is a dangerous place to work to start with. I've heard many times of a man getting a job . . . and going on the open hearth floor and seeing the charging machines and the overhead cranes run[ning] back and forth and the whistles blowing and the [furnace] doors opening up with the tremendous heat. . . . The heat was totally oppressive. The noise and activity was frightening. So, . . . many [individuals] quit after one turn or before one turn was over. [They] asked for a transfer or got the hell out of there."[17]

Those who stayed became part of a special breed of workers with a distinctive élan. As one keen observer of the mill work environment put it, the men of the open hearth

> wore the red neckerchiefs of railroad engineers and the tinted goggles of welders. They walked on shoes soled with rubber tires to keep their feet from getting burned on the brick floor. In summer as well as winter they cloaked themselves in protective long johns, denim coveralls, flame-retardant jackets, and by day's end what they wore was soaked in sweat. They drank steaming black coffee to keep their bodies hot and chewed Brown's Mule Plug tobacco to keep the dust out of their throats.

With incentive pay and prodigious effort, they earned high wages. With little or no formal training, they developed impressive skills in blacksmithing and metallurgy. Above all, their work required a close and careful interdependence—"like a Greek athletic event," one veteran of the open hearth remembered, "except that everyone is dirty and in heavy underwear."[18]

In this environment, with its traditions of physical prowess and work-based cooperation on one hand and racial exclusion on the other, the leadership of Local 1330 took an uncompromising stand against its own membership and won what turned out to be an ambiguous victory. The open hearth had always been segregated, with blacks confined to laborers' jobs in the "pit" and whites holding the higher-paying jobs as furnace men and crane men on the "floor" above them. According to Camens, efforts to change this situation met with "organized resistance" from white union members who were "quite vociferous in their opinions." But, he reported, "in the summer of 1948, due to vacations and labor shortage, management was forced to put a negro . . . to work as a slagger [furnace man] on the open hearth floor." The floor employees immediately organized a work stoppage that shut down every furnace. In a reversal of the usual conflict between blacks and whites in the steel industry, the white strikers claimed that the reason for their action was that the black man whom management promoted had worked in the mill for only ten days and that other (white) men with higher seniority should have been upgraded first.

With production stalled at a key point in the steelmaking process, management was prepared to cave in. But District Director Griffin and the Local 1330 leadership perceived the strike as racially motivated, and they stood their ground, with the result that the strikers returned to work within twenty-four hours. Sixteen days later, however, after two more black workers were upgraded on the open hearth, there was another wildcat strike. This time, there was no claim that seniority was an issue. Rather, white workers declared they were striking because of a series of long-standing grievances, especially the antiquated system of incentive pay, which denied the open hearth men their share of the company's vastly increased output. Once again, however, black workers were both the occasion and, to some degree, the cause of the walkout. Camens recalled strikers telling him that the company was "just bringing blacks in . . . [to] break our unity." Somehow, in spite of the exemplary—and highly visible—activism of a number of black unionists, many white workers still regarded their African American counterparts as a force that would disrupt the solidarity white men needed to maximize their tonnage pay and win their battles with management. Although local union leaders agreed to pursue the open hearth men's legitimate grievances, they continued to stand firm on the right of black workers to move from the pit to the floor, and the walkout ended within twenty-four hours. According to Camens, the principle of upgrading by departmental seniority had finally been established. "Today one negro has a job as a regular slagger," he reported in 1950, and others had moved up to better jobs in the department. "To my knowledge," he concluded proudly, "this is the only open hearth in this district where the sequences are now open on a strict seniority basis to all employees."[19]

But even with a formal agreement to open the department's lines of progression, white resistance continued and, in the circumstances of the open hearth, proved so daunting that few blacks were willing to take the physical risks they would have to confront in the higher-paying jobs that were now technically available to them. Even more than most areas of a steel mill, the open hearth was a dangerous place to work. Safety was contingent on the cooperation of everyone involved in the work process, and some whites were only too willing to engage in acts of sabotage that jeopardized the safety, even the lives, of their black fellow workers. Thus Weinstock remembered that one of the first blacks who was upgraded after the 1948 wildcat strike quit his new job almost immediately because "he was convinced that he would be killed." And Mann, who fought for the promotion rights of black workers at Brier Hill's open hearth, explained how realistic that fear was. If you were black and wanted to work on a furnace, he said, "you had to be able to take the heat," literally and figuratively. "Let's say a black guy was gonna go up there and try doing that job. He'd be shoveling [dolomite] into the furnace; the [furnace man] would pull the door all the way up, and the flames would shoot out twenty or thirty feet. It would discourage a fellow. If he had any common sense, he wouldn't want to work up there. And these were the games that were played. [The whites] would make it very difficult [for the blacks]." But at Brier Hill, Mann recalled, "we had some tough black guys that stayed and took it . . . and [eventually] moved up."[20]

Mann readily acknowledged that his inspiration for joining the fight against racial discrimination at Brier Hill came in significant measure from the example of the Ohio Works and Local 1330, where much of the union leadership was in the orbit of the Socialist Workers party (SWP). The SWP was a Trotskyist organization founded on New Year's Day in 1938. Although much smaller than the Communist party and generally much less influential than the CP in the ranks of labor, it had developed a significant leadership role among West Coast merchant seamen, Minneapolis teamsters, Akron rubber workers, and Flint (Michigan) autoworkers.[21] In the context of McCarthyism and the Korean War, some of the leading SWP members and sympathizers at the Ohio Works abandoned their ties to the party. But their transition to a more conventional trade unionism was a gradual one. For years the Trotskyist-unionist alliance in Local 1330 functioned as a creative outlet and leadership training school for men who were keenly intelligent but whose opportunities for advancement had been thwarted by the Great Depression or racial discrimination or, in some instances, channeled by conscious choice into the CIO.[22]

Camens served as president of Local 1330 for more than a decade, and he was followed by Weinstock for nearly as long. Ironically, in a plant with a labor force of forty-five hundred, there was only a handful of Jewish workers; and two of them were the leading figures in the Ohio Works local for nearly twenty-five years. The leadership group also included two outstanding black unionists, Harry Green and Nathaniel C. "Nate" Lee. Green was a grievance man in the mill and a leader of the Youngstown branch of the NAACP. Lee, a versatile and energetic man who loved opera almost as much as he cared about justice, was born in Jackson, Mississippi, in 1905. Although he graduated from Atlanta's Clark University, he found it impossible to maintain a decent job and live with dignity in his native South. In 1934 he went to Youngstown and tried, unsuccessfully, to obtain a teaching job in the city's schools. (The city hired its first black teacher, a woman, in 1940.) Determined to "make a living no matter what," he entered the mills during World War II and, in 1948, became a bricklayer's apprentice— the first black man to break the color line in the skilled trades at the Ohio Works. He served for many years as treasurer of Local 1330 and in 1965 was elected a teller in the international union. Like Green, he was also an NAACP activist; he eventually served not only as branch president in Youngstown but as president of the statewide NAACP in Ohio.[23]

Given the politics of the Local 1330 leadership, it is not surprising that the union mounted a determined campaign for racial equality in the mill and aggressively joined the fight against discrimination in the community as well. In reaching beyond the confines of the Ohio Works, Local 1330 activists played a key role in strengthening the ties between the CIO and civil rights organizations rooted in the black community. The most politicized activists had a larger mission: to merge the issues of class and race and to fuse the labor and civil rights movements into a mighty instrument of social transformation. During a "season of terrorism" in the fall of 1945, when "racial tension [was] seething" in Youngstown, the scheduled speakers at an overflow meeting to protest police brutality included Jerry Beck and Fred Dillard, a black steelworker from the Brier Hill Works. The NAACP's leaflet advertising the event accused the police chief of a "fascist attitude toward minorities" and expressed the hope that "the labor movement, together with the NAACP, [could] stamp out every least sign of approaching terrorism."[24]

The social character and political tone of this event suggests that in Youngstown, as in a number of other cities, there was indeed a historic moment during World War II and the immediate postwar years when the CIO and organizations based in the black community came together in a way that seemed to prefigure an unprecedented merging of the struggles for economic justice and civil rights. The leadership of this campaign came not from the CIO's centrist mainstream, which tended toward boldness in language and caution in practice, but from the Left. The power and sense of momentum that characterized this Left-led activism is evident in a confrontation that took place in September 1946 during the Ohio State CIO convention in Akron. The initiative came from members of Local 1330, in this case Harry Green and Tom Hood, the union's 270-pound vice-president. They went into an Akron restaurant for breakfast and were refused service because Green was African American. They reported this incident to the morning session of the convention, and at the noon recess "about fifty delegates went to the proprietor and they CONVINCED him that discrimination was a policy that the CIO would not tolerate." In the face of that kind of pressure in a union town, the owner quickly agreed that "he would serve anyone regardless of race, color or creed." He apologized to the entire delegation and to Green in particular, claiming "it was all a mistake."[25]

Members of Local 1330 became deeply involved in civil rights activism in the summer of 1949, when Youngstown's black community, with the support of the Mahoning County CIO Council and United Steelworkers locals 1330 and 1462, launched a campaign to integrate the city's public swimming pools. In spite of increasingly insistent challenges at the local level and a state law mandating equal access to public facilities, segregation had long been the norm at Youngstown's six swimming pools. In June 1949, however, with the issue of racial equality on the agenda in much of the nation, the city announced that all of its pools would be open to all Youngstown residents. Immediately, the plan aroused a storm of protest from some elements in the community, including the *Youngstown Vindicator*, which condemned the city's action for "giving public sanction to the attempt to force both races to swim together." When the city finally opened the pools, a number of black citizens took the lead in "testing the waters." Sometimes black swimmers encountered no resistance at all. More often, however, whites, or the great majority of them, left the pool in protest when blacks arrived and began to swim. And there were ugly incidents— including the stoning of a black youth; an especially violent confrontation in which two men, one white and one black, were stabbed; and frequent harassment and intimidation of black swimmers.[26]

In the midst of the escalating controversy, on the afternoon of July 5, Nate Lee was at the Local 1330 hall, when he suddenly informed Marvin Weinstock that he was "going swimming." Weinstock warned him that he would be lynched. But when Lee persisted, Weinstock announced, "I'm going with you," as did Ray Russo, the recording secretary of the local. The three men hurried to the East Side pool, where Weinstock, the "race traitor," was attacked and held under water by a group of white youths. Thanks to the quick intervention of the police, he recalled, "I didn't get drowned" or even seriously injured. But the incident received considerable publicity, including a front-page story in the *Youngstown Vindicator*.[27]

When Weinstock returned to work the next day, a number of people shouted angry epithets at him; others turned their backs as he approached them. But then, he remembered, "this carpenter sees me and starts screaming at me . . . and pulls a hatchet out and starts waving it in my face and I start to run and he starts to chase me . . . through the plant." Fortunately, Weinstock survived this confrontation too, although he was convinced that his days as an elected union official were over. But with the strong backing of the rest of the Local 1330 leadership, he was reelected chairman of the grievance committee and then, for five consecutive terms, became president of the local. His support came not only from the black workers who voted as a bloc but also from many whites in the mill, some of whom were no doubt endorsing his skill as an effective representative of their interests on the shop floor far more than his commitment to racial equality.[28]

On the shop floor and in the local union, the achievements of Local 1330's "Trotskyists" were impressive, and their commitment to trade

union democracy *and* racial equality is undeniable. But as they became
ensnared in the politics of the United Steelworkers at the district and
international levels, they compromised—and ultimately abandoned—
their vision of a transformed social order. Camens, Lee, and Weinstock
had been among the leading insurgents in Youngstown in the 1940s,
and Lee, at least, continued to support some activities of the Socialist
Workers party well into the 1950s. In 1946 all three men had actively
and enthusiastically supported Griffin's unprecedented "rebel" campaign for the district directorship—he ran, successfully, against an in-
cumbent director supported by Philip Murray—and they continued to
work closely with him. But gradually they became far more dependent
on Griffin than he was on them. His protection kept red-baiting rivals
at bay. His patronage facilitated Lee's many years of activity in the
NAACP, and he brought Camens and eventually Weinstock onto the
district staff. But over time Griffin became a symbol of entrenched
power in District 26 and the target of insurgent groups. For nearly
twenty years, moreover, he failed to appoint an African American to
a district staff job and thus convinced many Negro steelworkers that
he was antiblack. Finally, in 1965, he further undermined his reputation when he cast his lot with the lackluster McDonald regime against
international union secretary-treasurer I. W. Abel in the contest for
the USWA presidency. Although the stolid Abel was hardly a rebel,
virtually all of the forces of reform in the union rallied to his candidacy.
But Griffin harbored a number of grudges against Abel, and in pursuit
of his own ambition he agreed to serve as McDonald's campaign manager. Lee went along; so, reluctantly, did Camens. Lee even secured a
minor position on the McDonald slate and won the largest vote of any
candidate for international office. It was a personal triumph, but one
that revealed how much the politics of the "Trotskyists" had been shorn
of progressive content since the heyday of left-wing militancy in Local
1330.[29]

· · · · ·

Compared with the Ohio Works, the trajectory of unionism at Brier
Hill was more complex and contested, and it was much more clearly
shaped by issues of race and ethnicity. The founding generation at Brier
Hill was mainly Italian. The first person whom SWOC organizer Hugh
Carcella signed up in the local union was James "Baseball Jim" Mullidore, a man of enormous physical strength who, according to Carcella,
was "known by everybody . . . to be probably the strongest individual

Fig. 7.2. "98% Organized": United Steelworkers Local 1462 membership meeting, March 1944. *Second row, left,* President Jerry Beck; *front row, left,* Vice-President Dan Thomas. Credit: Archives of the Catholic University of America, Philip Murray Collection

around the Brier Hill [neighborhood.]" For years thereafter, names such as Ignazio, Naples, Liguore, Tombo, Deramo, and Thomas (an Anglicization of DiTommaso) predominated among Local 1462's officers. When it came to the top leadership of the local, however, Mullidore and other Italian Americans readily deferred to Jerry Beck, a relative newcomer to Brier Hill who was destined to blaze a meteoric path through the Mahoning Valley.[30]

Beck was a third-generation steelworker. His grandfather had been fired from his job at Apollo Steel in Apollo, Pennsylvania, during the upheaval that surrounded the famed Homestead strike of 1892 and "had to dig coal for the balance of his days." His father lost his job in the mill after the 1919 steel strike. Beck himself began work on the Pennsylvania Railroad a year later, at the age of sixteen, eventually becoming a locomotive fireman on freight runs that brought coal and iron ore from Lake Erie to the Mahoning Valley steel mills. When laid

off from the railroad, as he was each year after the freezing of the Great
Lakes halted the ore boats, he worked at Republic Steel's Youngstown
Works. He was among the Mahoning Valley steelworkers who heard
Philip Murray speak in Youngstown in April 1937, and again in May,
at the beginning of the Little Steel Strike. He was a picket captain at
the Bessemer Plant of Republic Steel's Youngstown Works, and when
the strike was defeated he was fired along with many other SWOC
partisans. In October 1939 he was hired at Brier Hill. Already well
known as a union activist, he was elected charter president of Local
1462.[31]

Although his daughter remembered him as a man of "socialistic no-
tions," Beck had no organizational ties with the Left. Nor was he the
kind of ethnic politician who built a career for himself on the basis
of his relationship to a particular immigrant nationality; he was too
obviously "American" for that. But in the polyglot environment of the
Brier Hill Works, he was remarkably successful in building a broadly
based leadership coalition across ethnic and racial lines. Above all,
though, Beck was a militant trade unionist whose main agenda was to
battle the company in the never-ending war of position that for him
was the essence of day-to-day working life. The Brier Hill rank and file
elected him president of Local 1462 four times, and he also served four
terms as president of the Mahoning County Industrial Union Council,
which made him second only to the USWA district director as a symbol
of CIO unionism in the Youngstown area.[32]

Given his high visibility and the controversy he engendered, it is
hardly surprising that Beck became not only the central figure but also
the alleged instigator of a momentous series of wildcat strikes at Brier
Hill in the spring and summer of 1945.[33] In spite of the United Steelworkers' strong commitment to the wartime no-strike pledge, there had
been twenty-three walkouts at Brier Hill since 1942. Most involved
small numbers of workers and lasted no more than a few hours. But the
1945 strikes were different. They eventually shut down the entire
plant, and the local union leadership—eleven officers elected on a
plantwide basis plus grievance men in every department—took a unified stand in support of the strikers. The wildcats started in May, with
a walkout by highly skilled maintenance men. They resumed in July
and this time halted production at the Brier Hill Works for more than
three weeks, in spite of orders from the company, the War Labor Board,
and Philip Murray himself to end the walkout. After receiving a second
telegram from Murray insisting that "you assume your responsibilities

and see to it that our membership returns to work immediately," Beck placed himself on the public record in defiance of the legendary president of the USWA and the CIO. "To execute your request," he wrote, "[would mean] the ordering of good union men into abject slavery" and would make "a mockery of unionism. . . . I could not do this and live with my conscience."[34]

What began as a strike had become an "insurrection," and the rebellious mood was evident not only at Local 1462 but throughout the Mahoning Valley. At a series of well-attended mass meetings, valley steelworkers expressed strong support for the Brier Hill strikers, with one unionist declaring that "if Jerry Beck is the master of double talk and the evil genius as [the *Youngstown Vindicator*] says, then we ought to have 75 more of him." But in the end the combined power of the employers, the international union, and the federal government overwhelmed the forces of insurgency at Brier Hill. Murray suspended all of Local 1462's officers and appointed a district staffer as administrator of the local's affairs. The company then fired most of the suspended union officials, including Beck. Eventually Beck became a CIO field representative and recalled engaging in many organizing campaigns, "from Maine to California and from the Great Lakes to the [G]ulf"— all of them far away from Youngstown.[35]

Beck's departure created an opening for Dan Thomas, a rough-edged but skillful ethnic politician who led the local for a decade and a half. The son of an immigrant railroad worker at Republic Steel, Thomas grew up in the Brier Hill section of Youngstown and worked as a slagger on the open hearth, then as a bricklayer. He was fired during the Little Steel Strike and, along with an honor roll of 265 other union members in Youngstown, Chicago, and Indiana Harbor, was restored to his job as a result of the agreement Sheet and Tube finally signed with SWOC in 1942. Even one of his leading critics conceded that he started out as "a very good unionist, very militant, [and] a very effective organizer. . . . Many people were pushed around on the job, terrorized by informants," John Barbero recalled. "Danny . . . was somehow able to counter [that], to put foremen up against the wall and say, 'You don't push that old man around again.' "[36]

Thomas became local vice-president in 1940, grievance committee chairman in 1942, and then, after a stint in the army, president in 1946. He quickly emerged as Griffin's main rival for the District 26 leadership, and the two men became the leading symbols of very different styles of unionism. Griffin was a devout Catholic in the Murray mold, an able administrator, and a skilled operator in the larger arena of community affairs and trade union politics. He repeatedly deplored "the Dan Thomas type of leadership" within the district and was especially appalled when Thomas was arrested in the company of two prostitutes, whom he tried to pass off as "organizers for the garment workers union." Thomas, in turn, denounced Griffin's alleged association with Trotskyism and tried to go over his head to enlist McDonald as an ally in the intraunion wars. But for the most part he remained a skillful accumulator of power at the local level. He created his machine not only by doing job-related and other favors for numerous individuals throughout the plant but also by using his sweeping power of appointment to develop a large network of shop stewards and other officials. These appointees constituted the impregnable core of the union. At the meetings, they ratified all of Thomas's initiatives, and anyone who disagreed became persona non grata or, worse, was labeled a "Commie" or "Trotskyite." Frank Leseganich, a persistent critic within the local, charged that Thomas used his presidency as "a platform to castigate and defame" members who opposed him as "reds" and "snakes in the grass." Archie Nelson declared that Thomas was a dictator who resorted to "threats, blackjacks, name calling, record changing, [and] rigged elections." Barbero maintained that "at every meeting you went to you were 'out of order.' No matter what you brought up, [Thomas] had such a well-organized machine it was 'sit down and shut up'; and he had the goons in the hall to enforce it."[37]

During World War II and the postwar era, the percentage of black workers at Brier Hill continued to increase until they constituted about one-third of the local union membership. Their numbers were more than sufficient to make them a major factor in the politics of Local 1462, but before they could play such a role they had to get out from under the Thomas machine. Nelson recalled that initially "a lot of blacks thought Danny Thomas was Jesus. They [were] crazy about him." It became part of the Thomas legend that back in "the early days," when there were still separate washrooms for blacks and whites at Brier Hill, he and a few other union representatives "picked up sledge hammers and we smashed down the walls that separated the blacks and the whites and dared the company to fire us." This story may well be apocryphal, a reflection of Thomas's remarkable ability to surround himself with layers of self-aggrandizing mythology. It is true, however, that he participated in CIO efforts to dismantle the informal but deeply rooted Jim Crow structure that prevailed in the Youngstown area, and that under his leadership Local 1462 developed a reputation not only for militancy but for a stronger commitment to the cause of racial equality than most Steelworkers' locals in the Mahoning Valley. Moreover, at the Brier Hill Works, on at least one noteworthy occasion, he publicly confronted—and condemned—a group of white bricklayers, most of whom were Italian Americans, when they engaged in a work stoppage to protest the upgrading of a black worker in the masonry department. Jim Davis, who worked in the department, recalled that Thomas made a powerful speech and "sounded like he was a champion of the black worker. To see a white man talking about black workers [having] a right to work was unheard of."[38]

Although Thomas's main commitment was to his Italian American base, he was careful to include a number of blacks in his leadership group. These men tended to be workers whose reputation in the plant derived in large measure from their membership in churches and fraternal organizations in the Negro community. Theo Wallace, the first black leader in Local 1462, was a high school graduate, an active Baptist, and a Prince Hall Mason. Alfred Jackson, the first black worker elevated to a skilled job in the plant—indeed, in the entire Mahoning Valley—fit the same profile. These men constituted the elite of the black working class. But in attempting to incorporate a few of them into the leadership of his machine, Thomas could go only so far. In the final analysis, he could not afford to alienate white workers who were opposed to any changes in the seniority structure that would—as they saw it—benefit blacks at their expense. As black workers demanded such changes and aggressively sought more representation within the local, most white union leaders naturally chose to side with their "own kind." Thomas extricated himself from an increasingly polarized environment when he moved up to the district staff in February 1960. But by that time a strategic core of black workers had already become convinced of the need to develop their own leadership and program.[39]

Three men played the key role in this process. The elder statesman of the group was Archie Nelson; the young militants were Jim Davis and Oliver Montgomery. Nelson was born in Mount Meigs, Alabama, in 1913. Before moving to Youngstown during World War II, he had worked as a dining-car waiter on the Louisville and Nashville Railroad, mostly on runs between Cincinnati and New Orleans. He left the Louisville and Nashville when he was assigned to "the lowest," and lowest-paying, job, serving black customers in the "colored" section of the dining car. At Youngstown Sheet and Tube, he worked in the condi-

Fig. 7.3. *Left*, Archie Nelson, with Local 1462 president Don Bernard and financial secretary Joe Clark, United Steelworkers Convention, Atlantic City, N.J., 1960. Credit: Archie Nelson

tioning yard, "scarfing" (removing the impurities from) steel, and over time he became the virtually unchallenged leader of the men, black and white, in that department. Barbero remembered him as "probably the best speaker we ever had in our local." His distinctively southern speech was richly colloquial; he was a man of genuine personal warmth and, considering his stature (five feet six inches tall), remarkable courage. At one union meeting, he grabbed a blackjack out of Danny Thomas's pocket, held it up to the membership, and accused the local president of "holdin' a blackjack meeting." But often his role was more conciliatory. According to Barbero, "When he got through speaking, people both black and white were saying Amen."[40]

Davis and Montgomery were younger than Nelson and more representative of the aggressive and uncompromising style of an emerging generation of black protest leaders. Both were born in Youngstown, and in comparison with the first generation of black union activists, their leadership qualifications derived less from membership in

271

churches and fraternal organizations than from their experience in the armed forces and their links to the Civil Rights movement. Davis was the third-oldest child in a family of thirteen. His father had migrated to Youngstown from South Carolina in the early 1920s and had worked at U.S. Steel's McDonald Works until he developed his own trucking business. With the coming of the Depression, the business failed and the elder Davis eventually returned to the mills as a bricklayer's helper. In the late 1940s Jim Davis went to work at Brier Hill, where, he recalled, the entry-level jobs available to blacks were coke plant labor, blast furnace labor, and masonry department labor. He worked in the masonry department until he was inducted into the army in 1949.[41]

With a number of white friends from high school, he went to Canton, Ohio, where they boarded a train for Fort Meade, Maryland. "When we got to Fort Meade," he recalled, "I don't know how they did it, but when they called the roster, all the blacks went one way and all the whites went the other." Even though President Truman had ordered the desegregation of the armed forces a year earlier, Davis found himself in a unit in which every recruit was black and all the officers were white. When his unit was transferred to Fort Benning, Georgia, he discovered that the swimming pool on the base was off-limits to blacks, including those who were preparing to ship out to Korea. "I began to look really hard at what was going on," he concluded, and "the more you look, the more you see." When he returned to Brier Hill in 1951, he saw that two-thirds of the workers in the masonry department were black but almost all of the bricklayers were white, and he decided, "We had to do something about that."[42]

His partner in "doing something about that" was Montgomery, a third-generation steelworker whose grandfather had moved to Youngstown from Albany, Georgia, in 1914 to work at Youngstown Sheet and Tube. His great-uncle had worked for U.S. Steel for more than half a century. His father worked at Republic Steel and Youngstown Sheet and Tube. Montgomery began working as a bricklayer's helper at the Campbell Works in 1948 and then at Brier Hill in 1950. He also served in the army during the Korean War era and went to school on the GI Bill. After graduating from Youngstown College, he rejoined Davis in the masonry department, where they launched a fight for the rights of black workers that spread from one department to the entire Brier Hill local to other steelworkers' locals in the Youngstown area and finally to affiliation with A. Philip Randolph's Negro American Labor Council and a national black caucus in the steelworkers' union.[43]

The crucible out of which this leadership emerged was the masonry department at Brier Hill. It was Dan Thomas's department; it was dominated by Italian Americans. They were the bricklayers, and the blacks were their helpers. After returning from the army, with a wife and two children to support, Davis began demanding that he and other blacks be given the opportunity to become bricklayer's apprentices. When management informed him that he had been accepted as an apprentice, he quickly discovered that many whites, in management and in the skilled trades, were reluctant to train black workers. Sometimes they tried to sabotage the process. Montgomery recalled, "Bricklaying is a dexterous craft and . . . you have to form the right habits immediately. They can't show you the wrong habits. If you practice those, they become ingrained. [But whites] would deliberately show blacks the wrong way to hold a trowel, the wrong way to spread the mud, that type of thing." In Davis's case, he had worked as a bricklayer with his father; he already knew the trade and was able to complete the apprenticeship. But the complaint of racially motivated sabotage became more frequent as black workers were upgraded and trained for higher-skilled jobs.[44]

By the end of the 1950s blacks at Brier Hill had decided to organize and compete as a group for leadership of the local union. With the impetus coming from the masonry department, they began to meet on their own and to train themselves in public speaking, parliamentary procedure, and the mechanics of office holding. For the 1960 local elections they organized a black slate and found themselves competing under unexpectedly favorable circumstances, because Dan Thomas had relinquished the presidency to move up to the district staff. With the whites relatively evenly divided between Italian and Slavic factions, the blacks, voting as a solid bloc, scored a stunning victory. Thomas's handpicked successor, Don Bernard, won the presidency, but the black slate won five offices, including Archie Nelson as vice-president and Joe Clark as financial secretary.[45]

There was little time for rejoicing, however. The black victory polarized the plant, and with the exception of progressives such as Barbero and Mann, white unionists concluded that they too needed to unite along racial lines to stave off the black workers' challenge. According to Mann, "nigger-baiting" and "red-baiting" became the norm in union politics even more than before. Montgomery recalled the threats: " 'You better not walk behind a furnace; we're gonna throw you in a ladle of steel.' These threats went on constantly. [Many of us] were just

273

back from the service and it was like we were on the front lines again. . . . The steel was hot; the jobs were dirty; and it was war." And insofar as the goal of the war was control of the union, blacks lost. In fact, said Montgomery, "We got slaughtered." In 1962 Clark defected to the reconstituted Thomas machine and was reelected, but every other black candidate was defeated.[46]

In some respects, the workers who organized a black caucus at Brier Hill were ahead of their time; they prefigured the Black Power movement that emerged in the second half of the 1960s. But they were also building on a foundation of black self-organization that had deep roots in the African American experience. Even in the 1950s, blacks and whites continued to occupy separate worlds. They lived in segregated neighborhoods, attended separate churches, and joined separate fraternal organizations; they socialized in separate taverns and worked in racially segmented occupations in the mills. Although they sometimes developed amicable relationships on the job, Nelson recalled with bitterness, "you'd see them [white] guys downtown, with their wives, . . . [and] they didn't know you. . . . They wouldn't speak to you downtown to save your life. They'd look at you like you was a fool down there if you tried to say you know 'em."[47]

In these circumstances, it was natural to build a racially separate caucus within the union, and there were plenty of precedents—most recently, A. Philip Randolph's Negro American Labor Council, which held its founding convention in 1960. Like Randolph, however, black workers at Brier Hill chose to organize separately to achieve the goal of racial integration. They did not speak the language of quotas or ask for "super seniority"; most of them were already high-seniority workers who were demanding the right to better jobs on the basis of their experience and ability. The backlash they encountered came not because they had repudiated an emerging consensus on issues of race; rather, they were exposing the limits of that consensus. Like their counterparts in Chicago and Detroit whose efforts to achieve access to housing outside the ghetto had run into an avalanche of resistance in the late 1940s and early 1950s, they were discovering that backlash was—and would continue to be—the principal response of white Americans to black demands for access to good jobs, decent housing, and quality education, in the North as well as the South.[48]

• • • • •

274

Fig. 7.4. *Left*, Oliver Montgomery, with A. Philip Randolph and Local 1462 union pioneer Alfred Jackson, at a meeting of the Negro American Labor Council, Youngstown, 1968. Credit: *Youngstown Vindicator*

But the sixties were about much more than backlash. As the momentum of this chaotic and exhilarating era continued to build, some of the key actors at Brier Hill reached beyond the local level in search of allies who could strengthen their campaign for racial justice and for a more democratic and progressive union. Montgomery became president of the Youngstown branch of the Negro American Labor Council, and in 1969 he moved up to the international union staff in Pittsburgh, where he continued to work with Davis and others to build a national caucus of black steelworkers. Likewise, Barbero and Mann reached beyond the confines of the Mahoning Valley to find allies in other districts. In the late sixties they became leading members of the Rank-and-File Team (RAFT), a caucus of militant unionists whose common denominator was their commitment to decentralized democracy in the United Steelworkers. Although RAFT aspired to be a national organization, it was headquartered in Youngstown and never amounted to much outside Ohio. But it played a vital role in building the leadership group that would finally win control of the Brier Hill local in the early

275

seventies. There were, to be sure, a number of fortuitous "external" developments that strengthened their hand and perhaps even made their victory possible. But one cannot discount the enduring vision and unrelenting determination of Mann and Barbero as midwives of change.[49]

Barbero was the embodiment of the progressive rank and filer. The son of an immigrant worker at Republic Steel, he enlisted in the army during World War II, went to language school to learn Japanese, became an interpreter, and in retrospect was enormously grateful that he "came through all of it without having to kill anybody." At war's end, he lived in Japan for two years and married a Japanese woman. As a result of his wartime and immediate postwar experiences, he became a pacifist. On one occasion, at an antiwar meeting, he explained that because his father was Italian, his mother Czech, and his wife Japanese, "in any imaginable war he would be fighting against a cousin."[50]

He returned to Youngstown in 1948, got a job at the Brier Hill Works, and enrolled in school at Youngstown College. He also became associated with a proudly unorthodox socialist organization, the United Labor party, which was based mainly in Akron but had a number of adherents in Youngstown as well. He later remembered it as "the one group I [joined] in my life where everybody seemed to trust each other." Beyond the personal bonds of friendship and solidarity, he was attracted to the group's intellectual openness and its advocacy of peace, racial equality, and economic democracy. Within Local 1462, in the early days of the Thomas regime, he became an almost singular voice of protest. Other workers have recalled that when no one else dared to challenge the machine, Barbero was there, speaking insistently but not stridently and without any personal ambition of his own. He was, said Nelson, "respected by everybody that knew him, and those that didn't know him, it didn't take me long to tell 'em about him."[51]

Barbero's close friend Ed Mann would also have a significant impact on the development of unionism at Brier Hill. He was born to Jewish parents in Toledo, Ohio, where his father was a salesman. In 1945, before graduating from high school, he enlisted in the Marine Corps; and in 1948, at the urging of Marine Corps friends, he moved to Youngstown, where, he recalled, "[i]t was so easy to get a job . . . at that time, I had eleven different jobs in one year and never got fired from one of them." After enrolling at Youngstown College, he met Barbero and through him became associated with the United Labor party and an interracial organization called the Intergroup Goodwill

Council. He also became aware of the presence of the Socialist Workers party, in the community and in Steelworkers' Local 1330. Although not much of a "joiner," he recalled, "These guys talked sense, in my estimation. They had ideas. They did things. I felt comfortable with them."[52] After another stint in the Marine Corps during the Korean War, he got a job at Brier Hill in 1952 and soon joined Barbero on the open hearth. Like his friend, Mann was comfortable with socialism; he believed in racial equality and was viscerally antiwar; he had a rank-and-file temperament. The two men formed the core of a small group of unionists who challenged the Thomas machine and, after a "long march," finally defeated it.[53]

Several conditions that prevailed in the steel industry in the 1960s and early 1970s facilitated their victory. First, steel contracts in the 1960s ushered in an era of wage stabilization after a sustained period of wage gains. Although negotiated fringe benefits enhanced steelworkers' welfare and made them the objects of envy among many other sectors of the wage-earning population, wage stabilization combined with the squeeze of taxes and inflation to engender a sense that something was amiss. This sensibility was magnified by the impact of mechanization and the rise of imported steel, which contributed to the loss of nearly one hundred thousand jobs between 1966 and 1974. It was inevitable that the Abel administration would feel the heat for these developments, especially since Abel had run for the presidency in 1965 promising to "return the union to its members" and seemed, in the eyes of many steelworkers, to have done nothing of the kind. The USWA remained as centralized under Abel as it had been under McDonald; and although Abel's widely publicized concessions to African American demands did not satisfy most black workers, they alienated many whites. The extent of the new administration's difficulties became clear when Emil Narick, an assistant general counsel in the USWA headquarters who was virtually unknown among the union's members, ran against Abel in 1969 and captured 40 percent of the vote. In basic steel, which accounted for a shrinking portion of the total membership, Narick won a stunning 63 percent.[54]

All of this discontent reverberated at the local level and worked to the advantage of Mann and Barbero. Using RAFT as their vehicle, they built a small caucus among Brier Hill steelworkers who shared their commitment to union democracy and, to some degree, their sympathetic relationship to the social movements that swept across the American landscape in the 1960s and early 1970s. When people looked

277

at them, Mann recalled, they thought, "Hey, look at these egg-heads, look at these radicals, look at these Reds." For years, many older workers had believed the accusation that Mann and Barbero were Communists and reflexively voted against them in local union elections. But by the late 1960s and early 1970s the composition of the Brier Hill workforce was changing in ways that made red-baiting less effective. Even as the industry downsized, individual plants continued to hire in certain departments, and many of the young men who entered the mills in the late 1960s reflected the rebellious and countercultural sentiments that were convulsing the larger society. Together with black workers, the newcomers provided the electoral foundation that made it possible for Mann and Barbero to reach a new plateau on a journey they had begun in the late 1940s. Mann ran for president of the local several times in the 1960s, and he was elected recording secretary in 1967. Three years later he ran for president again and was defeated by about a hundred votes. In 1973 he finally won, and Barbero was elected vice-president.[55]

"I was redbaited," Mann recalled of his years as Local 1462 president. "But I found that [most] people didn't really care what my politics were as long as I won grievances [and] did my job as a union officer." He helped build and strengthen a network of sixty-five elected shop stewards throughout the plant and claimed that during his first term the local filed "at least twice as many [grievances] as any previous administration." It also won more arbitration cases than any other steel local in the valley. The new regime established an award-winning monthly newspaper, the *Brier Hill Unionist*, and was careful to do the mundane, nonpolitical things that mattered to the membership, such as providing refreshments after every union meeting and negotiating with management to pave and fence in the main parking lot. In 1976 the "Ed Mann Team" ran for reelection, and four of the top five candidates on the slate, including Mann and Barbero, were victorious.[56]

The coalition that Mann and Barbero assembled was interracial, but only in a limited sense. (By this time, some allies of long standing were no longer available, because Montgomery had moved up to the international union staff in Pittsburgh and Nelson had become a foreman in the conditioning yard.) Mann could not have been elected without the support of black workers, and compared with his predecessors as president of Local 1462, he was aggressively pro–civil rights. He established an active civil rights committee, headed first by Jim Davis and then by Willie Aikens, a Korean War veteran whose father had worked in the masonry department at Brier Hill for forty-five years. But as a conscientious trade unionist and democrat with a small *d*, Mann was sensitive to the constraints that the will of the majority imposed on his conduct as president. Perhaps inevitably, tension developed between his agenda and the race-conscious concerns of black workers like Davis, who had recently been elected national president of the Ad Hoc Committee of Black Steelworkers. Davis's militant style and uncompromising demand for the elimination of racially based inequalities allowed some whites to label him a racist. He was, in a word, controversial. He believed that a key test of the Mann administration's bona fides was its willingness to incorporate blacks—above all, Davis himself—into the top elected positions in the local union. But this never happened. On the slate headed by Mann, nine of the eleven candidates for plantwide office were white, and Davis ended up running against Barbero for vice-president in 1976 and losing by forty-five votes.[57]

During Mann's tenure in office, the issue of race came to the fore—at Brier Hill and throughout much of the steel industry—in a way that dramatically sharpened the divisions between blacks and whites. The catalyst was a Consent Decree signed on April 15, 1974, by nine steel companies and the United Steelworkers international union on one side and the federal government on the other. The decree came at a time when the steel companies and the union had 408 cases against them pending with the federal Equal Employment Opportunity Commission (EEOC). In addition, both parties had suffered a number of stinging defeats in recent federal court cases brought by black workers and their allies in the NAACP and other civil rights organizations. These decisions mandated sweeping changes in union seniority practices and represented a dramatic turnaround on the part of the federal judiciary. In a decision involving the steel industry in 1959, Federal Judge John Minor Wisdom had denied relief to black plaintiffs in Houston because, in his words, "the Union and the Company have a contract that *from now on* is free from discrimination based on race." The judge recognized that black workers seeking skilled jobs would continue to be at a disadvantage as a result of past discrimination. But, he said, "[w]e cannot turn back the clock. Unfair treatment to their detriment in the past gives the plaintiffs no claim now to be paid back by unfair treatment in their favor." Title VII of the Civil Rights Act of 1964 was based on essentially the same premise—namely, that the basis of change was to be "prospective and not retrospective." "It was our understanding," said the United Steelworkers, "that so long as employers stopped discriminatorily assigning employees hired after the effective date of Title VII (July 2, 1965) no seniority changes would be required."[58]

But as the struggle for black equality continued to escalate in the streets, and more cases of job discrimination came before the judiciary, the courts took the position that an "affirmative duty . . . to undo past discrimination" permitted compensatory action on behalf of those who had been the victims of that discrimination. In 1971, in a case involving Bethlehem Steel, a federal judge characterized the seniority system negotiated by the company and the United Steelworkers as "illegal" and declared that "if relief under Title VII can be denied merely because the majority group of employees . . . will be unhappy about it, there will be little hope of correcting the wrongs to which the Act is directed." By 1974 rumors that the soon-to-be-announced Consent Decree would make it possible for high-seniority black workers to move up the job ladder on the basis of plant seniority, and "bump" white workers in the process, were sweeping through the mills.[59]

Actually, the USWA and the steel companies had initiated the negotiations that led to the Consent Decree as a means of preventing major changes and avoiding years of costly litigation. The international union informed the membership that its goal had been to short-circuit the creation of "unworkable and inconsistent seniority rules written by judges." Thus the decree established continuous service in the plant rather than departmental service as the basis of seniority but also sought to avoid "bumping," "leapfrogging," and other practices that, in the short term, would unduly disrupt existing seniority units and lines of progression. The decree did compel the posting of permanent vacancies throughout the plant and offered successful bidders two years of "rate retention," which meant that black workers—or whites, for that matter—could now afford to transfer from one department to another without fear of starting at a lower wage rate on their new job. The decree also established goals and timetables for the admission of minorities and women to the industry's most skilled jobs—the trade and craft positions—which had remained almost exclusively white and male; and it made $30,940,000 in back pay available to the fifty-five thousand minority and female workers covered by the agreement, with the stipulation that anyone who accepted a cash settlement would thereby forfeit the right to sue the companies or the union for discrimination.[60]

The Consent Decree did win some rank-and-file support, first and foremost among black workers. Thus the signers of an anonymous letter declared that "the Consent decree has been the most significant and just thing to happen to the American working people in 40 years." But many blacks were less than enthusiastic. Some found the decree's Byzantine complexity and arcane language daunting and were reluctant to take the risks associated with transferring from one job to another. Some refused to accept the cash settlement that the signatories offered until the decree was adjusted to allow pending or future litigation to proceed. The NAACP, which had been an indispensable ally of many black workers who challenged the companies and the union, was deeply disturbed because the aggrieved workers—and the association—had been allowed to play no role in shaping the decree and because of the limits on litigation. Meanwhile, many white workers refused to be mollified by the union's assurances that everyone would ultimately benefit from the decree's provisions. They saw the Consent Decree as an assault on their hard-won job security and condemned it as a coup imposed by a distant and uncaring minority. Indeed, the decree fed the fires of an angry populism that blamed liberal elites for the painful pressures that many white Americans were facing. But USWA leaders professed near complete satisfaction with the changes they had wrought. Howard Strevel of District 36 exulted that the "wails and disruptive efforts of some lawyers and dissident groups" had not succeeded. "Several years hence, when we look back," he concluded, "we will wonder how we ever lived under the pre-decree seniority rules."[61]

The experience of James Trevathan at the Campbell Works of Youngstown Sheet and Tube suggests that Strevel's glib optimism was unwarranted. Trevathan was born in Youngstown in 1925. In 1952, after graduating from high school and becoming the second black bus driver in the city's history, he went to work at the Struthers Rod and Wire Mill. When the mill shut down six years later, he transferred to the Campbell Works, where he served as a bricklayer's helper until 1974. Then, even though he was almost fifty, he took advantage of the Consent Decree and passed the test to become a machinist's apprentice. There was only one African American in the machine shop at the Campbell Works at the time (and none at Brier Hill). Bob Hill, a Youngstown native, high school graduate, and air force veteran, had been hired as a white-collar employee at Campbell in 1966. He became a machinist's apprentice later that year and completed his apprenticeship in 1970. He even served as an acting foreman on occasion and, according to his recollection, was fully accepted by management and his fellow workers. But the sudden entry of eight black apprentices into the machine shop created an entirely different dynamic. Although all had passed the necessary tests, the new men were, according to Hill, "tainted" by their association with the Consent Decree. The fact that they were high-seniority workers undoubtedly added to the resentment, because if they completed their apprenticeships their plant seniority would give them an advantage over some men with higher departmental seniority in the event of layoffs, job openings, vacation scheduling, and other phenomena governed by seniority.[62]

In any case, there was friction from the moment the new apprentices arrived in the shop, and it continued for years. Trevathan recalled that when the general foreman "assign[ed] you to a certain machine to work with a certain machinist, some would teach you, some would show you nothing. Some of them just let me sit there by the machine for eight hours." He estimated that "90 percent of them [wanted us to fail]." Fortunately, a black apprentice named Hubert Clardy excelled in mathematics, and the eight men gathered at his home to study the math they needed for the academic side of their training. But two of the eight dropped out of the program because they could not tolerate the unrelenting hostility in the shop and the stress it caused. Clardy's skill was so obvious and impressive, however, that he eventually was asked to become an acting foreman in the department. The first day that he wore the "white hat," all but two of the white machinists walked out.[63]

At Brier Hill, too, many whites resented the opportunities the Consent Decree offered to blacks. "There was a lot of friction," Mann recalled; "nothing physical, but a lot of hot language." Black workers who transferred to new jobs as a result of the decree faced the same problem that Davis and Montgomery had confronted when they became bricklayer's apprentices in the 1950s. Invariably, the men who trained them for their new positions were whites, who in many cases resented the presence of the newcomers and had no interest in making it easy for them to adjust to a new job in an unfamiliar environment. Willie Aikens, the chairman of the local civil rights committee, was hired into the coke plant in 1951. When the coke plant shut down in 1959, he was assigned to the labor pool, a department that gave new meaning to the term "dead-end job." It was predominantly black and made up entirely of unskilled workers who were routinely assigned to low-level jobs throughout the plant but were unable to accumulate seniority on any of those jobs. At one point Aikens was laid off for twenty-two months while the company continued to hire whites off the street for skilled and semiskilled positions. When—after seventeen years—Aikens finally got out of the labor pool and transferred to a more skilled job, white workers in his new department said, "I'm not gonna train *you* to take *my* job." Sometimes the black newcomers were much older than the men who were compelled to train them, and their old jobs had not prepared them for the hand-eye coordination and the dexterity that their new positions required. "It was a problem," said Mann. "Nobody would show them what to do."[64]

The Consent Decree created a dilemma for Mann and Barbero. Both men had been associated with organizations such as the Dues Protest Committee in the late 1950s, the Organization for Membership Rights in the early 1960s, and the Rank-and-File Team in the late 1960s and early 1970s. One of the common denominators of these organizations was the consistent demand for union democracy—the right of members to elect all of their officers, including stewards at the local level, and to ratify contracts and all major agreements negotiated on their behalf by the international union. The two activists had been "knocked down," red-baited, and accused of being antiunion because of their association with these organizations. But they had never been deterred from what they regarded as a principled and necessary course. For them trade union democracy and the rights of black workers went hand in hand; they had fought as hard for plantwide seniority as they had for the right to elect shop stewards at Brier Hill. So although Mann supported the implementation of the Consent Decree in practice, he called for the local to go on record in favor of "[s]crap[ping] the Consent Decree and any other agreement that is not ratified by the membership." (At a poorly attended meeting in March 1975, the membership resolved, by a four-vote margin, that "Local 1462 is strictly against the Consent Decree.")[65]

Black workers had their own criticisms of the decree, but they could not have looked to referendum democracy as a way of achieving racial justice. Beginning with the USWA's founding convention in 1942, they had urgently sought representation in the upper echelons of the union. Their reasoning was that such representation would give blacks a voice they otherwise lacked and a greater sense that the organization belonged to them too. Over the years, the leadership had offered token concessions but mostly had counseled patience, pointed to the union's electoral channels as the only solution, and chastised blacks for seeking "special privileges." In 1969, when an African American finally ran for district director in Baltimore with the international union's support, he was overwhelmingly rejected by the district's white rank and file. To blacks, then, union democracy as practiced in the United Steelworkers often served to reinforce the tyranny of the majority. Could they have expected anything different from a unionwide referendum on the Consent Decree?[66]

In August 1974 several hundred white steelworkers met at Philip Murray Hall in Youngstown to discuss ways of preventing the implementation of the decree. Only a week earlier, President Richard Nixon had resigned in disgrace as a result of fallout from the Watergate scandal. A spokesman for the group that called itself the Committee of Concern for Rights of Steelworkers compared the consent decree to Watergate. He complained—accurately—that the decree had been negotiated in secret, and according to the *Brier Hill Unionist*, he criticized the membership for "letting the Union get away with it." For the rank-and-file steelworkers who gathered at Philip Murray Hall that August afternoon, there was only one solution: "[G]et things back the way they were before the Consent Decree."[67]

But there was no going back to the wages of whiteness as they had evolved over several generations. Tragically, however, there was no going forward either, certainly not in Youngstown. At the end of the 1970s, layoffs hit the nation's steel valleys with a vengeance. Between 1979 and 1982, more than one hundred fifty thousand jobs were lost in steel, and the hemorrhaging continued well into the 1980s. For reasons that had nothing to do with the Consent Decree, the companies decided to shut down many of the historic centers of steel production in the United States. In September 1977 Youngstown Sheet and Tube announced the closing of its Campbell Works; a little more than a year later the Brier Hill Works shut down; and in November 1979, just in time for the holiday season, U.S. Steel informed the public and its dwindling workforce that steel production at the McDonald and Ohio Works was about to cease.[68]

Barbero was one of the last workers "on the clock" at Brier Hill. The day after the last heat of steel was poured, he returned to the open hearth with three other production workers and twenty maintenance men to "mothball" the department that had been his workplace for nearly thirty years. "It was a shock," he reported.

Fig. 7.5. "Save Our Valley": Jim Davis picketing at the Brier Hill Works, December 1978. Credit: Alice Lynd and Staughton Lynd, *We Are the Union*

Our normally clean locker . . . room resembled a garbage landfill. Looters had come in over the weekend and had taken everything that was useful. Everything else . . . was strewn about in one hellish mess. . . .

The last day I burned all the production records—"100,000,000 tons by 1970"—and the attendance and work records of the thousands of people who worked here for over 70 years. We have become non-persons. By the

285

time we left, the once awesome open hearths stood as skeletal ruins picked clean and probably abandoned forever. It reminded me of Hiroshima where I worked for a few months immediately after the bomb was dropped.[69]

The shuttering of the once-vibrant mills symbolized the power of capital to affect the lives of tens of thousands of workers and to alter the destiny of entire communities. But the steel mills of the Mahoning Valley also serve as a testament to the power of working-class agency in shaping patterns of racial inequality and struggles for equality during the overlapping CIO and Civil Rights eras. What stands out about Youngstown in this regard is not only the role of the employers in determining the complexion of steel's occupational structure, and of top union officials in addressing—or failing to address—these often stark inequalities, but the ways in which local union leaders and rank-and-file workers fought this battle on the shop floor and beyond it in the communities where they lived. At the Ohio Works, a sizable cadre of "Trotskyists" used the levers of collective bargaining to win numerous agreements that expanded the rights of black workers. But these officials quickly discovered that formal agreements by themselves could not bring about lasting change. Fortunately, Marvin Weinstock proved more fleet of foot than the carpenter who chased him with a hatchet in the summer of 1949, but over the years more covert forms of rank-and-file resistance often served to block the upgrading of black workers, even when it had contractual sanction. At Brier Hill blacks learned early on that they could not rely on union leaders to fight their battles for them. So they organized on the shop floor to fight on their own behalf. Sometimes they found white allies who stood with them; more commonly, they encountered various forms of resistance from the white rank and file—like the bricklayer who taught his apprentice "the wrong way to hold a trowel," the furnace man who used the door to the open hearth furnace as a flamethrower, and the machinists who openly proclaimed that their department was off-limits to blacks. This rank-and-file agency became a formidable force. Indeed, as Gerald Dickey discovered in 1968, it textured—and even helped to shape—the long-term pattern of race relations in the mills.[70]

Epilogue

"OTHER ENERGIES, OTHER DREAMS": TOWARD A
NEW LABOR MOVEMENT

GERALD DICKEY, an electrician at the last major mill that continues to
produce steel in the Mahoning Valley, is a third-generation steelworker—or, as he puts it, a "last-generation steelworker." His maternal
grandfather was a Slovak immigrant who came to Youngstown in the
1920s and got a job at Sheet and Tube's rod and wire mill in Struthers.
"As I look back on it," Dickey says, "he had to be one of the bravest
guys in the world—a mill laborer, living in a company house and buy-
ing his goods in a company store, who in 1937 went on strike against
the company and just laid everything on the line, everything." Dickey's
father worked in the pipe mill at Republic's Youngstown Works and
"always called himself a CIO man. . . . I can remember that growing
up. ['I'm a CIO man.'] It] was like a song, or slogan. That always stuck
with me."[1]

After graduating from high school and serving in the air force for
four years, Dickey went to work on the open hearth at Brier Hill in
1968. Although the military was not exactly a model of peaceful and
orderly racial integration, interaction between blacks and whites was
common in the air force, and among enlisted men it occurred on a
relatively equal basis. Thus Dickey was puzzled by a number of things
he encountered at Brier Hill. "I could see the remnants of segregation,"
he recalled in 1996. "It really hit me when I walked in[to] that mill.
The open hearth washroom was upstairs. The mason[ry] department
washroom was downstairs. The white guys changed clothes upstairs.
The black guys changed clothes downstairs. There was just no two ways
about it. And then [in] the masonry department, . . . there were two
halves." The bricklayers were all—or nearly all—white; the bricklayers'
helpers were all—or nearly all—black. "It was just an automatic thing."
This racial stratification was reflected, informally, in the masonry department washroom, which had a white section for the bricklayers and
a black section for the helpers. The few blacks who worked on the
open hearth went downstairs, to the black section, to wash up and
change clothes.[2]

Dickey was also struck by the nearly complete absence of African Americans on the floor of the open hearth. When he finally asked about it, white workers told him that blacks "can't do the job" and "can't take the heat." Of course, "they can't do the job" was a familiar rationalization for the exclusion of African Americans from the more desirable positions in the mills. But "they can't take the heat"? We have seen that over several generations black steelworkers were routinely assigned to the heaviest, dirtiest, and *hottest* jobs because the employers professed to believe that "the colored man likes the furnace business" and could "stand that kind of work better than the whites." Thus a racialized division of labor had evolved. It was, in the main, management's creation, but white workers had developed a clear stake in its continuation.[3]

At Brier Hill the self-serving myth that blacks "can't take the heat" obscured generations of agency on the part of white workers whose own sense of manhood depended on the exclusion and subordination of the racial Other. Hence Ed Mann's observation about the "games that were played" to keep blacks off the open hearth floor. "Let's say a black guy was gonna go up there and try doing that job," he recalled in 1988. "He'd be shoveling [dolomite] into the furnace; the [furnace man] would pull the door all the way up, and the flames would shoot out twenty or thirty feet." Other workers corroborated Mann's story. According to Sam Donnorumo, who worked with Mann on the open hearth, whites "didn't [want] blacks to go on the floor." He remembered a Puerto Rican man named Gonzales ("he was real dark, black"), who was promoted to slagger, and "they tried to burn him up." Ken Doran, who worked at Brier Hill from 1949 until the plant closed in the late 1970s, recalled: "I know blacks that went into the open hearth and worked two days and decided they didn't want the job, because they valued their lives." "A guy would go on [the open hearth floor] and they'd find a way to get him out," said Oliver Montgomery. "In fact, they used to take bets [on] how soon they could get rid of this black guy. They'd burn him up."[4]

Nineteen sixty-eight—the year Dickey became a steelworker—was also the year Martin Luther King, Jr., was assassinated. King's tragic death triggered uprisings in more than a hundred cities across the nation. One of the indelible images of 1968 is the picture of flames from the Washington, D.C., ghetto piercing the night sky and illuminating the Capitol. Coming on the heels of the fiery conflagrations in Watts, Newark, Detroit, and many other cities in the mid- and late 1960s, the fires that flickered in the nation's capital made it appear not that blacks could not "take the heat" but that in their rage they would "burn America down."

In this context, the Brier Hill open hearth workers' easy confidence in the unassailability of their racialized turf represents an anomaly that was profoundly out of sync with the fear and anxiety that were becoming the norm among many whites as the 1960s progressed. No one fed upon this anxiety, and channeled it into a new, populist insurgency, with more energy and skill than George Wallace. Before his inauguration as governor of Alabama in January 1963, few Americans outside his home state had ever heard of him. But his inaugural address, especially his ringing defense of "segregation now . . . segregation tomorrow . . . segregation forever," made him the leading symbol of massive resistance in the Deep South. In the spring of 1964, Wallace headed north. His mission was to prove that there was no Mason-Dixon line when it came to white attitudes toward issues of race and civil rights in American society. His chosen terrain was the Democratic primaries in Wisconsin, Indiana, and Maryland; his target, the popular and seemingly unassailable president Lyndon Baines Johnson.[5]

On the evening of April 1, 1964, Wallace spoke to an overflow crowd in Serb Memorial Hall, a community center run by the Saint Sava Serbian Orthodox Church on Milwaukee's south side. In retrospect, his appearance at Saint Sava marks one of the catalytic moments of the other sixties—the era not of progressive affirmation but of conservative revitalization, reactionary populism, and, ultimately, backlash. Wallace's audience that night was composed mainly of immigrants, and their offspring, from Yugoslavia, Poland, Hungary, and Czechoslovakia. Many of them were blue-collar workers and union members; most lived in the neighborhoods surrounding the church, where the threat of black "invasion" loomed ominously near. The leaders of organized labor had branded the Alabama governor as "a carpetbagger, a bigot, a racist, and one of the strongest anti-labor spokesmen in America." But this line of attack had little effect on the people gathered at Serb Memorial Hall. They listened intently as Wallace warned that the civil rights legislation Congress was about to enact would "destroy the union seniority system and impose racial quotas." In a forty-five-minute speech, Wallace received thirty-four sustained rounds of applause, including a five-minute standing ovation when he concluded that "a vote for this little governor will let the people in Washington know that we want them to leave our homes, schools, jobs, business and farms alone." Afterward, according to a Wallace bi-ographer, the governor was "mobbed" by hundreds of admirers. "They sought autographs, they made cash contributions, they wanted to touch him."[6]

Wallace "won without winning" in Wisconsin by capturing 34 per-cent of the ballots cast in the Democratic primary. In Indiana he picked up "only" 30 percent of the vote. In Maryland, the third and last pri-mary he entered, he carried sixteen of twenty-three counties and won a majority of the white vote and 42.7 percent of the total. His supporters included Republican crossover voters in Wisconsin and old-style Dix-iecrats on Maryland's rural Eastern Shore. But news reporters who fol-lowed his whirlwind campaign kept coming back to the white working-class men and women who supported him in all three states. In Indi-ana's Lake County, where steel mills dominated the landscape and blue-collar workers made up the bulk of the population, Wallace did not even campaign, but nevertheless it was one of three counties where he won a majority. The hub of Lake County was Gary, which was not only a quintessential steel town but also one of the few cities in the nation where the black population was nearly a majority. For Gary's white ethnic residents the growing black presence in "their" city seemed to portend the disintegration of everything they and their im-migrant parents and grandparents had labored to build. Wallace carried every white precinct in Gary, some by a better than two to one margin. One trade unionist summed up the prevailing sentiment when he told reporters that "we've got Negroes in my union and they're O.K., but eighty-five percent of the Negroes in this town are too pushy. It's time for the whites to enjoy some segregation."[7]

"White backlash" was exacerbated by cries of "Black Power" and by the violent ghetto uprisings that reached a terrifying crescendo in New-ark and Detroit in 1967. But no matter how large these phenomena loomed at the time, the fundamental cause of white backlash was the prospect of racial *integration* and the price that the incorporation of African Americans into the economic and social mainstream threat-ened to impose on White America.[8] This became painfully evident when Martin Luther King, Jr., and the Southern Christian Leadership Conference came to Chicago in 1965, seeking to achieve full citizen-ship for the city's African American population by nonviolent means. In the summer of 1966, King led open housing marches into several of Chicago's white neighborhoods and encountered a torrent of hate that even veterans of the movement in the Deep South found shocking. In Gage Park, according to one marcher, the scheduled hour-and-a-half march turned into a four-hour nightmare as we wandered haphazardly through the neighborhood, unable to get through the mob and back to our autos. . . . White persons in the line of march were targets of special abuse as the residents—especially older women—spat at us and called us "traitors, communists, white niggers" and ranged a long list of sexual perversion charges against us. . . . Many youths cried, "Burn them like Jews," and "white power." Others yelled, "Polish power."[9]

Gage Park and other contested neighborhoods on Chicago's Southwest Side were largely working class and white ethnic. More than half of the residents were foreign-born or of foreign or mixed parentage; many were of Czechoslovak, German, Lithuanian, or Polish descent. Apparently, Southwest Siders had accepted the Civil Rights movement in the Deep South as a "normal effort by people seeking a better way of life." But even during the movement's heyday, when its focus was southern and its rhetoric was resolutely Christian and nonviolent, they had bitterly opposed the extension of civil rights legislation to their community. The local alderman who guided a weak fair housing ordinance through the Chicago City Council in September 1963 became a pariah in his own neighborhood, and a year later an overwhelmingly Democratic Southwest Side constituency elected an "arch-conservative" Republican to the state senate, largely because of his outspoken opposition to "forced housing." Now, with King declaring that "my place is in Gage Park," Southwest Siders feared a dramatic decline in real estate values and the unraveling of the communal network of churches and fraternal organizations in which they had invested so much of themselves. Above all, their sense of who they were and what they had achieved was at stake; for as one local resident acknowledged, they measured their position in society by "how far they stand above the Negro."[10]

As "white ethnics" and "white backlash" became interchangeable terms in the late 1960s and early 1970s, sympathetic journalists and scholars began looking beneath the surface of events and finding plebeian voices that spoke compellingly of anxiety and pain, of proud pasts and a precarious future. One of the most compelling voices belonged to Alice McGoff, the widow and mother of seven children whom journalist J. Anthony Lukas rendered larger than life in his book on the Boston busing crisis of the 1970s. The descendant of Irish immigrants, McGoff lived in a public housing project in the gritty Charlestown section of the city. In addition to caring for her children, she worked at the officers' club of the Charlestown Navy Yard. When she heard of

Martin Luther King's death in 1968, it gave her pause, but not for long. "You had to admit he'd done one hell of a job for his people," McGoff reflected.

> If she were black, she would have been the first one in line behind him. And you had to support his crusade down South. No right-minded person wanted blacks to sit in the back of the bus, eat at separate lunch counters, or use different toilets. That sort of thing was just plain wrong. But when King turned northward, Alice had grown skeptical. When King held his big rally on the Boston Common, Alice had asked, "What the hell is he doing up here?"[11]

Even though her family had been loyal Democrats for generations, McGoff found herself increasingly at odds with the Kennedy brothers and their support for black civil rights. It seemed to her that the Kennedys and President Johnson had responded to the demands of African Americans by sanctifying their status as an oppressed minority. In the process they apparently had forgotten that the Irish had suffered discrimination in America; the Irish had succeeded against great odds; and many Irish—like Alice's friends and neighbors in Charlestown— were still struggling for a piece of the American Dream. Moreover, she knew who would be asked to pay the price for government policies designed to achieve equality for African Americans. Certainly not the Kennedys and their "limousine liberal" friends in the wealthy suburbs. No, as another Boston Irish mother who was "barely able to make ends meet" told psychiatrist Robert Coles, "we're the ones who get it; the final buck gets passed to us."[12]

From her own experience and that of her immigrant ancestors, McGoff constructed a past of real and imagined suffering that merged with the memories of countless others like herself to become a white ethnic narrative of history. It was a narrative that exalted white self-reliance and triumph over adversity, a narrative that required—and thus constructed—a counternarrative of black passivity and privilege. Insofar as it reflected its own distinctive historical context, it was a new creation, but it also had deep roots in the American past. Long before McGoff's Irish ancestors had settled in Boston, the labor movement of the early nineteenth century had developed a similar narrative. When trade unionists addressed the issue of chattel slavery, they often argued that there was "more real suffering among the landless whites of the North, than among the blacks of the South." Most trade unionists demonstrated no interest in building ties of sympathy and solidarity between southern slaves and northern wage earners. On the contrary, they often chastised abolitionists for deflecting attention from the evils of wage slavery and implied that in comparison with the unmerited suffering of the white worker, the oppression of the black slave was deserved. Moreover, just as the "slaves of America" were alleged to have "partake[n] of all the necessaries and comforts of life in abundance," so the Civil War was re-created as a contest in which the northern white soldier gladly made the supreme sacrifice "for the liberation of the slave," only to find that emancipated Negroes were marching northward, as strikebreakers, "for the enslavement of the whites." It became a self-justifying litany: whites, not blacks, were victims; white suffering alone was worthy of sympathy; whites had earned their status through hard work and sacrifice, whereas blacks demanded special privileges they had not earned.[13]

. . . . .

The responsibility of the historian is to acknowledge this underlying reality as central to the history of the white working class in the United States, to understand the role of workers' own agency in building and defending the ramparts of racially based inequality, and to recognize that among European immigrants the imperative to become "white" was a dynamic element in the historical construction of their identities as workers and as citizens.[14] In so understanding the past, historians can illuminate its relationship to the present. Indeed, one major lesson I learned in the course of writing this book is that economism can neither illuminate our history adequately nor point the way toward a better future. There are, to be sure, numerous economic issues around which blacks and whites, and workers of every race and nationality, can unite. But too often scholars and labor activists have sought to envelop race in the language of class, the "magic bullet" of broad-gauged social-democratic policy agendas, and the invocation of the "common dreams" that allegedly animated progressive social movements before the emergence of "identity politics." These ideological formulas and programmatic blueprints seek to hide race because of its volatility and proven capacity to divide. But given the ways in which race is encoded in working-class identities and definitions of self, there can be no economistic cure for the malady that is "whiteness."

Nor is there any escaping the basic fact that "class is lived through race and gender." Indeed, "working-class solidarity has been most effective and durable," Zachary Lockman argues, "when it has also been infused by other solidarities," not only of gender and race but of religion, ethnicity, and nationality.[15] This has clearly been the case in the American labor movement. In the late nineteenth century, it derived new energy from the force of Irish nationalism; in the early twentieth century, from Jewish socialism. During the CIO era, it was nourished by the remarkable convergence of Popular Front Marxism and new-immigrant rights consciousness. But organized labor in the Civil Rights era failed to draw on the extraordinary dynamism and moral authority of the Civil Rights movement. True, the United Auto Workers had a large contingent at the March on Washington, where Walter Reuther spoke from the podium with Martin Luther King, Jr.; and the NAACP acknowledged the vital importance of the AFL-CIO's lobbying effort on behalf of the Civil Rights Act of 1964.[16] But in general the social *movement* for black freedom set organized labor back on its heels, created deep fissures in the labor-liberal alliance, and provoked angry jeremiads against ungrateful African Americans (including, even, the impeccably dignified A. Philip Randolph) who—whites alleged—were "pushing too fast" and refusing to acknowledge that "we're doing the best we can."[17]

It is, perhaps, a hopeful sign of organized labor's regeneration that in their strike against the Pittston Coal Company in southwestern Virginia in the early 1990s, the leaders and members of the United Mine Workers of America sought to appropriate not only the memory and moral authority of Martin Luther King, Jr., but also the tactics of nonviolent civil disobedience as weapons of working-class struggle. The turn to this rich source of inspiration came a quarter-century after the Civil Rights movement's greatest triumphs, to be sure, but it was nonetheless remarkable. For from Bloody Ludlow to Bloody Harlan and beyond, the UMW's history has been marked by waves of violent confrontation between the forces of unionism on one side and the coal operators and their well-armed and -financed allies on the other. Coal, moreover, has been an industry in which technological innovation and the combined agency of labor and management have practically eliminated African Americans from a workforce where they once had a proud and enduring presence. Thus to see white southern workers and their families transform themselves into a nonviolent fighting force, led by a southern white union official who anointed King as the symbolic leader of this "new model army," suggests a quite stunning turnaround.[18] Indeed, the UMW's 1991 victory at Pittston was arguably an important stepping-

Fig. epi.1. Pittston strikers, 1989: Members of the United Mineworkers during the union's seizure of the Moss 3 coal-preparation plant (South Clinchfield, Va.). UMW members consciously emulated the CIO sit-down strikers of 1937 and the nonviolent Civil Rights movement of the 1960s. Credit: Earl Dotter stone toward the emergence of a new labor leadership that finally has recognized the need to draw upon "other energies" and "other dreams" in rebuilding organized labor.[19]

It is no longer possible to discuss organized labor and labor market segmentation mainly in the language of "black" and "white." Race has always been a complex and multifaceted phenomenon, and in the last generation it has become much more so, as millions of newcomers from Africa, Asia, and Latin America have changed the face of America and the complexion of its labor force. Once again, immigrants have reshaped much of the American landscape and have diversified its ethnocultural rhythms. Once again, organized labor has been forced to contend with the presence of a new immigrant workforce in an era of resurgent nativism. In this context, it is necessary to embrace new challenges in all their complexity, but it is equally important to recognize that addressing ancient enmities and long-standing patterns of inequality etched in black and white remains central to resolving the many problems of race relations in American society.

As the greatest social upheaval in twentieth-century America, the Civil Rights movement remains a fitting source of inspiration in this regard, and so does the Atlanta preacher who helped lead it. Even at the most perilous moments of the long journey that ended with his assassination, King recognized whites as oppressors of African Americans and yet uncompromisingly affirmed their capacity for redemption; he denounced his country's reckless aggression in Vietnam in the name of its highest ideals; and he preached a Christian gospel that transcended religious ethnocentrism. Before his death, he was actively exploring the linkages between race and class and seeking to fuse the moral energy of the Civil Rights movement with an economic agenda that could address America's deep structural inequalities. Indeed, he died supporting the strike of black sanitation workers in Memphis who were seeking union recognition but whose basic quest was to compel recognition of their dignity as human beings. (Hence the simple but eloquent declaration on their picket signs: "I Am a Man.") Perhaps at this fortuitous moment—the beginning of a new century and a new millennium—freedom and necessity will finally converge to facilitate the creation of the kind of solidarity that King died helping to build: a "civil-rights unionism" in which struggles for economic justice and racial equality will become "complementary and mutually reinforcing, rather than . . . antagonistic and divisive."[20]

296

Notes

INTRODUCTION
"SOMETHING IN THE 'ATMOSPHERE' OF AMERICA"

The quotation in the chapter title is from Noel Ignatiev, *How the Irish Became White* (New York: Routledge, 1995), 99.

1. Thanks to Staughton and Alice Lynd, Youngstown's recent labor history is not an untold story. See John Barbero et al., "A Common Bond," in *Rank and File: Personal Histories by Working-Class Organizers*, ed. Alice Lynd and Staughton Lynd (1973; reprint, New York: Monthly Review Press, 1988), 259–78; Staughton Lynd, *The Fight against Shutdowns: Youngstown's Steel Mill Closings* (San Pedro, Calif.: Singlejack Books, 1982); Staughton Lynd, "The Genesis of the Idea of a Community Right to Industrial Property in Youngstown and Pittsburgh, 1977–1987," *Journal of American History* 74 (December 1987): 926–58.

2. Archie Nelson, interview by author, Youngstown, Ohio, Nov. 19, 1990. Substantial segments of my interviews with Ed Mann on Dec. 14–15, 1988, appear in *We Are the Union: The Story of Ed Mann*, ed. Alice Lynd and Staughton Lynd (n.p., n.d. [1990]).

3. Herbert Hill, "Black Workers, Organized Labor, and Title VII of the 1964 Civil Rights Act: Legislative History and Litigation Record," in *Race in America: The Struggle for Equality*, ed. Herbert Hill and James E. Jones, Jr. (Madison: University of Wisconsin Press, 1993), quoted on 312.

4. Nell Irvin Painter, "The New Labor History and the Historical Moment," *Journal of Politics, Culture, and Society* 2 (spring 1989): 369, 370; Herbert Hill, "Myth-Making as Labor History: Herbert Gutman and the United Mine Workers of America," ibid. (winter 1988): 132; Herbert Hill, "The Problem of Race in American Labor History," *Reviews in American History* 24 (June 1996): 189.

5. See Herbert Hill, "Race, Ethnicity, and Organized Labor: The Opposition to Affirmative Action," *New Politics*, n. s. 1 (winter 1987): 31–82; Nick Salvatore et al., "Discussion: Race, Ethnicity, and Organized Labor," ibid. (summer 1987): 22–71; Herbert Hill, "Myth-Making as Labor History"; responses by Steven Shulman, Nell Irvin Painter, David Roediger, Martin Glaberman, Francille Rusan Wilson, Stephen Brier, Irving Bernstein, and Albert Fried, *Journal of Politics, Culture, and Society* 2 (spring 1989): 361–403; Herbert Hill, "Rejoinder," ibid. (summer 1989): 587–95; and most recently, Eric Arnesen, "Up from Exclusion: Black and White Workers, Race, and the

State of Labor History," *Reviews in American History* 26 (March 1998), especially 148–49.

6. J. Carroll Moody and Alice Kessler-Harris, eds., *Perspectives on American Labor History: The Problems of Synthesis* (DeKalb: Northern Illinois University Press, 1990). The seven authors are David Brody, Mari Jo Buhle, Alan Dawley, Leon Fink, Alice Kessler-Harris, Michael Reich, and Sean Wilentz. I quoted from Dawley, "Workers, Capital, and the State in the Twentieth Century," 160. I gladly acknowledge that I have learned much from the work of all these authors and readily concede that their work cannot be fully or altogether fairly assessed on the basis of their contributions to a single volume. What stands out about this volume, however, is its self-conscious effort to address problems of synthesis and to evaluate the overall development of the field since its emergence in the 1960s. For this very reason, its silences are—or, in the context of 1990, were—deafening. For a sharply different perspective that signified a new departure, see David Roediger, " 'Labor in White Skin': Race and Working-Class History," in *Reshaping the U.S. Left: Popular Struggles in the 1980s*, ed. Mike Davis and Michael Sprinkler (London: Verso, 1988), 287–308.

7. Michael Goldfield, "Race and the CIO: Reply to Critics," *International Labor and Working-Class History* 46 (fall 1994), quoted on 148.

8. Bruce Nelson, *Workers on the Waterfront: Seamen, Longshoremen, and Unionism in the 1930s* (Urbana: University of Illinois Press, 1988); E. P. Thompson, *The Making of the English Working Class* (New York: Pantheon, 1964), 10; William H. Sewell, Jr., "How Classes Are Made: Critical Reflections on E. P. Thompson's Theory of Working-Class Formation," in *E. P. Thompson: Critical Perspectives*, ed. Harvey J. Kaye and Keith McClelland (Philadelphia: Temple University Press, 1990), 51.

9. Nancy Quam-Wickham, "Who Controls the Hiring Hall? The Struggle for Job Control in the ILWU during World War II," in *The CIO's Left-Led Unions*, ed. Steve Rosswurm (New Brunswick, N.J.: Rutgers University Press, 1992), 67; Bruce Nelson, "Class, Race, and Democracy in the CIO: The 'New' Labor History Meets the 'Wages of Whiteness,' " *International Review of Social History* 41 (December 1996): 359.

10. Joe William Trotter, Jr., *Coal, Class, and Color: Blacks in Southern West Virginia, 1915–32* (Urbana: University of Illinois Press, 1990); Earl Lewis, *In Their Own Interests: Race, Class, and Power in Twentieth-Century Norfolk, Virginia* (Berkeley: University of California Press, 1991); Robin D. G. Kelley, *Hammer and Hoe: Alabama Communists during the Great Depression* (Chapel Hill: University of North Carolina Press, 1990); Robin D. G. Kelley, " 'We Are Not What We Seem': Rethinking Black Working-Class Opposition in the Jim Crow South," *Journal of American History* 80 (June 1993): 75–112, quoted on 100; Robin D. G. Kelley, *Race Rebels: Culture, Politics, and the Black Working Class* (New York: Free Press, 1994); Tera W. Hunter, *To 'Joy My Free-*

dom: Southern Black Women's Lives and Labors after the Civil War (Cambridge, Mass.: Harvard University Press, 1997).

11. David R. Roediger, *The Wages of Whiteness: Race and the Making of the American Working Class* (London: Verso, 1991). In highlighting the linkage between race and class, and the central importance of race in shaping the consciousness of American workers in the nineteenth century, Roediger had a distinguished predecessor in Alexander Saxton, author of *The Indispensable Enemy: Labor and the Anti-Chinese Movement in California* (Berkeley: University of California Press, 1971) and *The Rise and Fall of the White Republic: Class Politics and Mass Culture in Nineteenth-Century America* (London: Verso, 1990). Recently, historians of the American working class have finally begun to recognize *The Indispensable Enemy* as an early classic of the new labor history.

12. Roediger, *The Wages of Whiteness*, 9, 13, and passim; David R. Roediger, "Race and the Working-Class Past in the United States: Multiple Identities and the Future of Labor History," *International Review of Social History* 38 (December 1993), supplement 1, 127–43, quoted on 130–31; Bruce Nelson, "Ethnicity, Race, and the Logic of Solidarity: Dock Workers in International Perspective," in *Studies in the International History of Dock Labour, c. 1790s-1970s,* ed. Sam Davies et al. (Liverpool, Eng.: Ashgate, forthcoming); Kathleen Neils Conzen et al., "The Invention of Ethnicity: A Perspective from the U.S.A.," *Journal of American Ethnic History* 12 (fall 1992): 3–41; Howard Winant, "Racial Dualism at Century's End," in *The House That Race Built: Black Americans, U.S. Terrain,* ed. Wahneema Lubiano (New York: Pantheon, 1997), 87–115.

13. Roediger, "Race and the Working-Class Past," 135; Saxton, *The Indispensable Enemy,* 268–78; Saxton, *The Rise and Fall,* 313; Catherine Collomp, "Unions, Civics, and National Identity: Organized Labor's Reaction to Immigration, 1881–1897," *Labor History* 29 (fall 1988): 450–74; Matthew Frye Jacobson, *Whiteness of a Different Color: European Immigrants and the Alchemy of Race* (Cambridge, Mass.: Harvard University Press, 1998).

14. Rick Halpern, *Down on the Killing Floor: Black and White Workers in Chicago's Packinghouses, 1904–54* (Urbana: University of Illinois Press, 1997), 24, 39.

15. E. Franklin Frazier, "A Negro Industrial Group," *Howard Review* 1 (June 1924): 198; Ignatiev, *How the Irish Became White,* 92–121; Cheryl Harris, "Whiteness as Property," *Harvard Law Review* 106 (June 1993): 1709–91.

16. Robert Orsi, "The Religious Boundaries of an Inbetween People: Street *Feste* and the Problem of the Dark-Skinned Other in Italian Harlem, 1920–1990," *American Quarterly* 44 (September 1992): 313–47; James R. Barrett and David Roediger, "Inbetween Peoples: Race, Nationality, and the 'New Immigrant' Working Class," *Journal of American Ethnic History* 16 (spring 1997): 3–44; Roediger, *The Wages of Whiteness,* 115–27; Saxton, *The Rise and*

Fall, 165–81; Eric Lott, *Love and Theft: Blackface Minstrelsy and the American Working Class* (New York: Oxford University Press, 1995).

17. Roediger, *The Wages of Whiteness*, 72–76, 140–43, Douglas quoted on 142; Saxton, *The Rise and Fall*, 127–54, Whitman quoted on 154.

18. I am deeply indebted to Grace Elizabeth Hale, *Making Whiteness: The Culture of Segregation in the South, 1890–1940* (New York: Pantheon, 1998), especially 121–97.

19. Ira Berlin, *Many Thousands Gone: The First Two Centuries of Slavery in North America* (Cambridge, Mass.: Harvard University Press, 1998), 1; Hale, *Making Whiteness*, quoted on 195.

20. James R. Barrett, *Work and Community in the Jungle: Chicago's Packinghouse Workers, 1894–1922* (Urbana: University of Illinois Press, 1987), 188–231; James R. Grossman, *Land of Hope: Chicago, Black Southerners, and the Great Migration* (Chicago: University of Chicago Press, 1989), 208–45; Halpern, *Down on the Killing Floor*, 65–72. On the athletic clubs, which one contemporary observer characterized as "athletic only with their fists and brass knuckles and guns," see Chicago Commission on Race Relations, *The Negro in Chicago: A Study of Race Relations and a Race Riot* (Chicago: University of Chicago Press, 1922), 11–17.

21. James R. Barrett, "Americanization from the Bottom Up: Immigration and the Remaking of the Working Class in the United States, 1880–1930," *Journal of American History* 79 (December 1992): 1002.

22. David Doyle points out that although the Irish constituted only 7.5 percent of the American labor force in 1900, they accounted for one-sixth of the teamsters, metalworkers, and masons and nearly one-third of plumbers, steam fitters, and boilermakers. David Doyle, "The Irish and American Labour, 1880–1920," *Saothar* 1 (1975): 43.

23. Robert Anthony Orsi, *The Madonna of 115th Street: Faith and Community in Italian Harlem, 1880–1950* (New Haven, Conn.: Yale University Press, 1985), 199; Thomas Bell, *Out of This Furnace* (1941; reprint, Pittsburgh: University of Pittsburgh Press, 1976), 123, 160; James T. Farrell, *Studs Lonigan: A Trilogy Comprising Young Lonigan, the Young Manhood of Studs Lonigan, and Judgment Day* (1932, 1934, 1935; reprint, Urbana: University of Illinois Press, 1993), 79–80, 327, 402, 425–26.

24. Doyle, "The Irish and American Labour," 44; Barrett, *Work and Community*, 138–42, 227; Barrett and Roediger, "Inbetween Peoples," 21–26; Steven P. Erie, *Rainbow's End: Irish-Americans and the Dilemmas of Urban Machine Politics, 1840–1985* (Berkeley: University of California Press, 1988), 100–106.

25. Eric Foner, "Class, Ethnicity, and Radicalism in the Gilded Age: The Land League and Irish-America," *Marxist Perspectives* 1 (summer 1978): 6–55; David Brundage, " 'Green over Black' Revisited: Ireland and Irish-Americans in the New Histories of American Working-Class 'Whiteness' " (paper presented at "Racializing Class, Classifying Race: Labour and Difference in Af-

rica, USA and Britain," St. Antony's College, University of Oxford, July 11–13, 1997). With regard to issues of race and broad-gauged solidarity, Declan Kiberd argues that Irish nationalism vacillated between two poles—one embraced all anticolonial struggles and sought to make common cause with Indian nationalists, in particular, and the other was "a strain of white triumphalism, which ... would never countenance such a solidarity." Declan Kiberd, *Inventing Ireland: The Literature of the Modern Nation* (London: Jonathan Cape, 1995), 259.

26. Richard Oestreicher, "Terence V. Powderly, the Knights of Labor, and Artisanal Republicanism," in *Labor Leaders in America*, ed. Melvyn Dubofsky and Warren Van Tine (Urbana: University of Illinois Press, 1987), 31; Peter Rachleff, *Black Labor in Richmond, 1865–1890* (1984; reprint, Urbana: University of Illinois Press, 1989), 117–20, 169–76, quoted on 176; Edward P. Johanningsmeier, *Forging American Communism: The Life of William Z. Foster* (Princeton, N.J.: Princeton University Press, 1994), 10, 88–110; L. A. O'Donnell, "John Fitzpatrick, 1871–1946: American Labor Leader," *Eire-Ireland* 26 (summer 1991): 42–61; Elizabeth McKillen, "American Labor, the Irish Revolution, and the Campaign for a Boycott of British Goods, 1916–1924," *Radical History Review* 61 (winter 1995): 35–61.

27. Roediger, *The Wages of Whiteness*, 133–56; Betty Wood, *The Origins of American Slavery: Freedom and Bondage in the English Colonies* (New York: Hill and Wang, 1997), 21–22.

28. Halpern, *Down on the Killing Floor*, quoted on 51; Herbert G. Gutman, "The Negro and the United Mine Workers of America: The Career and Letters of Richard Davis and Something of Their Meaning, 1890–1900," in *Work Culture and Society in Industrializing America: Essays in American Working-Class and Social History* (New York: Alfred A. Knopf, 1976), 190–91; Saxton, *The Indispensable Enemy*, 272–73.

29. Bruce Nelson, "Organized Labor and the Struggle for Black Equality in Mobile during World War II," *Journal of American History* 80 (December 1993): 953; Harold Preece, "The South Stirs," *The Crisis* 48 (October 1941): 318; White quoted in *Cleveland Call and Post*, Feb. 27, 1943, A3; Robert H. Zieger, *The CIO, 1935–55* (Chapel Hill: University of North Carolina Press, 1995), 155; Lizabeth Cohen, *Making a New Deal: Industrial Workers in Chicago, 1919–1939* (New York: Cambridge University Press, 1991), 337; Nelson Lichtenstein, *The Most Dangerous Man in Detroit: Walter Reuther and the Fate of American Labor* (New York: Basic Books, 1995), 442.

30. Robert Korstad and Nelson Lichtenstein, "Opportunities Found and Lost: Labor, Radicals, and the Early Civil Rights Movement," *Journal of American History* 75 (December 1988): 787.

31. One of the major themes of Robert Zieger's history of the CIO is the gulf between the liberalism of its leadership and the more conservative stance of its rank-and-file membership. Although Zieger paints too monolithic a por-

trait of that rank and file, his extensive use of polling data, social surveys, and organizers' reports from the field adds considerable weight to his assertions. Zieger finds "little evidence that industrial workers had much stomach for the kinds of root-and-branch confrontation with the American state that a more radical program would have required." To those who lament the decline of militancy in the CIO after World War II, he responds that "it was precisely the CIO's reputation for strikes and confrontation that dissuaded potential members." Zieger, The CIO, 374, 345; Bruce Nelson, "Zieger's CIO: In Defense of Labor Liberalism," Labor History 37 (spring 1996): 157–62.

32. Nelson Lichtenstein, The Most Dangerous Man, 442; Bruce Nelson, "Autoworkers, Electoral Politics, and the Convergence of Class and Race: Detroit, 1937–1945," in Organized Labor and American Politics, 1894–1994: The Labor-Liberal Alliance, ed. Kevin Boyle (Albany: State University of New York Press, 1998), 121–47, especially 145–47; Arthur Kornhauser, Detroit as the People See It: A Survey of Attitudes in an Industrial City (Detroit: Wayne University Press, 1952), 82–105; Thomas J. Sugrue, "Crabgrass-Roots Politics: Race, Rights, and the Reaction against Liberalism in the Urban North, 1940–1964," Journal of American History 82 (September 1995), quoted on 556; Thomas J. Sugrue, The Origins of the Urban Crisis: Race and Inequality in Postwar Detroit (Princeton, N.J.: Princeton University Press, 1996); Kevin Boyle, "The Kiss: Racial and Gender Conflict in a 1950s Automobile Factory," Journal of American History 84 (September 1997): 496–523.

33. Michael Rogin, "Making America Home: Racial Masquerade and Ethnic Assimilation in the Transition to Talking Pictures," Journal of American History 79 (December 1992): 1050–77, especially 1054; James Trevathan, interview by author, Youngstown, Ohio, May 14, 1996; James C. Davis, interview by author, Girard, Ohio, Oct. 27, 1996; George Lipsitz, A Life in the Struggle: Ivory Perry and the Culture of Opposition (Philadelphia: Temple University Press, 1988), 38–63; Arnold R. Hirsch, Making the Second Ghetto: Race and Housing in Chicago, 1940–1960 (New York: Cambridge University Press, 1983), 186–211; David R. Roediger, "Whiteness and Ethnicity in the History of 'White Ethnics' in the United States," in Towards the Abolition of Whiteness: Essays on Race, Politics, and Working Class History (London: Verso, 1994), 181–98; Andrew Hurley, Environmental Inequalities: Class, Race, and Industrial Pollution in Gary, Indiana, 1945–1980 (Chapel Hill: University of North Carolina Press, 1995), 108–9.

34. See Nelson, "Class, Race, and Democracy"; Elizabeth Faue, " 'Anti-Heroes of the Working Class: A Response to Bruce Nelson," International Review of Social History 41 (December 1996): 375–88; Thomas J. Sugrue, "Segmented Work, Race-Conscious Workers: Structure, Agency, and Division in the CIO Era," ibid., 389–406; Bruce Nelson, "Working-Class Agency and Racial Inequality," ibid., 407–20; Michael Goldfield, The Color of Politics: Race and the Mainsprings of American Politics (New York: New Press, 1997), 240;

Staughton Lynd, "History, Race, and the Steel Industry," *Radical Historians' Newsletter* 76 (June 1977): 1, 13–16; Brundage, " 'Green over Black' Revisited"; Arnesen, "Up from Exclusion," 152–53.

35. David Roediger argues, however, that Irish loathing of black "savagery" was combined with an intense attraction to black people as living symbols of a half-imagined rural idyll that famine, emigration, and industrialization had destroyed. Following Frantz Fanon, Roediger identifies a persistent historical tendency to define blacks as "natural, erotic, sensual and animal," and he argues that as the Irish adjusted to the urban environment and industrial regime in the United States, they "shunt[ed] anxieties and desires regarding relationships to nature and to sexuality onto Blacks." Roediger, *The Wages of Whiteness*, 150–56, quoted on 155. Eric Lott extends this argument to the white working class as a whole in *Love and Theft*.

36. Gilbert Osofsky, "Abolitionists, Irish Immigrants, and the Dilemmas of Romantic Nationalism," *American Historical Review* 80 (October 1975): 905, 900; Peter Way, *Common Labour: Workers and the Digging of North American Canals, 1780–1860* (Cambridge, Eng.: Cambridge University Press, 1993), 93, 17; Roediger, *The Wages of Whiteness*, 144 (emphasis added); Brundage, " 'Green over Black' Revisited."

37. Kerby A. Miller, *Emigrants and Exiles: Ireland and the Irish Exodus to North America* (New York: Oxford University Press, 1985), 193; Albert J. von Frank, *The Trials of Anthony Burns: Freedom and Slavery in Emerson's Boston* (Cambridge, Mass.: Harvard University Press, 1998), 37–38; Ignatiev, *How the Irish Became White*, 97–98; Thomas Mooney, *Nine Years in America* (Dublin: James McGlashin, 1850), 84; David Noel Doyle, "The Remaking of Irish America, 1845–80," in *A New History of Ireland*, vol. 6, *Ireland under the Union, II, 1870–1921*, ed. W. E. Vaughan (Oxford: Clarendon Press, 1996), 753.

38. Theodore W. Allen, *The Invention of the White Race*, vol. 1, *Racial Oppression and Social Control* (London: Verso, 1994), 179–84, 186, 190–92, 198–99; Sean Wilentz, *Chants Democratic: New York City and the Rise of the American Working Class* (New York: Oxford University Press, 1984), 327–35, 356; S. J. Connolly, ed., *The Oxford Companion to Irish History* (New York: Oxford University Press, 1998), quoted on 537; Miller, *Emigrants and Exiles*, quoted on 241; Douglas C. Riach, "Daniel O'Connell and American Anti-Slavery," *Irish Historical Studies* 20 (March 1976): 3–25; Riach, "O'Connell and Slavery," in *The World of Daniel O'Connell*, ed. Donal McCartney (Dublin and Cork: Mercier Press, 1980), 175–85; William Lloyd Garrison to Theobald Mathew, July 26, 1849, in *The Letters of William Lloyd Garrison*, vol. 3, *No Union with Slaveholders, 1841–1849*, ed. Walter M. Merrill (Cambridge, Mass.: Belknap Press of Harvard University Press, 1973), 641.

39. Riach, "Daniel O'Connell and American Anti-Slavery"; Riach, "O'Connell and Slavery," 176; William S. McFeely, *Frederick Douglass* (New

York: W. W. Norton, 1990), 126. As early as 1824, English abolitionist James Cropper had witnessed the suffering of the Irish peasantry and concluded that with regard to food, clothing, and shelter, these "civil, kind-hearted, and generous-minded poor people . . . must be infinitely worse off than many of the slaves." David Brion Davis, *Slavery and Human Progress* (New York: Oxford University Press, 1984), 184.

40. Von Frank, *The Trials of Anthony Burns*, 240–44; Riach, "Daniel O'Connell and American Anti-Slavery," 10; Albon P. Man, Jr., "The Church and the New York City Draft Riots of 1863," *Records of the American Catholic Historical Society of Philadelphia* 62 (March 1951): 33–50; Charles R. Morris, *American Catholic: The Saints and Sinners Who Built America's Most Powerful Church* (New York: Times Books, 1997), 75–79, *Freeman's Journal* quoted on 78. Historian David Wilson has pointed out that many Irish Protestant immigrants embraced the white racial attitudes that would later evolve among Irish Catholic immigrants to the United States. This was true even of the republicans who came to America after the collapse of Ireland's 1798 Rebellion. Many of these exiles were deeply influenced by the egalitarianism of the American and French Revolutions. But "despite anti-slavery sentiment within Ireland," Wilson writes, "and despite early signs of solidarity between Irish radicals and African Americans, it proved increasingly difficult for immigrants who sought acceptance and respectability to identify with people whom white Americans regarded as an inferior race." For Protestants and Catholics alike, then, becoming white had far more to do with the "atmosphere" of America than with the cultural baggage they transported from Ireland. David A. Wilson, *United Irishmen, United States: Immigrant Radicals in the Early Republic* (Ithaca, N.Y.: Cornell University Press, 1998), 137.

41. Ignatiev, *How the Irish Became White*, 99; Roediger, *The Wages of Whiteness*, 13, 19–20, 35; Lott, *Love and Theft*, 122.

42. "The People v. George Angus," Apr. 10, 1818, District Attorney Indictment Papers, Municipal Archives of New York City (in author's possession, courtesy of Shane White); Roger Swift, "The Outcast Irish in the British Victorian City: Problems and Perspectives," *Irish Historical Studies* 25 (May 1987): 272; Dale T. Knobel, *Paddy and the Republic: Ethnicity and Nationality in Antebellum America* (Middletown, Conn.: Wesleyan University Press, 1986), 68–103, especially 100; Jacobson, *Whiteness of a Different Color*, 48; L. Perry Curtis, Jr., *Apes and Angels: The Irishman in Victorian Caricature*, rev. ed. (Washington, D.C.: Smithsonian Institution Press, 1997), 63, 100; Miller, *Emigrants and Exiles*, 107.

43. Allen, *The Invention of the White Race*, Hughes quoted on 181; Brundage, " 'Green over Black' Revisited." Alexander Saxton points out that disputes about race often "pitted white egalitarians (characterized by the hardest side of racism) against white elitists (necessarily characterized by a degree of racial tolerance) who sought to use non-white populations as bulwarks of class

NOTES TO CHAPTER ONE

privilege." Relative to employers, especially employers in labor-intensive industries, workers were much "more likely to speak for segregation, denial of training, [and] exclusion from labor markets." Saxton, *The Rise and Fall*, 148–49, 296–98.

44. Sugrue, "Segmented Work," 395; Laura Lee Downs, "Identities and Differences II," *Social History* 22 (May 1997): 204.

45. St. Clair Drake and Horace R. Cayton, *Black Metropolis: A Study of Negro Life in a Northern City* (New York: Harcourt, Brace, 1945), 325.

46. Roediger, *The Wages of Whiteness*, 12; Jonathan Schneer, "London's Docks in 1900: Nexus of Empire," *Labour History Review* 59 (winter 1994): 20–33; Nelson, "Ethnicity, Race."

47. Miller, *Emigrants and Exiles*, 280, 346.

48. Federal Writers' Project, *New York Panorama: A Companion to the WPA Guide to New York City* (1938; reprint, New York: Pantheon, 1984), 336; Edward E. Swanstrom, *The Waterfront Labor Problem: A Study in Decasualization and Unemployment Insurance* (New York: Fordham University Press, 1938), 8; David F. Selvin, *A Terrible Anger: The 1934 Waterfront and General Strikes in San Francisco* (Detroit: Wayne State University Press, 1996), 69.

49. *Louisiana Weekly*, Sept. 19, 1959, 1.

50. Allen, *The Invention of the White Race*, 170.

CHAPTER ONE
THE LOGIC AND LIMITS OF SOLIDARITY, 1850s–1920s

1. Ernest Poole, "The Ship Must Sail on Time," *Everybody's Magazine* 19 (August 1908): 176–86; "Longshore Labor Conditions in the United States," part 1, *Monthly Labor Review* 31 (October 1930): 812; Citizens Waterfront Committee, *The New York Waterfront: A Report to the Public of New York City by the Citizens Waterfront Committee Setting Forth Our Oldest and Most Urgent Civic Problem—the Condition of the Waterfront* (New York: Citizens Waterfront Committee, 1946), 18–24.

2. Federal Writers' Project, *New York Panorama*, 325–42; Swanstrom, *The Waterfront Labor Problem*, 7–9; U.S. Commission on Industrial Relations, *Final Report and Testimony Submitted to Congress by the Commission on Industrial Relations*, 11 vols., 64th Cong., 1st sess., S. Doc. 415, hereafter cited as U.S. CIR), 3:2061, 2068, 2091, 2109, 2128, 2134, 2158.

3. Eric Arnesen, *Waterfront Workers of New Orleans: Race, Class, and Politics, 1863–1923* (New York: Oxford University Press, 1991), 38; David Montgomery, *The Fall of the House of Labor: The Workplace, the State, and American Labor Activism, 1865–1925* (New York: Cambridge University Press, 1987), 96–109; Lester Rubin, with the assistance of William S. Swift, *The Negro in the Longshore Industry*, The Racial Policies of American Industry, Report No. 29 (Philadelphia: Industrial Research Unit, Wharton School, University of

Pennsylvania, 1974), 9–13; Charles B. Barnes, *The Longshoremen* (New York: Survey Associates, 1915), 28–54; Charles P. Larrowe, *Shape-up and Hiring Hall: A Comparison of Hiring Methods and Labor Relations on the New York and Seattle Waterfronts* (Berkeley: University of California Press, 1955), 52; Jeff Kisseloff, *You Must Remember This: An Oral History of Manhattan from the 1890s to World War II* (New York: Harcourt Brace Jovanovitch, 1989), 543.

4. Theodore Dreiser, "The Waterfront," in *The Color of a Great City* (New York: Boni and Liveright, 1923), 11; Poole, "The Ship Must Sail on Time," 176; Charles H. Farnham, "A Day on the Docks," *Scribner's Monthly* 18 (May 1879): 34; J. Anthony Lukas, *Common Ground: A Turbulent Decade in the Lives of Three American Families* (New York: Alfred A. Knopf, 1985), 148. See also David M. Katzman, "Black Longshoremen" (paper presented at the annual meeting of the Organization of American Historians, San Francisco, April 11, 1980).

5. E. L. Taplin, *Liverpool Dockers and Seamen* (Hull: University of Hull Publications, 1974), 9; U.S. CIR, 3:2056, 2126; Mayor's Committee on Unemployment, New York City, *Report on Dock Employment in New York City and Recommendations for Its Regularization* (New York: Mayor's Committee on Unemployment, 1916), 10; Barnes, *The Longshoremen*, 8–13; Frazier, "A Negro Industrial Group," 208.

6. Barnes, *The Longshoremen*, 51–54; James Sexton, the president of the National Union of Dock Labourers, quoted in P. J. Waller, *Democracy and Sectarianism: A Political and Social History of Liverpool, 1868–1939* (Liverpool: Liverpool University Press, 1981), 3; "Longshore Labor Conditions," part 1, 812. See also E. J. Hobsbawm, "National Unions on the Waterside," in *Labouring Men: Studies in the History of Labour* (London: Weidenfeld and Nicholson, 1964), 204–23, especially 207.

7. U.S. CIR, 3:2150; Ernest Poole, "The Men on the Docks," *Outlook*, May 25, 1907, 144; Kisseloff, *You Must Remember This*, 521.

8. Barnes, *The Longshoremen*, 98–99, 114–15, 126–27.

9. U.S. CIR, 3:2104, 2148, 2150; Gwendolyn Mink, *Old Labor and New Immigrants in American Political Development: Union, Party, and State, 1875–1920* (Ithaca, N.Y.: Cornell University Press, 1986), 96; Saxton, *The Indispensable Enemy*, 271–72. Both Mink and Saxton cite the American Federation of Labor pamphlet *Some Reasons for Chinese Exclusion. Meat vs. Rice. American Manhood Against Asiatic Coolieism. Which Shall Survive?* (Washington, D.C.: American Federation of Labor, 1901), which apparently was coauthored by AFL president Samuel Gompers.

10. Joshua B. Freeman, "Hardhats: Construction Workers, Manliness, and the 1970 Pro-War Demonstrations," *Journal of Social History* 26 (summer 1993): 725–44; U.S. CIR, 3:2147, 2153; Taplin, *Liverpool Dockers and Seamen*, 10; Eric Taplin, "The History of Dock Labour: Liverpool, circa 1850–1914," in *Port Reports Prepared for the Conference, Comparative International History of*

Dock Labour, c. 1790–1970 [hereafter, *Port Reports*] (Amsterdam: International Institute of Social History, 1997), 2:5. The experience of hard labor and "bull-driving" as a threat to manhood was clearly an international if not a universal phenomenon on the waterfronts of the world. Thus, in the South African river port of East London, Gary Minkley found dock laborers complaining that the work regime "sucked the blood of men," "emptied our insides until we were not men," and "stole our manliness." Gary Minkley, " 'Did Not Come to Work on Monday': Dock Workers, the River Port and the Tensions of Empire, the East London Waterfront in Comparative Perspective, c. 1930–63" (paper presented at "Racializing Class, Classifying Race—A Conference on Labour and Difference in Africa, USA, and Britain," St. Antony's College, University of Oxford, July 11–13, 1997).

11. William W. Pilcher, *The Portland Longshoremen: A Dispersed Urban Community* (New York: Holt, Rinehart, and Winston, 1972), 25–26; Robert Cherny, "San Francisco Longshoremen, 1890–1940," in *Port Reports*, 2:12; Kisseloff, *You Must Remember This*, 442, 478.

12. Elizabeth Ogg, *Longshoremen and Their Homes: The Story of a Housing "Case" Study Conducted under the Auspices of Greenwich House* (New York: Greenwich House, 1939), 52; Kisseloff, *You Must Remember This*, 522.

13. Gareth Stedman Jones, *Outcast London: A Study in the Relationship between Classes in Victorian Society* (1971; reprint, New York: Pantheon, 1984), 53; Malcolm Johnson, *Crime on the Labor Front* (New York: McGraw-Hill, 1950), 133–34. In 1914 International Longshoremen's Association official John Riley offered a brief description of the shape-up in the port of New York. "The men congregate in something of a horseshoe form," said Riley, "and the man known as the stevedore, he stands out in the doorway calling in different gangs. . . . [H]e calls out first No. 1 deck gang, then . . . No. 1 hold gang, and No. 1 dock gang, then right straight down the line until he has probably 15 or 16 gangs." Riley's description was far more prosaic than Mayhew's and Johnson's, but it remains important for its emphasis that, in the better organized parts of the port at least, the men were hired in gangs rather than as individuals. U.S. CIR, 3:2054.

14. Liverpool employers collaborated with the National Union of Dock Labourers to effect a major decasualization scheme in 1912, only to encounter sustained resistance from the union rank and file, at both ends of the employment spectrum. According to Liverpool historian P. J. Waller, "Aristocrats" resented the scheme because they "cherished their freedom of working long spells and relaxing," whereas "the under-employed feared displacement." Larrowe, *Shape-up and Hiring Hall*, 26, 54–68, 74–77; Montgomery, *The Fall of the House of Labor*, 104; Hobsbawm, "National Unions on the Waterside," 209; Waller, *Democracy and Sectarianism*, 253–54, 262–64. See also Jonathan Schneer, "The War, the State, and the Workplace: British Dockers during 1914–1918," in *Social Conflict and the Political Order in Modern Britain*, ed.

James E. Cronin and Jonathan Schneer (New Brunswick, N.J.: Rutgers University Press, 1982), 98, 105.

15. Vernon H. Jensen, *Hiring of Dock Workers and Employment Practices in the Ports of New York, Liverpool, London, Rotterdam, and Marseilles* (Cambridge, Mass.: Harvard University Press, 1964), 23–33; Ogg, *Longshoremen and Their Homes*, 18; Howard Kimeldorf, *Reds or Rackets? The Making of Radical and Conservative Unions on the Waterfront* (Berkeley: University of California Press, 1988), 151–52, 209; Daniel Bell, "The Racket-Ridden Longshoremen: The Web of Economics and Politics," in *The End of Ideology: On the Exhaustion of Political Ideas in the Fifties* (Glencoe, Ill.: Free Press, 1960), 163–64. Bell and Kimeldorf argue, erroneously, that regular gangs did not develop until World War II.

16. U.S. CIR, 3:2054; Ogg, *Longshoremen and Their Homes*, quoted on 34, 42–47, 50.

17. Katzman, "Black Longshoremen," 8–10; Antonio Salcido, interview by author (via telephone), Long Beach, Calif., June 2, 1994; David Montgomery, *The Fall of the House of Labor*, 98–100.

18. Albon P. Man, Jr., "Labor Competition and the New York Draft Riots of 1863," *Journal of Negro History* 36 (October 1951): 392; Barnes, *The Longshoremen*, 5. On the development of a labor market niche as a means to further the economic status and security of an ethnic group, see Suzanne Modell, "The Ethnic Niche and the Structure of Opportunity: Immigrants and Minorities in New York," in *The "Underclass" Debate: Views from History*, ed. Michael B. Katz (Princeton, N.J.: Princeton University Press 1993), 161–93.

19. Ira Berlin, "Time, Space, and the Evolution of Afro-American Society on British Mainland North America," *American Historical Review* 85 (February 1980): 48–49; Gary B. Nash, "Forging Freedom: The Emancipation Experience in the Northern Seaport Cities, 1775–1820," in *Slavery and Freedom in the Age of the American Revolution*, ed. Ira Berlin and Ronald Hoffman (Urbana: University of Illinois Press, 1986), 6, 8–10; W. Jeffrey Bolster, *Black Jacks: African American Seamen in the Age of Sail* (Cambridge, Mass.: Harvard University Press, 1997).

20. Shane White, " 'We Dwell in Safety and Pursue Our Honest Callings': Free Blacks in New York City, 1783–1810," *Journal of American History* 75 (September 1988): 445–70, especially 453–54; White, *Somewhat More Independent: The End of Slavery in New York City, 1770–1810* (Athens: University of Georgia Press, 1991), 159; Bolster, *Black Jacks*, 235; James Weldon Johnson, *Black Manhattan* (1930; reprint, New York: Da Capo Press, 1991), 45–46; Paul A. Gilje, *The Road to Mobocracy: Popular Disorder in New York City, 1763–1834* (Chapel Hill: University of North Carolina Press, 1987), 160–70; Ignatiev, *How the Irish Became White*, quoted on 97–98; Nash, "Forging Freedom," 47; Linda K. Kerber, "Abolitionists and Amalgamators: The New York City

Race Riots of 1834," *New York History* 48 (January 1967), 28–39; Wilentz, *Chants Democratic*, 264–66.

21. Amy Bridges, *A City in the Republic: Antebellum New York and the Origins of Machine Politics* (1984; reprint, Ithaca, N.Y.: Cornell University Press, 1987), 39–40; Richard B. Stott, *Workers in the Metropolis: Class, Ethnicity, and Youth in Antebellum New York City* (Ithaca, N.Y.: Cornell University Press, 1990), 71–72; Graham Hodges, " 'Desirable Companions and Lovers': Irish and African Americans in the Sixth Ward, 1830–1870," in *The New York Irish*, ed. Ronald H. Bayor and Timothy J. Meagher (Baltimore: Johns Hopkins University Press, 1996), 110; Douglass quoted in Man, "Labor Competition," 377.

22. Miller, *Emigrants and Exiles*, 193, 198; Edward O'Donnell, " 'The Scattered Debris of the Irish Nation': The Famine Irish and New York City, 1845–55," in *The Hungry Stream: Essays on Emigration and Famine*, ed. E. Margaret Crawford (Belfast: Centre for Irish Studies, Ulster-American Folk Park, and Institute of Irish Studies, Queen's University of Belfast, 1997), 49–60.

23. Way, *Common Labour*, 90–99; Knobel, *Paddy and the Republic*, 76–79; Robert James Scally, *The End of Hidden Ireland: Rebellion, Famine, and Emigration* (New York: Oxford University Press, 1995), 160; John Belchem, "Introduction: The Peculiarities of Liverpool," in *Popular Politics, Riot, and Labour: Essays in Liverpool History, 1790–1940*, ed. John Belchem (Liverpool: Liverpool University Press, 1992), 10; Waller, *Democracy and Sectarianism*, 8; Peter Way, "Evil Humors and Ardent Spirits: The Rough Culture of Canal Construction Laborers," *Journal of American History* 79 (March 1993): 1420; Miller, *Emigrants and Exiles*, 328; William H. A. Williams, *'Twas Only an Irishman's Dream: The Image of Ireland and the Irish in American Popular Song Lyrics, 1800–1920* (Urbana: University of Illinois Press, 1996).

24. Robert Ernst, *Immigrant Life in New York City, 1825–1863* (1949; reprint, Syracuse, N.Y.: Syracuse University Press, 1994), 66–69, 216; Mooney, *Nine Years in America*, 84–86; Taplin, "The History of Dock Labour," 13–14; John Belchem, "Liverpool in the Year of Revolution: The Political and Associational Culture of the Irish Immigrant Community in 1848," in *Popular Politics*, 70; William Kenefick, "Irish Dockers and Trade Unionism on Clydeside," *Irish Studies Review* 19 (summer 1997): 22–29; John Lovell, *Stevedores and Dockers: A Study of Trade Unionism in the Port of London, 1870–1914* (London: Macmillan, 1969), 57; Lovell, "The Irish and the London Dockers," *Bulletin of the Society for the Study of Labour History* 35 (autumn 1977): 16–17; Lynn Hollen Lees, *Exiles of Erin: Irish Migrants in Victorian London* (Ithaca, N.Y.: Cornell University Press, 1979), 241.

25. Stott, *Workers in the Metropolis*, 59; Iver Bernstein, *The New York City Draft Riots: Their Significance for American Politics and Society in the Age of the Civil War* (New York: Oxford University Press, 1990), 114–22; Kisseloff, *You Must Remember This*, 477–88, 516–18. It is important to emphasize that a

block, or an entire neighborhood, was often identified as Irish or German or Italian, even when the predominant ethnic group constituted a minority of the area's residents. Predominance came through control of local institutions such as churches, Tammany Hall clubs, trade unions, and youth gangs, rather than through majority status. See Bruce Nelson, "Longshoremen in the Port of New York, 1850–1940," in *Studies in the International History of Dock Labour*, ed. Davies et al.; Orsi, *The Madonna of 115th Street*, 15–17, 28–42.

26. David Montgomery, "The Irish and the American Labor Movement," in *America and Ireland, 1776–1976: The American Identity and the Irish Connection*, ed. David Noel Doyle and Owen Dudley Edwards (Westport, Conn.: Greenwood Press, 1980), 213; *New York Tribune*, Oct. 16, 1852, 4, 7; Edwin G. Burrows and Mike Wallace, *Gotham: A History of New York City to 1898* (New York: Oxford University Press, 1999), 772.

27. *New York Times*, July 1, 1854, 3; *New York Tribune*, Jan. 18, 1855, 5, Jan. 19, 1863, 7.

28. Gilje, *The Road to Mobocracy*, 178–87; Paul A. Gilje and Howard B. Rock, eds., *Keepers of the Revolution: New Yorkers at Work in the Early Republic* (Ithaca, N.Y.: Cornell University Press, 1992), 204–7; Robert G. Albion, *The Rise of New York Port, 1815–1860* (1939; reprint, Newton Abbott, Eng.: David & Charles, 1970), 223–24; Barnes, *The Longshoremen*, 93; Man, "Labor Competition," 393; Wilentz, *Chants Democratic*, 250–51, 288; Ernst, *Immigrant Life in New York City*, 107.

29. Risa L. Faussette, " 'We Know No Distinction but That of Merit': New York City's Longshoremen and the Construction of Racial Identity, 1825–1863" (graduate seminar paper, SUNY, Binghamton, 1993), 4–9; Gilje and Rock, *Keepers of the Revolution*, 204, 207; Wilentz, *Chants Democratic*, 109–10.

30. *New York Times*, July 1, 1854, 3; *New York Tribune*, Oct. 16, 1852, 4; Man, "Labor Competition," 393, 394; Williams, *'Twas Only an Irishman's Dream*, 111.

31. Ignatiev, *How the Irish Became White*, 120–21.

32. Robert Ernst, "The Economic Status of New York City Negroes, 1850–1863," in *The Making of Black America*, vol. 1, *The Origins of Black Americans*, ed. August Meier and Elliott Rudwick (New York: Atheneum, 1969), 250–61, especially "Special Statistical Note," 261; Man, "Labor Competition," 380–81, 395–400; Charles Lionel Franklin, *The Negro Labor Unionist of New York* (1936; reprint, New York: AMS Press, 1968), 25; Warren C. Whatley, "African-American Strikebreaking from the Civil War to the New Deal," *Social Science History* 17 (winter 1993): 530; Sterling D. Spero and Abram L. Harris, *The Black Worker: The Negro and the Labor Movement* (1931; reprint, New York: Atheneum, 1968), 197; *Fincher's Trades Review*, July 11, 1863, 2. See also Emerson David Fite, *Social and Industrial Conditions in the North during the Civil War* (New York: Macmillan, 1910), 189–90.

33. Bernstein, *The New York City Draft Riots*, 7–8, 17–42, 118–20; Man, "The Church and the New York Draft Riots," 43, 45; Man, "Labor Competition," 392–402.

34. Roediger, *The Wages of Whiteness*, 10–13, 149–50; Knobel, *Paddy and the Republic*, 68–103; Ignatiev, *How the Irish Became White*, 111–12.

35. Man, "Labor Competition," 402; Farnham, "A Day on the Docks," 32, 41.

36. Barnes, *The Longshoremen*, 5, 102–9; U.S. CIR, 3:2061–62.

37. Williams, *'Twas Only an Irishman's Dream*, 118–204, especially 175; Roger Daniels, *Not Like Us: Immigrants and Minorities in America, 1890–1924* (Chicago: Ivan Dee, 1997), 19; Miller, *Emigrants and Exiles*, 492–533.

38. Barnes, *The Longshoremen*, 8; U.S. CIR, 3:2196.

39. U.S. CIR, 3:2125, 2054, 2196; Barnes, *The Longshoremen*, 11.

40. *New York Times*, June 15, 1907, 3.

41. Poole, "The Men on the Docks," 142–43; U.S. CIR, 3:2159; Caroline F. Ware, *Greenwich Village, 1920–1930: A Comment on American Civilization in the Post-War Years* (Boston: Houghton Mifflin, 1935), 52; Ogg, *Longshoremen and Their Homes*, 28–29.

42. Barnes, *The Longshoremen*, 7–9, 83, 90; U.S. CIR, 3:2069, 2171; John Higham, *Strangers in the Land: Patterns of American Nativism, 1860–1925* (New Brunswick, N.J.: Rutgers University Press, 1955), 173.

43. Frazier, "A Negro Industrial Group," 220. See Barrett, "Americanization from the Bottom Up," 1002; Roediger, *Towards the Abolition of Whiteness*, 181–94.

44. Barnes, *The Longshoremen*, 9; Frazier, "A Negro Industrial Group," 198. On at least one occasion between 1887 and 1895, blacks regained access to waterfront employment in the port on New York by serving as strikebreakers. According to New York State's Board of Mediation and Arbitration, in December 1889 "about 200 longshoremen, who were employed by a foreign steamship company, went on strike because they were required to work with colored men. These colored men were employed in June, 1889, to take the places of longshoremen who were then on strike, and from time to time thereafter the white men complained of being compelled to work with them. The company refused to discharge their colored employes, and engaged other men to take the places of those who had gone on strike." *Fourth Annual Report of the Board of Mediation and Arbitration of the State of New York* (Albany, N.Y.: James B. Lyon, 1891), 275.

45. Frazier, "A Negro Industrial Group," 198; Rubin, *The Negro in the Longshore Industry*, 58; Mary White Ovington, *Half a Man: The Status of the Negro in New York* (New York: Longman's, Green, 1911), 85; Claude McKay, *Home to Harlem* (1928; reprint, Boston: Northeastern University Press, 1987), 48.

46. *Brooklyn Daily Eagle*, May 2, 1907, 1, May 4, 1907, 5; Calvin Winslow, " 'Men of the Lumber Camps Come to Town': New York Longshoremen in

the Strike of 1907," in *Waterfront Workers: New Perspectives on Race and Class*, ed. Calvin Winslow (Urbana: University of Illinois Press, 1998), 62–96; Winslow, "On the Waterfront: Black, Italian, and Irish Longshoremen in the New York Harbour Strike of 1919," in *Protest and Survival: Essays for E. P. Thompson*, ed. John Rule and Robert Malcolmson (London: Merlin Press, 1993), 355–93; *New York Times*, May 29, 1907, 2, June 15, 1907, 3.

47. *Brooklyn Daily Eagle*, Oct. 14, 1919, 1, 2, Oct. 20, 1919, 1; *New York Times*, Oct. 12, 1919, 1, 2; Winslow, "On the Waterfront," 373, 382; Franklin, *The Negro Labor Unionist*, 189–90; Kimeldorf, *Reds or Rackets?* 46–49.

48. "Decision of the Colored Longshoremen Engaged in the Breaking of the Irish Patriotic Strike," Sept. 13, 1920, folder 6, Peter Golden Papers, National Library of Ireland, Dublin; David Brundage, "The 1920 New York Dockers' Boycott: Class, Gender, Race, and Irish-American Nationalism" (paper presented at the annual meeting of the Organization of American Historians, Chicago, April 1992). There was strong support for the Irish independence struggle in some sectors of the trade union movement, notably in municipal labor councils. The preeminent example was the Chicago Federation of Labor, under the leadership of Irish-born John Fitzpatrick. In close conjunction with Irish nationalist organizations in the United States, there was also a trade union boycott of British goods in 1920. However, the strike on the New York waterfront appears to have had no connection with the boycott activity sanctioned by organized labor. See McKillen, "American Labor."

49. Joe Doyle, "Striking for Ireland on the New York Docks," in *The New York Irish*, ed. Bayor and Meagher, 357, 360, 365, 372; Michael Kenny, *The Road to Freedom: Photographs and Memorabilia from the 1916 Rising and Afterwards* (Dublin: Country House, 1993), 41, 44.

50. Dermot Keogh, "Mannix, de Valera, and Irish Nationalism," in *The Irish Emigrant Experience in Australia*, ed. John O'Brien and Pauric Travers (Dublin: Poolbeg, 1991), 196–201; Doyle, "Striking for Ireland," 363–64; John Belchem, "Ethnicity, Labour History, and Irish Migration" (paper presented at "Racializing Class, Classifying Race—A Conference on Labour and Difference in Africa, the USA, and Britain," St. Antony's College, University of Oxford, July 11–13, 1997); *New York Evening Sun*, July 31, 1920, 1; *New York Times*, July 21, 1920, 17, July 31, 1920, 1, Aug. 1, 1920, 1, 4, Aug. 9, 1920, 1.

51. *New York Times*, Aug. 6, 1920, 9, Aug. 7, 1920, 1, Aug. 8, 1920, 5, Aug. 9, 1920, 1, Aug. 10, 1920, 1, Aug. 16, 1920, 3, Aug. 23, 1920, 4; Doyle, "Striking for Ireland," 365.

52. Brundage, "The 1920 New York Dockers' Boycott," 1, 9–10; Doyle, "Striking for Ireland," 357–73, 664 n. 50; *New York Times*, Aug. 28, 1920, 1, 3; *New York World*, Aug. 29, 1920, sec. 2, 1; *New York Tribune*, Aug. 28, 1920, 1; Miller, *Emigrants and Exiles*, 548–51.

53. Doyle, "Striking for Ireland," 368–69; *The Sun and New York Herald*, Aug. 28, 1920, 1.

54. "Longshoremen! Stokers! Oilers! Seamen! Trimmers! Every Red-Blooded Workingman . . . Mass Meeting," n.d., folder 6, Peter Golden Papers; Helen Golden to "Dear Friend," Sept. 16, 1920, ibid.

55. Ovington, *Half a Man*, 44; P. O. Huaithne, "The Irish and the Negro," *The Messenger* 1 (October 1919): 32; Frazier, "A Negro Industrial Group," 198; "Decision of the Colored Longshoremen"; Brundage, "The 1920 New York Dockers' Boycott," 10–11; Doyle, "Striking for Ireland," 366–67, 370; *New York World*, Aug. 29, 1920, sec. 2, 2, sec. 1, 4; *New York Times*, Aug. 28, 1920, 3. Apparently, participation in the boycott was uneven in the first several days, with some longshoremen joining it, then returning to work, then joining up with the boycotters again. Thus, at first, most New York newspapers characterized the boycott as a failure and made light of the dockworkers' participation. But on August 31 the *Journal of Commerce* acknowledged that according to officials of the shipping companies, the loading and unloading of vessels was "going on very slowly. A few small forces were at work, but they were Italians and Americans, and it was said not a single man of Irish blood could be found among them." Moreover, according to the *Journal*, all of the streets along the Chelsea waterfront "were noticeably abandoned by the crowds of negroes who usually serve as stevedores and longshoremen's helpers." *Journal of Commerce*, Aug. 31, 1920, 5.

56. *New York Tribune*, Aug. 28, 1920, 1; *New York World*, Aug. 29, 1920, sec. 1, 4, sec. 2, 2; *New York Times*, Sept. 3, 1920, 1; Doyle, "Striking for Ireland," 371.

57. Brundage, "The 1920 New York Dockers' Boycott," 11–12; Robert A. Hill, "General Introduction," in *The Marcus Garvey and Universal Negro Improvement Association Papers*, ed. Robert A. Hill (Berkeley: University of California Press, 1983), 1:lxx–lxxviii; "Report by Special Agent P-138," Sept. 20, 1920, ibid., 3:12–13.

58. Ronald Schaffer, *America in the Great War: The Rise of the War Welfare State* (New York: Oxford University Press, 1991), 75–90; David M. Kennedy, *Over Here: The First World War and American Society* (New York: Oxford University Press, 1980), 158–63, 199–200, 279–84; Grossman, *Land of Hope*; Ira De A. Reid, *The Negro Immigrant: His Background, Characteristics, and Social Adjustment, 1899–1937* (New York: Columbia University Press, 1939), 153; Paul Gilroy, *The Black Atlantic: Modernity and Double Consciousness* (Cambridge, Mass.: Harvard University Press, 1993); Wayne F. Cooper, *Claude McKay: Rebel Sojourner in the Harlem Renaissance: A Biography* (Baton Rouge: Louisiana State University Press, 1987), 109, 256. McKay re-created the world of black emigrants in Marseilles in his novel *Banjo: A Story without a Plot* (New York: Harper and Brothers, 1929).

59. On the experience of African Americans in the armed forces of the United States during World War I, see Arthur E. Barbeau and Florette Henri, *The Unknown Soldier: Black American Troops in World War I* (Philadelphia:

Temple University Press, 1974), and Tyler Stovall, *Paris Noir: African Americans in the City of Light* (Boston: Houghton Mifflin, 1996), 5–24. Most black American troops became "laborers in uniform." Many of these laborers worked as "stevedores," or longshoremen, unloading military cargo. One especially—and grotesquely—evocative portrayal of these laborers in uniform is the "Reminiscences of Edwin P. Arpin, Jr." Arpin, an army officer from Wisconsin, observed the working lives and leisure activities of African American longshoremen in Bordeaux through the lenses of a reflexively white-supremacist worldview. According to Arpin, "[T]hese men were recruited from the waterfronts of New Orleans, Galveston, and other Southern Gulf ports, and needless to say, among them were a large number of probably the toughest niggers in the U.S." See Ira Berlin, ed., "A Wisconsinite in World War I: Reminiscences of Edward P. Arpin, Jr.," part 1, *Wisconsin Magazine of History* 51 (autumn 1967): 18.

60. Winston James's *Holding Aloft the Banner of Ethiopia: Caribbean Radicalism in Early Twentieth-Century America* (London: Verso, 1998), 50–69, provides an excellent overview of the travail of the British West Indies Regiment and of the repercussions of that experience not only in the Anglophone Caribbean but in New York, where a number of BWIR veterans settled in the 1920s. James points out that whereas 1,071 men of the British West Indies Regiment died of sickness, mainly pneumonia, only 185 were killed in combat or died of combat-related wounds.

61. Peter Fryer, *Staying Power: The History of Black People in Britain* (London: Pluto Press, 1984), 298–316; W. F. Elkins, "Black Power in the British West Indies: The Trinidad Longshoremen's Strike of 1919," *Science and Society* 33 (winter 1969): 71–75; Tony Martin, "Revolutionary Upheaval in Trinidad, 1919: Views from British and American Sources," *Journal of Negro History* 58 (July 1973): 313–26; Bridget Brereton, *A History of Modern Trinidad, 1783–1962* (Kingston, Jamaica: Heinemann, 1981), 157–64; Irma Watkins-Owens, *Blood Relations: Caribbean Immigrants and the Harlem Community, 1900–1930* (Bloomington: University of Indiana Press, 1996), 1–4; Philip Kasinitz, *Caribbean New York: Black Immigrants and the Politics of Race* (Ithaca, N.Y.: Cornell University Press, 1992), 23–25; James, *Holding Aloft the Banner*, 63–66, 69.

62. Huaithne, "The Irish and the Negro"; Claude McKay, "How Black Sees Red and Green," *Liberator* 4 (June 1921), reprinted in *The Passion of Claude McKay: Selected Poetry and Prose, 1912–1948*, ed. Wayne F. Cooper (New York: Shocken Books, 1973), 58–62.

63. James, *Holding Aloft the Banner*, 155–84; Robert Hill, "General Introduction," lxx–lxxi; "Approaching Irish Success," *The Crusader* 1 (August 1919): 8; Cyril V. Briggs, "Heroic Ireland," ibid. 3 (February 1921): 5. See also "The Irish Fight for Liberty," ibid. 2 (July 1920): 16, and "British Rule in Ireland," ibid. 3 (December 1920): 10. Although most of Briggs's statements on Ireland in *The Crusader* appeared after the Irish Patriotic Strike, his and

other black political activists' interest in the Irish independence struggle clearly predated the longshoremen's boycott of British shipping. As early as August 1919 the Military Intelligence Division of the Justice Department reported that "all the Colored speakers in Harlem [were] using the Irish question in their discussions." Judith Stein, *The World of Marcus Garvey: Race and Class in Modern Society* (Baton Rouge: Louisiana State University Press, 1986), 53.

64. "The Irish Boycott on British Goods," *The Crusader* 4 (March 1921): 9–10; *New York Times*, Mar. 13, 1920, 7, Mar. 18, 1920, 19, Aug. 17, 1920, 6, Sept. 3, 1920, 2; Ware, *Greenwich Village*, 51.

65. *New York Times*, Sept. 11, 1920, 7; "Report by Special Agent P-138;" "Decision of Colored Longshoremen."

66. "Report by Special Agent P-138"; "Decision of Colored Longshoremen"; Helen Golden to Mr. Welch, Sept. 19, 1920, folder 6, Peter Golden Papers; Helen Golden to Miss Cleary, Sept. 21, 1920, ibid.

67. Doyle, "Striking for Ireland," 372; Keogh, "Mannix, de Valera," 219–20; Frazier, "A Negro Industrial Group," 220.

68. Frazier, "A Negro Industrial Group," 198; Brundage, "The 1920 New York Dockers' Boycott," 14.

69. Charles S. Johnson, "The New Frontage on American Life," in *The New Negro: Voices of the Harlem Renaissance*, ed. Alain Locke (1925; reprint, New York: Atheneum, 1992), 292; Ware, *Greenwich Village*, 51; Gilbert Osofsky, *Harlem: The Making of a Ghetto: Negro New York, 1890–1930*, 2d ed. (New York: Harper and Row, 1971), 127–31; Sherrill Wilson and Larry A. Greene, "Blacks," in *The Encyclopedia of New York City*, ed. Kenneth T. Jackson (New Haven, Conn.: Yale University Press, 1995), 113; Frazier, "A Negro Industrial Group," 196–97, 206–11, 214–15.

70. Frazier, "A Negro Industrial Group," 202–3, 212–14, 221–22.

71. Ibid., 224.

72. Ibid., 225.

73. Ibid., 226–27 (emphasis added).

74. Barnes, *The Longshoremen*, 9–12; Rubin, *The Negro in the Longshore Industry*, 55–56; Frazier, "A Negro Industrial Group," 198–99, 224–27; Kisseloff, *You Must Remember This*, 520–22, 543; Kimeldorf, *Reds or Rackets?* 45–46; Larrowe, *Shape-up and Hiring Hall*, 58.

75. Maud Russell, *Men Along the Shore* (New York: Brussel and Brussel, 1966), 244; "Longshore Labor Conditions," part 1, 825; U.S. Department of Commerce, Bureau of the Census, *Fifteenth Census of the United States: 1930*, vol. 4, *Occupations, by States* (Washington, D.C.: U.S. Government Printing Office, 1933), 729; Bureau of the Census, *Census of Population: 1950*, vol. 2, *Characteristics of the Population*, part 21, *Massachusetts* (Washington, D.C.: U.S. Government Printing Office, 1952), 224; Bureau of the Census, *Census of*

Population: 1960, vol. 1, *Characteristics of the Population*, part 23, *Massachusetts* (Washington, D.C.: U.S. Government Printing Office, 1961), 274, 389; Rubin, *The Negro in the Longshore Industry*, 43–50. In March 1989 I had the opportunity to tour Boston's Moran Terminal with a group of Irish American dockworkers, who quite unashamedly bragged about the exclusion of African Americans from what remained of the city's working waterfront.

76. "Longshore Labor Conditions," part 1, 826–29; Spero and Harris, *The Black Worker*, 182–84, 192–97; William C. Hine, "Black Organized Labor in Reconstruction Charleston," *Labor History* 25 (fall 1984): 504–17; Eric Arnesen, "Biracial Waterfront Unionism in the Age of Segregation," in *Waterfront Workers*, ed. Winslow, 19–61; Bruce Nelson, "Class and Race in the Crescent City: The ILWU, from San Francisco to New Orleans," in *The CIO's Left-Led Unions*, ed. Rosswurm, 39; George B. Tindall, *The Emergence of the New South, 1913–1945* (Baton Rouge: Louisiana State University Press, 1967), 162–64; William Regensburger, "The Emergence of Industrial Unionism in the South, 1930–1945: The Case of Coal and Metal Miners," in *How Mighty a Force? Studies of Workers' Consciousness and Organization in the United States*, ed. Maurice Zeitlin (Los Angeles: Institute of Industrial Relations, University of California, 1983), 95–96; "Longshore Labor Conditions in the United States," part 2, *Monthly Labor Review* 31 (November 1930): 1058.

77. Howard Kimeldorf and Robert Penney, " 'Excluded' by Choice: Dynamics of Interracial Unionism on the Philadelphia Waterfront," *International Labor and Working-Class History* 51 (spring 1997): 50–71, especially 50–55. See also Lisa McGirr, "Black and White Longshoremen in the IWW: A History of the Philadelphia Marine Transport Workers Industrial Union Local 8," *Labor History* 37 (summer 1995): 377–402.

78. Kimeldorf and Penney, " 'Excluded' by Choice," 55–67; "Longshore Labor Conditions," part 1, 826.

79. Eric Arnesen, "Waterfront Unions and Race in the American South, 1880–1920: The Case of New Orleans, Galveston, Mobile, Savannah, and Baltimore," in *Port Reports*, 1:1–5; Arnesen, *Waterfront Workers of New Orleans*, 3–145.

80. Bruce Nelson, "Class and Race in the Crescent City," 24–25; Bruce Nelson, "Race and Democracy," part 1, *The Nation* 252 (June 17, 1991): 821; Arnesen, *Waterfront Workers of New Orleans*, 156–203. See also Daniel Rosenberg, *New Orleans Dockworkers: Race, Labor, and Unionism, 1892–1923* (Albany: State University of New York Press, 1988), especially 69–92.

81. Arnesen, *Waterfront Workers of New Orleans*, 176–210, 244–52; Bruce Nelson, "Class and Race in the Crescent City," 25.

82. Bruce Nelson, "Class and Race in the Crescent City," 25–45.

83. "Longshore Labor Conditions," part 1, 822.

84. Budd Schulberg, "Joe Docks: Forgotten Man of the Waterfront," *New York Times Magazine*, Dec. 28, 1952, reprinted in *American Labor Since the*

New Deal, ed. Melvyn Dubofsky (Chicago: Quadrangle Books, 1971), 210–11; Roediger, *The Wages of Whiteness*, 12. Nicholas Lemann offers a vivid evocation of white ethnic privilege and black disadvantage in *The Promised Land: The Great Black Migration and How It Changed America* (New York: Alfred A. Knopf, 1991), 93–94.

85. Ann Douglas, *A Terrible Honesty: Mongrel Manhattan in the 1920s* (New York: Farrar, Strauss and Giroux, 1995), 73.

86. Arnesen, "Waterfront Unions," 7–10; Arnesen, "Biracial Waterfront Unionism"; Nelson, "Class and Race in the Crescent City," 41–42.

87. Barrett and Roediger, "Inbetween Peoples"; Thompson, *The Making of The English Working Class*, 9–11; Brundage, " 'Green over Black' Revisited"; Nelson, "Working-Class Agency and Racial Inequality."

Chapter Two
New York: "They . . . Helped to Create Themselves Out of What They Found Around Them"

The quotation in the chapter title is from Ralph Ellison, "An American Dilemma: A Review," in *Shadow and Act* (New York: Random House, 1964), 315.

1. Daniel Bell, "Last of the Business Rackets," *Fortune* 43 (June 1951): 89.

2. Ellison, "An American Dilemma," 315.

3. Ibid.

4. "Longshoremen's Association; International (ILA)," in *Labor Unions*, ed. Gary M. Fink (Westport, Conn.: Greenwood Press, 1977), 192–94; Charles P. Larrowe, *Maritime Labor Relations on the Great Lakes* (East Lansing: Labor and Industrial Relations Center, Michigan State University, 1959), 15–20; Russell, *Men Along the Shore*, 61–74. See also Brenda K. Shelton, "The Buffalo Grain Shovellers' Strike of 1899," *Labor History* 9 (spring 1968): 210–38.

5. Allen Raymond, *Waterfront Priest* (New York: Henry Holt, 1955), 69. "Under the Communists' strategy," said AFL official George Meany, "if they can control the means of communication and the means of transportation, . . . then they don't worry much about parliaments or congresses or politicians." In 1952, during the height of the cold war, a journalist chimed in with the observation that the port of New York offered hundreds of opportunities for sabotage. "Atomic bombs planted at strategic places could disrupt the port for months." International Longshoremen's Association, *Proceedings of the Thirty-fifth Quadrennial Convention* (New York, July 27–31, 1951), 18; Larry Hennessy, "I Faced Death on the Waterfront," *Bluebook* 95 (October 1952): 55. See also Nelson, *Workers on the Waterfront*, 91–93, 292–93.

6. International Longshoremen's Association, *Proceedings of the Thirty-second Convention* (New York, July 10–14, 1939), 28.

7. International Longshoremen's Association, AFL-CIO, *Proceedings of Fortieth Convention* (Miami Beach, Fla., July 15–18, 1963), 41–42.

8. Barnes, *The Longshoremen*, 181–87.

9. John Dwyer, interview by Bruce Nelson and Debra Bernhardt, New York City, May 22, 1997.

10. Robert P. Bass [and Horace B. Drury], *Marine and Dock Labor: Work, Wages, and Industrial Relations during the Period of the War*, Report of the Director of the Marine and Dock Industrial Relations Division, United States Shipping Board (Washington, D.C.: Government Printing Office, 1919), 29–30; Bell, "The Racket-Ridden Longshoremen," 163, 175; Alfred D. Chandler, Jr., *The Visible Hand: The Managerial Revolution in American Business* (Cambridge, Mass.: Harvard University Press, 1977), 189–92; Montgomery, *The Fall of the House of Labor*, 97–104; Kimeldorf, *Reds or Rackets?* 57–60.

11. U.S. CIR, 3:2053–67.

12. Ibid., 2115–24, 2195–96.

13. Mayor's Committee on Unemployment, "Agreement of International Longshoremen's Association with Certain New York Employers," [Sept.? 1916], in *Report on Dock Employment*, 73.

14. Bass, *Marine and Dock Labor*, 136; Citizens Waterfront Committee, *The New York Waterfront*, 26–27; Johnson, *Crime on the Labor Front*, 145, 231.

15. In 1864 the New York State legislature chartered the Longshoremen's Union Protective Association (LUPA). It was, no doubt, the successor of the Longshoremen's United Benevolent Society, but why the one organization declined and the other emerged in its place is not clear. Between 1864 and 1914, the year the second Longshoremen's Union Protective Association of Greater New York merged with the ILA, at least ten other organizations of dockworkers, many of them with variations on the same name, were formed in the port of New York. See Russell, *Men Along the Shore*, 298–302.

16. Citizens Waterfront Committee, *The New York Waterfront*, 12–13; U.S. CIR, 3:2060, 2062.

17. Meany, quoted in Joseph C. Goulden, *Meany* (New York: Atheneum, 1972), 20; Citizens Waterfront Committee, *The New York Waterfront*, 12–13; "Longshoremen's Association," 194; Rubin, *The Negro in the Longshore Industry*, 18–19; Larrowe, *Shape-up and Hiring Hall*, 9–26; Chandler, *The Visible Hand*, 189–92; Montgomery, *The Fall of the House of Labor*, 101–4; Kimeldorf, *Reds or Rackets?* 51–79.

18. Maurice Rosenblatt, "Joe Ryan and His Kingdom," *The Nation*, Nov. 24, 1945, 548; Mary Heaton Vorse, "The Pirate's Nest of New York," *Harper's* 204 (April 1952): 33; Russell, *Men Along the Shore*, 96–97; Federal Writers' Project, *The WPA Guide to New York City* (1939; reprint, New York: Pantheon, 1982), 151; Kisseloff, *You Must Remember This*, 477–85, 488, 511, 524; Raymond, *Waterfront Priest*, 41, 37–39; Lester Velie, "A Waterfront Priest Battles the Big Port's Big Boss," *Collier's*, Feb. 16, 1952, 18–19, 56–57.

19. Peter McDonough, *Men Astutely Trained: A History of the Jesuits in the American Century* (New York: Free Press, 1992), 110; Miller, *Emigrants and Exiles*, 525–26; Joshua B. Freeman, *In Transport: The Transport Workers Union in New York City, 1933–1966* (New York: Oxford University Press, 1989), 35; Kisseloff, *You Must Remember This*, 528. See also Schulberg, "Joe Docks."

20. Rosenblatt, "Joe Ryan and His Kingdom," 548; Russell, *Men Along the Shore*, 93–112, 142; Larrowe, *Shape-up and Hiring Hall*, 16; Irving Bernstein, *Turbulent Years: A History of the American Worker, 1933–1941* (Boston: Houghton Mifflin, 1970), 266; Kimeldorf, *Reds or Rackets?* 15; International Longshoremen's Association, Ind., *Proceedings of Special Convention* (Philadelphia, Nov. 16–18, 1953), 57; Johnson, *Crime on the Labor Front*, 163–64; Nelson, *Workers on the Waterfront*, 142–44.

21. Larrowe, *Shape-up and Hiring Hall*, 17; Bell, "The Racket-Ridden Longshoremen," 160; Alan Block, *East Side–West Side: Organizing Crime in New York, 1930–1950* (New Brunswick, N.J.: Transaction Books, 1980), 163–95; Steven Fraser, *Labor Will Rule: Sidney Hillman and the Rise of American Labor* (New York: Free Press, 1991), 242–54.

22. Joshua B. Freeman, *Working-Class New York: Life and Labor since World War II* (New York: The New Press, 2000), 38–39; Jerry Della Femina and Charles Sopkin, *An Italian Grows in Brooklyn* (Boston: Little, Brown, 1978), 35–66.

23. Larrowe, *Shape-up and Hiring Hall*, 17; Raymond, *Waterfront Priest*, 63–65; Bell, "The Racket-Ridden Longshoremen," 159–90; A. H. Raskin, "How the Docks Shape up Now," *New York Times Magazine*, June 12, 1955, 13, 35, 37; Budd Schulberg, "How One Pier Got Rid of the Mob," ibid., Sept. 27, 1953, 17. The most detailed treatment of gangsterism and industrial racketeering on the New York waterfront is Johnson's *Crime on the Labor Front*, 90–238. For brief overviews, see Bell, "Last of the Business Rackets," 89–91, 194 ff.; Block, *East Side–West Side*, 183–95.

24. Larrowe, *Shape-up and Hiring Hall*, 20; Russell, *Men Along the Shore*, 142; Charles H. Logan to Louis Stark, Feb. 27, 1953, box 24, William M. Leiserson Papers, State Historical Society of Wisconsin, Madison.

25. International Longshoremen's Association, *Proceedings of the Thirty-fourth Quadrennial Convention of the International Longshoremen's Association* (New York City, July 14–18, 1947), 5–15; Larrowe, *Shape-up and Hiring Hall*, 16–17; Raymond, *Waterfront Priest*, 42–45; Lester Velie, "Big Boss of the Big Port," *Collier's*, Feb. 9, 1952, 38.

26. Bell, "The Racket-Ridden Longshoremen," 174–80; Vorse, "The Pirate's Nest of New York," 35; Velie, "Big Boss of the Big Port," 18–19, 38–40, quoted on 39.

27. "The Reminiscences of Paul O'Dwyer" (Oral History Office, Columbia University, New York, 1962), 39–40; Paul O'Dwyer, *Counsel for the Defense:*

The Autobiography of Paul O'Dwyer (New York: Simon and Schuster, 1979), 141–42; Kisseloff, *You Must Remember This*, 527.

28. Spero and Harris, *The Black Worker*, 201, 196–97; Herbert R. Northrup, *Organized Labor and the Negro* (New York: Harper and Brothers, 1944), 141, 146; Abram L. Harris, "Hampton Roads District, International Longshoremen's Association," n.d., folder 9, box 43-1, Abram Lincoln Harris Papers, Moorland-Spingarn Research Center, Howard University, Washington, D.C. Harris acknowledged that the "rather hard and fast lines of racial separation" in the district were not always advantageous to blacks. "There are Negro time keepers, pay masters, [and] foremen," he reported, "but there are no Negro checkers and weighers. The white longshoremen usually work on top deck, the Negro usually works below."

29. Frazier, "A Negro Industrial Group," 221–23; Spero and Harris, *The Black Worker*, 202, 199; Marian Wynn Perry to Clarence Mitchell ("Memorandum re. International Longshoremen['s] Association"), Mar. 3, 1949, box B89, group 2, NAACP Papers.

30. Franklin, *The Negro Labor Unionist*, 189; Cheryl Lynn Greenberg, *Or Does It Explode? Black Harlem in the Great Depression* (New York: Oxford University Press, 1991), 86–91.

31. Spero and Harris discovered exactly the same sentiment that Frazier had encountered a decade earlier. An official of Local 968 told them, "We are in the union today because the white man had to take us in for his own protection. Outside the organization the Negro could scab on the white man. Inside he can't." Franklin, *The Negro Labor Unionist*, 189–91; "International Longshoremen's Association[,] Local 1124, General Cargo Workers," Aug. 13, 1935, folder 7, box 131-125, E. Franklin Frazier Papers, Moorland-Spingarn Research Center; Frazier, "A Negro Industrial Group," 222; Spero and Harris, *The Black Worker*, 199.

32. John T. Clark, "Report in re. the Bush Terminal," Sept. 8, 1917, box 87, ser. 6, National Urban League Papers, 1911–1960, Manuscript Division, Library of Congress, Washington, D.C.; Harold X. Connolly, *A Ghetto Grows in Brooklyn* (New York: New York University Press, 1977), 52–55; Spero and Harris, *The Black Worker*, 200.

33. Kimeldorf, *Reds or Rackets?* 124–25; Helen Lawrenson, *Stranger at the Party: A Memoir* (New York: Random House, 1975), 210–11; *Daily Worker*, July 25, 1939, 3, July 26, 1939, 1; *New York Times*, Jan. 30, 1941, 1, 14, Feb. 7, 1941, 40; William Mello, "Pete Panto: Rank and File Radical on the Brooklyn Waterfront" (paper presented at the conference entitled "The Lost World of Italian American Radicalism: Labor, Politics, and Culture," New York, May 14, 1997), 1–9.

34. Nathan Glazer and Daniel P. Moynihan, *Beyond the Melting Pot: The Negroes, Puerto Ricans, Jews, Italians, and Irish of New York City*, 2d ed. (Cambridge, Mass.: MIT Press, 1970), 190–91; Block, *East Side–West Side*, 186–

87; Bell, "The Racket-Ridden Longshoremen," 174–75; Raymond, *Waterfront Priest*, 11, 28, 33; Mello, "Pete Panto," 7–10, 13–15.

35. Marc Karson, *American Labor Unions and Politics, 1900–1918* (Carbondale: Southern Illinois University Press, 1958), 221–24.

36. Ronald H. Bayor, *Neighbors in Conflict: The Irish, Germans, Jews, and Italians of New York City, 1929–1941* (Baltimore: Johns Hopkins University Press, 1978), 1–56; Erie, *Rainbow's End*, especially 85–91, 118–22, 133; Bell, "The Racket-Ridden Longshoremen," 171; Montgomery, *The Fall of the House of Labor*, 303; Glazer and Moynihan, *Beyond the Melting Pot*, 221–29.

37. Bayor, *Neighbors in Conflict*, 87–108; David J. O'Brien, *American Catholics and Social Reform: The New Deal Years* (New York: Oxford University Press, 1968), 81–82; Montgomery, *The Fall of the House of Labor*, 308–9; Steve Fraser, "The 'Labor Question,'" in *The Rise and Fall of the New Deal Order, 1930–1980*, ed. Steve Fraser and Gary Gerstle (Princeton, N.J.: Princeton University Press, 1989), 73.

38. Alden V. Brown, *The Tablet: The First Seventy-Five Years* (n.p.: Tablet Publishing, 1983), 32–33; O'Brien, *American Catholics and Social Reform*, 179.

39. According to journalist James Weschler, "There are 12,000 Irish Catholic policemen in New York. The speeches delivered at their communion breakfasts often differ in intensity rather than in kind from Coughlin propaganda." Although Weschler acknowledged in passing the growing importance of the German American Bund in the Coughlinite movement and the frustrations of unemployed workers and economically hard pressed shopkeepers, his portrayal of the movement's social base otherwise focused almost exclusively on its Irish and Catholic dimensions. James Weschler, "The Coughlin Terror," *Nation*, July 22, 1939, 92–97. In the last two months of 1938, Scanlan reported receiving 3,150 communications in regard to Father Coughlin, all but 42 of them favorable. Brown, *The Tablet*, 34–39.

40. Gerald H. Gamm, *The Making of New Deal Democrats: Voting Behavior and Realignment in Boston, 1920–1940* (Chicago: University of Chicago Press, 1989), 155; Nelson, *Workers on the Waterfront*, 90–91, 170–71, 245–46; *Irish World*, Dec. 10, 1938, 7.

41. William V. Shannon, *The American Irish: A Social Portrait*, 2d ed. (Amherst: University of Massachusetts Press, 1989), 327–57; Chris McNickle, *To Be Mayor of New York: Ethnic Politics in the City* (New York: Columbia University Press, 1993), 42–43; O'Brien, *American Catholics and Social Reform*; Freeman, *In Transit*, 26–35, 45–57, 159; Joshua B. Freeman, "Catholics, Communists, and Republicans: Irish Workers and the Organization of the Transport Workers Union," in *Working-Class America: Essays on Labor, Community, and American Society*, ed. Michael H. Frisch and Daniel J. Walkowitz (Urbana: University of Illinois Press, 1982), 256–83.

42. Marion R. Casey, "'From the East Side to the Seaside': Irish Americans on the Move in New York City," in *The New York Irish*, ed. Bayor and Meagher,

395–415; Ware, *Greenwich Village*, 203–21, especially 208–11; Freeman, *In Transit*, 14–15, 31, 62, 84–85; CIO Maritime Committee, "For Immediate Release," [Oct. 1937], reel 7, part 1, *The CIO Files of John L. Lewis* (microfilm ed.); Nelson, "Class and Race in the Crescent City," 23.

43. Swanstrom, *The Waterfront Labor Problem*, 3; Thurgood Marshall to Joseph P. Ryan, Apr. 10, 1940, box A338, group 2, NAACP Papers.

44. Rubin, *The Negro in the Longshore Industry*, 58; Franklin, *The Negro Labor Unionist*, 189; Dwyer, interview.

45. Fraser, *Labor Will Rule*, 377.

46. Freeman, *In Transit*, 35; Kimeldorf, *Reds or Rackets?* 43; Charles Leinenweber, "The Class and Ethnic Bases of New York City Socialism, 1904–1915," *Labor History* 22 (winter 1981): 47–49; *New York Sun*, Aug. 28, 1920, 1.

47. Logan to Stark, Feb. 27, 1953; Kimeldorf, *Reds or Rackets?* 154–56; Maurice Rosenblatt, "The Scandal of the Waterfront," *Nation*, Nov. 17, 1945, 517–19; Larrowe, *Shape-up and Hiring Hall*, 26–34, 37–41; Vernon H. Jensen, *Strife on the Waterfront: The Port of New York since 1945* (Ithaca, N.Y.: Cornell University Press, 1974), 36–94; Kimeldorf, *Reds or Rackets?* 154–56.

48. Raymond, *Waterfront Priest*, 3, 45; Larrowe, *Shape-up and Hiring Hall*, 81; Bell, "The Racket-Ridden Longshoremen," 183; Russell, *Men Along the Shore*, 143, 168; "Report and Recommendations of AFL-CIO Executive Council Committee Respecting Application of International Longshoremen's Association (Independent) for Affiliation with the AFL-CIO," Aug. 17, 1959, in *AFL-CIO Executive Council Statements and Reports, 1956–1975*, ed. Gary M. Fink (Westport, Conn.: Greenwood Press, 1977), 1: 499.

49. *New York Times*, June 27, 1963, 33; Jensen, *Strife on the Waterfront*, 95–111, 121–35; Raymond, *Waterfront Priest*, 21; Raskin, "How the Docks Shape up Now," 35.

50. Father [John M.] Corridan, "Waterfront," *America*, Oct. 8, 1955, 40–41; Larrowe, *Shape-up and Hiring Hall*, 196–205; Jensen, *Strife on the Waterfront*, 116–20, 136–46.

51. Raymond, *Waterfront Priest*, 72; Kimeldorf, *Reds or Rackets?* 153–54; Sanford Gottlieb, "The Man Who Shut Down the Port of New York," *Reporter*, Apr. 27, 1954, 28–31; Kisseloff, *You Must Remember This*, 517, 525, 528; Dwyer, interview; John Dwyer, "Merger or Mockery," [1959], folder 34, Johnny Dwyer Collection, Tamiment/Bobst Library, New York University, New York.

52. Raymond, *Waterfront Priest*, 76–79; Schulberg, "How One Pier Got Rid of the Mob," 17, 58–59; Gottlieb, "The Man Who Shut Down the Port," 29.

53. Schulberg, "Joe Docks," 214; Larrowe, *Shape-up and Hiring Hall*, 27n., 33, 34n.; *New York Times*, Nov. 11, 1948, 1, 31; Velie, "Big Boss of the Big Port," 18, 40; Vorse, "The Pirate's Nest of New York," 35, 36; Charles Garrett, *The La Guardia Years: Machine and Reform Politics in New York City* (New Brunswick, N.J.: Rutgers University Press, 1961), 305, 311. Daniel Bell offers

an excellent brief portrait of Sampson in "Labor: Wildcats and Gorillas," *Fortune* 44 (December 1951): 48, 50.

54. Dennis Howard, "Waterfront Underground," *Jubilee* 1 (May 1953): 17–23; Johnson, *Crime on the Labor Front*, 214–26; Raymond, *Waterfront Priest*, 4–6, 58; Schulberg, "How One Pier Got Rid of the Mob," 58–59.

55. Joshua B. Freeman and Steve Rosswurm, "The Education of an Anti-Communist: Father John F. Cronin and the Baltimore Labor Movement," *Labor History* 33 (spring 1992): 217–47, quoted on 226; Gary Gerstle, *Working-Class Americanism: The Politics of Labor in a Textile City, 1914–1960* (New York: Cambridge University Press, 1989), 247–59, 279–89; Jules Weinberg, "Priests, Workers, and Communists: What Happened in a New York Transit Workers Union," *Harper's* 197 (November 1948): 49–56; John M. Corridan, "Longshoremen's Case," *America*, Nov. 20, 1948, 176–78; *Irish World*, Jan. 22, 1938, 7. See also Joseph M. McShane, S.J., " 'The Church Is Not for the Cells and the Cave': The Working Class Spirituality of the Jesuit Labor Priest," *U.S. Catholic Historian* 9 (summer 1990): 289–304; Steve Rosswurm, "The Catholic Church and the Left-Led Unions: Labor Priests, Labor Schools, and the ACTU," in *The CIO's Left-Led Unions*, ed. Rosswurm, 119–37; McDonough, *Men Astutely Trained*, 98–118, 309–16.

56. Ronald Schatz, *The Electrical Workers: A History of Labor at General Electric and Westinghouse, 1923–60* (Urbana: University of Illinois Press, 1983), 188–221; Rosswurm, "The Catholic Church"; Morris, *American Catholic*, 209–11; Frank Fiano to John M. Corridan, May 23, 1954, folder 1, box 11, Records of the Xavier Institute of Industrial Relations, Fordham University Archives, Fordham University, Bronx, N.Y.; James Troiano and family to John M. Corridan, May 21, 1954, ibid.; "The Son of a Longshoreman" to John M. Corridan, May 17, 1953, ibid.

57. Handwritten, undated notes to John M. Corridan, folder 1, box 11, Records of the Xavier Institute of Industrial Relations; International Longshoremen's Association, *Proceedings of the Thirty-fourth Quadrennial Convention*, 7–8.

58. Raymond, *Waterfront Priest*, 201, 237; Howard, "Waterfront Underground," 23; Jensen, *Strife on the Waterfront*, 123–24; *New York Times*, Oct. 20, 1953, 51; "Waterfront Alert" (leaflet), n.d., folder 1, box 11, Records of the Xavier Institute of Industrial Relations. According to Allen Raymond, the leadership of Local 791 "announced to the press that they had sent a warning to Father Corridan to keep his hands out of waterfront politics and to confine himself to spiritual advice to the dock workers. As Father Corridan recalls it, he never received any such message of warning and disregarded with a shrug the news in the papers that such a warning had been sent." Raymond, *Waterfront Priest*, 199.

59. Frank Fiano, a checker who had worked at the Waterman Steamship Company dock in Hoboken for twelve years and who voted for the ILA in

the representation elections, informed Corridan: "The situation at Waterman SS Co. is that no ILA man is hired as checker or clerk. All men are hired thru [sic] the AFL headquarters. . . . Six clerks, all on steady salary, were let go without a word of explanation.

"None of us are goons. None of us with a record of any kind. Two are veterans of World War 1 and two are veterans of World War 2. All of us men with families who worked [our way] . . . up to what we considered positions of reasonable security only to be knocked out by a deal between the AFL and a company official who is a bosom buddy of Mr. Paul Hall." (Paul Hall was the president of the Seafarers' International Union.) Fiano to Corridan, May 23, 1954; see also Troiano and family to Corridan, May 21, 1954.

60. Jensen, *Strife on the Waterfront*, 134–35; Raymond, *Waterfront Priest*, 240, 246, 81; Larrowe, *Shape-up and Hiring Hall*, 209; Everett C. Parker, "How Chelsea Was Torn Apart," *Christian Century*, Feb. 3, 1960, 130–33; John T. McGreevy, *Parish Boundaries: The Catholic Encounter with Race in the Twentieth-Century Urban North* (Chicago: University of Chicago Press, 1996), 114–17; Fraser, "The 'Labor Question,' " 73.

61. Perry to Mitchell, "Memorandum," Mar. 3, 1949; Cleophas Jacobs, "Answer of Local 968 before New York District Council on July 18, 1949, to Complaint Filed"; Roy Wilkins to Joseph Ryan, June 8, 1949, box B89, group 2, NAACP Papers; *New York Sun*, June 6, 1949, 12.

62. Jacobs, "Answer of Local 968"; *New York Amsterdam News*, June 18, 1949, 15.

63. W[illia]m Glazier to Harry Bridges, Aug. 19, 1948, box 1, International Longshoremen's Association Collection, 1933–89, Tamiment/Bobst Library, New York University [hereafter, ILA Collection/NYU]; Bell, "The Racket-Ridden Longshoremen," 163; Jacobs, "Answer of Local 968"; *New York Sun*, June 6, 1949, 1, 12; *New York Amsterdam News*, June 11, 1949, 1, 21, June 18, 1949, 11, 15; *New York Times*, June 7, 1949, 55.

64. *New York Times*, June 8, 1948, 1, 18, June 9, 1949, 55; *New York Sun*, June 7, 1949, 1, 14; *New York Amsterdam News*, June 11, 1949, 1, 21. The battle was not strictly racial. The ILA loyalists may have included some black longshoremen, and the ranks of the protesters apparently included many whites, from left-wing unions in New York.

65. In a letter to a member of the Catholic Interracial Council, Father Corridan expressed the belief that "the demonstration the other day was really the Chelsea longshoremen's resentment against the Communist activities in their section. They did not counter-picket just to bail out Ryan." John M. Corridan to George K. Hunton, June 10, 1949, folder 20, box 11, Records of the Xavier Institute of Industrial Relations.

66. *New York Times*, June 8, 1948, 1, 18; *New York Amsterdam News*, June 18, 1949, 6. An official of the NAACP, an organization whose anti-Communist credentials were clear and well established, expressed the belief that the

leadership of Local 968 was not political and that "the political question has just been thrown in to try to kill the Local." Marian [Wynn Perry], "Memorandum to Messrs. [Thurgood] Marshall and [Clarence] Mitchell from Miss Perry," July 15, 1949, box B89, group 2, NAACP Papers.

67. Schulberg, "Joe Docks," 210–11; *New York Sun*, Mar. 15, 1949, night edition, 7; Larrowe, *Shape-up and Hiring Hall*, 72–73.

68. President's Committee on Government Contracts, "Waterfront Hiring Meeting Proceedings," Washington, D.C., Jan. 25, 1960 (a copy of the stenographic transcript is available at the U.S. Department of Labor Library, Washington, D.C.); Douglas G. Pugh (Urban League of Greater New York), "An Indictment: Of the 'Shape-up' Hiring System in the Port of New York which Fosters Racial and Individual Discrimination" (June 1959), 2–4, box 39, series 4, NUL Papers, 1911–60. Pugh's report is incorporated into the "Waterfront Hiring Meeting Proceedings," 44–64.

69. Rubin, *The Negro in the Longshore Industry*, 67.

70. Pugh, "An Indictment," 8–9.

71. Ibid., 5; Kisseloff, *You Must Remember This*, 520–21.

72. President's Committee on Government Contracts, "Waterfront Hiring Meeting Proceedings," 73; *New York Times*, June 4, 1959, 62; Rubin, *The Negro in the Longshore Industry*, 68.

73. Spero and Harris, *The Black Worker*, 201–2; *New York Times*, Jan. 19, 1952, 31, June 23, 1959, 1, 20; ILA Local 1814, AFL-CIO, "News Release: Local 1814 Celebrates Tenth Anniversary June 6[,] Mayor Proclaims Date 'Local 1814, ILA Day,' " May 29, 1964, box 3, ILA Collection/NYU; Jensen, *Strife on the Waterfront*, 160, 232.

74. *New York Times*, June 23, 1959, 20; ILA Local 1814, AFL-CIO, "News Release"; ILA Local 1814, AFL-CIO, "Local 1814 Report to the Membership: Local 1814 Marches for Justice and Freedom," Sept. 5, 1963, box 3, ILA Collection/NYU; "Why We Protest: A joint Statement by Anthony Scotto, President, Local 1814, International Longshoremen's Association, George Houser, Executive Director, American Committee on Africa, James Farmer, National Director, Congress of Racial Equality," Oct. 9, 1963, folder 3, box 280, Claude A. Barnett Papers, Chicago Historical Society; Jensen, *Strife on the Waterfront*, 160, 288.

75. A. Philip Randolph to George Meany, Oct. 9, 1961, and [A. Philip Randolph], "Job Discrimination and Racial Intimidation on the New York Piers," [1961], box 23, A. Philip Randolph Papers, Manuscript Division, Library of Congress, Washington, D.C.; Herman D. Bloch, *The Circle of Discrimination: An Economic and Social Study of the Black Man in New York* (New York: New York University Press, 1969), 115, 118; Rubin, *The Negro in the Longshore Industry*, 67. See also Herbert Hill, "Labor and Segregation," *New Leader*, Oct. 19, 1959, 3–4.

76. Rubin, *The Negro in the Longshore Industry*, 62–66; Jan Morris, *The Great Port: A Passage through New York* (1969; reprint, New York: Oxford University Press, 1985), 78.

77. Corridan, "Waterfront," 40. The classic challenge to assimilationist hypotheses, with New York City as its frame of reference, is Glazer and Moynihan's *Beyond the Melting Pot*, which first appeared in 1963. A more recent affirmation of the importance of ethnicity in the distribution of employment opportunities in New York is Roger Waldinger's *Still the Promised City? African-Americans and New Immigrants in Postindustrial New York* (Cambridge, Mass.: Harvard University Press, 1996).

78. Frazier, "A Negro Industrial Group," 198, 225; Spero and Harris, *The Black Worker*, 200; Marshall to Ryan, Apr. 10, 1940; Randolph to Meany, Oct. 9, 1961; [Randolph], "Job Discrimination."

79. Ignatiev, *How the Irish Became White*, 42; Waldinger, *Still the Promised City?* 30.

CHAPTER THREE
WATERFRONT UNIONISM AND "RACE SOLIDARITY": FROM THE CRESCENT CITY TO THE CITY OF ANGELS

This chapter draws on—and extends the analysis in—my earlier published work on this subject, namely: "Class and Race in the Crescent City: The ILWU, from San Francisco to New Orleans," 19–45; "Harry Bridges, the ILWU, and Race Relations during the CIO Era," Occasional Paper Series, working paper no. 2 (Center for Labor Studies, University of Washington, Seattle, 1995); and "The 'Lords of the Docks' Reconsidered: Race Relations among West Coast Longshoremen, 1933–61," 155–92.

1. Richard White, "Race Relations in the American West," *American Quarterly* 38 (1986): 396–416; Robert M. Fogelson, *The Fragmented Metropolis: Los Angeles, 1850–1930* (Cambridge, Mass.: Harvard University Press, 1967), 76, 78; Gerald D. Nash, *The American West Transformed: The Impact of the Second World War* (Bloomington: Indiana University Press, 1985), 99; Saxton, *The Indispensable Enemy*, 18; Tomas Almaguer, *Racial Fault Lines: The Historical Origins of White Supremacy in California* (Berkeley: University of California Press, 1994), 153–82; Paul Scharrenberg, the editor of the *Seamen's Journal* and secretary of the California State Federation of Labor, quoted in Nelson, *Workers on the Waterfront*, 49.

2. Albert S. Broussard, *Black San Francisco: The Struggle for Racial Equality in the West, 1900–1954* (Lawrence: University Press of Kansas, 1993), 48–50; Quintard Taylor, *The Forging of a Black Community: Seattle's Central District from 1870 through the Civil Rights Era* (Seattle: University of Washington Press, 1994), 52–53; Horace Cayton, Jr., *Long Old Road: An Autobiography* (1965; reprint, Seattle: University of Washington Press, 1970), 112–13.

3. The key figure was ILWU president Harry Bridges. Throughout his long career Bridges continued to express sympathy for the Communist party (CPUSA) but steadfastly denied that he was—or ever had been—a member. However, the recent opening of the archives of the Communist party of the Soviet Union to scholars has revealed that Bridges was not only a party member in the 1930s but—briefly, at least—a member of the CPUSA's central committee. See Harvey Klehr and John Haynes, "Communists and the CIO: From the Soviet Archives," *Labor History* 35 (summer 1994): 442–46; Robert W. Cherny, "Harry Bridges and the Communist Party: New Evidence, Old Questions; Old Evidence, New Questions" (paper presented at the annual meeting of the Organization of American Historians, Indianapolis, Apr. 4, 1998).

4. Broussard, *Black San Francisco*, 98–99, 102–5; *Chicago Defender*, Jan. 14, 1933, quoted in Halpern, *Down on the Killing Floor*, 109. See also "Negro Editors on Communism: A Symposium of the American Negro Press," in *Voices of a Black Nation: Political Journalism in the Harlem Renaissance*, ed. Theodore G. Vincent (1973; reprint, Trenton, N.J.: Africa World Press, [1991]), 203–9. On John Pittman and the relationship between the *Daily People's World* and the Communist party, see Al Richmond, *A Long View from the Left* (1972; reprint, New York: Delta Books, 1977), 270–73, 289; Dorothy Healey and Maurice Isserman, *Dorothy Healey Remembers: A Life in the American Communist Party* (New York: Oxford University Press, 1990), 182. In 1961 Healey encountered Pittman in the Soviet Union, where he was the *Daily Worker*'s Soviet correspondent.

5. Michael K. Honey, *Southern Labor and Black Civil Rights: Organizing Memphis Workers* (Urbana: University of Illinois Press), 227; Korstad and Lichtenstein, "Opportunities Found and Lost," 791. Other sources that illuminate the Communists' role in the struggles of African American workers include Nell Irvin Painter, *The Narrative of Hosea Hudson: His Life as a Negro Communist in the South* (Cambridge, Mass.: Harvard University Press, 1979); Mark Naison, *Communists in Harlem during the Depression* (Urbana: University of Illinois Press, 1983); Freeman, *In Transit*; Kelley, *Hammer and Hoe*; Halpern, *Down on the Killing Floor*; and Roger Horowitz, *"Negro and White, Unite and Fight!": A Social History of Industrial Unionism in Meatpacking, 1930–90* (Urbana: University of Illinois Press, 1997).

6. Freeman, *In Transit*, 26–27, 30, 154–56. A more extensive examination of the TWU's relationship to the struggle for black equality is August Meier and Elliott Rudwick's "Communist Unions and the Black Community: The Case of the Transport Workers Union, 1934–1944," *Labor History* 23 (spring 1982): 165–97. Meier and Rudwick conclude, "[T]he TWU's early history demonstrates that the response of a Communist-dominated union leadership to race discrimination in the job market was anything but simple. That leadership, regardless of its ideals, was dependent for survival in office on a white

membership characterized by pervasive prejudices."Ibid., 195. See also Naison, *Communists in Harlem*, 265; Alex Lichtenstein, " 'Scientific Unionism' and the 'Negro Question': Communists and the Transport Workers Union in Miami, 1944–1949," in *Southern Labor in Transition, 1940–1995*, ed. Robert H. Zieger (Knoxville: University of Tennessee Press, 1997), 58–85.

7. George Murphy, Jr., "Memorandum," Nov. 16, 1938, quoted in Meier and Rudwick, "Communist Unions," 166.

8. The port of Los Angeles is located on San Pedro Bay, twenty-five miles south of the city's center. In 1909 the waterfront communities of San Pedro and Wilmington were absorbed by Los Angeles, and they became the site of its Harbor District. For many years, ILWU Local 13 was located in San Pedro, and in the dialect of West Coast dockworkers it was common to refer to the port as San Pedro, or "Peedrow," rather than as Los Angeles. Writers' Program, Works Projects Administration, *Los Angeles: A Guide to the City and Its Environs* (1941; reprint, St. Claire Shores, Mich.: Somerset Publishers, 1972), 215.

9. Nelson, "Harry Bridges," 19.

10. *Louisiana Weekly*, Sept. 19, 1959, 1.

11. Halpern, *Down on the Killing Floor*, 245. For a brief summation emphasizing the "adverse effect" of the purge of the Left on black workers, see William H. Harris, *The Harder We Run: Black Workers since the Civil War* (New York: Oxford University Press, 1982), 124, 137–41. For the record, I share Rick Halpern's admiration for the United Packinghouse Workers and his belief that the UPWA's course—"The Path Not Taken" by most CIO unions— was indeed the better path to take. But New Orleans clearly demonstrates that black workers sometimes freely chose another course.

12. See David Lee Wells, "The ILWU in New Orleans: CIO Radicalism in the Crescent City, 1937–1957" (M.A. thesis, University of New Orleans, 1979), 48–73; Adam Fairclough, *Race and Democracy: The Civil Rights Struggle in Louisiana, 1915–1972* (Athens: University of Georgia Press, 1995), 136– 47.

13. Lewis, *In Their Own Interests*, passim.

14. On the Big Strike, see Irving Bernstein's *Turbulent Years: A History of the American Worker, 1933–1941* (Boston: Houghton Mifflin, 1970), 252–98; Kimeldorf, *Reds or Rackets?* 99–110; Charles P. Larrowe, *Harry Bridges: The Rise and Fall of Radical Labor in the United States* (New York: Lawrence Hill, 1972), 32–93; Nelson, *Workers on the Waterfront*, 127–55; Mike Quin, *The Big Strike* (Olema, Calif.: Olema Publishing, 1949); and Selvin, *A Terrible Anger*.

15. Nelson, *Workers on the Waterfront*, 157–63; Gregory Harrison, *Maritime Strikes on the Pacific Coast: A Factual Account of Events Leading to the 1936 Strike of Marine and Longshore Unions*, Statement before the United States Maritime Commission, San Francisco, Nov. 2, 1936 (San Francisco: Waterfront Employers Association, 1936), 21; *Waterfront Worker*, June 24, 1935, 7; *Voice of the Federation*, July 5, 1935, 4, Feb. 6, 1936, 4. See also Herb Mills

and David Wellman, "Contractually Sanctioned Job Action and Workers' Control: The Case of the San Francisco Longshoremen," *Labor History* 28 (spring 1987): 167–95.

16. Nelson, *Workers on the Waterfront*, 156–88; *Voice of the Federation*, July 12, 1935, 2.

17. Nelson, *Workers on the Waterfront*, 48–50; Robert Cherny, "San Francisco Longshoremen, 1848–1940," in *Studies in the International History of Dock Labour*, ed. Davies et al.; Mary Joy Renfro, "The Decline and Fall of the Riggers' and Stevedores' Union of San Francisco: A History of the Years 1916 through 1919" (senior honors thesis, San Francisco State University, 1995), 16–17; Taylor, *The Forging of a Black Community*, 53–54; Cayton, *Long Old Road*, 118; U.S. Department of Commerce, Bureau of the Census, *Fourteenth Census of the United States Taken in the Year 1920*, vol. 4, *Occupations* (Washington, D.C.: U.S. Government Printing Office, 1923), 1233.

18. Cherny, "San Francisco Longshoremen"; Eugene Dennis Vrana, *The ILWU Story: Six Decades of Militant Unionism* (San Francisco: International Longshoremen's and Warehousemen's Union, 1997), 68; Germaine Bulcke, "Longshore Leader and ILWU-PMA Arbitrator," an oral history interview by Estolv Ward (Regional Oral History Office, Bancroft Library, University of California, Berkeley, 1984), 38; Robert Coleman Francis, "A History of Labor on the San Francisco Waterfront" (Ph.D. diss., University of California, Berkeley, 1934), 182–83; Northrup, *Organized Labor and the Negro*, 152–53.

19. Nelson, *Workers on the Waterfront*, 114–16, 123–25; *Waterfront Worker*, Oct. 3, 1933; Robert W. Cherny, "Harry Bridges, Labor Radicalism, and the State" (paper delivered at a conference entitled "Harry Bridges and the Tradition of Dissent among Waterfront Workers," University of Washington, Seattle, Jan. 29, 1994), 5; *Dispatcher*, Dec. 18, 1942, 7. See also Broussard, *Black San Francisco*, 128–30, and Selvin, *A Terrible Anger*, 96.

20. Kimeldorf, *Reds or Rackets?* 146–51, quoted on 146; "Note for File," Dec. 5, 1946, folder on membership statistics—Negroes, ILWU History Files, International Longshoremen's and Warehousemen's Union Archives [hereafter, ILWUA], Anne Rand Research Library, International Longshoremen's and Warehousemen's Union, San Francisco; Lincoln Fairley to David Mitchell, Jan. 3, 1951, ibid.; [Lincoln Fairley], "Memorandum, Subject: Estimate of Negro Membership in ILWU as of January 1, 1964," Mar. 17, 1964, folder on minorities—longshore, ibid.

21. "American Minorities and the Case of Harry Bridges" (pamphlet, n.d.), folder on minorities—blacks, 1960, ILWU History Files; (San Francisco) *Sun-Reporter*, Sept. 29, 1951, 10; Cy W. Record, "Willie Stokes at the Golden Gate," *The Crisis* 56 (June 1949): 188. See also Broussard, *Black San Francisco*, 156. Broussard states that "as far as blacks were concerned, the ILWU stood head and shoulders above other Bay Area locals in virtually every respect."

22. Fairley to Mitchell, Jan. 3, 1951; "Per Cent Distribution of Hawaiian Sugar and Pineapple Workers by Race; ILWU Members, 10/46," Dec. 5, 1946, folder on membership statistics—Negroes, ILWU History Files; Steve Rosswurm, "Introduction: An Overview and Preliminary Assessment of the CIO's Expelled Unions," in *The CIO's Left-Led Unions*, ed. Rosswurm, 3–4.

23. Harvey Schwartz, "A Union Combats Racism: The ILWU's Japanese-American 'Stockton Incident' of 1945," *Southern California Quarterly* 62 (summer 1980): 161–76.

24. International Longshoremen's and Warehousemen's Union, *The ILWU Story: Two Decades of Militant Unionism* (San Francisco: International Longshoremen's and Warehousemen's Union, 1955), 62–63; Harry Bridges to Officers and Executive Board Members, Local 10, ILWU, Oct. 9, 1947, box 18A, ILWU Officer's Correspondence, 1934–77, ILWUA; U.S. Congress, House of Representatives, Committee on Merchant Marine and Fisheries, *Study of Harbor Conditions in Los Angeles and Long Beach*, Hearings, Oct. 19, 20, and 21, 1955 (Washington, D.C.: U.S. Government Printing Office, 1955), 325.

25. *Local 10 Longshore Bulletin*, Feb. 19, 1948; Committee on Merchant Marine and Fisheries, *Study of Harbor Conditions*, 328–29; Record, "Willie Stokes at the Golden Gate," 175; Davis McEntire and Julia R. Tarnopol, "Postwar Status of Negro Workers in San Francisco Area," *Monthly Labor Review* 70 (June 1950): 616.

26. *Local 13 Bulletin*, [July 1951]; Pilcher, *The Portland Longshoremen*, 69; Larrowe, *Harry Bridges*, 368; Ralph Freedman, "The Attitudes of West Coast Maritime Unions in Seattle toward Negroes in the Maritime Industry" (M.A. thesis, State College of Washington, 1952), 47; "Walter E. Williams Oral History Interview," conducted by Tony Salcido, Nov. 10, 1988, and by Tony Salcido and Robert G. Marshall, Oct. 4, 1990, International Longshoremen's and Warehousemen's Union, Local 13, Oral History Project (hereafter, ILWU Local 13 OHP), Urban Archives Center, California State University, Northridge (CSUN), 84–86. (Because the two interviews are combined in one transcript, I will not make separate reference by date hereafter but will simply identify them as the "Walter E. Williams Oral History Interview.") "Oral History Interview of George W. Love," conducted by Tony Salcido, May 16, 19, 30, 1989, ibid., 100.

27. John Gunther, *Inside U.S.A.*, 50th anniversary ed. (1947; reprint, New York: New Press, 1997), 88; *Portland Oregonian*, Sept. 16, 1959, clipping in folder on minorities—blacks, 1960, ILWU History Files; Rubin, *The Negro in the Longshore Industry*, 145, 148; Nash, *The American West Transformed*, 99; Edward Balloch Debra, "An Injury to One: The Politics of Racial Exclusion in the Portland Local of the International Longshoremen's and Warehousemen's Union" (B.A. honors thesis, University of Oregon, 1992), 24, 58 (quoted). See also Larrowe, *Harry Bridges*, 366–68; Pilcher, *The Portland Longshoremen*, 67–76.

28. Freedman, "The Attitudes of West Coast Maritime Unions," 47.

29. Cherny, "San Francisco Longshoremen"; U.S. Department of Commerce, Bureau of the Census, *Fifteenth Census of the United States: 1930*, vol. 4, *Occupation by States*, 1709, 1715; Bureau of the Census, *Sixteenth Census of the United States: 1940*, vol. 3, *The Labor Force*, part 5, *Pennsylvania-Wyoming* (Washington, D.C.: U.S. Government Printing Office, 1943), 853, 864.

30. [Bjorne Halling], "Report to the First Convention of the International Longshoremen['s] and Warehousemen's Union," Apr. 6, 1938, box 12, ILWU Organizing Files, ILWUA; R. R. Tisdale to J. S. Potofsky, Sept. 27, 1937, folder 5, box 221, Records of the Amalgamated Clothing Workers of America, Labor-Management Documentation Center, Catherwood Library, Cornell University, Ithaca, N.Y.

31. *Voice of the Federation*, June 3, 1937, 4; Mervyn Rathborne to John L. Lewis, July 14, 1937, box A7-28, Records of the Congress of Industrial Organizations (CIO), Department of Archives and Manuscripts, Catholic University of America, Washington, D.C; Mervyn Rathborne to John L. Lewis, Aug. 27, 1937, ibid.

32. CIO Maritime Committee, "For Immediate Release," [Oct. 1937].

33. Ben Jones to Mervyn Rathborne et al., Dec. 12, 1937, box 12, ILWU Organizing Files; Paul Heide to Matt Meehan, Oct. 22, 1938, ibid. The statement "the white man will lead the negro out of the pit" was made by Caleb Green, a white southerner who in 1939 became the ILWU's principal organizer and spokesman in the Gulf. *Proceedings of the Third Annual Convention of the International Longshoremen's and Warehousemen's Union* (North Bend, Ore., Apr. 1–11, 1940), 140.

34. Herbert R. Northrup, "The New Orleans Longshoremen," *Political Science Quarterly* 57 (December 1942): 532–33; Rubin, *The Negro in the Longshore Industry*, 100; International Longshoremen's Association, *Proceedings of the Thirtieth Convention* (New York, July 13–18, 1931), 53.

35. Northrup, "The New Orleans Longshoremen," 533–34; Robert C. Francis, "Dock Trouble in New Orleans," *The Crisis* 42 (December 1935): 373; Robert C. Francis, "Longshoremen in New Orleans: The Fight Against 'Nigger' Ships," *Opportunity* 14 (March 1936): 82–85, 93; "Statement by the New Orleans Steamship Association on the New Orleans Longshore Labor Situation," Dec. 9, 1935, box 1320, Records of the National Labor Relations Board (NLRB), Record Group (RG) 25, National Archives and Records Administration (NARA), Suitland, Md.

36. United States of America, Before the National Labor Relations Board (NLRB), "In the Matter of Aluminum Line [et al.] and the International Longshoremen['s] and Warehousemen's Union," Sept. 29, 1938, box 3, Disbanded Locals Files, ILWUA; Charles H. Logan to William Leiserson, Sept. 4, 1934, and Logan to National Labor Relations Board, Oct. 19, 1935, box 23, Leiserson Papers (unless otherwise noted, all of Logan's correspondence

cited in this chapter is from box 23 of the Leiserson Papers); Northrup, "The New Orleans Longshoremen," 534–37; Francis, "Longshoremen in New Orleans," 85, 93; Gilbert Mers, *Working the Waterfront: The Ups and Downs of a Rebel Longshoreman* (Austin: University of Texas Press, 1988), 137–38, 157; [Halling], "Report to the First Convention"; *New Orleans Times-Picayune*, June 29, 1938, 9. See also Paul H[o]rtman, "Negro Longshoremen Make Gains," *American Federationist* 47 (June 1940): 585.

37. "Longshore Labor Conditions," part 1, 11–13; "Strike of Longshoremen on the Gulf Coast," *Monthly Labor Review* 42 (February 1936): 392; Charles H. Logan to Louis Stark, Feb. 27, 1953, box 24, Leiserson Papers; [Halling], "Report to the First Convention."

38. Charles H. Logan to William M. Leiserson, Dec. 6, 1939, and Oct. 25, 1940; "Official Report of Proceedings Before the National Labor Relations Board, Case No. XV-R-168, in the Matter of Aluminum Line, et al and International Longshoremen['s] and Warehousemen's Union" (New Orleans, June 27, 1938), 504–8, 529; Avery C. Alexander, interview by author (via telephone), July 29, 1993; Donald E. DeVore, "The Rise from the Nadir: Black New Orleans between the Wars" (M.A. thesis, University of New Orleans, 1983), 55; *New Orleans Item*, Oct. 24, 1940, 1, 27, Oct. 25, 1940, 1, 2, Oct. 27, 1940, 1, 6; [Halling], "Report to the First Convention"; Charles H. Logan, "Memorandum in Re New Orleans Steamship Association, Collectively, and Its Several Members, Individually, and International Longshoremen['s] and Warehousemen's Union and International Longshoremen's Association, Locals 1418, 1419, 1497, 1515, and 854," Apr. 6, 1938, box 378, NLRB Records, RG 25, NARA.

39. *Proceedings of the Second Annual Convention of the International Longshoremen's and Warehousemen's Union* (San Francisco, Apr. 3–14, 1939), 142; "Minutes of the Full District Executive Board Meeting, International Longshoremen's and Warehousemen's Union, . . . San Francisco, California, Sunday, October 23, 1938," box 12, ILWU Organizing Files; United States of America, Before the National Labor Relations Board, Fifteenth Region, "In the Matter of Aluminum Line [et al.] and the International Longshoremen['s] and Warehousemen's Union," Oct. 19, 1938, box 378, NLRB Records, RG 25, NARA.

40. Felix Siren to Anthony Wayne Smith, Oct. 22, 1938, box 3, Disbanded Locals Files, ILWUA; Bjorne Halling to Nathan Witt, Oct. 29, 1938, ibid.; Matt Meehan to J. R. Robertson, Apr. 29, 1939, box 12, ILWU Organizing Files; J. R. (Bob) Robertson, interview by Harvey Schwartz, San Rafael, Calif., Dec. 29, 1972 (in author's possession, courtesy of Harvey Schwartz); Burt Nelson, interview by Philip Lelli, Seattle, Mar. 28, 1987 (in author's possession, courtesy of Ron Magden); Ruby Heide, "Terror in New Orleans," *The Ledger*, n.d., in "Beginnings of the CIO Unions in New Orleans, June 24, 1938 to July 8, 1938" (a collection of newspaper clippings), box 2034, American

Civil Liberties Union Archives, Seeley G. Mudd Manuscript Library, Princeton University, Princeton, N.J.; Nelson, "Class and Race in the Crescent City," 31–34.

41. "Minutes of the Full District Executive Board Meeting, International Longshoremen's and Warehousemen's Union, . . . San Francisco, California, Sunday, October 23, 1938"; Heide to Meehan, Oct. 22, 1938; Nelson, "Class and Race in the Crescent City," 38–39.

42. J. R. Robertson to Harry Bridges, Aug. 9, 1938, box 12, ILWU Organizing Files; Heide to Meehan, Oct. 22, 1938; Arnold R. Hirsch, "Simply a Matter of Black and White: The Transformation of Race and Politics in Twentieth-Century New Orleans," in *Creole New Orleans: Race and Americanization*, ed. Arnold R. Hirsch and Joseph Logsdon (Baton Rouge: Louisiana State University Press, 1992), 265–67; William Pickens, "Note to Office," Dec. 15, 1937, box G-83, group 1, NAACP Papers; Fairclough, *Race and Democracy*, 58; Jones to Rathborne et al., Dec. 12, 1937; [Halling], "Report to the First Convention"; *New Orleans Item*, Oct. 24, 1940, 1, 27, Oct. 25, 1940, 1, 2, Oct. 27, 1940, 1, 6; DeVore, "The Rise from the Nadir," 55.

43. F. Ray Marshall, *Labor in the South* (Cambridge, Mass.: Harvard University Press, 1967), 207; New Orleans Colored Citizens Committee to "My dear Longshoremen," Oct. 12, 1938, box 12, ILWU Organizing Files. See also "Stink-Mouth Bridges Can't Get Away with This Scheme!" [Oct. 1938], ibid.

44. Logan to Leiserson, Apr. 6, 1939; J. R. Robertson to Matt Meehan, Mar. 27, 1939, box 14, ILWU Organizing Files; J. R. Robertson, "To the Officers and Members of All ILWU Locals," Apr. 28, 1939, ibid.; Nelson, "Class and Race in the Crescent City," 37, 40. In the case of the cotton compress workers, Robertson reported the outcome as ILWU, 508 votes; AFL, 10.

45. Mers, *Working the Waterfront*, 147–48; Francis, "Dock Trouble in New Orleans," 373; Logan to Leiserson, Oct. 25, 1940; Northrup, "The New Orleans Longshoremen," 540–42; Alexander, interview; Richard A. Dowling to Lee Pressman, October 19, 1938, box 12, ILWU Organizing Files; Siren to Smith, Oct. 22, 1938 (emphasis in original).

46. Heide to Meehan, Oct. 22, 1938; Dowling to Pressman, Oct. 19, 1938; "Gulf News: First Hand Report by Paul Heide on New Orleans Elections," *Voice of the Federation*, undated clipping in "Beginnings of the CIO Unions in New Orleans, June 24, 1938 to July 8, 1938."

47. *New Orleans Times-Picayune*, July 2, 1938, 1, 3; Felix Siren to John L. Lewis, June 28, 1938, box 12, ILWU Organizing Files; *Proceedings of the Third Annual Convention*, 140; Neil R. McMillen, *Dark Journey: Black Mississippians in the Age of Jim Crow* (Urbana: University of Illinois Press, 1989), 260; Wells, "The ILWU in New Orleans," 10.

48. Kimeldorf, *Reds or Rackets?* 141; Al Langley, interview by Howard Kimeldorf, Feb. 4, 1982 (hereafter, Langley, interview by HK); "Alfred E. Langley Oral History Interview," conducted by Tom W. Brown, Apr. 3, 1984, and

by Tony Salcido, May 13, 1986, ILWU Local 13 OHP, Urban Archives Center, CSUN, 39, 62; Tony Salcido, interview by author (via telephone), June 2, 1994. An analysis published in 1967, after extensive investigation by the international union, concluded that "prior to 1943, . . . there was not a single Negro longshoreman employed" on the Los Angeles–Long Beach waterfront. Ben Margolis, "Brief on Behalf of International Longshoremen's and Warehousemen's Union, Local 13," Apr. 4, 1967, 34, Local 13 Case Files, Local Files, ILWUA. Assuming the accuracy of Langley's assertion that two black longshoremen were registered in November 1942, the international union's statement should be modified accordingly.

49. Kimeldorf, *Reds or Rackets?* 142–44; *Local 13 Bulletin*, May 1, 1942, July 9, 1942; Langley, interview by HK; "Alfred E. Langley Oral History Interview," 43–45; Margolis, "Brief on Behalf of International Longshoremen's," 35; Bill Lawrence to Agnes Quave, Jan. 5, 1945, folder on membership statistics—Negroes, ILWU History Files.

50. Arthur Kaunisto, interview by Harvey Schwartz, Sept. 23, 1982, ILWU–National Endowment for the Humanities (NEH) Oral History Project (OHP); Corky Wilson, interview by Harvey Schwartz, Dec. 7, 1983, ibid.

51. Henry Schmidt, *Secondary Leadership in the ILWU, 1933–1966* (Regional Oral History Office, Bancroft Library, University of California, Berkeley, 1983), 40–41; Victor Silverman, "Left-Led Unions and Racism: A History of ILWU Local 10, 1940–1960" (undergraduate seminar paper, University of California, Berkeley, 1983), 4–5; Wilson, interview; Al Langley, interview by Harvey Schwartz, Nov. 19, 1981, ILWU–NEH OHP.

52. Joe Stahl, interview by Harvey Schwartz, Dec. 7, 1983, ILWU–NEH OHP; Walter Williams, interview by Harvey Schwartz, Mar. 30, 1984, ibid.

53. "Walter E. Williams Oral History Interview," 28–30 (on his background), quoted on 20, 30, 61.

54. Quam-Wickham, "Who Controls the Hiring Hall?" 66; "Alfred E. Langley Oral History Interview," 38–40; Langley, interview, Nov. 19, 1981. See also Frank Sunstedt, interview by Harvey Schwartz, Mar. 26, 1984, ILWU–NEH OHP. Sunstedt maintained that "any time a black man was about ready to get a gang, the promotions committee members would go around and entice anyone else to get a gang, just to keep a black man out."

55. Bill Lawrence to Harry Bridges, Apr. 24, 1946, box 18D, ILWU Officers' Correspondence, 1934–77.

56. Margolis, "Brief on Behalf of International Longshoremen's," 6; Lawrence to Bridges, Apr. 24, 1946; Harry Bridges to L. B. Thomas, Sept. 8, 1947, box 18D, ILWU Officers' Correspondence, 1934–77.

57. Williams, interview, Mar. 30, 1984; Lawrence to Bridges, Apr. 24, 1946; Arthur D. Guy, Jr., to Harry Bridges, Aug. 28, 1947, box 18D, ILWU Officers' Correspondence, 1934–77; Nash, *The American West Transformed*, 96.

58. Lawrence to Bridges, Apr. 24, 1946; Margolis, "Brief on Behalf of International Longshoremen's," 16–20, 25, 28; *Local 13 Bulletin*, July 9, 1942; L. B. Thomas to Harry Bridges, Aug. 9, 1947, box 18D, ILWU Officers' Correspondence, 1934–77.

59. Margolis, "Brief on Behalf of International Longshoremen's," 10; Guy to Bridges, Aug. 28, 1947; Arthur D. Guy, Jr., to International Longshoremen's and Warehousemen's Union, Executive Board, Sept. 16, 1947, box 18D, ILWU Officers' Correspondence, 1934–77.

60. Margolis, "Brief on Behalf of International Longshoremen's," 31–33, 35–36.

61. Ibid., 32; Bridges to Thomas, Sept. 8, 1947; *Local 13 Bulletin*, Dec. 8, 1950; *Dispatcher*, Dec. 22, 1950, 7.

62. Langley, interview by HK. See Margolis, "Brief on Behalf of International Longshoremen's"; Adolph M. Koven, "Arbitrator's Opinion and Award, in the Matter of a Controversy between International Longshoremen's and Warehousemen's Union, Local 13, and Pacific Maritime Association, Involving Walter Williams et al," June 5, 1970, Local 13 Case Files, Local Files, ILWUA; "Opinion and Decision of Sam Kagel, Coast Arbitrator, in the Matter of an Arbitration between International Longshoremen's and Warehousemen's Union, Local No. 13, Complainant, and Pacific Maritime Association, Respondent, Involving Walter E. Williams et al," Mar. 11, 1971, ibid.

63. *Local 13 Bulletin*, [July 1951]. In the immediate postwar period, John Gunther found that "anti-Negro prejudice" in Los Angeles was "steeply rising." Gunther, *Inside U.S.A.*, 61.

64. *Local 13 Bulletin*, [July 1951]; "George W. Love Oral History Interview," 38–39, 49; Salcido, interview; John Pandora, interview by author (via telephone), Jan. 26, 1994. Salcido was registered as part of a group of 1,000 "limited registrants," or "B" men, in 1949; Pandora, as part of a group of 450 "B" men in 1955. Pandora did not recall "a single black" in his group, and after recalling none in his, Salcido checked the list of "B" registrants in 1949 and identified about a dozen men whom he knew to be black, plus a few men of "mixed parentage" who spoke with a "hint of a Cajun twang" and "passed" for white. Tony Salcido to author, June 4, 1994. "Note for File," Dec. 5, 1946; Bill Piercy, Jr., to Lincoln Fairley, Feb. 19, 1964, folder on membership statistics—Negroes, ILWU History Files; [Fairley], "Memorandum, Subject: Estimate of Negro Membership in ILWU as of January 1, 1964," Mar. 17, 1964; Langley, interview by HK. I am grateful to Tony Salcido for confirming, on the basis of his own research in the records of Local 13, that the local voted in July 1951 to impose the ten-year residency rule for prospective members.

65. "Walter E. Williams Oral History Interview," 117; Tony Salcido to author, June 3, 1994; Salcido, interview; Walter Williams, interview by author (via telephone), July 15, 1994.

66. H. R. Bridges to John H. Williams, March 26, 1946, box 18D, ILWU Officers' Correspondence, 1934–77; Bridges to Thomas, Sept. 8, 1947.

67. Richard Alan Liebes, "Longshore Labor Relations on the Pacific Coast, 1934–1942" (Ph.D. diss., University of California, Berkeley, 1942), 186a–90; Nelson, *Workers on the Waterfront*, 262.

68. Mickey Mahon, interview by Harvey Schwartz, Apr. 20, 1983, ILWU–NEH OHP.

69. Ibid.; Mike Davis, *City of Quartz: Excavating the Future of Los Angeles* (London: Verso, 1990), 160–64, 398–401; Kelley, " 'We Are Not What We Seem,' " 96–97; Lewis, *In Their Own Interests*, 58. In his study of black migration, Lawrence de Graaf concluded that by the end of the 1930s "Negroes had become much more concentrated in a small section of Los Angeles and were almost totally excluded from large sections of the city and most suburban areas." Lawrence Brooks de Graaf, "Negro Migration to Los Angeles, 1930 to 1950" (Ph.D. diss., University of California, Los Angeles, 1962), 130.

70. "George W. Love Oral History Interview," 95, 114.

71. Guy to Bridges, Aug. 28, 1947; Guy to International Longshoremen's and Warehousemen's Union, Executive Board, Sept. 16, 1947; Williams, interview, Mar. 30, 1984. In his letter to the ILWU Executive Board, attorney Arthur Guy stated that "certain members of the group [had] proceeded to employ the various remedial processes available within the Union to obtain reinstatement." When they failed in that endeavor, "I was employed as legal counsel for the unemployed group on or about the 15th day of July, 1947." By mid-September, ninety-nine members had formally requested that Guy represent them.

72. Williams, interview, July 15, 1994; Harold Irving Roth to Local Executive Board, ILWU Local 13, Oct. 28, 1950 (in author's possession, courtesy of Tony Salcido); Committee on Merchant Marine and Fisheries, *Study of Harbor Conditions*, 324–25, 345.

73. Debra, "An Injury to One," 66. This issue continued to drive a wedge between blacks and whites. In his investigation of the Los Angeles waterfront during the 1980s, William Finlay found that a group of black longshoremen sued the Pacific Maritime Association (PMA), charging that access to the much coveted position of steady crane operator was racially discriminatory. As a result, the PMA and Local 13 "were required to add an affirmative action criterion" in selecting candidates for crane-operator training. This challenge to seniority was, according to Finlay, "another blow to union solidarity," because "the senior men regard the black workers as interlopers arrogating their job opportunities." William Finlay, *Work on the Waterfront: Worker Power and Technological Change in a West Coast Port* (Philadelphia: Temple University Press, 1988), 171. See also "Willie McGee Oral History Interview," conducted by Tony Salcido, Feb. 25, 1991, ILWU Local 13 OHP, Urban Archives Center, CSUN, 21–33.

74. Langley, interview by HK; "Men Who Are Eligible for Registration," [Nov. 1934] (in author's possession, courtesy of Tony Salcido); Tony Salcido to author, Apr. 15, 1994; Max Chavez, interview by Tony Salcido, Dec. 28, 1983, ILWU Local 13 OHP; Henry Gaitan, interview by Daniel Beagle and David Wellman, May 14, 1983, ILWU-NEH OHP; Salcido, interview; Joe Uranga, quoted in Harvey Schwartz, ed., "A Long Struggle for Equality: The Mexican American Longshoremen of Local 13, 1934–1975," *Dispatcher*, April 1999, 6–7.

75. Williams, interview, July 15, 1994; "Alfred E. Langley Oral History Interview," 87; Nash, *The American West Transformed*, 108; Ricardo Romo, *East Los Angeles: History of a Barrio* (Austin: University of Texas Press, 1983), 170. See also George J. Sanchez, *Becoming Mexican American: Ethnicity, Culture, and Identity in Chicano Los Angeles, 1900–1945* (New York: Oxford University Press, 1993), 239–44 and passim. Sanchez makes it clear that ethnic Mexicans played a significant role in organizing CIO-affiliated unions in Los Angeles in the late 1930s and early 1940s. This, too, set them apart from African Americans.

76. Modell, "The Ethnic Niche"; Gaitan, interview; Salcido, interview; Williams, interview, July 15, 1994; Neil Foley, "Becoming Hispanic: Mexican Americans and the Faustian Pact with Whiteness," in *Reflexiones 1997: New Directions in Mexican American Studies*, ed. Neil Foley (Austin: Center for Mexican American Studies, University of Texas at Austin, 1998), 53–70; Mike Davis, "Magical Urbanism: Latinos Reinvent the US Big City," *New Left Review* 234 (March–April 1999): 11.

77. "Walter E. Williams Oral History Interview," 22–30; Alonzo Smith and Quintard Taylor, "Racial Discrimination in the Workplace: A Study of Two West Coast Cities during the 1940s," *Journal of Ethnic Studies* 8 (spring 1980): 42–44; Herbert Hill, *Black Labor and the American Legal System: Race, Work, and the Law* (1977; reprint, Madison: University of Wisconsin Press, 1985), 185–208, quoted on 200.

78. Bridges to Thomas, Sept. 8, 1947; Larrowe, *Harry Bridges*, 369 (quoted); Williams, interview, July 15, 1994; Williams, interview, Mar. 30, 1984.

79. "Walter E. Williams Oral History Interview," 34–35.

80. "American Minorities"; Bruce Minton and John Stuart, *Men Who Lead Labor* (New York: Modern Age Books, 1937), 179–80; Kimeldorf, *Reds or Rackets?* 143–51; *Local 10 Longshore Bulletin*, Aug. 21, 1947, Feb. 17, 1948; *San Francisco Chronicle*, Jan. 14, 1948, 12; Larrowe, *Harry Bridges*, 366.

81. Langley, interview by HK; *Local 13 Bulletin*, Mar. 5, 1942, June 27, 1944, June 28, 1945; L. B. Thomas to Harry Bridges, Apr. 29, 1946, box 18D, ILWU Officers' Correspondence, 1934–77.

82. "Walter E. Williams Oral History Interview," 84; "George W. Love Oral History Interview," 68, 69; Finlay, *Work on the Waterfront*, 60, 86.

83. Finlay, *Work on the Waterfront*, 171; *Dispatcher*, May 5, 1961, 12.

84. Larrowe, *Harry Bridges*, 379–81. In January 1969, on the Johnson administration's last day in office, Attorney General Ramsey Clark filed suit against the ILA, its South Atlantic and Gulf Coast district, and thirty-seven ILA locals. The Nixon administration added a separate suit against ILA longshore locals in Baltimore on April 22, 1969. Herb Mills, " 'ILA — Discrimination': Report to the Stewards Workshop, [Longshore Local 10, ILWU]," Aug. 26, 1970, box 3, ILA Collection/NYU; *New York Times*, July 14, 1970, 23.

85. Wayne Hardin, "Pros and Cons of Merger Stir Two ILA Locals," *Baltimore Evening Sun*, Apr. 29, 1969, clipping in box 3, ILA Collection/NYU; Al Prince, "ILA Merger Opinion to Be Cited in Texas," *Houston Post*, Sept. 14, 1970, ibid.; Rubin, *The Negro in the Longshore Industry*, 111.

86. Leon F. Litwack, *Trouble in Mind: Black Southerners in the Age of Jim Crow* (New York: Alfred A. Knopf, 1998), xvi.

87. *Louisiana Weekly*, Sept. 19, 1959, 1; Fairclough, *Race and Democracy*, 146–47; Wells, "The ILWU in New Orleans," 48–73.

88. Northrup, "The New Orleans Longshoremen," 544; James P. Baughman, "Gateway to the Americas," in *The Past as Prelude: New Orleans, 1718–1968*, ed. Hodding Carter (New Orleans: Pelican Publishing House, 1968), 285–86; "New Orleans Makes a Play for Imports," *Business Week*, Mar. 13, 1948, 54, 56; "South's Port Trade Booms," ibid., Aug. 21, 1948, 24; "The Great New Orleans 'Steal,' " *Fortune* 38 (November 1948): 102; "The Internationalists of New Orleans," ibid. 45 (June 1952): 127, 130, 136; *Newsweek*, Sept. 9, 1952, 80.

89. *Louisiana Weekly*, Sept. 29, 1951; Jan. 3, 1953, 1, Jan. 31, 1953, June 27, 1953, 1, July 11, 1953; *Waterfront Investigation: Hearings Before a Subcommittee of the Committee on Interstate and Foreign Commerce*, U.S. Senate, 83d Cong., 1st sess., Pursuant to S. Res. 41 on Waterfront Racketeering and Port Security, part 2, *New Orleans Waterfront, June 24–26, 1953* (Washington, D.C.: U.S. Government Printing Office, 1953), 795, 806, 815, 883–93; Charles Frederick Ortique, "A Study of the Longshore Industry in New Orleans with Emphasis on Negro Longshoremen" (M.A. thesis, University of Illinois, 1956), 22–25; *Color* 6 (August 1950): 29–30, 36–37.

90. *Waterfront Investigation*, 721–22, 734–45; *New Orleans Times-Picayune*, June 25, 1953, 9.

91. *Louisiana Weekly*, July 2, 1938, 1, June 27, 1953, 1, 6, July 11, 1953, August 15, 1953, 1, 6; *New Orleans Times-Picayune*, June 17, 1953, 1, June 23, 1953, 1, June 24, 1953, 1, 3, June 27, 1953, 1; Alexander, interview; Ortique, "A Study of the Longshore Industry," 71–73; Carroll George Miller, "A Study of the New Orleans Longshoremen's Unions from 1850 to 1962" (M.A. thesis, Louisiana State University, 1962), 42–48; Fairclough, *Race and Democracy*, 211, 513 n. 44.

92. *Louisiana Weekly*, Oct. 10, 1953, 8, Sept. 12, 1959, 1, Dec. 1, 1956, 1, 7, Dec. 25, 1957, 1, 8; Edward F. Haas, *DeLesseps S. Morrison and the Image of*

Reform: New Orleans Politics, 1946–61 (Baton Rouge: Louisiana State University Press, 1974), 251; Alexander, interview; Miller, "A Study of the New Orleans Longshoremen's Unions," 48–51.

93. Hirsch, "Simply a Matter of Black and White," 274–81; Alexander, interview; *Louisiana Weekly*, Oct. 3, 1952; Perry H. Howard, "Louisiana: Resistance and Change," in *The Changing Politics of the South*, ed. William C. Havard (Baton Rouge: Louisiana State University Press, 1972), 551; Haas, *DeLesseps S. Morrison*, 71–74, 80–81, 247–48.

94. *Black Worker* 30 (August 1959): 5; *Third Constitutional Convention of the American Federation of Labor and Congress of Industrial Organizations, 1959 Proceedings* (San Francisco, Calif., Sept. 23, 1959, Report of Fifth Day—Wednesday Afternoon Session), 134–35; *New York Times*, Sept. 24, 1959, 1; *Louisiana Weekly*, Oct. 17, 1959, 2.

95. Hirsch, "Simply a Matter of Black and White," 273–304, quoted on 299. According to Adam Fairclough, the Deacons for Defense and Justice were driven far less by ideology than by the practical realization that civil rights activity in rural mill towns such as Bogalusa and Jonesboro would be impossible unless blacks were capable of deterring the Ku Klux Klan and other rabid partisans of white supremacy. Fairclough concludes that the Deacons "showed no signs of being tainted by left-wing or black nationalist ideas." Fairclough, *Race and Democracy*, 295–96, 342–60, quoted on 359.

96. Kim Lacy Rogers, *Righteous Lives: Narratives of the New Orleans Civil Rights Movement* (New York: New York University Press, 1993), 111–14, 124. Jerome Smith had a brief—and revealing—moment of fame in May 1963, during a meeting between Attorney General Robert Kennedy and civil rights activists, arranged by the novelist James Baldwin. In a group that featured luminaries such as Harry Belafonte, Lena Horne, Lorraine Hansberry, and Baldwin himself, Smith was a relative unknown. But he quickly seized center stage when he told Kennedy, "You don't have no idea what trouble is. Because I'm close to the moment where I'm ready to take up a gun." By this time, Smith had endured a "series of beatings" while attempting to integrate the bus terminal in McComb, Mississippi, and had served a stint in the infamous Parchman Penitentiary. His growing fury, and visceral repudiation of nonviolence, foreshadowed the imminent rise of Black Power. Taylor Branch, *Parting the Waters: America in the King Years, 1954–63* (New York: Simon and Schuster, 1988), 809–11; Rogers, *Righteous Lives*, 143.

97. *New Orleans Times-Picayune*, Oct. 1, 1962, 1; Forrest E. LaViolette, "The Negro in New Orleans," in *Studies in Housing and Minority Groups*, ed. Nathan Glazer and Davis McEntire (Berkeley: University of California Press, 1960), 116, 122–23, 133; *Louisiana Weekly*, Feb. 2, 1957, 1; Fairclough, *Race and Democracy*, 149–51; Haas, *DeLesseps S. Morrison*, 76–78.

98. Rubin, *The Negro in the Longshore Industry*, 105–10; Miller, "A Study of the New Orleans Longshoremen's Unions," 64.

99. Rubin, *The Negro in the Longshore Industry*, 111; Dave Wells and Jim Stodder, "A Short History of New Orleans Dockworkers," *Radical America* 10 (January–February 1976): 63; Miller, "A Study of the New Orleans Longshoremen's Unions," 64; Andrew Young, *An Easy Burden: The Civil Rights Movement and the Transformation of America* (New York: HarperCollins, 1996), 22; LaViolette, "The Negro in New Orleans," 115, 117–29, 133; Fairclough, *Race and Democracy*, 435–62, quoted on 446, 447. See also Daphne Spain, "Race Relations and Residential Segregation in New Orleans: Two Centuries of Paradox," *Annals of the American Academy of Political and Social Science* 441 (January 1979): 82–96.

100. "Longshoreman Says Merger Will Hurt Blacks," *Houston Post*, Sept. 10, 1970, clipping in box 3, ILA Collection/NYU; Leroy Hoskins, former president of ILA Local 851 (Galveston, Texas), remarks at panel on "Life and Work on the Waterfront: From San Francisco to New Orleans" (annual meeting of the American Studies Association, New Orleans, Nov. 4, 1990); Rubin, *The Negro in the Longshore Industry*, 111; Wells and Stodder, "A Short History of New Orleans Dockworkers," 63.

101. Nelson, "Harry Bridges," 19–20; Finlay, *Work on the Waterfront*, 43–44; "Walter E. Williams Oral History Interview," 117, 36.

102. Rubin, *The Negro in the Longshore Industry*, 104–7.

103. Du Bois, quoted in Hirsch, "Simply a Matter of Black and White," 307; "George W. Love Oral History Interview," 96, 114, 115 (emphasis added). By then the conception of "turf" that Love articulated in 1989 had become a staple ingredient of the backlash that political and social analysts wrongly saw as new among northern whites in the mid- and late 1960s. Politicians such as George Wallace, Richard Nixon, and Ronald Reagan broadened the basis of their electoral appeal by endowing whites' determination to defend their turf with an aura of moral high ground. As Nixon declared in 1972, "There is no reason to feel guilty about wanting to enjoy what you get and what you earn. . . . Those are not values to be ashamed of; those are values to be proud of." See Thomas Byrne Edsall with Mary D. Edsall, *Chain Reaction: The Impact of Race, Rights, and Taxes on American Politics* (New York: W. W. Norton, 1991), Nixon quoted on 97.

104. See Harris, "Whiteness as Property"; George Lipsitz, *The Possessive Investment in Whiteness: How White People Profit from Identity Politics* (Philadelphia: Temple University Press, 1998).

CHAPTER FOUR
ETHNICITY AND RACE IN STEEL'S NONUNION ERA

1. Commission of Inquiry, Interchurch World Movement, *Report on the Steel Strike of 1919* (New York: Harcourt, Brace and Howe, 1920), 132–33.

2. David Brody, *Labor in Crisis: The Steel Strike of 1919* (Philadelphia: Lippincott, 1965), 42.

3. Barrett and Roediger, "Inbetween Peoples"; Thomas C. Holt, "Marking: Race, Race-Making, and the Writing of History," *American Historical Review* 100 (February 1995): 1–20, quoted on 16.

4. Olivier Zunz, *The Changing Face of Inequality: Urbanization, Industrial Development, and Immigrants in Detroit, 1880–1920* (Chicago: University of Chicago Press, 1982), quoted on 398.

5. Bridge, quoted in Katherine Stone, "The Origins of Job Structures in the Steel Industry," in *Labor Market Segmentation*, ed. Richard C. Edwards, Michael Reich, and David M. Gordon (Lexington, Mass.: Lexington Books, 1975), 36; John A. Fitch, *The Steel Workers* (1910; reprint, Pittsburgh: University of Pittsburgh Press, 1989), 3; Montgomery, *The Fall of the House of Labor,* 28, 40–41; Abraham Berglund, *The United States Steel Corporation: A Study of the Growth and Influence of Combination in the Iron and Steel Industry,* Columbia University Studies in the Social Sciences, 73 (1907; reprint, New York: AMS Press, 1979), 78; Thomas K. McCraw, *Prophets of Regulation* (Cambridge, Mass.: Harvard University Press, 1984), quoted on 64.

6. For a telling critique of steel's—and especially U.S. Steel's—relative backwardness, see "The Corporation," *Fortune* 13 (March 1936): 173–74, 176, 178, 180.

7. On the organization and character of work in the automobile industry, see Nelson Lichtenstein and Stephen Meyer, eds., *On the Line: Essays on the History of Auto Work* (Urbana: University of Illinois Pres, 1989), especially Meyer, "The Persistence of Fordism: Workers and Technology in the American Automobile Industry, 1900–1960."

8. On employment patterns in steel, see Stone, "The Origins of Job Structures"; Montgomery, *The Fall of the House of Labor,* 9–46; Jack Stieber, *The Steel Industry Wage Structure: A Study of the Joint Union-Management Job Evaluation Program in the Basic Steel Industry* (Cambridge, Mass.: Harvard University Press, 1959); Robert Ruck, "Origins of the Seniority System in Steel" (University of Pittsburgh, 1977). On the immigrants, I have relied mainly on Margaret Byington, *Homestead: The Households of a Mill Town* (1910; reprint, Pittsburgh: University Center for International Studies, University of Pittsburgh, 1974), 131–68; David Brody, *Steelworkers in America: The Nonunion Era* (1960; reprint, New York: Harper and Row, 1969), 96–111; John Bodnar, Roger Simon, and Michael P. Weber, *Lives of Their Own: Blacks, Italians, and Poles in Pittsburgh, 1900–1960* (Urbana: University of Illinois Press, 1982), especially 29–151; John Bodnar, *Workers' World: Kinship, Community, and Protest in an Industrial Society, 1900–1940* (Baltimore: Johns Hopkins University Press, 1982); John Bodnar, *The Transplanted: A History of Immigrants in Urban America* (Bloomington: University of Indiana Press, 1985); Ewa Morawska, *For Bread with Butter: The Life-Worlds of East Central Europeans in Johnstown, Pennsylvania, 1890–1940* (Cambridge, Eng.: Cambridge University Press, 1985); Charles Tilly, "Transplanted Networks," in *Immigration Reconsidered:*

History, Sociology, and Politics, ed. Virginia Yans-McLaughlin (New York: Oxford University Press, 1990), 79–95.

9. Fitch, *The Steel Workers,* 147; Brody, *Steelworkers in America,* 120; John Bodnar, *Immigration and Industrialization: Ethnicity in an American Mill Town, 1870–1940* (Pittsburgh: University of Pittsburgh Press, 1977), 38.

10. Alois B. Koukol, "A Slav's a Man for A' That," in *Wage-Earning Pittsburgh,* ed. Paul Underwood Kellogg (New York: Survey Associates, 1914), 74–75.

11. Fitch, *The Steel Workers,* 10–11, 147; Brody, *Labor in Crisis,* 39–43; Brody, *Steelworkers in America,* 121; Morawska, *For Bread with Butter,* 237; Paul S. Taylor, *Mexican Labor in the United States: Chicago and the Calumet Region,* University of California Publications in Economics 7, no. 2 (Berkeley: University of California Press, 1932), 159.

12. Reports of the Immigration Commission, *Immigrants in Industries,* part 2, *Iron and Steel Manufacturing* (Washington, D.C.: Government Printing Office, 1911), 1: 387; Fitch, *The Steel Workers,* 12; Brody, *Steelworkers in America,* 119–21; Brody, *Labor in Crisis,* 42.

13. In Johnstown a Polish worker recalled the role of his priest in providing employment in the mills. If any of "his people needed a job or maybe a green-horn came seeking employment, it was enough for Father to write a little note, and [a] job was waiting there for the asking." In return, the Cambria Steel Company made regular deductions from Polish workers' paychecks for the upkeep of Saint Casimir's Church. Morawska, *For Bread with Butter,* 98, 101, 117–18.

14. Bodnar, *Workers' World,* 131; Bodnar, Simon, and Weber, *Lives of Their Own,* 62.

15. Dennis C. Dickerson, *Out of the Crucible: Black Steelworkers in Western Pennsylvania, 1875–1980* (Albany: State University of New York Press, 1986), 25; Brody, *Steelworkers in America,* 107–8, 138–39. In his study of the Duquesne Works of Carnegie Steel, Jim Rose found that by 1920, 55 percent of the crane men were immigrants from southern and eastern Europe and that the sons of new immigrants held another 20 percent of these jobs. James D. Rose, "The United States Steel Duquesne Works, 1886–1941: The Rise of Steel Unionism" (Ph.D. diss., University of California, Davis, 1997), 28–29.

16. Commission of Inquiry, Interchurch World Movement, *Report on the Steel Strike of 1919,* 117–18, 135–36, 139; Bell, *Out of This Furnace,* 184–85.

17. "The U.S. Steel Corporation: III," *Fortune* 13 (May 1936): 97; James Rose, " 'The Problem Every Supervisor Dreads': Women Workers at the U.S. Steel Duquesne Works during World War II," *Labor History* 36 (winter 1995): 24–51; Mark Reutter, *Sparrows Point: Making Steel: The Rise and Ruin of American Industrial Might* (New York: Summit Books, 1988), 360–78.

18. Montgomery, *The Fall of the House of Labor,* 204–5; Byington, *Homestead,* 112, 171–73; Fitch, *The Steel Workers,* 233; Bodnar, *Workers' World,* 89.

19. S. J. Kleinberg, *The Shadow of the Mills: Working-Class Families in Pittsburgh, 1870–1907* (Pittsburgh: University of Pittsburgh Press, 1989), xvii; Byington, *Homestead*, 75–80, 106; Elizabeth Fee, Linda Shopes, and Linda Zeidman, eds., *The Baltimore Book: New Views of Local History* (Philadelphia: Temple University Press, 1991), 178.

20. Byington, *Homestead*, 164, 109; Fitch, *The Steel Workers*, 204.

21. Byington, *Homestead*, 142, 145, 153–55; Thomas Bell, quoted in Kleinberg, *The Shadow of the Mills*, 222.

22. Leslie Woodcock Tentler, *Wage-Earning Women: Industrial Work and Family Life in the United States, 1900–1930* (New York: Oxford University Press, 1979); Bodnar, *The Transplanted*, 80–83; Robert A. Slayton, *Back of the Yards: The Making of a Local Democracy* (Chicago: University of Chicago Press, 1986), 65–75, 84; Kleinberg, *The Shadow of the Mills*, 144–52, 240–50; Ileen A. DeVault, *Sons and Daughters of Labor: Class and Clerical Work in Turn-of-the-Century Pittsburgh* (Ithaca, N.Y.: Cornell University Press, 1990), 73–104; Byington, *Homestead*, 125–28.

23. Bodnar, *Immigration and Industrialization*, 36–37; Sam Camens, interview by author, Youngstown, Ohio, Sept. 22, 1991.

24. Oliver Montgomery, interview by author, Pittsburgh, Pa., Oct. 22, 1990; Frank Leseganich, interview by author, Canfield, Ohio, June 17, 1992.

25. Angela Campana, interview by Philip Bracy, Dec. 13, 1982 (Youngstown State University Oral History Program, Youngstown Steel Strike Project, 1937 "Little Steel" Strike, O. H. 243), 1–4.

26. Ewa Morawska, "East European Laborers in an American Mill Town, 1890–1940: The Deferential-Proletarian-Privatized Workers?" *Sociology* 19 (August 1985): 364–83; Byington, *Homestead*, quoted on 168.

27. Jay Dolan, *The American Catholic Experience: A History from Colonial Times to the Present* (Garden City, N.Y.: Doubleday, 1985), 195–240; Slayton, *Back of the Yards*, 79–81, 118–23; Leslie Woodcock Tentler, "On the Margins: The State of American Catholic History," *American Quarterly* 45 (March 1993): 104–27; McGreevy, *Parish Boundaries*, 7–28.

28. Dolan, *The American Catholic Experience*, 200–8; McGreevy, *Parish Boundaries*, 7–53.

29. Dolan, *The American Catholic Experience*, 225; John Bodnar, "Immigration, Kinship, and the Rise of Working-Class Realism in Industrial America," *Journal of Social History* 14 (fall 1980): 45–65; Bodnar, *Workers' World*; Jack Metzgar, "Plant Shutdowns and Worker Response: The Case of Johnstown, Pa.," *Socialist Review* 53 (September–October 1980): 9–49; Raymond A. Mohl and Neil Betten, *Steel City: Urban and Ethnic Patterns in Gary, Indiana, 1906–1950* (New York: Holmes and Meier, 1986), 43–47, 108–78; Ronald Filippelli, "The History Is Missing, Almost: Philip Murray, the Steelworkers, and the Historians," in *Forging a Union of Steel: Philip Murray, SWOC, and the United*

Steelworkers, ed. Paul F. Clark, Peter Gottlieb, and Donald Kennedy (Ithaca, N.Y.: ILR Press, 1987), 8–9.

30. David J. Saposs, "The Mind of the Immigrant Communities in the Pittsburgh District," in *Public Opinion and the Steel Strike: Supplementary Reports of the Investigators*, by Commission of Inquiry, Interchurch World Movement (New York: Harcourt, Brace, 1921), 226–42; Montgomery, *The Fall of the House of Labor*, 384–85; Commission of Inquiry, Interchurch World Movement, *Report on the Steel Strike of 1919*, 150–51. For a sympathetic treatment of the skilled workers' reluctance to strike in 1919, emphasizing their memory of prior defeats dating from the early 1890s, see Robert Asher, "Painful Memories: The Historical Consciousness of Steelworkers and the Steel Strike of 1919," *Pennsylvania History* 45 (January 1978): 61–86.

31. Bodnar, *Immigration and Industrialization*, 144; Morawska, "East European Laborers," 367, 372, 376–77; Morawska, *For Bread with Butter*, 167, 180–81, 273–74. See also Richard Oestreicher, "Working-Class Formation, Development, and Consciousness in Pittsburgh, 1790–1960," in *City at the Point: Essays in the Social History of Pittsburgh*, ed. Samuel P. Hays (Pittsburgh: University of Pittsburgh Press, 1989), 111–50, especially 137.

32. James Gilbert, *Another Chance: Postwar America, 1945–1985*, 2d ed. (Chicago: Dorsey Press, 1986), 21–24; Nelson Lichtenstein, "Labor in the Truman Era: Origins of the 'Private Welfare State,' " in *The Truman Presidency*, ed. Michael J. Lacey (New York: Cambridge University Press, 1989), 128–55; Helen M. Gould, "Aliquippa—Town of Smoke, Fog, and Steel Unionism," *Labor and Nation* 1 (April–May 1946): 27–30; Mary Heaton Vorse, "An Altogether Different Strike," *Harper's* 200 (February 1950): 50–57; Warner Bloomberg, Jr., "Gary's Industrial Workers as Full Citizens: They Mean to Use Their New-Won Status and Power," *Commentary* 18 (September 1954): 202–10; William Kornblum, *Blue Collar Community* (Chicago: University of Chicago Press, 1974), 108–9; Bodnar, *Immigration and Industrialization*, 147.

33. Barrett and Roediger, "Inbetween Peoples," 7–9, 24, 32; John Hinshaw, "Dialectic of Division: Race and Power among Western Pennsylvania Steelworkers, 1937–1975" (Ph.D. diss., Carnegie Mellon University, 1995), 54; James Green, "Democracy Comes to 'Little Siberia': Steelworkers Organize in Aliquippa, Pennsylvania, 1933–1937," *Labor's Heritage* 5 (summer 1993): 14; Reports of the Immigration Commission, *Immigrants in Industries*, part 2, *Iron and Steel Manufacturing*, 2: 205; Orsi, "The Religious Boundaries," 313–19.

34. Mink, *Old Labor and New Immigrants*, 96–97; Barrett and Roediger, "Inbetween Peoples," 21–28; Mae M. Ngai, "The Architecture of Race in American Immigration Law: A Reexamination of the Immigration Act of 1924," *Journal of American History* 86 (June 1999): 75.

35. Fitch, *The Steel Workers*, 147; Brody, *Steelworkers in America*, 119.

36. W. David Lewis, *Sloss Furnaces and the Rise of the Birmingham District: An Industrial Epic* (Tuscaloosa: University of Alabama Press, 1994), 83–84;

Charles B. Dew, *Ironmaker to the Confederacy: Joseph R. Anderson and the Tredegar Iron Works* (New Haven, Conn.: Yale University Press, 1966), 22–30, 239, 250, quoted on 24.

37. Dew, *Ironmaker to the Confederacy*, 313–14; Montgomery, *The Fall of the House of Labor*, 26; Spero and Harris, *The Black Worker*, quoted on 249; Paul Krause, *The Battle for Homestead, 1880–1892: Politics, Culture, and Steel* (Pittsburgh: University of Pittsburgh Press, 1992), quoted on 114.

38. Krause, *The Battle for Homestead*, 116; Spero and Harris, *The Black Worker*, 250; Dickerson, *Out of the Crucible*, 11–12; Rachleff, *Black Labor in Richmond*, 101–2.

39. Charles S. Johnson, "Negro Workers and the Unions," *Survey*, Apr. 15, 1928, 113–15, quoted on 113; Spero and Harris, *The Black Worker*, 251–55, quoted on 253–54. On white unionists' attitudes toward black workers in the iron and steel industry, see also Henry M. McKiven, Jr., *Iron and Steel: Class, Race, and Community in Birmingham, Alabama, 1875–1920* (Chapel Hill: University of North Carolina Press, 1995), 114, 123–26.

40. Spero and Harris, *The Black Worker*, 246; Dickerson, *Out of the Crucible*, 36; Grossman, *Land of Hope*, 197; Horace R. Cayton and George S. Mitchell, *Black Workers and the New Unions* (Chapel Hill: University of North Carolina Press, 1939), 18–19.

41. Kenneth Warren, *The American Steel Industry, 1850–1970: A Geographical Interpretation* (Oxford: Clarendon Press, 1973), 136; Richard R. Wright, "One Hundred Negro Steel Workers," in *Wage-Earning Pittsburgh*, ed. Kellogg, 97–100, 105; Helen A. Tucker, "The Negroes of Pittsburgh," *Charities and the Commons*, Jan. 2, 1909, 599–608, quoted on 603.

42. Wright, "One Hundred Negro Steel Workers," 99.

43. Ibid., 102–5.

44. Ibid., 105–6; Dickerson, *Out of the Crucible*, 23; Bodnar, Simon, and Weber, *Lives of Their Own*, 59; Francis G. Couvares, *The Remaking of Pittsburgh: Class and Culture in an Industrializing City, 1877–1919* (Albany: State University of New York Press, 1984), 90–91.

45. Cayton and Mitchell, *Black Workers and the New Unions*, 6, 7 (quoted), 12–15; Dickerson, *Out of the Crucible*, 36, 45; Mohl and Betten, *Steel City*, 75.

46. Spero and Harris, *The Black Worker*, 258; Fitzpatrick, quoted in Cayton and Mitchell, *Black Workers and the New Unions*, 77.

47. William M. Tuttle, Jr., *Race Riot: Chicago in the Red Summer of 1919* (New York: Atheneum, 1970), 108–56; Peter Gottlieb, *Making Their Own Way: Southern Blacks' Migration to Pittsburgh, 1916–30* (Urbana: University of Illinois Press, 1987), 89–182; Grossman, *Land of Hope*, 181–245, quoted on 215.

48. Kenneth L. Kusmer, *A Ghetto Takes Shape: Black Cleveland, 1870–1930* (Urbana: University of Illinois Press, 1976), 196–97; Spero and Harris, *The*

Black Worker, 259–63, quoted on 259, 260; Mohl and Betten, *Steel City*, 32; Foster, quoted in Cayton and Mitchell, *Black Workers and the New Unions*, 78.

49. Fitzpatrick, quoted in Cayton and Mitchell, *Black Workers and the New Unions*, 79; Interchurch World Movement, quoted in ibid., 80; Foster, quoted in Johanningsmeier, *Forging American Communism*, 144.

50. John T. Clark, "The Negro in Steel," *Opportunity* 2 (October 1924): 299; Commission of Inquiry, Interchurch World Movement, *Public Opinion and the Steel Strike*, 205; Mary Heaton Vorse, *Men and Steel* (London: Labour Publishing, 1922), 64–67, 84; Cayton and Mitchell, *Black Workers and the New Unions*, 180.

51. Gottlieb, *Making Their Own Way*, 146–82, quoted on 174–75. Gottlieb provides an excellent analysis of black workers' attitude toward unions, as does Grossman, *Land of Hope*, 208–45.

52. Gottlieb, *Making Their Own Way*, 92–93; Cayton and Mitchell, *Black Workers and the New Unions*, 18–20.

53. Cayton and Mitchell, *Black Workers and the New Unions*, 24; Robert J. Norrell, "Caste in Steel: Jim Crow Careers in Birmingham, Alabama," *Journal of American History* 73 (December 1996): 671; Warren, *The American Steel Industry*, 205; Hinshaw, "Dialectic of Division," 47; Gottlieb, *Making Their Own Way*, 89–94, 103.

54. Cayton and Mitchell, *Black Workers and the New Unions*, 20; Mohl and Betten, *Steel City*, 74–75, 92; Edward Greer, "Racism and U.S. Steel, 1906–1974," *Radical America* 10 (September–October 1976): 50–52; Cohen, *Making a New Deal*, 165–67; Taylor, *Mexican Labor in the United States*, quoted on 93, 94.

55. Cayton and Mitchell, *Black Workers and the New Unions*, 32; Norrell, "Caste in Steel," 669.

56. Ed Mann, interview by author, Hubbard, Ohio, Dec. 14, 1988; Archie Nelson, interview, Nov. 19, 1990; Oliver Montgomery, interview, Oct. 22, 1990; Norrell, "Caste in Steel," 669; Roderick N. Ryon, "An Ambiguous Legacy: Baltimore Blacks and the CIO, 1936–1941," *Journal of Negro History* 65 (winter 1980): 23; Cayton and Mitchell, *Black Workers and the New Unions*, 38; Abram Lincoln Harris, Jr., "The New Negro Worker in Pittsburgh" (M.A. thesis, University of Pittsburgh, 1924), 52; Ira De Augustine Reid, "The Negro in the Major Industries and Building Trades of Pittsburgh" (M.A. thesis, University of Pittsburgh, 1925), 28; Gottlieb, *Making Their Own Way*, quoted on 99.

57. "The Gary Project: Summary and Recommendations," [1937], folder 1, box 280, Claude A. Barnett Papers, Chicago Historical Society; Cayton and Mitchell, *Black Workers and the New Unions*, 32, 33; McKiven, *Iron and Steel*, 123.

58. Morawska, *For Bread with Butter*, 113; Vorse, *Men and Steel*, 32–34, 36.

59. [Edward Wieck], "Summary of Observations o[f] SWOC Campaign to Organize the Steel Workers during Trip Beginning September 1, 1936 . . . ," Sept. 23, 1936, box 10, Edward A. Wieck Papers, Archives of Labor History and Urban Affairs, Walter P. Reuther Library, Wayne State University, Detroit; Bodnar, *Workers' World*, 124–25.

60. Green, "Democracy Comes to 'Little Siberia,' " 8; Michael J. Zahorsky, interview by Steven Kocherzat, June 20, 1978, Records of the Beaver Valley Labor History Society [BVLHS], UE/Labor Archives, University of Pittsburgh. In Duquesne the Democratic party simply "withered" during the 1920s, and by 1929 it was no longer fielding candidates in local elections. According to Jim Rose, mill managers at Carnegie Steel's Duquesne Works "fired workers who voted Democratic." Rose, "The United States Steel Duquesne Works," 55.

61. Green, "Democracy Comes to 'Little Siberia,' " 7; "The U.S. Steel Corporation: III," 93–94, 134, 147.

62. Brody, *Steelworkers in America*, 87–93, 109–11, 165–70, 185–90; "The U.S. Steel Corporation: III," 134.

63. Judith Stein, "Southern Workers in National Unions: Birmingham Steelworkers, 1936–1951," in *Organized Labor in the Twentieth-Century South*, ed. Robert H. Zieger (Knoxville: University of Tennessee Press, 1991), 186; Harris, "The New Negro Worker in Pittsburgh," 14–25.

64. Dickerson, *Out of the Crucible*, 101–17; Rob Ruck, *Sandlot Seasons: Sport in Black Pittsburgh* (Urbana: University of Illinois Press, 1987), 23–30; John P. Davis, " 'Plan 11'—Jim Crow in Steel," *The Crisis* 43 (September 1936): 262; William Serrin, *Homestead: The Glory and Tragedy of an American Steel Town* (New York: Times Books, 1992), 21–23, Leonard quoted on 23; Cayton and Mitchell, *Black Workers and the New Unions*, 40–41; Mohl and Betten, *Steel City*, 60.

65. Dennis C. Dickerson, "The Black Church in Industrializing Western Pennsylvania, 1870–1950," *Western Pennsylvania Historical Magazine* 64 (October 1981): 329–44; "Heritage: A Black History of Johnstown," *Johnstown Tribune-Democrat*, Feb. 12, 1980, 4; *Steel Labor*, Dec. 1960, 13; George Powers, *Cradle of Steel Unionism: Monongahela Valley, Pa.* (East Chicago, Ind.: Figueroa, 1972), 42.

66. Cayton and Mitchell, *Black Workers and the New Unions*, 389–93, quoted on 390; Kleinberg, *The Shadow of the Mills*, 163–64; Gretchen Lemke-Santiago, *Abiding Courage: African American Migrant Women and the East Bay Community* (Chapel Hill: University of North Carolina Press, 1996), 43–44, 155–62; Dickerson, *Out of the Crucible*, 64–72; Harris, "The New Negro Worker in Pittsburgh," 77; William P. Young, "The First Hundred Negro Workers," *Opportunity* 2 (January 1924): 18.

67. Powers, *Cradle of Steel Unionism*, 42; Horace R. Cayton, "Changed Attitudes: Press and Church Have Done an About-Face on Labor Matters," *Pittsburgh Courier*, Feb. 16, 1946, 7.

68. Kelley, *Hammer and Hoe*, 107, 148–49; Brenda McCallum, "Songs of Work and Songs of Worship: Sanctifying Black Unionism in the Southern City of Steel," *New York Folklore* 14 (1988): 9–33, quoted on 24, 27.

69. Painter, *The Narrative of Hosea Hudson*, 75–76; Ruck, *Sandlot Seasons*, 58.

70. Meyer Bloomfield, *Labor and Compensation* (New York: Industrial Extension Institute, 1921), 295; Clark, "The Negro in Steel," 300.

71. Gottlieb, *Making Their Own Way*, 124–27; Clark, "The Negro in Steel," 301.

72. Harris, "The New Negro Worker in Pittsburgh," 51; [Urban League of Pittsburgh], "Absenteeism in the Ovens Department, Jones & Laughlin Steel Corporation, South Side Works, By-Products Plant," July 27, 1945, folder 1, box 1, Records of the United Steelworkers of America, Civil Rights Department, Historical Collections and Labor Archives, Paterno Library, Pennsylvania State University, University Park, Pa. (hereafter, HCLA/PSU). In a nationwide study conducted by the Urban League in 1945, investigators concluded that excessive absenteeism among Negro workers was *not* a problem in 232 of the 300 plants it surveyed. The league concluded that where absenteeism was a problem, it occurred mainly in plants in which "personnel practices limited the Negro workers to certain jobs or departments, and there were no chances for improving skills and advancing." National Urban League, *Industrial Relations News Letter*, May 1945, 2.

73. Irving Bernstein, *The Lean Years: A History of the American Worker, 1920–1933* (Boston: Houghton Mifflin, 1960), 506–7; Carroll R. Daugherty, Melvin G. de Chazeau, and Samuel S. Stratton, *The Economics of the Iron and Steel Industry* (New York: McGraw-Hill, 1937), 885; Cohen, *Making a New Deal*, 242–43; Mohl and Betten, *Steel City*, 98–107. See also Francisco A. Rosales and Daniel T. Simon, "Chicano Steel Workers and Unionism in the Midwest, 1919–1945," *Aztlan* 6 (1975): 267–75, especially 269.

74. Taylor, *Mexican Labor in the United States*, 109–10.

75. Daugherty, de Chazeau, and Stratton, *The Economics of the Iron and Steel Industry*, 902; Stein, "Southern Workers in National Unions," 186; Northrup, *Organized Labor and the Negro*, 174, 175 (quoted).

76. Mohl and Betten, *Steel City*, 48–90; Cayton and Mitchell, *Black Workers and the New Unions*, 41; J. Harvey Kerns, *A Study of the Social and Economic Conditions of the Negro Population of Gary, Indiana* (New York: National Urban League, 1944), 62.

77. Linda J. Evans, "Claude A. Barnett and the Associated Negro Press," *Chicago History* 12 (spring 1983): 44–56.

78. [Claude A. Barnett] to J. Carlisle McDonald, July 25, 1936; Claude A. Barnett, "Memo for Mr. J. Carlise McDonald," Oct. 31, 1936; [Claude A. Barnett], "Memorandum for Mr. Stephens," Jan. 27, 1937, all in folder 1, box 280, Barnett Papers.

79. Barnett, "Memo for Mr. J. Carlisle McDonald." In an early communication with U.S. Steel executives, Barnett proposed beginning his project in Gary and then moving on to South Chicago. He also offered his services to Inland Steel but apparently received no encouragement from management there. [Barnett], "Memo for Mr. John A. Stephens," Aug. 1, 1936; Claude A. Barnett to W. Sykes, July 25, 1936, all in folder 1, box 280, Barnett Papers.

80. [Barnett], "Memorandum for Mr. Stephens."

81. Ibid.; "The Gary Project."

82. Ibid.

83. [Barnett], "Memorandum for Mr. Stephens"; Mohl and Betten, *Steel City*, 71–72; H. D. Gould, "An Analysis of Results Obtained during First Ten Days Operation of the Gary Project," [1937], folder 1, box 280, Barnett Papers; "The Gary Project."

84. "Memorandum to Mr. Barnett," [1937], folder 1, box 280, Barnett Papers; Gould, "An Analysis of Results."

85. [H. D. Gould], "Special Memorandum to Mr. Barnett," [1937], folder 1, box 280, Barnett Papers.

86. Ibid.; [Barnett] to McDonald, July 25, 1936; "The Gary Project"; "Memorandum to Mr. Barnett."

CHAPTER FIVE
"REGARDLESS OF CREED, COLOR OR NATIONALITY": STEELWORKERS
AND CIVIL RIGHTS (I)

The quotation in the chapter title is from Van A. Bittner, *Industrial Unionization of Steel and the Negro Worker* (n.p., [ca. June 1936]), no page numbers, in reel 12, part 1, *The CIO Files of John L. Lewis*.

1. Frederick H. Harbison, "Steel," in *How Collective Bargaining Works: A Survey of Experience in Leading American Industries*, ed. Harry A. Millis et al. (New York: Twentieth Century Fund, 1942), 535; John Chamberlain, "The Steelworkers," *Fortune* 39 (February 1944): 166; David Brody, "The Origins of Modern Steel Unionism: The SWOC Era," in *Forging a Union of Steel*, ed. Clark, Gottlieb, and Kennedy, 14.

2. "Statement by Philip Murray," Nov. 8, 1936, folder USWA 1, box A7-33, CIO Records.

3. Robert H. Zieger, *John L. Lewis: Labor Leader* (Boston: Twayne, 1988), xv–xvi; Walter Galenson, *The CIO Challenge to the AFL: A History of the American Labor Movement, 1935–1941* (Cambridge, Mass.: Harvard University Press, 1960), 83–84; Robert R. R. Brooks, *As Steel Goes, . . . Unionism in*

a Basic Industry (New Haven, Conn.: Yale University Press, 1940), 155; David J. McDonald, *Union Man* (New York: E. P. Dutton, 1969), 91. For concise evaluations of SWOC, see Bernstein, *Turbulent Years*, 497–98; Brody, "The Origins of Modern Steel Unionism," 13–29; Zieger, *The CIO*, 34–39.

4. Bernstein, *Turbulent Years*, 441–47; profile of Philip Murray, attached to John G. Ramsay to Stanley H. Ruttenberg, Aug. 3, 1950, folder 1, box 3, John G. Ramsay Papers, 1928–79, Southern Labor Archives, Georgia State University (hereafter, SLA/GSU), Atlanta; Jonathan Mitchell, "Murray: CIO's New Boss," *New Republic*, Dec. 30, 1940, 896–97; Alice M. Hoffman, "Oral History Interview #1 with Pat Fagan," Sept. 24, 1968 (United Steelworkers of America Oral History Project [hereafter, USWA/OHP], HCLA/PSU), 9.

5. Bernstein, *Turbulent Years*, 443; Dominic Del Turco, interview by Steven Kocherzat, Sept. 14, 1978, BVLHS. See also Ronald W. Schatz, "Philip Murray and the Subordination of the Industrial Unions to the United States Government," in *Labor Leaders in America*, ed. Dubofsky and Van Tine, 234–57; Melvyn Dubofsky, "Labor's Odd Couple: Philip Murray and John L. Lewis," in *Forging a Union of Steel*, ed. Clark, Gottlieb, and Kennedy, 30–44.

6. Ronald L. Lewis, *Black Coal Miners in America: Race, Class, and Community Conflict, 1780–1980* (Lexington: University Press of Kentucky, 1987), 99; Melvyn Dubofsky and Warren Van Tine, *John L. Lewis: A Biography* (New York: Quadrangle / New York Times Books, 1977), 3–14; Bernstein, *Turbulent Years*, 441–43; McDonald, *Union Man*, 15–19; Hoffman, "Oral History Interview #1 with Pat Fagan," 1–2.

7. Brooks, *As Steel Goes*, 47. On Clarence Irwin and the rank-and-file movement in the Amalgamated Association, see ibid., 46–74; Staughton Lynd, "The Possibility of Radicalism in the Early 1930s: The Case of Steel," in *Workers' Struggles Past and Present: A "Radical America" Reader*, ed. James Green (Philadelphia: Temple University Press, 1983), 190–208.

8. Brooks, *As Steel Goes*, 1–20, 84–88, 95; Powers, *Cradle of Steel Unionism*, 135; Alice M. Hoffman, "The Reminiscences of John J. Mullen . . . : Organizational Activities and Political Efforts of the United Steelworkers of America in Clairton, Penna.," fall 1966 (USWA/OHP); Eric Leif Davin, "The Littlest New Deal: How Democracy and the Union Came to Western Pennsylvania" (paper presented at the annual meeting of the Organization of American Historians, Chicago, Apr. 3, 1992), 22; Ralph Norman Mould, "Steel Strike Town," *Christian Century*, June 23, 1937, 806; Lynd and Lynd, *Rank and File*, 83–86.

9. Lynd and Lynd, *Rank and File*, 85–86; Hoffman, "The Reminiscences of John J. Mullen"; Davin, "The Littlest New Deal," 23–28, 34–36; Len De Caux, *Labor Radical—From the Wobblies to CIO: A Personal History* (Boston: Beacon Press, 1970), 280; John Herling, *Right to Challenge: People and Power in the Steelworkers Union* (New York: Harper and Row, 1972), 224.

10. Powers, *Cradle of Steel Unionism*, 125; E. Robert Livernash et al., *Collective Bargaining in the Basic Steel Industry: A Study of the Public Interest and the Role of Government* (Washington, D.C.: U.S. Department of Labor, 1961), 79–80; Zieger, *John L. Lewis*, xv; Northrup, *Organized Labor and the Negro*, 168; Lewis, *Black Coal Miners in America*, 99–118, quoted on 103, 106; Workers' Bureau, National Urban League, "The Organization of Steel Workers and Its Importance to Negro Labor," Bulletin no. 12, Aug. 7, 1936, folder 1, box 280, Barnett Papers. On the racial practices of the United Mine Workers, in addition to Ronald Lewis's comprehensive study cited earlier, see Spero and Harris, *The Black Worker*, 206–45; Northrup, *Organized Labor and the Negro*, 154–71; Gutman, "The Negro and the United Mine Workers"; Herbert Hill, "Myth-Making as Labor History"; Trotter, *Coal, Class, and Color*, especially 102–19; Daniel Letwin, *The Challenge of Interracial Unionism: Alabama Coal Miners, 1878–1921* (Chapel Hill: University of North Carolina Press, 1998).

11. Workers' Bureau, National Urban League, "The Organization of Steel Workers"; *The Crisis* 43 (September 1936): 273; [Barnett], "Memo for Mr. John A. Stephens."

12. On John P. Davis, see Patricia Sullivan, *Days of Hope: Race and Democracy in the New Deal Era* (Chapel Hill: University of North Carolina Press, 1996), 46–53. According to Davis, the National Negro Congress was a "federation of several hundred organizations, both local and national, both Negro and white, committed to a broad policy of improving the social and economic status of the Negro people." It grew out of a conference at Howard University in May 1935 on the economic status of the Negro. The congress itself was founded in Chicago in February 1936. Its president, until 1940, was A. Philip Randolph, the president of the Brotherhood of Sleeping Car Porters and the nation's leading African American trade unionist. See [John P. Davis], "Proposed Plan for Organization of Negro Steel Workers in Youngstown, Ohio," June 10, 1936, box 20, part 1, National Negro Congress Papers, Schomburg Center for Research in Black Culture, New York Public Library, New York; Cayton and Mitchell, *Black Workers and the New Unions*, 415–24; Lawrence S. Wittner, "The National Negro Congress: A Reassessment," *American Quarterly* 22 (winter 1970): 883–901; Harvard Sitkoff, *A New Deal for Blacks* (New York: Oxford University Press, 1978), 258–60; August Meier and Elliott Rudwick, *Black Detroit and the Rise of the UAW* (New York: Oxford University Press, 1979), 28–29.

13. [John P. Davis], "Proposed Plan"; John P. Davis, " 'Plan Eleven,' " 276.

14. "Statement by Philip Murray"; Bill Gebert, "The Steel Drive and the Tasks of Communists in Mass Organizations," *Party Organizer* 9 (September 1936): 12–15; Roger Keeran, "The International Workers Order and the Origins of the CIO," *Labor History* 30 (summer 1989): 385–408; Max Gordon, "The Communists and the Drive to Organize Steel, 1936," ibid. 23 (spring 1982): 255–56.

15. "Statement by Philip Murray"; Philip S. Foner, *Organized Labor and the Black Worker, 1619–1973* (New York: Praeger, 1974), 220; Adam Lapin, "Negro America Works to Build Steel Union," in *The Black Worker: A Documentary History from Colonial Times to the Present*, ed. Philip S. Foner and Ronald L. Lewis, vol. 7, *The Black Worker from the Founding of the CIO to the AFL-CIO Merger, 1936–1955* (Philadelphia: Temple University Press, 1983), 46–48, first published in *Daily Worker*, Feb. 8, 1937; "Steel," *Opportunity* 15 (May 1937): 133; "Blood for the Cause," *The Crisis* 44 (July 1937): 209; Hank [Johnson] to Ben [Careathers], Feb. 25, 1937, box 10, part 1, National Negro Congress Papers.

16. John P. Davis to Carl Murphy, July 22, 1936, box 6, part 1, National Negro Congress Papers; George S. Schuyler, "Negro Workers Lead in Great Lakes Steel Drive," *Pittsburgh Courier*, July 31, 1937, 1, 14; Philip Bonosky, "The Story of Ben Careathers," *Masses and Mainstream* 6 (July 1953): 34–44; Foner, *Organized Labor and the Black Worker*, 219. On the legendary Henry "Hank" Johnson, see Stephen Brier, "Labor, Politics, and Race: A Black Worker's Life," *Labor History* 23 (summer 1982): 416–21; Halpern, *Down on the Killing Floor*, 137–38, 168, 196–98; Horowitz, *"Negro and White,"* 71–72, 128–33, 135.

17. Gordon, "The Communists," quoted on 254; De Caux, *Labor Radical*, 269, 270.

18. Brody, "The Origins of Modern Steel Unionism," 21; Mary Heaton Vorse, *Labor's New Millions* (New York: Modern Age Books, 1938), 111–17; "It Happened in Steel," *Fortune* 15 (May 1937): 91–94, 176, 179–80; Galenson, *The CIO Challenge*, 91–96; Bernstein, *Turbulent Years*, 466–73; Livernash et al., *Collective Bargaining*, 61; Richard M. Locke and Ann C. Frost, "The Paradox of Politics: Local Unions and Workplace Change in the U.S. Steel Industry" (Cambridge, Mass., n.d.), 7.

19. Cayton and Mitchell, *Black Workers and the New Unions*, 216–17; *Chicago Defender*, June 5, 1937, national edition, 3. On the Little Steel Strike, see Benjamin Stolberg, *The Story of the CIO* (New York: Viking Press, 1938), 80–115; Brooks, *As Steel Goes*, 130–52; Galenson, *The CIO Challenge*, 96–109; Bernstein, *Turbulent Years*, 478–97; James L. Baughman, "Classes and Company Towns: Legends of the 1937 Little Steel Strike," *Ohio History* 87 (spring 1978): 175–92.

20. "Negro and White Stick—Steel Lockout Fails," in *The Black Worker*, ed. Foner and Lewis, 7: 45, first published in *Daily Worker*, Jan. 12, 1937; Schuyler, "Negro Workers Lead," 14.

21. George S. Schuyler, "Schuyler Visits Steel Centers in Ohio and Pennsylvania; Finds Race Workers Loyal to Companies; Making Big Money," *Pittsburgh Courier*, July 24, 1937, 1, 14.

22. Morawska, *For Bread with Butter*, 160; Schuyler, "Schuyler Visits Steel Centers," 1, 14; Richard B. Sherman, "Johnstown vs. the Negro: Southern

Migrants and the Exodus of 1923," *Pennsylvania History* 30 (October 1963): 454–64.

23. Nelson Lichtenstein, *Labor's War at Home: The CIO in World War II* (New York: Cambridge University Press, 1982), 14; Thomas A. Van Evera to John L. Lewis, Aug. 18, 1938, BVLHS; Harold J. Ruttenberg and Stanley Ruttenberg, "Live Steel—Dead Jobs," *New Republic*, Oct. 14, 1940, 519.

24. Brooks, *As Steel Goes*, 162; Norrell, "Caste in Steel," 675; Stein, "Southern Workers in National Unions," 189–91; Hinshaw, "Dialectic of Division," 61–64, Powell quoted on 63. See also Barbara Warne Newell, *Chicago and the Labor Movement: Metropolitan Unionism in the 1930's* (Urbana: University of Illinois Press, 1961), 144–46.

25. Greer, "Racism and U.S. Steel," 55; Cook, quoted in Harold Preece, "CIO Means Something to Us, Say Chicago's Leading Negroes," *Sunday Worker*, Jan. 28, 1940, sec. 2, 2.

26. Drake and Cayton, *Black Metropolis*, 326, 338, 330; Cayton and Mitchell, *Black Workers and the New Unions*, 218.

27. Gunnar Myrdal, *An American Dilemma: The Negro Problem and American Democracy* (New York: Harper and Brothers, 1944), 587; Morton T. Elder, "Labor and Race Relations in the South: A Report to the Southern Regional Council," Oct. 1956, quoted on 24, box 108, Fund for the Republic Papers, Seeley G. Mudd Manuscript Library, Princeton University, Princeton, N.J.; Nelson, "Organized Labor," 979–81; Boyle, "The Kiss"; Gerald Zahavi, "Passionate Commitments: Race, Sex, and Communism at Schenectady General Electric, 1932–1954," *Journal of American History* 83 (September 1996): 514–48; George S. Schuyler, "Firestone Plant like Heaven Now, Says Akron Worker; Inter-Racial Union Picnic Symbolizes New Labor Deal," *Pittsburgh Courier*, Aug. 28, 1937, 14.

28. Congress of Industrial Organizations, *The CIO and the Negro Worker: Together for Victory* (Washington, D.C., 1942), 10, folder 7, box 280, Barnett Papers; Fraser, *Labor Will Rule*, 349–432. See also Fraser, "The 'Labor Question' "; Bayor, *Neighbors in Conflict*, 87–108; Nelson Lichtenstein, *The Most Dangerous Man*, 74–131.

29. Drake and Cayton, *Black Metropolis*, 332.

30. Ibid., 332–33.

31. Melvyn Dubofsky, "Not So 'Turbulent Years': Another Look at the American 1930s," *Amerikastudien* 24 (January 1979): 5–20; Peter Friedlander, *The Emergence of a UAW Local, 1936–1939: A Study in Class and Culture* (Pittsburgh: University of Pittsburgh Press, 1975); Cayton and Mitchell, *Black Workers and the New Unions*, quoted on 221. It is important to emphasize that although southern white migrants added to the volatility of race relations during World War II, they were not the sole, or even the main, cause of the backlash against African American migrants. In his article on postwar Detroit, Thomas Sugrue identifies new immigrants as the key source of hostility toward

black aspirations, and he declares that "although southern whites were frequently blamed for racial tension in the city, their role was greatly exaggerated." Sugrue, "Crabgrass-Roots Politics," 558. See also James N. Gregory, "Southernizing the American Working Class: Post-war Episodes of Regional and Class Transformation," *Labor History* 39 (May 1998): 135–54, especially 144–45.

32. Bernstein, *Turbulent Years*, 727–33; Hinshaw, "Dialectic of Division," 63; USWA, "Proceedings of the International Executive Board," Sept. 21–23, 1943, 318, folder 8, box 41, International Executive Board (IEB) Proceedings, USWA, HCLA/PSU; *Pittsburgh Courier*, May 30, 1942, 1, 4; Livernash et al., *Collective Bargaining*, 81–82.

33. Murray's statement to the 1944 CIO convention, quoted in Drake and Cayton, *Black Metropolis*, 341.

34. The term "class-essentialist" is Robert Zieger's in *The CIO*, 158.

35. George L.-P. Weaver, "The Stake of Organized Labor and the Negro in the Post-war Period" (speech to the Southern Negro Youth Congress, Atlanta, Dec. 3, 1944), folder 7, box 280, Barnett Papers; Philip Murray, "Modernizing Postwar America," *Opportunity* 23 (October–December 1945): 202 (emphasis added); Walter Reuther, "The Negro Worker's Future," ibid., 206.

36. Congress of Industrial Organizations, *The CIO and the Negro Worker*, 10; Drake and Cayton, *Black Metropolis*, 341; USWA, "Proceedings of the International Executive Board," Sept. 21–23, 1943, 334–35.

37. "Report of the United Steelworkers of America Committee on Civil Rights," Jan. 28, 1949, 12, folder 23, box 3, Civil Rights Department, USWA; Zieger, *The CIO*, 155–61.

38. USWA, "Proceedings of the International Executive Board," May 5, 1944, 94–95, box 41, IEB Proceedings, USWA; Dennis C. Dickerson, "Wilson, Boyd L.," in *Biographical Dictionary of American Labor*, ed. Gary Fink, 2d ed. (Westport, Conn.: Greenwood Press, 1984), 586–87; *Pittsburgh Courier*, May 30, 1942, 1, 4; "The Old Members Won't Forget! . . . The New Members Shouldn't Forget!" *Steel Labor*, June 1961, 20; Schuyler, "Negro Workers Lead," 14; Preece, "CIO Means Something to Us"; Foner, *Organized Labor and the Black Worker*, 263; Jack Spiese, "An Interview with Boyd Wilson," Oct. 23, 1967 (USWA/OHP), 1–6.

39. United Steelworkers of America, *Proceedings of the Fourth Constitutional Convention* (Boston, May 11–15, 1948), 226–27; USWA, Committee on Civil Rights, *The Steel Problem on Civil Rights* (n.p., [1950]), 14, folder 1, box 29, District 31 Papers, USWA, Chicago Historical Society; Spiese, "An Interview with Boyd Wilson," 9–12, quoted on 12. Not surprisingly, Frank Shane's recollection was quite different. In 1967 he recalled that when Murray informed him of his appointment, "he said, and I quote him, 'Francis, I am asking you to take this position because I feel that you believe in the cause of social

justice and civil rights. . . . But make no mistake[,] you will probably be the most misunderstood and one of the most disliked people in our international office for a long time.' " "Statement by Francis C. Shane," Pittsburgh, Pa., May 23, 1967 (in author's possession, courtesy of John Hoerr).

40. Spiese, "An Interview with Boyd Wilson," 12.

41. United Steelworkers of America, *Proceedings of the Fifth Constitutional Convention* (Atlantic City, N.J., May 9–12, 1950), 164–73.

42. Francis C. Shane to David J. McDonald ("Re: Report of United Steelworkers of America Committee on Civil Rights, January 1, 1952 through December 31, 1952"), Jan. 1, 1953, folder 11, box 5, Civil Rights Department, USWA; David J. McDonald to Boyd L. Wilson, Aug. 9, 1956, folder 15, box 7, ibid.; "Report of the United Steelworkers," 3, 4; Murray, quoted in United Steelworkers of America, *Proceedings of the Fifth Constitutional Convention,* 166; United Steelworkers of America, "Report of Officers to the Eighth Constitutional Convention" (Los Angeles, Sept. 17–21, 1956), 82–102, quoted on 82, 84.

43. USWA, Committee on Civil Rights, *The Steel Problem,* 15; Francis C. Shane to Roy Wilkins, Jan. 9, 1950, folder 7, box 1, Civil Rights Department, USWA; Shane to McDonald, Jan. 1, 1953; *Pittsburgh Courier,* Sept. 14, 1954, cited in Hinshaw, "Dialectic of Division," 248; United Steelworkers of America, *Proceedings of the Seventh Constitutional Convention* (Atlantic City, N.J., Sept. 20–24, 1954), 163.

44. Committee on Civil Rights, United Steelworkers of America, *Steelworkers Fight for Human Equality* (n.p., n.d.), 9, folder on civil rights, box 29, District 31 Papers, USWA; "Report of the United Steelworkers," 12; USWA, Committee on Civil Rights, *The Steel Problem,* 15; N. A. Zonarich to David J. McDonald, June 8, 1954, folder 52, box 7, Civil Rights Department, USWA.

45. "Report of the United Steelworkers," 12, 14; "Remarks of David J. McDonald," Philadelphia, Feb. 19, 1950, folder 24, box 3, Civil Rights Department, USWA.

46. David J. McDonald, I. W. Abel, and James G. Thimmes, "To All USA District Directors, Staff Representatives and Local Union Recording Secretaries" ("Re: Union Policy against Racial Discrimination in Plants"), Aug. 31, 1954, folder 52, box 7, Civil Rights Department, USWA; Paul E. Schremp to Thomas Shane, Mar. 19, 1950, folder 21, box 3, ibid.

47. J. Thomas Watson to Thomas Shane, Mar. 10, 1950, ibid.

48. Harry H. Powell to Thomas Shane, Mar. 14, 1950, ibid.; Jerome Wilczewski to Thomas Shane, Mar. 14, 1950, ibid.; Joe Cook to Thomas Shane, Mar. 6, 1950, ibid.

49. Herbert Hill to Roy Wilkins ("Memorandum Re: United States Steel Corporation and United Steelworkers of America, AFL-CIO[,] Birmingham, Alabama"), Sept. 13, 1965, box A195, group 3, NAACP Papers. On the pat-

tern of racial discrimination in the Birmingham-Bessemer area, see Norrell, "Caste in Steel."

50. Charles Alford to Thomas Shane, Mar. 12, 1950, folder 21, box 3, Civil Rights Department, USWA; Jack Greenberg et al., "In the Supreme Court of the United States, October Term, 1981, Pullman-Standard, a Division of Pullman Incorporated, Petitioner, no. 80–1190, United Steelworkers of America, AFL-CIO and Local 1466, United Steelworkers of America, AFL-CIO, Petitioners, no. 80–1193, v. Louis Swint and Willie Johnson et al, . . . Brief for Respondents," [1981], Personal Papers of Herbert Hill, Madison, Wisc.

51. Herbert Hill to Wilkins, Sept. 13, 1965; Herbert Hill, "Black Workers," 309–13; Norrell, "Caste in Steel."

52. Joseph Bazdar to Thomas Shane, Mar. 9, 1950, folder 21, box 3, Civil Rights Department, USWA.

53. Thomas Shane to "All Local Union Presidents, Directors and Staff Representatives," Feb. 17, 1950; Harold E. Park to Thomas Shane, Feb. 27, 1950; Cornice C. Milton to Thomas Shane, Feb. 28, 1950; Carl Jones to Thomas Shane, Feb. 28, 1950; Harry Wallis to Thomas Shane, Feb. 20, 1950; George Hill to Thomas Shane, Mar. 7, 1950. All in folder 21, box 3, Civil Rights Department, USWA.

54. Ambrose Airaudi to Thomas Shane, Mar. 9, 1950; Carl Hartie to Thomas Shane, Mar. 13, 1950; Velma Garren to Thomas Shane, Feb. 20, 1950; Orlando Anness to Thomas Shane, Mar. 13, 1950; Ray Matthews to Thomas Shane, Feb. 25, 1950; Jesse C. Walters to Thomas Shane, Feb. 21, 1950; James H. McElfresh to Thomas Shane, Mar. 7, 1950; Larry Laughlin to Thomas Shane, Mar. 8, 1950; Robert Harter to Thomas Shane, Feb. 28, 1950. All in folder 21, box 3, Civil Rights Department, USWA.

55. Harry Doty to Thomas Shane, Mar. 8, 1950, ibid.; Powell to Shane, Mar. 14, 1950.

56. Sam Camens to Tom Shane, Mar. 10, 1950, folder 21, box 3, Civil Rights Department, USWA.

57. USWA, Committee on Civil Rights, *The Steel Problem*, 15–17.

58. McCallum, "Songs of Work," 26–27.

59. "Notes on a Meeting Held Saturday Morning, July 10, 1943, in Office of Noel R. Beddow, B'ham, Ala.," box A4-2, Philip Murray Papers, Department of Archives and Manuscripts, Catholic University of America, Washington, D.C.; Vernon H. Jensen, *Nonferrous Metals Industry Unionism, 1932–1954*, Cornell Studies in Industrial and Labor Relations, 5 (Ithaca, N.Y.: Cornell University Press, 1954), 233–45; Arthur W. Hepner, "Union War in Birmingham," *Reporter*, July 5, 1949, 12–14; Horace Huntley, "The Red Scare and Black Workers in Alabama: The International Union of Mine, Mill, and Smelter Workers, 1945–53," in *Labor Divided: Race and Ethnicity in United*

States Labor Struggles, 1835–1960, ed. Robert Asher and Charles Stephenson (Albany: State University of New York Press, 1990), 129–45; Zieger, *The CIO,* 281–82; Alan Draper, "The New Southern Labor History Revisited: The Success of the Mine, Mill, and Smelter Workers Union in Birmingham, 1934–1938," *Journal of Southern History* 62 (February 1996): 87–108.

60. For a beautiful evocation of the family and community lives of African American women in Bessemer, see Deborah E. McDowell, *Leaving Pipe Shop: Memories of Kin* (New York: Scribner, 1996).

61. Miles Otwell et al. to Philip Murray, July 25, 1946, box A4-78, Murray Papers.

62. James G. Thimmes to Philip Murray, "Memorandum" ("Re: Conditions Affecting Our Union and Our Relationships with the Tennessee Coal, Iron and Railroad Co., at Birmingham, Alabama"), Apr. 19, 1951, box A4-87, ibid.; J. J. Lindsay to Philip Murray, July 22, 1951, and other letters praising Strevel's work at TCI, ibid.; Norrell, "Caste in Steel," 684–88, quoted on 687; Stein, "Southern Workers in National Unions," 202–6; remarks of [James?] Ward, District 37, "United Steelworkers of America Conference on Fair Employment Practices," Pittsburgh, Pa., Sept. 29, 1953, folder 10, box 5, Civil Rights Department, USWA.

63. Herbert Hill, interview by author, Madison, Wisc., Aug. 19–21, 1994; Herbert Hill to John L. Yanc[e]ly, Mar. 10, 1952, box A586, group 2, NAACP Papers; "Biographical Sketch of Herbert Hill," ibid.; Herbert Hill to August Meier, Mar. 26, 1990 (in author's possession, courtesy of Herbert Hill); Constance Webb, *Richard Wright: A Biography* (New York: Putnam, 1968), 397; Michael Harrington, *Fragments of the Century* (New York: Saturday Review Press, 1973), 97–98.

64. Karen Budd, "An Interview with Jimmy Jones," Philadelphia, May 4, 1971 (USWA/OHP), 27; Herbert Hill, "Confidential Memorandum to: Mr. Walter White[,] Re: Birmingham Bessemer Area CIO NAACP Relations," May 8–17, 1953, folder 27, box 6, Civil Rights Department, USWA.

65. USWA, International Executive Board, "Proceedings," Mar. 2–4, 1955, 353–55, box 45, IEB Proceedings, USWA; J. F. Vance to W. H. Crawford, Feb. 22, 1926, box 4, District 36 Papers, USWA, HCLA/PSU; J. F. Vance to W. H. Crawford, [Feb. 1926], ibid.; Margaret Tinney to William Crawford, Mar. 10, 1942, ibid.; W. H. Crawford to David J. McDonald, Mar. 5, 1942, folder 12, box 44, USWA—President's Office: David J. McDonald (hereafter, USWA/McDonald), USWA, HCLA/PSU; "Atlanta and Labor Lose a Very Good Friend," *Atlanta Constitution,* Dec. 21, 1954, 4; Congress of Industrial Organizations, *Proceedings of the Sixteenth Constitutional Convention* (Los Angeles, Dec. 6–10, 1954), 387; W. H. Crawford to David J. McDonald, Dec. 4, 1953, folder 52, box 7, Civil Rights Department, USWA. On the sharply limited role of black staff members and organizers in the district, see W. H.

Crawford to David J. McDonald, Feb. 4, 1946, folder 13, box 44, USWA/ McDonald; W. H. Crawford to David J. McDonald, Feb. 26, 1946, ibid.; W. H. Crawford to David J. McDonald, Aug. 31, 1950, folder 15, ibid. See also Philip Taft, *Organizing Dixie: Alabama Workers in the Industrial Era* (Westport, Conn.: Greenwood Press, 1981), 98, 100, 106. Taft incorrectly identified Crawford as a native Alabamian.

66. Harris, *The Harder We Run*, 128; Julius A. Thomas to Louis Mason, Jr. ("Subj.: Field Visit—Cleveland, Ohio, July 23–24, 1951"), Oct. 23, 1951, box 11, series 4, group 1, National Urban League Papers; Sterling Tucker to Julius A. Thomas ("Subj.: Summary Statements of Information about Employment Needs of Major Companies Included in Field Reports of Mr. Louis Mason, Jr."), Jan. 21, 1952, ibid.

67. Paul A. Tiffany, *The Decline of American Steel: How Management, Labor, and Government Went Wrong* (New York: Oxford University Press, 1988), 27; Mark McColloch, "Modest but Adequate: Standard of Living for Mon Valley Steelworkers in the Union Era" (1995), 8–11; Stein, "Southern Workers in National Unions," 200–201; USWA, *Proceedings of the Seventh Constitutional Convention*, 164. McColloch points out that a modest standard of living was very modest indeed. The Bureau of Labor Statistics "envisioned a family of four, living in a rented apartment, consisting of a kitchen, bath, and three other rooms. The family had hot running water and owned a washing machine" but "did not own a car and there was no money in the budget for any vacation." McColloch, "Modest but Adequate," 5–6. See also David Dempsey, "Steelworkers: Not Today's Wage, Tomorrow's Security," in *American Labor Since the New Deal*, ed. Dubofsky, 192–201, first published in *New York Times Magazine*, Aug. 7, 1949.

68. Louis Mason, Jr., to Julius A. Thomas ("Subj.: Field Visit: Baltimore, Maryland—July 11–13, 1951"), Aug. 14, 1951, box 11, series 4, group 1, National Urban League Papers; Louis Mason, Jr., to Julius A. Thomas ("Subj.: Field Report—Youngstown, Ohio—October 8, 1951"), Dec. 18, 1951, ibid.; USWA, *Proceedings of the Seventh Constitutional Convention*, 170. See also Hinshaw, "Dialectic of Division," 218–33.

69. Warner Bloomberg, Jr., "Five Hot Days in Gary, Indiana," *Reporter*, Aug. 11, 1955, 38. In July 1955 Bloomberg, who was both a steelworker and a sociologist at the University of Chicago, attended a mass meeting in Gary on the eve of what many thought would be a nationwide steel strike; he reported that the meeting attracted "some three hundred of Gary's thirty-five thousand millhands."

70. Elder, "Labor and Race Relations," 12; Crawford to McDonald, Dec. 4, 1953; Herbert Hill, "Confidential Memorandum To: Mr. Walter White[,] Re: Birmingham Bessemer Area CIO NAACP Relations."

CHAPTER SIX
"WE ARE DETERMINED TO SECURE JUSTICE NOW": STEELWORKERS
AND CIVIL RIGHTS (II)

The quote in the chapter title is by unnamed members of Local 1033 to "President Xavier Smykowski and the [Local] Executive Board," n.d., attached to Joseph P. Molony to Joseph Germano, Aug. 23, 1966, folder 6, box 178, Records of District 31, United Steelworkers of America, Chicago Historical Society.

1. See, especially, Todd Gitlin, *The Twilight of Common Dreams: Why America Is Wracked by Culture Wars* (New York: Metropolitan Books, 1995); Michael Tomasky, *Left for Dead: The Life, Death, and Possible Resurrection of Progressive Politics in America* (New York: Free Press, 1996); and Robin D. G. Kelley's critique of Gitlin, Tomasky, et al. in *Yo Mama's Disfunktional! Fighting the Culture Wars in Urban America* (Boston: Beacon Press, 1997), 103–24.

2. Judith Stein, "History of an Idea," *Nation*, Dec. 14, 1998, 13; Stein, "Southern Workers in National Unions," quoted on 207. Stein develops this argument at much greater length in *Running Steel, Running America: Race, Economic Policy, and the Decline of Liberalism* (Chapel Hill: University of North Carolina Press, 1998).

3. Melvyn Dubofsky, *The State and Labor in Modern America* (Chapel Hill: University of North Carolina Press, 1994), quoted on 225.

4. Drake and Cayton, *Black Metropolis*, 338.

5. See Kelley, *Yo Mama's Disfunktional!* 109, and Zachary Lockman, *Comrades and Enemies: Arab and Jewish Workers in Palestine, 1906–1948* (Berkeley: University of California Press, 1996), 361–62.

6. Stein, "Southern Workers in National Unions," quoted on 211. The experience of the United Steelworkers clearly contradicts the argument of historians Numan Bartley and Alan Draper that southern white workers relied on unions to defend their "class" interests and on organizations such as the White Citizens Councils to protect their "caste" interests. For white steelworkers, especially but not exclusively in the South, their caste and class interests were closely intertwined. See Numan V. Bartley, *The Rise of Massive Resistance: Race and Politics in the South during the 1950s* (Baton Rouge: Louisiana State University Press, 1969), 305–12, especially 310; Alan Draper, *Conflict of Interests: Organized Labor and the Civil Rights Movement in the South, 1954–1968* (Ithaca, N.Y.: ILR Press, 1994), 166.

7. E. T. Earp et al. to Philip Murray, June 12, 1950, folder 13, box 3, Civil Rights Department, USWA.

8. Arthur J. Goldberg to "All CIO Regional Directors and CIO Industrial Union Councils" ("Subject: Segregated Facilities in CIO Offices and Halls"),

Apr. 24, 1950, folder 26, box 5, ibid.; R. E. Farr to Philip Murray, May 19, 1950, folder 13, box 3, ibid.

9. Earp et al. to Murray, June 12, 1950.

10. Norrell, "Caste in Steel," 685; Herbert Hill, "Confidential Memorandum to: Mr. Walter White."

11. Farr to Murray; Francis C. Shane to R. E. Farr, Dec. 19, 1949, folder 13, box 3, Civil Rights Department, USWA; Francis C. Shane to Philip Murray, May 23, 1950, ibid.; Francis C. Shane to R. E. Farr, June 19, 1953, folder 27, box 6, ibid.; Francis C. Shane to R. E. Farr, Apr. 29, 1954, ibid.

12. Robert J. Norrell, "Labor Trouble: George Wallace and Union Politics in Alabama," in *Organized Labor in the Twentieth-Century South*, ed. Zieger, 258; "Report of O. L. Garrison on Investigation Made at Direction of President McDonald in District #36 with Regard to Segregation Issue," Apr. 16, 1956, folder 3, box 140, USWA/McDonald; Alton Hornsby, Jr., "A City That Was Too Busy to Hate: Atlanta Businessmen and Desegregation," in *Southern Businessmen and Desegregation*, ed. Elizabeth Jacoway and David Colburn (Baton Rouge: Louisiana State University Press 1982), 120–36; Draper, *Conflict of Interests*, 28; Elder, "Labor and Race Relations," 10–11.

13. "Report of O. L. Garrison"; John Broome, "Regarding the Appeal by Colored Members of Local 309," n.d., folder 52, box 7, Civil Rights Department, USWA; Howard Strevel, remarks, "United Steelworkers of America Conference on Fair Employment Practices," Pittsburgh, Pa., Sept. 29, 1953, folder 10, box 5, ibid.

14. Chamberlain, "The Steelworkers," 210; McDonald, *Union Man*, 15; Herling, *Right to Challenge*, 23, 133.

15. McDonald, *Union Man*, 15–33; Robert H. Zieger, "Leadership and Bureaucracy in the Late CIO," *Labor History* 31 (summer 1990): 253–70, quoted on 256, 258–59; Herling, *Right to Challenge*, 2, 25, 42; Eisenhower, quoted in Tiffany, *The Decline of American Steel*, 147.

16. Herling, *Right to Challenge*, 96–100, 133; John A. Orr, "The Rise and Fall of Steel's Human Relations Committee," *Labor History* 14 (winter 1973): 69–82; Local Union 1013 to David J. McDonald, June 12, 1963, box 49, USWA/McDonald.

17. "Plant Visitation: B. F. Fairless, D. J. McDonald, and Party, Youngstown District Works, January 13, 1954" (in author's possession, courtesy of Agnes Griffin); Herling, *Right to Challenge*, 25, 97, 99; De Caux, *Labor Radical*, 409.

18. David L. Stebenne, *Arthur J. Goldberg: New Deal Liberal* (New York: Oxford University Press, 1996), 100; Allen J. Matusow, *The Unraveling of America: A History of Liberalism in the 1960s* (New York: Harper and Row, 1984), 3–21; John Hoerr, notes on Francis C. Shane press conference, May 23, 1967 (in author's possession, courtesy of John Hoerr).

19. John G. Deedy, Jr., "Civil Rights and the Steelworkers," *America*, May 6, 1961, quoted on 251; Boyd Wilson to David J. McDonald ("Re: Survey on

Fair Employment Practices in the Steel Industry and the United Steelworkers of America"), May 14, 1959, folder 3, box 166, USWA/McDonald; United Steelworkers of America, District no. 26, "An Introduction to District 26. . . . United Steelworkers of America, 27 Years of Progress, 1936–1963," folder 32, box 48, ibid.; Francis C. Shane to "All Members USA Committee on Civil Rights," [Apr. 1961], folder 9, box 6, Howard R. Hague Papers, USWA, HCLA/PSU; Francis C. Shane to David J. McDonald, Dec. 9, 1964, folder 6, box 27, USWA/McDonald. In a January 1965 letter to McDonald, Shane stated: "[W]e have 649 committees on file out of 2,725 local unions in the United States. This is only 23.8% of the total." Francis C. Shane to David J. McDonald, ibid.

20. Francis C. Shane to Alfred Baker Lewis, Feb. 3, 1953, folder 38, box 6, Civil Rights Department, USWA; Hinshaw, "Dialectic of Division," 219.

21. Joseph Neal et al. to David J. McDonald ("Memorandum Re: Civil Rights Program of the United Steelworkers of America"), Sept. 14, 1960, folder 8, box 6, Hague Papers.

22. Walter A. Jackson, *Gunnar Myrdal and America's Conscience: Social Engineering and Racial Liberalism, 1938–1987* (Chapel Hill: University of North Carolina Press, 1990), 172–211; Lewis, quoted in Alan B. Batchelder, "Decline in the Relative Income of Negro Men," *Quarterly Journal of Economics* 78 (November 1964): 526. Jackson's *Gunnar Myrdal and America's Conscience* is indispensable for understanding liberal attitudes toward race in the postwar era. Nicholas Lemann, in *The Promised Land: The Great Black Migration and How It Changed America* (New York: Alfred A. Knopf, 1991), 113–17, effectively conveys the failure of liberal opinion makers and policy elites to understand the crisis that was brewing in northern cities as the Great Migration accelerated.

23. Joseph Chapman and R. R. Jefferson, report on interview with "Mr. Alfred Rebollo, Staff Representative, United Steel Workers, CIO," July 30 1948, box 19, series 4, group 1, National Urban League Papers; "Gary Turns Her Back on Bias," *Ebony* 11 (July 1956): 17–20, 22–23; Warner Bloomberg, Jr., "They'll Go Democratic Anyway: The Negro in Gary, Indiana," *New Republic*, Oct. 15, 1956, 13–15; Mohl and Betten, *Steel City*, 59, 79.

24. Bloomberg, "They'll Go Democratic Anyway," 14; Warner Bloomberg, Jr., "The State of the American Proletariat, 1955: Working Day and Living Time in Gary, Indiana," *Commentary* 19 (March 1955): 212–13; Foner, *Organized Labor and the Black Worker*, 326–27.

25. Ben C. Cashaw, "An Open Inquiry to E. G. Grace, Chairman of the Board of Directors, A. B. Homer, President of the Bethlehem Steel Company, David J. McDonald, President of USWA, Eugene Morris, Director of District 13[,] and the Local Union[s] of District 13," [1955], box 19, series 4, group 1, National Urban League Papers; "Heritage: A Black History of Johnstown," *The Tribune-Democrat*, Feb. 12, 1980, 7–9.

26. Lemann, *The Promised Land*, 53–71; Harold M. Baron and Bennett Hymer, "The Negro Worker in the Chicago Labor Market: A Case Study of De Facto Segregation," in *The Negro and the American Labor Movement*, ed. Julius Jacobson (New York: Doubleday, 1968), 232–85; Gavin Wright, *Old South, New South: Revolutions in the Southern Economy Since the Civil War* (New York: Basic Books, 1986), 241–47.

27. Halpern, *Down on the Killing Floor*, 167–68, 247–49, quoted on 249; Thomas N. Maloney and Warren C. Whatley, "Making the Effort: The Contours of Racial Discrimination in Detroit's Labor Markets, 1920–1940," *Journal of Economic History* 55 (September 1995): 465–93; Thomas J. Sugrue, "The Structures of Urban Poverty: The Reorganization of Space and Work in Three Periods of American History," in *The "Underclass" Debate*, ed. Katz, 100–109; Thomas J. Sugrue, " 'Forget about Your Inalienable Right to Work': Deindustrialization and Its Discontents at Ford, 1950–1953," *International Labor and Working-Class History* 48 (fall 1995): 112–30; Matthew A. Kessler, "Economic Status of Nonwhite Workers, 1955–62," *Monthly Labor Review* 86 (July 1963): 78; Harris, *The Harder We Run*, 127–33.

28. Hirsch, *Making the Second Ghetto*, 68–99, 171–211; Arnold R. Hirsch, "Massive Resistance in the Urban North: Trumbull Park, Chicago, 1953–1966," *Journal of American History* 82 (September 1995): 522–50; McGreevy, *Parish Boundaries*, 79–110. See also Frank London Brown, *Trumbull Park: A Novel* (Chicago: Regnery, 1959), an extraordinary, and chilling, insider's account by a black tenant.

29. United Packinghouse Workers vice-president Russell Lasley, quoted in Congress of Industrial Organizations, *Proceedings of the Sixteenth Constitutional Convention*, 389; Charles Spencer, *Blue Collar: An Internal Examination of the Workplace* (Chicago: Lakeside Charter Books, 1977), 87. Herbert Hill also acknowledged that "members of various trade unions, including some in the Steelworkers' Union," were among the rioters at Trumbull Park. USWA, *Proceedings of the Seventh Constitutional Convention*, 164.

30. Hirsch, *Making the Second Ghetto*, 171–211, quoted on 187, 171, 186, 196; Thurgood Marshall's appeal for the "striking down of race" is quoted in Hugh Davis Graham, *The Civil Rights Era: Origins and Development of National Policy, 1960–1972* (New York: Oxford University Press, 1990), 370.

31. Horace R. Cayton, interview by Herbert Hill, New York, Nov. 19, 1955, quoted in Herbert Hill, "The Problem of Race," 199; Robert H. Zieger, "George Meany: Labor's Organization Man," in *Labor Leaders in America*, ed. Dubofsky and Van Tine, 334, 342–44; Harvard Sitkoff, *The Struggle for Black Equality, 1954–1980* (New York: Hill and Wang, 1981), 23, 37–39, 83–85.

32. Meany, quoted in Jervis Anderson, *A. Philip Randolph: A Biographical Portrait* (1973; reprint, Berkeley: University of California Press, 1986), 302; Oliver Montgomery, interview, Oct. 22, 1990; James C. Davis, interview by author, Niles, Ohio, Feb. 18, 1989; "Negro Pressure on Unions," *Business*

Week, Apr. 30, 1960, 139; Paula F. Pfeffer, *A. Philip Randolph: Pioneer of the Civil Rights Movement* (Baton Rouge: Louisiana State University Press, 1990), 218. Randolph was referring to the wave of student-led sit-ins in restaurants and other public accommodations that began in Greensboro, North Carolina, in February 1960 and spread like wildfire across much of the South.

33. Roy Wilkins to A. Philip Randolph, Feb. 6, 1959, Personal Papers of Herbert Hill; Herbert Hill, "The ILGWU—Fact and Fiction: A Reply to Gus Tyler," *New Politics* 2 (winter 1963): 8; Will Herberg, "The Old-Timers and the Newcomers: Ethnic Group Relations in a Needle Trades Union," *Journal of Social Issues* 9 (1953): 12–19; Herbert Hill, "Race, Ethnicity, and Organized Labor," 53–54.

34. Herbert Hill, "Race, Ethnicity, and Organized Labor," 55; *New York Times*, July 8, 1962, 66, Sept. 20, 1962, 23.

35. *New York Times*, Oct. 12, 1962, 20, Oct. 19, 1962, 15, Nov. 10, 1962, 1, 13; Herbert Hill, "The ILGWU," 26; Roy Wilkins to Emanuel Muravchik, Oct. 31, 1962, Personal Papers of Herbert Hill. On the development of the controversy between the ILGWU and the NAACP, see also Herbert Hill, "The ILGWU Today: The Decay of a Labor Union," *New Politics* 1 (summer 1962): 6–17; Gus Tyler, "The Truth about the ILGWU," ibid. 2 (fall 1962): 6–17; Herbert Hill, "The ILGWU," 7–27. For an early attempt at a dispassionate summation, see Ray Marshall, *The Negro and Organized Labor* (New York: John Wiley and Sons, 1965), 73–79.

36. *New York Times*, Oct. 12, 1962, 20; Wilkins to Muravchik, Oct. 31, 1962; Roy Wilkins to George Meany, Dec. 7, 1962, Personal Papers of Herbert Hill; Peter B. Levy, *The New Left and Labor in the 1960s* (Urbana: University of Illinois Press, 1994), 20; *Atlanta Daily World*, Nov. 23, 1962, 5.

37. For a fuller treatment of events at Atlantic Steel, see Bruce Nelson, " 'CIO Meant One Thing for the Whites and Another Thing for Us': Steelworkers and Civil Rights, 1936–1974," in *Southern Labor in Transition*, ed. Zieger, 112–45.

38. Glenn W. Gilman and James W. Sweeney, *Atlantic Steel Company and United Steelworkers of America: A Case Study*, Causes of Industrial Peace under Collective Bargaining, Case Study no. 12 (Washington, D.C.: National Planning Association, 1953), 1–22.

39. Joseph A. Rabun to David J. McDonald, [Nov. 1955], folder 31, box 718, District 35 Records, 1940–73, United Steelworkers of America, SLA/GSU; Rayfield Mooty to Frank Shane, Aug. 31, 1955, folder 53, box 7, Civil Rights Department, USWA; *Atlanta Constitution*, Oct. 4, 1955, 4. On the Till case, see Stephen J. Whitfield, *A Death in the Delta: The Story of Emmett Till* (New York: Free Press, 1988).

40. Rabun to McDonald. There is a brief portrait of Rabun in John Egerton, *Speak Now Against the Day: The Generation Before the Civil Rights Movement in the South* (New York: Alfred A. Knopf, 1994), 423–24.

41. Rabun to McDonald, [Nov. 1955]; Lorne H. Nelles to David J. McDonald, Dec, 14, 1955, folder 31, box 718, District 35 Papers, 1940–73. Crawford died in December 1954 and was succeeded by Lorne Nelles as district director.

42. Report of Labor and Industry Committee, [Atlanta Branch, NAACP], Apr. 7, 1957, Personal Papers of Herbert Hill; "Memorandum to Mr. Wilkins from Herbert Hill: Re: The Atlantic Steel Company, Atlanta, Georgia," May 27, 1958, box A184, group 3, NAACP Papers.

43. U.S. Commission on Civil Rights, *Employment: 1961 Commission on Civil Rights Report* (Washington, D.C.: U.S. Government Printing Office, 1961), 137.

44. Herbert Hill to Boyd L. Wilson, Aug. 1, 1957, Personal Papers of Herbert Hill.

45. Herbert Hill to J. H. Calhoun, Aug. 6, 1958, ibid.; Nathaniel Brown et al. to President's Committee on Equal Employment Opportunity, Sept. 11, 1961, ibid.; U.S. Commission on Civil Rights, *Employment*, 136–37; Gilman and Sweeney, *Atlantic Steel Company*, 62–66; Wilbur F. Glenn to United Steelworkers of America, June 17, 1959, box A195, group 3, NAACP Papers; David E. Feller to Roy Wilkins, Nov. 9, 1962, ibid.; "Memorandum to Mr. Wilkins from Herbert Hill"; Robert L. Carter and Maria L. Marcus, "Memorandum Supporting Motion," in the case of Atlantic Steel Company and United Steelworkers of America, Local 2401, Before the National Labor Relations Board, Oct. 29, 1962, ibid.

46. Gwendolyn Young Richburg, quoted in Hinshaw, "Dialectic of Division," 244; Spiese, "An Interview with Boyd Wilson," 19–20; Dickerson, *Out of the Crucible*, 195–99; Boyd L. Wilson to Julius C. Wynn, Aug. 21, 1958, Personal Papers of Herbert Hill; Herbert Hill to J. H. Calhoun, Aug. 6, 1958, ibid. For a general statement about the dilemma Wilson faced, see William Kornhauser, "The Negro Union Official: A Study of Sponsorship and Control," *American Journal of Sociology* 57 (March 1952): 443–52.

47. Trezzvant W. Anderson, "G[eorgi]a Steelworkers Say Union Is 'Selling Out,' " *Pittsburgh Courier*, July 23, 1960, copy in folder 15, box 13, Hague Papers.

48. Francis C. Shane to Herbert Hill ("Subject: United Steelworkers of America–National Association for the Advancement of Colored People Joint Committee"), June 30, 1960, box A195, group 3, NAACP Papers; Francis C. Shane to Herbert Hill, June 1, 1962, ibid.

49. William B. Gould, *Black Workers in White Unions: Job Discrimination in the United States* (Ithaca, N.Y.: Cornell University Press, 1978), 68; Shane to Hill, June 30, 1960.

50. Roy Wilkins to David E. Feller, Dec. 13, 1962, box A195, group 3, NAACP Papers; Nathaniel Brown et al. to President's Committee on Equal Employment Opportunity, Sept. 11, 1961, folder 3, box 2900, District 35 Records, 1945–87, United Steelworkers of America, SLA/GSU; Jerome A.

Cooper to Bernard Kleiman, Jan. 20, 1967, ibid. Cooper, an attorney representing Local 2401, pointed out that from the beginning of the union's efforts to resolve the matter black workers had wanted opportunities for promotion but "did not wish in any way to jeopardize their accumulated seniority on their old jobs."

51. Wilkins to Feller, Dec. 13, 1962; Nathaniel Brown, interview by Herbert Hill, Atlanta, Oct. 21, 1962, Personal Papers of Herbert Hill.

52. Wilkins to Feller, Dec. 13, 1962; Stuart Rothman to Robert L. Carter, Apr. 8, 1963, folder 2, box 2888, District 35 Records, 1945–87; Roy Wilkins to George Meany, Dec. 7, 1962, Personal Papers of Herbert Hill; *New York Times*, Oct. 31, 1962, 13; Herbert Hill to author, Feb. 6, 1995.

53. Feller to Wilkins, Nov. 9, 1962; Shane to Hill, June 30, 1960; Wilkins to Feller, Dec. 13, 1962.

54. *Steel Labor*, July 1962, 13.

55. Ibid., June 1961, 20–22.

56. Branch, *Parting the Waters*, 808–922; "Statement by Francis C. Shane"; Hoerr, notes on Francis C. Shane press conference.

57. USWA, "Meeting of International Executive Board, United Steelworkers of America" (Chicago, Oct. 23, 1963), 13, box 48, IEB Proceedings, USWA.

58. Ibid., 14–15.

59. Ibid., 18–27.

60. Ibid., 30–31.

61. Ibid., 34–35.

62. USWA, *Proceedings of the Fifth Constitutional Convention*, 169; John P. Hoerr, *And the Wolf Finally Came: The Decline of the American Steel Industry* (Pittsburgh: University of Pittsburgh Press, 1988), Abel quoted on 646; Herling, *Right to Challenge*, 355–59.

63. Drake and Cayton, *Black Metropolis*, 341, 313; Martin Bauml Duberman, *Paul Robeson: A Biography* (New York: Alfred A. Knopf, 1989), 305–11, Revels Cayton quoted on 310.

64. Williams, interview, July 15, 1994. Rogers wrote a regular column, "Your History," in the *Pittsburgh Courier* and was the author of several popular books, including *The World's Greatest Men and Women of African Descent* (1931) and *A Hundred Amazing Facts about the Negro* (1934). Although these books were virtually unknown to whites and had little credibility among African American intellectuals, they were enormously popular in the black community. On Rogers, see Jeffrey C. Stewart and Fath Davis Ruffins, "A Faithful Witness: Afro-American Public History in Historical Perspective, 1828–1984," in *Presenting the Past: Essays on History and the Public*, ed. Susan Porter Benson, Stephen Brier, and Roy Rosenzweig (Philadelphia: Temple University Press, 1986), 323, 411–12; James, *Holding Aloft the Banner*, 40, 99, 109.

65. Vrana, *The ILWU Story*, 66; Philip W. Nyden, "Evolution of Black Political Influence in American Trade Unions," *Journal of Black Studies* 13 (June 1983): 379–98; Ruth Needleman, "Diplomats and Rabble Rousers: Black Leadership in Northwest Indiana's Steel Mills, Local Unions, and Communities" (paper presented at the annual meeting of the Organization of American Historians, Indianapolis, Apr. 1998), 5; Hurley, *Environmental Inequalities*, 80–81, 115–16; Kevin Boyle, *The UAW and the Heyday of American Liberalism, 1945–1968* (Ithaca, N.Y.: Cornell University Press, 1995), 129–31; Nelson Lichtenstein, *The Most Dangerous Man in Detroit*, 370–81, quoted on 376; Herbert Hill, "The Problem of Race," 196.

66. Drake and Cayton, *Black Metropolis*, 324–25.

67. Unnamed members of Local 1033 to "President Xavier Smykowski and the [Local] Executive Board," n.d., and statistical tables, attached to Molony to Germano, Aug. 23, 1966; photocopy of John C. Daniels, "Letter to Editor," [1966], folder 6, box 178, District 31 Records; Trevathan, interview, May 14, 1996.

68. Unnamed members of Local 1033 to I. W. Abel, folder 6, box 178, District 31 Records; unnamed members of Local 1033 to "President Xavier Smykowski and the [Local] Executive Board"; Spencer, *Blue Collar*, 86–113.

69. Brown, interview; Bruce Nelson, " 'CIO Meant One Thing,' " 136–38; Michael Goldfield, *The Decline of Organized Labor in the United States* (Chicago: University of Chicago Press, 1987), 134–35; James Trevathan, interview by Alice and Staughton Lynd, Nov. 1998 (in author's possession, courtesy of Staughton Lynd). See also Michael Honey, "Black Workers Remember: Industrial Unionism in the Era of Jim Crow," in *Race, Class, and Community in Southern Labor History*, ed. Gary M. Fink and Merl E. Reed (Tuscaloosa: University of Alabama Press, 1994), 121–37. Honey points out that in Memphis black unionists such as George Holloway of the United Auto Workers and Clarence Coe of the United Rubber Workers believed that their unions *did* serve as an important weapon in the fight against Jim Crow. But as Honey emphasizes, "the union" in this case "represented black self-activity, not rights handed down from the international or white union leaders."

70. Nelson, "Class, Race, and Democracy," 368; Irwin Barkan to Robert Carter, Sept. 4, 1968, Personal Papers of Herbert Hill.

CHAPTER SEVEN
"THE STEEL WAS HOT, THE JOBS WERE DIRTY, AND IT WAS WAR":
CLASS, RACE, AND WORKING-CLASS AGENCY IN YOUNGSTOWN

The quotation in the chapter title is from Oliver Montgomery, interview, Oct. 22, 1990.

1. Thomas G. Fuechtmann, *Steeples and Stacks: Religion and Steel Crisis in Youngstown* (New York: Cambridge University Press, 1989), 10–17; Warren,

The American Steel Industry, 55–57, 168–75; William D. Jenkins, *Steel Valley Klan: The Ku Klux Klan in Ohio's Mahoning Valley* (Kent, Ohio: Kent State University Press, 1990), 17–18; Galenson, *The CIO Challenge to the AFL*, quoted on 104.

2. Warren, *The American Steel Industry*, 173, 296.

3. Ibid., 168–75, 296–97; Janice Cafaro, "Interview with John Weed Powers," Aug. 5, 1986 (Youngstown State University Oral History Program, History of Industry in Youngstown Project, Youngstown Sheet & Tube O. H. 488), 6–7. Powers, a member of Sheet and Tube's board of directors, acknowledged that "it cost about $5 more a ton to produce steel in Youngstown than it did in Chicago."

4. Warren, *The American Steel Industry*, 296–300; United Steelworkers of America, District no. 26, "An Introduction to District 26. . . . United Steelworkers of America, 27 Years of Progress, 1936–1963," box 48, USWA/McDonald; "Steelworkers for the Canal," *Youngstown Vindicator*, Mar. 27, 1962, ibid.; Lynd, *The Fight against Shutdowns*, 16; Fuechtmann, *Steeples and Stacks*, 41–42; Stein, *Running Steel, Running America*, 241–43.

5. Lynd, "The Genesis of the Idea"; Lynd, *The Fight against Shutdowns*, 138–40, 151–57, quoted on 139, 154; *Youngstown Vindicator*, Jan. 28, 1980, 1, 6, Jan. 29, 1980, 1, 6; Lynd and Lynd, *We Are the Union*, 54–57.

6. Lynd and Lynd, *We Are the Union*, quoted on 57; Charles R. Walker, *Steeltown: An Industrial Case History of the Conflict between Progress and Security* (New York: Harper, 1950), 28; Bodnar, *Workers' World*, 165; Ronald Filippelli, "The History Is Missing, Almost: Philip Murray, the Steelworkers, and the Historians," in *Forging a Union of Steel*, ed. Clark, Gottlieb, and Kennedy, 8, 9; Stolberg, *The Story of the CIO*, quoted on 83; Clinton S. Golden and Harold J. Ruttenberg, *The Dynamics of Industrial Democracy* (New York: Harper and Brothers, 1942), 109–18.

7. Stanley Aronowitz, *False Promises: The Shaping of American Working Class Consciousness* (New York: McGraw-Hill, 1973), quoted on 235; Goldfield, "Race and the CIO," 156–59; Barbero et al., "A Common Bond," 276; Oliver Montgomery, interview, Oct. 22, 1990.

8. Jenkins, *Steel Valley Klan*, 16–19; Alan Williams, interview by author, Charlottesville, Va., June 1, 1997. Williams, a professor of history at the University of Virginia for many years, was born and raised in Youngstown. His father's family emigrated from Wales to the coal mines of southern Ohio and then to the Mahoning Valley, where his father was a foreman at the Brier Hill Works. Williams first went to work at the Campbell Works in June 1944, when he turned sixteen, and he continued to work there intermittently until 1954. As a boy and even as a young man, he was deeply enmeshed in the Anglo-Protestant culture of the supervisors and skilled workers at Youngstown Sheet and Tube. I have relied on his recollections.

9. Jenkins, *Steel Valley Klan*, 19–20, and passim; Steel Workers Organizing Committee, *The SWOC Wins at Youngstown Sheet and Tube and Youngstown Metal Products* (Pittsburgh, [1941]), box 167, USWA/McDonald; "Youngstown Sheet and Tube Negotiating Committee," Sept. 10, 1941, attached to David J. McDonald to Clinton S. Golden, Sept. 10, 1941, folder 4, box 167, USWA/McDonald; "Negotiating Committee—Youngstown Sheet and Tube," [1945], attached to David J. McDonald to Joseph Germano, Feb. 9, 1945, ibid.; Agnes Griffin, interview by author, Youngstown, Ohio, Dec. 12, 1991; Fuechtmann, *Steeples and Stacks*, 27, 79; Camens, interview, Sept. 22, 1991; Nelson Lichtenstein, "Walter Reuther and the Rise of Labor-Liberalism," in *Labor Leaders in America*, ed. Dubofsky and Van Tine, 293–94; Reutter, *Sparrows Point*, 378.

10. Richard L. Rowan, *The Negro in the Steel Industry*, part 4 of Herbert R. Northrup, Carl B. King, and Richard L. Rowan, *Negro Employment in Basic Industry: A Study of Racial Policies in Six Industries*, vol. 1, *Studies of Negro Employment* (Philadelphia: Industrial Research Unit, Wharton School of Finance and Commerce, University of Pennsylvania, 1970), 279; U.S. Department of Commerce, Bureau of the Census, *1970 Census of Population*, vol. 1, *Characteristics of the Population*, part 37, *Ohio*, sec. 2 (Washington, D.C.: U.S. Government Printing Office, 1973), 1524; "Black/White Unemployment Patterns in Industrial and 'Postindustrial' Cities: Cleveland and Youngstown, Ohio, 1940–1980" (table compiled from census data by Iris Chiu, July–Aug. 1992, in author's possession).

11. Annetta Dieckmann, "The Relations of Trade Unions and Negro Workers in Youngstown, Ohio," Oct. 1925, box 89, series 6, group 1, National Urban League Papers; "Occupation[al] Statistics for Youngstown, Ohio" (tables compiled from census data by Andrew Schopler, Jan.–Mar. 1992, in author's possession); Daniel P. Thomas, interview by author, Youngstown, Ohio, Dec. 12, 1991; Arlette Gatewood, interview by Donna DeBlasio, Youngstown, Ohio, Apr. 21, 1991, Youngstown Historical Center of Industry and Labor/ Ohio Historical Society (hereafter, YHCIL/OHS); Donnorumo, interview, Apr. 4, 1991; James C. Davis, interview by Donna DeBlasio, Sept. 26, 1991, ibid.

12. T. Arnold Hill, "The Negro and the C.I.O.," *Opportunity* 15 (August 1937): 243; Schuyler, "Schuyler Visits Steel Centers," 1, 14; Romare Bearden, "The Negro in 'Little Steel,'" *Opportunity* 15 (December 1937): 364–65.

13. Archie Nelson, interview, Nov. 19, 1990.

14. Mann, interview, Dec. 14, 1988; Trevathan, interview, May 14, 1996.

15. Camens to Shane, Mar. 10, 1950; *Youngstown Vindicator*, May 5, 1957, clipping in box 43, Hague Papers.

16. Camens, interview; Camens to Shane, Mar. 10, 1950.

17. Marvin Weinstock, interview by author, Youngstown, Ohio, Sept. 17, 1989; Mann, interview, Dec. 14, 1988; Ed Mann, interview by author, Hub-

bard, Ohio, Dec. 15, 1988; Ed Mann, interview by author (via telephone), Nov. 14, 1991.

18. Reutter, *Sparrows Point*, 310–14.

19. Camens to Shane, Mar. 10, 1950; Harry Wines to James P. Griffin, Oct. 19, 1948, box 19, series 4, National Urban League Papers; *Youngstown Vindicator*, Aug. 10, 1948, 1, Aug. 26, 1948, 1, 22; Camens, interview.

20. Weinstock, interview; Mann, interview, Dec. 14, 1988; Barbero et al., "A Common Bond," 273.

21. Mann, interview, Nov. 14, 1991; James P. Cannon, *The History of American Trotskyism: Report of a Participant* (New York: Pioneer, 1944), 234–52; Constance Ashton Myers, *The Prophet's Army: Trotskyists in America, 1928–1941* (Westport, Conn.: Greenwood Press, 1977), 145; Alan Wald, *The New York Intellectuals: The Rise and Decline of the Anti-Stalinist Left from the 1930s to the 1980s* (Chapel Hill: University of North Carolina Press, 1987), 164–92, 295–310. The Socialist Workers party's membership reached a high of 1,470 in 1946, and due to internal factionalism and the pressure of McCarthyism and the cold war, it declined to 825 in 1950 and 480 in 1954.

22. Merlin Luce, interview by author, Youngstown, Ohio, Nov. 17, 1990. For similar examples of left-wing organizations serving as leadership-training schools for working-class activists, see Friedlander, *The Emergence of a UAW Local*; Nelson Lichtenstein, "Life at the Rouge: A Cycle of Workers' Control," in *Life and Labor: Dimensions of Working-Class History*, ed. Charles Stephenson and Robert Asher (Albany: State University of New York Press, 1986), 237–59; Korstad and Lichtenstein, "Opportunities Found and Lost"; Zahavi, "Passionate Commitments."

23. Camens, interview; Weinstock, interview; *Ohio Works Organizer*, Feb. 19, 1947, 2; Nathaniel C. Lee, Jr., interview by author (via telephone), Nov. 20, 1991; Vivian Lee, interview by author (via telephone), Feb. 1, 1992; "Obsequies of Nathaniel C. Lee, 1905–1982," Oct. 21, 1982 (in author's possession, courtesy of Vivian Lee); Herling, *Right to Challenge*, 223, 273–74.

24. Ethel Dostal to Ruby Hurley, Dec. 11, 1945, box C152, group 2, NAACP Papers; William H. Staton to Ella J. Baker, Sept. 25, 1945, ibid.; "Protest Meeting against Police Brutality in Youngstown" (leaflet, [Sept. 1945]), ibid.; *Cleveland Call and Post*, Oct. 6. 1945, 1-B, Oct. 13, 1945, 1-B, 4-B.

25. Korstad and Lichtenstein, "Opportunities Found and Lost"; *Ohio Works Organizer*, Sept. 20, 1946, 4.

26. *Youngstown Vindicator*, June 20, 1949, 1, 2, June 23, 1949, 1, 22, June 25, 1949, 1, 2, June 26, 1949, 1, June 28, 1949, 1, 12, July 5, 1949, 1, 12, July 6, 1949, 1, 12; *The Militant*, July 4, 1949, 4; Weinstock, interview.

27. Weinstock, interview; *Youngstown Vindicator*, July 6, 1949, 1, 12.

28. Weinstock, interview.

29. *Ohio Works Organizer*, Jan. 13, 1947, 1; [Statement of Nathaniel C. Lee], July 19, 1956, box C127, group 3, NAACP Papers; "Memorandum to Mr. Wilkins . . . from Mr. Current, Re: Youngstown Branch Dispute," Sept. 5, 1956, ibid.; Camens, interview; Oliver Montgomery, interview by author, Pittsburgh, Pa., Oct. 25, 1996; John S. Barbero, review of *Right to Challenge*, *Brier Hill Unionist*, Mar. 1974, 4; Herling, *Right to Challenge*, 103, 115, 151, 223, 273–74, 289.

30. Donald L. Martin, "Oral History Interview with Hugh Carcella," Philadelphia, Pa., Nov. 7, 1967 (USWA/OHP), 7, 13–14; Daniel P. Thomas, interview

31. Betsy Murphy, interview by author, Youngstown, Ohio, Oct. 27, 1996; Emmett C. Shaffer, "Interview with Carl E. Beck," May 8, 1974 (Youngstown State University Oral History Program, Steel Industry Labor and Management, Labor and Union Experience, O. H. 8), quoted on 7, 8, 20, 24; Carl E. Beck, "Autobiography," [1970s] (in possession of Betsy Murphy, Youngstown, Ohio).

32. Murphy, interview; James B. Gent to Joseph Scanlon ("Memorandum, Re: Youngstown, Ohio"), June 14, 1943, box A4-2, Murray Papers; *Youngstown Vindicator*, June 4, 1947, 1; Joseph Scanlon to Philip Murray, David J. McDonald, and Clinton S. Golden ("Memorandum, Re: Youngstown, Ohio"), June 15, 1943, box A4-2, Murray Papers.

33. Beck had plenty of detractors. The *Youngstown Vindicator* denounced him as a "trouble maker," a "bad," even "vicious," leader, and an "evil genius." Critics within the United Steelworkers accused him of running a political machine, "gagging" opponents within Local 1462, slandering the leadership of the district union, and cultivating a boisterous, hard-drinking group of followers who were bent on creating "as much hell and dissension as they possibly could." *Youngstown Vindicator*, May 31, 1945, 1, 8, June 1, 1945, 10, Aug. 3, 1945, 10, Aug. 22, 1945, 8, Aug. 23, 1945, 14. Robert Purnell to Philip Murray, Feb. 3, 1945, folder 21, box 1, Local Union Appeals, IEB/USWA; "Statement of James P. Griffin, Staff Representative[:] Chronological Order of the Actions of Carl E. Beck and Other Officers of Local Union 1462 in Their Attempt to Get James C. Quinn Removed from Office," n.d., ibid.; James B. Gent to Joseph Scanlon ("Re: Show Cause Hearing, Cleveland, Youngstown Sheet & Tube Work Stoppage"), Aug. 8, 1945, ibid.

34. Philip Murray to Carl E. Beck and Samuel W. Evans, July 31, 1945, and Aug. 8, 1945; "Outcome of Meeting Held with Members of Local Union 1462 Involving Youngstown Sheet and Tube Co. Brier Hill Works . . . Maintenance Dept. Issue," attached to Ernest Konesky to Joe Scanlon, Aug. 2, 1945; Gent to Scanlon, Aug. 8, 1945; Carl E. Beck to Philip Murray, Aug. 9, 1945; James Robb and Howard N. Porter, "In the Matter of: Unauthorized Stoppage of Work at Brier Hill Plant of the Youngstown Sheet and Tube Company,

Youngstown, Ohio[,] Supplementing Our Telegram to You of August 12, 1945," n.d., all in folder 21, box 1, Local Union Appeals, IEB/USWA.

35. Robb and Porter, "In the Matter of"; *Youngstown Vindicator*, Aug. 22, 1945, 1, 4.

36. Daniel P. Thomas, interview; Dan Thomas, interview by Emmett C. Shaffer, Aug. 1, 1974 (Youngstown State University Oral History Program, Steel Industry Labor and Management, Mahoning Valley Labor, O. H. 5), 2; Steel Workers Organizing Committee, *The SWOC Wins at Youngstown Sheet and Tube and Youngstown Metal Products*; 12, box 167; Barbero et al., "A Common Bond," 265.

37. Dan Thomas, interview by Emmett C. Shaffer, 3; *Youngstown Vindicator*, Apr. 25, 1949, 2, July 28, 1949, 1, Feb. 9, 1953, 1, Mar. 26, 1955, 1, 2, July 10, 1956, 12, May 29, 1960, 1, 10; Mann, interview, Dec. 14, 1988; Oliver Montgomery, interview, Oct. 22, 1990; "Trial Board Report on Charges against President Dan Thomas by Frank Leseganich," Oct. 15, 1954, folder 33, box 5, Local Union Appeals, IEB/USWA; Barbero et al., "A Common Bond," 265.

38. Oliver Montgomery, interview, Oct. 25, 1996; Archie Nelson, interview; Dan Thomas, interviewed by Emmett C. Shaffer, 4–6; *Ohio Works Organizer*, Feb. 19, 1947, 2; James C. Davis, interview, Feb. 18, 1989.

39. Oliver Montgomery, interviews, Oct. 22, 1990, and Oct. 25, 1996; Archie Nelson, interview; Heybert Moyer, interview by author, Youngstown, Ohio, Oct. 28, 1996; James C. Davis, interview, Sept. 26, 1991.

40. Archie Nelson, interview; Barbero et al., "A Common Bond," 270. On the blackjack incident, see *Youngstown Vindicator*, July 4, 1956, 1, 2, July 10, 1956, 12.

41. James C. Davis, interview, Feb. 18, 1989.

42. Ibid., Oct. 27, 1996. On black soldiers' experience in the army during the Korean War era, see Lipsitz, *A Life in the Struggle*, 39–63.

43. Oliver Montgomery, interview, Oct. 22, 1990.

44. Trevathan, interview, May 14, 1996; James C. Davis, interview, Feb. 18, 1989; Oliver Montgomery, interview, Oct. 22, 1990; Willie Aikens, interview by author, Youngstown, Ohio, Dec. 14, 1988.

45. Oliver Montgomery, interview, Oct. 22, 1990; *Youngstown Vindicator*, July 1, 1960, 1.

46. Mann, interview, Nov. 14, 1991; Oliver Montgomery, interview, Oct. 22, 1990; *Youngstown Vindicator*, June 29, 1962, 5.

47. Andrew Hurley, *Environmental Inequalities*, 33; Archie Nelson, interview.

48. The common experience of backlash did not compel all black workers to draw the same lessons. Davis and Montgomery concluded that separate organization was more important than ever, but others came to the conclusion that in spite of its limitations, the interracial leadership group that had charac-

terized the Dan Thomas era was the only way to achieve representation and incremental gains for blacks at Brier Hill. Thus Joe Clark's defection to the Thomas machine was not merely an individual act. It reflected the thinking of other African Americans and indicated that there would be no unified black response to problems of racial discrimination in the plant and the union. Moyer, interview.

49. Oliver Montgomery, interview, Oct. 22, 1990; Barbero et al., "A Common Bond," 259–60; Lynd and Lynd, *We Are the Union*, 22–23.

50. Barbero et al., "A Common Bond," 259, 262–64.

51. Ibid., 268; Archie Nelson, interview. On the United Labor party, see Burr McCloskey, "I Appeal the Ruling of the Chair," in *Rank and File*, ed. Lynd and Lynd, 141–54; Staughton Lynd, "A Chapter from History: The United Labor Party, 1946–1952," *Liberation* 18 (December 1973): 38–45.

52. Mann, interview, Dec. 14, 1988; Lynd and Lynd, *We Are the Union*, 1–10. Mann may have been a member of the Socialist Workers party at some point in the early 1950s. According to one sympathetic source, he attended SWP meetings at that time and finally "ended his formal association with the party" in 1953. Shirley Pasholk and Leonard Grbinick, "Ed Mann, 1928–1992: An Appreciation of a Trade Unionist Who Always Put the Working Class First," *Socialist Action* 10 (May 1992): 6.

53. Mann, interview, Dec. 14, 1988; Lynd and Lynd, *We Are the Union*, 12–15.

54. Philip W. Nyden, *Steelworkers Rank-and-File: The Political Economy of a Union Reform Movement* (New York: Praeger, 1984), 43–53; Casey Ichniowski, "Have Angels Done More? The Steel Industry Consent Decree," National Bureau of Economic Research, working paper no. 674 (Cambridge, Mass.: National Bureau of Economic Research, 1981), 3–5; Herling, *Right to Challenge*, 96–101, 330–37, 342–80; Hurley, *Environmental Inequalities*, 104–5.

55. Nyden, *Steelworkers Rank-and-File*, 50–51; Mann, interview, Dec. 14, 1988; Gerald Dickey, interview by author, Boardman, Ohio, Oct. 28, 1996; Barbero et al., "A Common Bond," 261–78; Lynd and Lynd, *We Are the Union*, 20–23, 45–48.

56. Lynd and Lynd, *We Are the Union*, 45–50, quoted on 45; *Brier Hill Unionist*, Sept. 1973, 3–4, May, 1976, 3; Dickey, interview.

57. Oliver Montgomery, interview, Oct. 22, 1990; Lynd and Lynd, *We Are the Union*, 26; Aikens, interview; James C. Davis, interview, Oct. 27, 1996; Dickey, interview; "Examine the Record," [Apr. 1976], and " 'I Am a Radical,' " [Apr. 1976] (campaign leaflets, in author's possession, courtesy of Ed Mann); "Let's Get the Local Union Back in Order[.] Elect Jim Davis and Jim Porter" (campaign leaflet, [Apr. 1976]), folder 25, box M219-1, Gerald Dickey Collection, YHCIL/OHS.

58. Herbert Hill, "The Steel Industry Consent Decree," n.d. (in author's possession, courtesy of Herbert Hill); Gould, *Black Workers in White Unions*,

quoted on 70, 71; "Statement of Policy on Seniority Adopted by the International Executive Board, USWA, June 26–27, 1973, Pittsburgh, Pa.," attached to John S. Johns to "All District Directors," July 5, 1973, folder 7, box 7, USWA—President's Office: I. W. Abel (hereafter, USWA/Abel), USWA, HCLA/PSU.

59. Gould, *Black Workers in White Unions*, 71–78; Herbert Hill, "Black Workers," 263–341, quoted on 310.

60. Ben Fischer, "Evaluating the Steel Industry Consent Decree" (Rutgers University Equal Employment Opportunity Symposium, Newark, N.J., Nov. 28–29, 1975); Ruck, "Origins of the Seniority System," 105–11; Bernard Kleiman to the Members of the International Executive Board, June 5, 1973, folder 7, box 7, USWA/Abel; In the United States District Court for the Northern District of Alabama (Southern Division), "Consent Decree I," April 12, 1974 , passim, especially 27, Personal Papers of Herbert Hill; Mann, interview, Dec. 15, 1988; Herbert Hill, "The Steel Industry Consent Decree."

61. Stein, *Running Steel, Running America*, 178–80; Herbert Hill, "The Steel Industry Consent Decree"; Ruck, "Origins of the Seniority System," 109–11, Strevel quoted on 110.

62. Bob Hill, interview by author (via telephone), Nov. 13, 1996; "Summary of Seniority Civil Rights Decree," supplement to *Brier Hill Unionist*, May 1974, no page numbers; Trevathan, interview, May 14, 1996.

63. Trevathan, interview, May 14, 1996.

64. Lynd and Lynd, *We Are The Union*, 31, 29; Aikens, interview.

65. Barbero et al., "A Common Bond," 270–75; Lynd and Lynd, *We Are the Union*, 20–22; *Brier Hill Unionist*, Aug. 1974, 1, Apr. 1975, 3.

66. Foner, *Organized Labor and the Black Worker*, 263; Herling, *Right to Challenge*, 355–59, 377, 379.

67. *Brier Hill Unionist*, Aug. 1974, 1.

68. David Bensman and Roberta Lynch, *Rusted Dreams: Hard Times in a Steel Community* (New York: McGraw-Hill, 1987), 3; Lynd, *The Fight against Shutdowns*.

69. Lynd, *The Fight against Shutdowns*, 126–27.

70. Weinstock, interview; Oliver Montgomery, interviews, Oct. 22, 1990, and Oct. 25, 1996.

EPILOGUE
"OTHER ENERGIES, OTHER DREAMS": TOWARD A
NEW LABOR MOVEMENT

The quotation in the chapter title is from Lockman, *Comrades and Enemies*, 362.

1. Dickey, interview, Oct. 28, 1996.

2. Ibid.

3. Lewis, *Sloss Furnaces*, quoted on 90, 435; Cayton and Mitchell, *Black Workers and the New Unions*, 26–35.

4. Mann, interview, Dec. 14, 1988; Donnorumo, interview, Apr. 4, 1991; Ken Doran, interview by author, Kinsman, Ohio, Feb. 19, 1989; Oliver Montgomery, interview, Oct. 25, 1996.

5. Dan T. Carter, *The Politics of Rage: George Wallace, the Origins of the New Conservatism, and the Transformation of American Politics* (New York: Simon and Schuster, 1995), 9–11, 108–9, 205–7.

6. Ibid., quoted on 205, 207; Stephan Lesher, *George Wallace: American Populist* (Reading, Mass.: Addison-Wesley, 1994), quoted on 284.

7. Carter, *The Politics of Rage*, 208–15; Matusow, *The Unraveling of America*, 138–39; Kenneth Durr, "When Southern Politics Came North: The Roots of White Working-Class Conservatism in Baltimore, 1940–1964," *Labor History* 37 (summer 1996): 309–31; "Gary Turns Her Back on Bias," 17–20, 22–23; Bloomberg, "They'll Go Democratic Anyway," 13–15; Victor Hoffman and John Strietelmeier, "Gary's Rank-and-File Reaction," *Reporter*, Sept. 10, 1964, 28–29, quoted on 29; Hurley, *Environmental Inequalities*, 96.

8. Jack M. Bloom, *Class, Race, and the Civil Rights Movement* (Bloomington: Indiana University Press, 1987); Gary Orfield, "Race and the Liberal Agenda: The Loss of the Integrationist Dream, 1965–1974," in *The Politics of Social Policy in the United States*, ed. Margaret Weir, Ann Shola Orloff, and Theda Skocpol (Princeton, N.J.: Princeton University Press, 1988), 313–55.

9. David J. Garrow, *Bearing the Cross: Martin Luther King, Jr. and the Southern Christian Leadership Conference* (New York: William Morrow, 1986), 431–525; James Ralph, Jr., *Northern Protest: Martin Luther King, Jr., Chicago, and the Civil Rights Movement* (Cambridge, Mass.: Harvard University Press, 1993), 114–29; Alan B. Anderson and George W. Pickering, *Confronting the Color Line: The Broken Promise of the Civil Rights Movement in Chicago* (Athens: University of Georgia Press, 1986), quoted on 224.

10. Ralph, *Northern Protest*, 124–26, 279–80n.70.

11. Lukas, *Common Ground*, 21–28. The words in the extract are Lukas's, based on his extensive interviews with McGoff.

12. Ibid., 27; Robert Coles, "The White Northerner: Pride and Prejudice," *Atlantic Monthly* 217 (June 1966): 53–57.

13. Ignatiev, *How the Irish Became White*, 80, 20; W. E. Burghardt Du Bois, *Black Reconstruction in America* (1935; reprint, New York: Russell and Russell, 1966), 17–31; Eric Foner, *Politics and Ideology in the Age of the Civil War* (New York: Oxford University Press, 1980), 57–93; Charles Sellers, *The Market Revolution: Jacksonian America, 1815–1846* (New York: Oxford University Press, 1991), 404–5; Roediger, *The Wages of Whiteness*, 68–69, 178–81; Barry Goldberg, "Slavery, Race, and the Languages of Class: 'Wage Slaves' and White 'Niggers,' " *New Politics* 5 (summer 1991): 64–83; Gottlieb, *Making Their Own Way*, 156.

14. It is also the responsibility of the historian to acknowledge that these generalizations—as valid and important as they are—cannot stand without qualification. Measuring the extent of the "public and psychological wage" that "whiteness" has proffered will no doubt continue to generate considerable disagreement. But it is undeniable that for some—notably for many of Alice McGoff's neighbors in Charlestown and South Boston—the fruits of "whiteness" have provided precious little nourishment in recent years. In his memoir of growing up poor in South Boston, Michael Patrick MacDonald chronicles not only the "primal fear of being thrown back into blackness," which drove his neighbors to desperate acts of racist violence in the mid-1970s, but the relentless deterioration in the quality of life that continues to stalk "Southie," separating it even further from Boston's flourishing zones of wealth and conspicuous consumption. See Michael Patrick MacDonald, *All Souls: A Family Story from Southie* (Boston: Beacon Press, 1999); Brent Staples, "A Prayer for the Dead," *New York Times Book Review*, Oct. 3, 1999, 13–14, quoted on 13.

15. Kelley, *Yo Mama's Disfunktional!* 109; Lockman, *Comrades and Enemies*, 362.

16. Nelson Lichtenstein, *The Most Dangerous Man in Detroit*, 382–87; Ronald L. Filippelli, *Labor in the USA: A History* (New York: Alfred A. Knopf, 1984), 267.

17. These accusations had become a familiar part of the (white) discourse on race by the late 1950s, so much so that Randolph's close associate Milton Webster of the Brotherhood of Sleeping Car Porters felt compelled to point out that "many white men in and out of the trade union movement [believe] they have all the answers [to] these problems" and assumed that it was their right and obligation to "tell us how we ought to proceed." Milton P. Webster, "Webster Answers Attack on Randolph," *Black Worker* 31 (January 1960): 2.

18. The southern white union official is Cecil Roberts, a fourth-generation West Virginia coal miner who was then vice-president of the UMW and is now the union's president. During the Pittston strike, Roberts began his speeches to rank-and-file miners and strike supporters with the words, "Welcome to class warfare in southwest Virginia!" But according to a strike participant, "Cecil's other oratorical claim to fame is his unabashed use of the word 'love' and his admiration for Dr. Martin Luther King. He has begun quoting entire passages of King's speeches from memory, and his Appalachian audiences have listened in rapt attention." Jim Sessions and Fran Ansley, "Singing across Dark Spaces: The Union/Community Takeover of the Pittston Company's Moss 3 Coal Preparation Plant," in *Nonviolence in America: A Documentary History*, ed. Staughton Lynd and Alice Lynd, rev. ed. (Maryknoll, N.Y.: Orbis Books, 1995), 374–96.

19. Lockman, *Comrades and Enemies*, 362.

20. Historian Charles Payne sees Martin Luther King, Jr., as the outstanding example of the Civil Rights movement's "community-mobilizing tradi-

tion, focused on large-scale, relatively short-term public events." This is the tradition that most observers have come to regard as emblematic of the movement's history, with Birmingham, the March on Washington, and Selma as its normative events. In *I've Got the Light of Freedom*, however, Payne explores the historical reality and contemporary relevance of the more democratic and egalitarian community-organizing tradition, which placed a premium on developing leadership skills among ordinary men and women. This is the tradition of the Student Nonviolent Coordinating Committee (SNCC) and the Mississippi movement of the early and mid-1960s. Significantly, this movement was shaped by women such as Ella Baker and Septima Clark and led, in part, by women such as the legendary Fannie Lou Hamer in Mississippi. In the long term, this tradition may provide the most appropriate foundation on which to rebuild the labor movement. But it also offers a greater challenge to organized labor's leadership and rank and file. See Charles M. Payne, *I've Got the Light of Freedom: The Organizing Tradition and the Mississippi Movement* (Berkeley: University of California Press, 1995), 3–4, 440–41, and passim, quoted on 3; Glenn T. Eskew, *But for Birmingham: The Local and National Movements in the Civil Rights Struggle* (Chapel Hill: University of North Carolina Press, 1997).

21. Garrow, *Bearing the Cross*, 575–624; David J. Garrow, "The Man Who Was King," *New York Review of Books*, Apr. 13, 2000, 40, 42–43; Michael Honey, "Martin Luther King, Jr., the Crisis of the Black Working Class, and the Memphis Sanitation Strike," in *Southern Labor in Transition*, ed. Zieger, 146–75, quoted on 148. There are, of course, no blueprints for the development of civil rights unionism. For the ambiguous results of one union's efforts in this direction, see Leon Fink and Brian Greenberg, *Upheaval in the Quiet Zone: A History of Hospital Workers' Union, Local 1199* (Urbana: University of Illinois Press, 1989), especially 129–80.

Index

Abel, I.W., 246, 265, 277

Abbott, Robert, 91

abolitionists, xxviii, xxxiv-xxxv, xxxvii, 13, 293; and Ireland, 304n.40

Ad Hoc Committee of Black Steelworkers, 279

AFL. *See* American Federation of Labor

AFL-CIO: and Civil Rights movement, 232, 243, 294; founding of, 232; and racial discrimination, 235; and racial equality, 232, 294

African Americans, xxviii, 89, 129; in Gary, 180–84, 228; and Great Depression, 178, 179–80, 183–84, 256–57; and Korean War, 216, 229, 272; on Los Angeles waterfront, xlii-xliii, 110–28, 139–41; in New Orleans, 42–45, 101,106–10, 129–40; in 1950s, 212, 216–17, 227–32; in port of New York, 13, 19, 21, 24–25, 38–40, 44–45, 51, 79–80, 83–84, 86–87, 311n.44; religious activity of, 38, 174–76, 182, 231; and residential segregation, 63–64, 110, 120, 138, 180, 228, 274, 290–91, 336n.69; on San Francisco waterfront, 95–99, 126–27; in steel industry, xli-xlii, 145, 146–47, 155, 159, 160–70, 229, 237–38, 240–41, 257–61, 269–74, 286; as strikebreakers, 18, 19, 24–26, 35–36, 41, 63, 90, 160–61, 166–67, 194–95, 196, 257, 293, 311n.44; as strikers, 25–26, 30–31, 165–66, 194–95; and World War I, 31, 87, 164, 165, 167, 314n.59; and World War II, 96–97, 100, 110, 207, 214, 219, 229, 262, 269; as victims of European immigration, 13–14, 164; unemployment among, 99, 230, 256; in Youngstown, 255–58, 262, 269–74

African Black Brotherhood, 34

Afro-American Labor Protective Society, 115, 247

Aikens, Willie, xxi, 278–79, 282–83

Alexander, Rev. Avery, 133

Alford, Charles, 208

Amalgamated Association of Iron, Steel, and Tin Workers, 161, 170, 175, 188, 216

American Committee on Africa, 85

American Federation of Labor (AFL), xxxiii, 47, 73–74, 77, 93, 100, 181, 192, 200; and CIO, 102, 105; expulsion of ILA, 72; and Great Steel Strike, 165; and merger with CIO, 232; in New Orleans, 105, 107; and racial discrimination, xxxii, 118, 165, 201; role of Irish in, xxx, 65–66

American Women Pickets for the Enforcement of America's War Aims, 28–30, 37

Anastasia, Anthony, 65, 84, 85

Anaya, Gilbert, 204

Anderson, Joseph, 160

anti-Chinese movement, 89, 95

Antonik, Andrew, 149–50

Arnesen, Eric, 42

Association of Catholic Trade Unionists, 75

Atlantic Steel, 235–42; and case of Joseph Rabun, 236–37; racial discrimination in, 235–36, 237–38, 241; and racial equality, 236

Barbero, John, xl, 254, 268, 269, 271, 273; and closing of Brier Hill Works, 284–86; portrait of, 276; radical reputation of, 278; and Rank-and-File Team, 275–76, 277, 283; and steel industry Consent Decree, 283; as vice-president of Local 1462, 278, 279

Barnes, Charles B., 6, 7–8, 12, 21, 22, 52

Barnett, Claude A., 180–84, 190

Barrett, James, xxix, xxx

Bazdar, Joseph, 209, 211

Beck, Jerry, 253, 263, 266, 370n.33; career of, 266–68

Bell, Daniel, 46, 47, 50

Bell, Thomas, xxix-xxx, xli, 152

POLITICS AND SOCIETY IN TWENTIETH-CENTURY AMERICA

Civil Defense Begins at Home:
Militarization Meets Everyday Life in the Fifties
by Laura McEnaney

Cold War Civil Rights: Race and the Image of American Democracy
by Mary L. Dudziak

Divided We Stand: American Workers and the Struggle for Black Equality
by Bruce Nelson